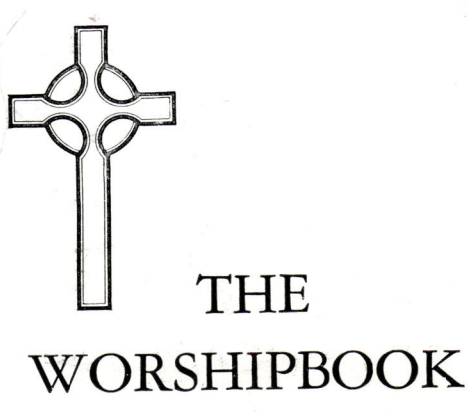

THE WORSHIPBOOK

Presented to the glory of God as a memorial to perpetuate the growth of our Christian discipleship.

FIRST PRESBYTERIAN CHURCH
OTTUMWA, IOWA

The Worshipbook
Services and Hymns

The Worshipbook

Services and Hymns·

Prepared by The Joint Committee on Worship *for* Cumberland Presbyterian Church · Presbyterian Church in the United States · The United Presbyterian Church in the United States of America

Philadelphia

COPYRIGHT © MCMLXX, MCMLXXII, THE WESTMINSTER PRESS

All rights reserved—no part of this publication may be reproduced in any form without permission in writing from the publisher.

ACKNOWLEDGMENTS

Doubleday & Company, Inc., for quotations from *The Jerusalem Bible*. Copyright © 1966 by Darton, Longman & Todd, Ltd., and Doubleday & Company, Inc.

The Macmillan Company, for quotations from *The New Testament in Modern English*, translated by J. B. Phillips. © 1958 by J. B. Phillips.

The National Council of Churches, Division of Christian Education, for Scripture quotations from the Revised Standard Version of the Bible, copyrighted 1946 and 1952.

Oxford University Press, Inc., and Cambridge University Press, for quotations from *The New English Bible*. Copyright © the Delegates of the Oxford University Press and the Syndics of the Cambridge University Press 1961, 1970.

Oxford University Press, Inc., for litanies abridged and adapted from *The Kingdom, the Power, and the Glory*. Copyright 1933 by Oxford University Press, Inc., and Renewed 1961 by Bradford Young.

Second Printing

PUBLISHED BY THE WESTMINSTER PRESS®
PHILADELPHIA, PENNSYLVANIA

Printed in the United States of America

Preface

THE WORSHIPBOOK is in two forms. Chronologically, *The Worshipbook—Services* is first. *The Worshipbook—Services and Hymns* is second, following the first after a passage of years. All the pages of *The Worshipbook—Services* constitute the first pages of *The Worshipbook—Services and Hymns*. The second book is different from the first only in the way that the subtitles suggest. The second offers hymns. The first does not.

The Worshipbook—Services is the successor to *The Book of Common Worship* (1946). *The Worshipbook—Services and Hymns* is the successor to *The Book of Common Worship* and, for many congregations, *The Hymnal* (1933) or *The Hymnbook* (1955).

Three Churches have produced *The Worshipbook*. They are: the Cumberland Presbyterian Church, the Presbyterian Church in the United States, and The United Presbyterian Church in the United States of America. They have been served by the Joint Committee on Worship and by The Committee on Selection of Hymns, the latter reporting to the several denominations through the former. Sessions of the Joint Committee on Worship have been attended by an observer from the Reformed Church of America.

At the point in *The Worshipbook—Services and Hymns* where the hymns begin, there is a further statement about the music and hymnody in the book. This preface, therefore, contains only generalizations as to hymns, and a degree of greater detail about the services.

A principal dimension of *The Worshipbook* is its attempt to employ contemporary English in worship. The word *contemporary* needs definition. It does not mean *idiom* or *slang*, or the selection of words that will call attention to their jarring strangeness, or language that reveals more the cleverness of the writer than the reality of God. It means the straightforward use of words and language in current, contemporary use in the last third of the twentieth century.

Moreover, so much of *The Worshipbook* is in the language of Scripture that the words of the new translations of the Bible have been employed. Thus, the other principal dimension of *The Worshipbook* is that it rests upon the foundation of the Holy Scriptures.

There has been no attempt to write new theology. Because the Joint Committee on Worship prepared the Directory for Worship which became part of the Constitution of The United Presbyterian Church in the United States of America, that directory has been the standard which *The Worshipbook* obeys. Nevertheless, care has been taken not to trespass against the Constitutions of the other two Churches.

The Worshipbook is a Presbyterian book. It is faithful to that tradition. *The Worshipbook* is an ecumenical book. It attempts to adopt, both in services and hymns, the best that fellow Christians in other Churches and traditions offer.

Presbyterians value freedom and variety in worship, but they emphasize equally the virtue of orderliness. It is hardly necessary to state that the book is for voluntary use. Congregations will find options offered in *The Worshipbook*. In addition, they will supply their own variations. To do so will be to please, not disappoint, those who have prepared the book. All that is claimed is that *The Worshipbook*, notably in the Service for the Lord's Day, offers one orderly and responsible way to plan for the worship of God.

There is contemporaneity in the hymns. New hymns have been written. Old hymns have been altered, where copyright and literary structure permit, so that archaic language is eliminated, and excessive introspective use of first person singular pronouns is diminished. There are folk hymns and spirituals.

The hymns have been selected, of course, in adherence to many standards. Due consideration has been given to sound theology, musical integrity, variety in the texts, variety in the tunes, and the blending of the old with the new.

There has been, however, one primary standard by which the hymns have been chosen. They have been chosen to support the services in *The Worshipbook*, particularly the Service for the Lord's

Day. If the assignment of The Committee on Selection of Hymns had been to create a general hymnal to succeed another, older hymnal, it would have offered many more hymns, with diverse and diffuse potential uses. Here, on the other hand, is a book that seeks the integrity of unity. Music is a part of worship, not apart from worship. In *The Worshipbook*, congregations should find services through which they can intelligently worship God. They should also find, in the same volume, hymns that are appropriate to those services.

The Joint Committee has been enriched in its work by the renewal of worship in other Churches. The Lord's Prayer, as it appears in the text of *The Worshipbook*, at various places, is in a version prepared by the International Consultation on English Texts. That body was composed of representatives of Roman Catholic and Protestant Churches in twenty countries, including Great Britain and the United States, where English is spoken. It is a remarkable achievement in Christian unity, blending a wide variety of both traditions and nationalities.

The same International Consultation prepared the versions of the Apostles' Creed and the Nicene Creed that *The Worshipbook* employs. For the convenience of congregations not yet ready to adopt the admittedly unfamiliar new versions of the prayer and the creeds, the Lord's Prayer, the Apostles' Creed, and the Nicene Creed are published in traditional form on the end papers of this book.

After the Second Vatican Council, the Roman Catholic Church greatly modified its Christian year, omitting many of the saints' days. In that connection, it published an entirely new lectionary, which is a list of Scripture passages, from the Old and New Testaments, for use on each Lord's Day. The members of the Joint Committee on Worship, like many other Protestants, discovered that the new Roman Catholic selections, and the manner of their organization, were remarkably in harmony with the teachings of the Reformation. The excellence of the lectionary commended itself to the committee, and with a few alterations it is offered in *The Worshipbook*.

As is known, Presbyterians are not required to follow a lectionary as they plan for worship on the Lord's Day. On the other hand, the following of a lectionary, with flexibility, helps assure a congregation that it will not, in the course of a period of years, neglect the great teachings of the Bible.

It is customary, in the preface of such a book as this, to list the members of the committee that prepared it. Inevitably, in a committee that has worked for more than a decade, there have been those who have had to leave the committee and give their attention elsewhere. They should not be held accountable for the final product of the others, but their names will nevertheless be listed.

The list does not indicate membership on one committee or the other, or membership in one church or another. It does not distinguish between laymen and ministers. It does not separate consultants from committee members. It is in alphabetical order, and the omission of further identification symbolizes the unity of the book as well as the unity of those who have served:

James Appleby, James H. Blackwood, Eugene Carson Blake, Scott Francis Brenner, Lewis A. Briner, Frank A. Brooks, Jr., Robert McAfee Brown, Wanzer H. Brunelle, David G. Buttrick, Frank H. Caldwell, Donald F. Campbell, Robert Carwithen, Dwight M. Chalmers, Rex S. Clements, Harold Davis, Theodore A. Gill, Richard W. Graves, Robert E. Grooters, Warner L. Hall, Robert H. Heinze, Thomas Holden, Edward J. Humphrey, Donald D. Kettring, Norman F. Langford, Cecil W. Lower, Joseph E. McAllaster, Dalton E. McDonald, Earl W. Morey, Jr., Marian S. Noecker, Richard M. Peek, Mary H. Plummer, John Ribble, David W. Romig, Garrett C. Roorda, Joan M. Salmon, Donald W. Stake, Jean Woodward Steele, Robert F. Stevenson, Howard S. Swan, James Rawlings Sydnor, H. William Taeusch, Hubert V. Taylor, William P. Thompson, Leonard J. Trinterud, Richard D. Wetzel, James T. Womack, Jr., H. Davis Yeuell.

Richard W. Graves died in 1969. Robert McAfee Brown was the principal writer-editor for the Directory for Worship. David G. Buttrick was the principal writer-editor for the services in *The Worshipbook*. Robert Carwithen was the editor for the musical portions of the book.

At the date of publication the chairman of the Joint Committee on Worship was Robert H. Heinze. Serving as chairmen, at successive stages of the work, were Scott Francis Brenner, Dwight M. Chalmers, Thomas Holden, and David W. Romig. The secretary was H. Davis Yeuell. He was preceded by Robert H. Heinze. John Ribble was publishing consultant.

The chairman of The Committee on Selection of Hymns was Cecil W. Lower. The secretary was Donald F. Campbell.

PREFACE

The Worshipbook is a new book with a new name, offered in the hope that it will serve a new age in the church. The old and well-loved title of the former book, *The Book of Common Worship*, has been sacrificed because the word *common* is no longer used as it was in times gone by. The change in title is symbolic of the attempt to help Christians, and those who may become Christians, to hear God's word, and worship him, in the language of their needs and aspirations, today.

The committees hope that *The Worshipbook* will find favor with the churches, but more, that it may be an instrument blessed by God for those who praise and serve him.

THE JOINT COMMITTEE ON WORSHIP

Memphis
Richmond
Philadelphia

Contents

	Page
PREFACE	5

PREPARATION FOR WORSHIP
- Prayers for Use Before Worship ... 15
- The Law of God ... 17
- Summary of the Law ... 17

ORDERS FOR THE PUBLIC WORSHIP OF GOD
- An Outline, Including the Sacrament of the Lord's Supper ... 21
- An Outline, Including the Sacrament of Baptism ... 22
- An Outline, When the Sacraments Are Omitted ... 23
- Service for the Lord's Day ... 25
- The Sacrament of Baptism ... 43
- The Commissioning of Baptized Members ... 48
  - The Order for Confirmation ... 48
  - The Reception of Members from Other Churches ... 51
- A Brief Order for the Lord's Supper ... 53
- Morning Prayer ... 56
- Evening Prayer ... 59
- Order for an Agape ... 62
- The Marriage Service ... 65
- A Service for the Recognition of a Marriage ... 69
- Witness to the Resurrection—Funeral Service ... 71
  - —Committal Service ... 87
- A Service for Ordination and Installation ... 89
- The Installation of a Commissioned Church Worker ... 96
- Recognition of Trustees ... 98
- Recognition of Church School Teachers ... 100

LITANIES
- Of the Beatitudes ... 105
- Of Confession ... 109
- Of Intercession ... 111
- Of Thanksgiving ... 114
- For the Church ... 116
- For the Unity of Christ's Church ... 119
- Of the Names of the Church ... 121
- For World Peace ... 124

CONTENTS

  For the Nation 127
  For Those Who Work 130

THE CHRISTIAN YEAR
  Advent 135
  Christmastide 137
  Epiphany 139
  Lent 142
  Palm Sunday and Holy Week 144
  Maundy Thursday 146
  Good Friday 147
  Eastertide 148
  Ascension Day 150
  Pentecost 152

SPECIAL DAYS
  New Year's Eve or Day 158
  Christian Unity 159
  World Communion 160
  Reformation Sunday 161
  Thanksgiving Day 162
  Day of Civic or National Significance 163

LECTIONARY FOR THE CHRISTIAN YEAR 167

OTHER PRAYERS FOR CHRISTIAN WORSHIP 179

PRAYERS FOR USE AT HOME 205

MUSICAL RESPONSES AND HYMNS
  Musical Responses—Contents 208
  Preface to the Musical Responses and Hymns 209
  Musical Responses 211–272
  Hymns 273–646

INDEXES
  Index of Scripture and Scriptural Allusions 648
  Guide for the Use of Prayers 653
  Guide for the Use of Hymns 659
  Index of Familiar Hymns with Unfamiliar First Lines 675
  Index of Authors, Translators, and Sources 677
  Index of Composers, Arrangers, and Sources 680
  Alphabetical Index of Tunes 684
  Metrical Index of Tunes 686

Preparation for Worship

Preparation for Worship

PRAYERS FOR USE BEFORE WORSHIP

The session will guide a congregation's preparation for worship. As people gather on the Lord's Day, they may pray, or, when there is instrumental music, give silent attention; they may wish to sing or read hymns, or to greet one another, talking together as neighbors in faith.

The following prayers may be used by members of the congregation before worship:

Eternal God: you have called us to be members of one body. Join us in Spirit with those who in all times and places have praised your name; that, having one faith, we may show the unity of your church, and bring honor to our Lord and Savior, Jesus Christ. Amen.

God our king: rule over us as we meet together, and so fill us with your Spirit, that in faith, hope, and love we may worship you, and proclaim your mighty deeds; through Jesus Christ our Lord. Amen.

Merciful God, who sent Jesus to eat and drink with sinners: lead us to your table and be present with us, weak and sinful people; that, fed by your love, we may live to praise you, remembering Jesus Christ our Savior. Amen.

Lord God: we cannot pray unless your Spirit prays in us; we cannot forgive ourselves unless your word tells mercy.

Lord God: speak your word, and send your Spirit to help us worship as we ought; for the sake of our Lord Jesus Christ. Amen.

A doxology may be sung with the choir as they make ready for worship, or one of the following prayers may be used:

God of grace: you have given us minds to know you, hearts to love you, and voices to sing your praise. Fill us with Holy

Spirit, so we may celebrate your glory, and truly worship you; through Jesus Christ our Lord. **Amen.**

Great God: you have been generous and marvelously kind. Give us such wonder, love, and gratitude that we may sing praises to you, and joyfully honor your name; through Jesus Christ our Lord. **Amen.**

Give to the Lord glory and praise!

> **His loving-kindness is forever.**

Lift up your hearts.

> **We lift them to the Lord.**

Praise the Lord.

> **The Lord's name be praised.**

Amen.

> **And Amen.**

When elders meet before worship, they may wish to say one of the following prayers:

God our Father: without your word we have nothing to say, and without your Spirit we are helpless. Give us Holy Spirit, so that we may lead your people in prayer, proclaim the good news, and gratefully praise your name; through Jesus Christ our Lord. **Amen.**

Startle us, O God, with your truth, and open our minds to your Spirit; that we may be one with your Son our Lord, and serve as his disciples; through Jesus Christ. **Amen.**

Almighty God: you have set a table before us, and called us to feast with you. Prepare us in mind and spirit to minister in your name, and to honor your Son, our Lord, Jesus Christ. **Amen.**

THE LAW OF GOD

In preparation for worship, the people may wish to think on the law of God.

The law, or the summary of the law given by our Lord Jesus, may be used in the Service for the Lord's Day immediately after the Declaration of Pardon, as a guide for the forgiven Christian who will live obedient to God.

God spoke all these words, saying, I am the Lord your God.

You shall have no other gods before me.

You shall not make for yourself a graven image, or any likeness of anything that is in heaven above, or that is in the earth beneath, or that is in the water under the earth; you shall not bow down to them or serve them.

You shall not take the name of the Lord your God in vain.

Remember the Sabbath day, to keep it holy.

Honor your father and your mother.

You shall not kill.

You shall not commit adultery.

You shall not steal.

You shall not bear false witness against your neighbor.

You shall not covet your neighbor's house; you shall not covet your neighbor's wife, or anything that is your neighbor's.

SUMMARY OF THE LAW

Our Lord Jesus said:

You shall love the Lord your God with all your heart, and with all your soul, and with all your mind. This is the great and first commandment. And a second is like it, You shall love your neighbor as yourself. On these two commandments depend all the law and the prophets.

Orders for the
Public Worship of God

OUTLINE OF THE SERVICE FOR THE LORD'S DAY
Including the Sacrament of the Lord's Supper

THE BASIC STRUCTURE	ADDITIONS AND VARIANT FORMS
CALL TO WORSHIP	
	Versicle
HYMN OF PRAISE	
CONFESSION OF SIN	
DECLARATION OF PARDON	
RESPONSE	(Gloria, Hymn, or Psalm)
PRAYER FOR ILLUMINATION	(Or, the Collect for the Day)
OLD TESTAMENT LESSON	
	Anthem, Canticle, or Psalm
NEW TESTAMENT LESSON(S)	
SERMON	
	Ascription of Praise
	AN INVITATION
CREED	
	Hymn
	Concerns of the Church
THE PRAYERS OF THE PEOPLE	
THE PEACE	
OFFERING	
	Anthem or Special Music
	Hymn or Doxology
INVITATION TO THE LORD'S TABLE	
THE THANKSGIVING	
THE LORD'S PRAYER	
THE COMMUNION	
RESPONSE	
HYMN	
CHARGE	
BENEDICTION	

OUTLINE OF THE SERVICE FOR THE LORD'S DAY
Including the Sacrament of Baptism

THE BASIC STRUCTURE	ADDITIONS AND VARIANT FORMS
CALL TO WORSHIP	
	Versicle
HYMN OF PRAISE	
CONFESSION OF SIN	
DECLARATION OF PARDON	
RESPONSE	(Gloria, Hymn, or Psalm)
PRAYER FOR ILLUMINATION	(Or, the Collect for the Day)
OLD TESTAMENT LESSON	
	Anthem, Canticle, or Psalm
NEW TESTAMENT LESSON(S)	
SERMON	
	Ascription of Praise
	AN INVITATION
APOSTLES' CREED	
THE SACRAMENT OF BAPTISM	
	Hymn
	Concerns of the Church
THE PRAYERS OF THE PEOPLE	
THE PEACE	
OFFERING	
	Anthem or Special Music
	Hymn or Doxology
PRAYER OF THANKSGIVING	
THE LORD'S PRAYER	
HYMN	
CHARGE	
BENEDICTION	

OUTLINE FOR THE SERVICE FOR THE LORD'S DAY
When the Sacraments Are Omitted

THE BASIC STRUCTURE	ADDITIONS AND VARIANT FORMS
CALL TO WORSHIP	
	Versicle
HYMN OF PRAISE	
CONFESSION OF SIN	
DECLARATION OF PARDON	
RESPONSE	(Gloria, Hymn, or Psalm)
PRAYER FOR ILLUMINATION	(Or, the Collect for the Day)
OLD TESTAMENT LESSON	
	Anthem, Canticle, or Psalm
NEW TESTAMENT LESSON(S)	
SERMON	
	Ascription of Praise
	AN INVITATION
CREED	
	Hymn
	Concerns of the Church
THE PRAYERS OF THE PEOPLE	
THE PEACE	
OFFERING	
	Anthem or Special Music
	Doxology or Response
PRAYER OF THANKSGIVING	
THE LORD'S PRAYER	
HYMN	
CHARGE	
BENEDICTION	

ORDER FOR THE
PUBLIC WORSHIP OF GOD

Service for the Lord's Day

CALL TO WORSHIP

Let the people stand. The minister shall call the people to the worship of God, saying:

Let us worship God.

The minister shall say one or more of the following:

Our help is in the name of the Lord, who made heaven and earth.

God loved the world so much that he gave his only Son, so that everyone who believes in him may not be lost but may have eternal life.

Thank God, the God and Father of our Lord Jesus Christ, that in his great mercy we men have been born again into a life full of hope, through Christ's rising from the dead.

God was in Christ reconciling the world to himself—not counting their sins against them—and has commissioned us with the message of reconciliation.

The kingdom of the world has become the kingdom of our Lord and his Christ, and he will reign forever and ever.

At the name of Jesus every knee should bow and every tongue confess that Jesus Christ is Lord, to the glory of God the Father.

In the name of the Father, and of the Son, and of the Holy Spirit.

And, the following may be sung or said:

Praise the Lord.

The Lord's name be praised.

Let the people sing a psalm or a hymn of praise.

CONFESSION OF SIN

The minister shall say:

If we claim to be sinless, we are self-deceived and strangers to the truth. If we confess our sins, God is just, and may be trusted to forgive our sins and cleanse us from every kind of wrong.

Let us admit our sin before God:

> **Almighty God: in Jesus Christ you called us to be a servant people, but we do not do what you command. We are often silent when we should speak, and useless when we could be useful. We are lazy servants, timid and heartless, who turn neighbors away from your love. Have mercy on us, O God, and, though we do not deserve your care, forgive us, and free us from sin; through Jesus Christ our Lord. Amen.**

Or,

The proof of God's amazing love is this: while we were sinners Christ died for us. Because we have faith in him, we dare with confidence to approach God.

Let us ask God to forgive us.

> **Almighty God: you love us, but we have not loved you; you call, but we have not listened. We walk away from neighbors in need, wrapped up in our own concerns. We have gone along with evil, with prejudice, warfare, and greed. God our Father, help us to face up to ourselves, so that, as you move toward us in mercy, we may repent, turn to you, and receive forgiveness; through Jesus Christ our Lord. Amen.**

The people may pray silently.

DECLARATION OF PARDON

One of the following may be said:

Hear the good news!

> This statement is completely reliable and should be universally accepted: Christ Jesus entered the world to rescue sinners.

He personally bore our sins in his body on the cross, so that we might be dead to sin and be alive to all that is good.

> Or,

Who is in a position to condemn? Only Christ, and Christ died for us, Christ rose for us, Christ reigns in power for us, Christ prays for us.

If a man is in Christ, he becomes a new person altogether— the past is finished and gone, everything has become fresh and new.

> And,

Friends: Believe the good news of the gospel.

In Jesus Christ, we are forgiven.

> Then the minister may say one of the following exhortations; or read the Summary of the Law (see page 17):

As God's own people, be merciful in action, kindly in heart, humble in mind. Be always ready to forgive as freely as the Lord has forgiven you. And, above everything else, be loving, and never forget to be thankful for what God has done for you.

> Or,

Let us now obey the Lord. This is his command: to give allegiance to his Son Jesus Christ and to love one another.

> Then the people may stand to sing or say the following response; or some other thanksgiving:

Give thanks to God, for he is good, his love is everlasting.

> **You are the Lord, giver of mercy!**
> **You are the Christ, giver of mercy!**
> **You are the Lord, giver of mercy!**

PRAYER FOR ILLUMINATION

> Before the reading of the Scripture lessons, the Collect for the Day may be used; or one of the following Prayers for Illumination, or a like prayer, may be said by the reader or by the people in unison:

Prepare our hearts, O Lord, to accept your word. Silence in us any voice but your own; that, hearing, we may also obey your will; through Jesus Christ our Lord. **Amen.**

Or,

O God, tell us what we need to hear, and show us what we ought to do to obey your Son, Jesus Christ. **Amen.**

OLD TESTAMENT LESSON

Before the Old Testament lesson, let the reader say:

The lesson is . . .
Listen for the word of God!

After the Old Testament lesson, the reader may say:

Amen.

After the lesson, there may be an anthem, a canticle, or a psalm.

NEW TESTAMENT LESSON(S)

Before the reading of the New Testament lesson, or lessons, let the reader say:

The lesson is . . .
Listen for the word of God!

After the New Testament lesson, or lessons, the reader may say:

Amen.

SERMON

When the Scripture has been read, its message shall be proclaimed in a Sermon. The Sermon may be followed by an Ascription of Praise:

Amen. Praise and glory and wisdom and thanksgiving and honor and power and strength to our God forever and ever. **Amen.**

Or,

Now to the King of all worlds, undying, invisible, the only God, be honor and glory forever and ever. **Amen.**

After the Sermon, an INVITATION may be given to any who wish to answer God's word by declaring their faith, or by renewing their obedience to Christ.

CREED

The people may stand to sing or say a Creed of the church; or some Affirmation of Faith drawn from Scripture:

Let us say what we believe.

> We believe in one God,
>> the Father, the Almighty,
>> maker of heaven and earth,
>> of all that is seen and unseen.
>
> We believe in one Lord, Jesus Christ,
>> the only Son of God,
>
> eternally begotten of the Father,
> God from God, Light from Light,
> true God from true God,
> begotten, not made, one in Being with the Father.
> Through him all things were made.
> For us men and for our salvation
>> he came down from heaven:
>
> by the power of the Holy Spirit
>> he was born of the Virgin Mary, and became man.
>
> For our sake he was crucified under Pontius Pilate;
> he suffered, died, and was buried.
>> On the third day he rose again
>>> in fulfillment of the Scriptures;
>>
>> he ascended into heaven
>>> and is seated at the right hand of the Father.
>
> He will come again in glory to judge the living
>> and the dead,
>> and his kingdom will have no end.
>
> We believe in the Holy Spirit, the Lord,
>> the giver of life,
>
> who proceeds from the Father and the Son.
> With the Father and the Son he is worshiped
>> and glorified.
>
> He has spoken through the prophets.
> We believe in one holy catholic and apostolic church.
> We acknowledge one baptism for the forgiveness of sins.
> We look for the resurrection of the dead,
>> and the life of the world to come. Amen.

Or,

I believe in God, the Father almighty,
   creator of heaven and earth.

I believe in Jesus Christ, his only Son, our Lord.
   He was conceived by the power of the Holy Spirit
      and born of the Virgin Mary.
   He suffered under Pontius Pilate,
      was crucified, died, and was buried.
   He descended to the dead.
   On the third day he rose again.
   He ascended into heaven,
      and is seated at the right hand of the Father.
   He will come again to judge the living and the dead.

I believe in the Holy Spirit,
   the holy catholic church,
   the communion of saints,
   the forgiveness of sins,
   the resurrection of the body,
   and the life everlasting. Amen.

Or,

This is the good news which we received, in which we stand, and by which we are saved: that Christ died for our sins according to the Scriptures, that he was buried, that he was raised on the third day; and that he appeared to Peter, then to the Twelve and to many faithful witnesses.

We believe he is the Christ, the Son of the living God. He is the first and the last, the beginning and the end, he is our Lord and our God. Amen.

A hymn may be sung.

CONCERNS OF THE CHURCH

Announcements concerning the life of the church may be made.

THE PRAYERS OF THE PEOPLE

Prayers of Intercession may be said by a leader, or leaders, to express concerns of the church.

Or, a few or many of the following prayers may be used with the people responding, or by the people in unison.

The response, "Hear our prayer, O God," may be said instead of "Amen" after each intercession.

The following may be sung or said:

The Lord is risen.

He is risen indeed.

Then, the minister may say:

Let us pray.

Father, whose Son Jesus Christ taught us to pray: let our prayers for others be the kind you want, and not just ways of getting what we want, who already have so much in Jesus Christ, our Savior. **Amen.**

Let us pray for the world.

Silent prayer.

Lord of all the worlds that are, Savior of men: we pray for the whole creation. Order the unruly powers, deal with injustice, feed and satisfy the longing peoples, so that in freedom your children may enjoy the world you have made, and cheerfully sing your praises; through Jesus Christ our Lord. **Amen.**

Let us pray for the church.

Silent prayer.

Gracious God: you called us to be the church of Jesus Christ. Keep us one in faith and service, breaking bread together, and telling good news to the world; that men may believe you are love, and live to give you glory; through Jesus Christ our Lord. **Amen.**

Let us pray for peace.

Silent prayer.

Eternal God: send peace on earth, and put down greed, pride, and anger, which turn man against man and set nation against nation. Speed the day when wars will end and all men call you Father; through Jesus Christ our Lord. **Amen.**

Let us pray for enemies.

>   **Silent prayer.**

O God, whom we cannot love unless we love our brothers: remove hate and prejudice from us and all men, so that your children may be reconciled with those they fear, resent, or threaten; and live together in your peace; through Jesus Christ our Lord. **Amen.**

Let us pray for those who govern us.

>   **Silent prayer.**

Almighty God, ruler of men: direct those who make, administer, and judge our laws; the President of the United States and others in authority among us (especially _____); that, led by your wisdom, they may lead us in the way of righteousness; through Jesus Christ our Lord. **Amen.**

Let us pray for world leaders.

>   **Silent prayer.**

Great God our hope: give vision to those who serve the United Nations, or govern people; that, with goodwill and justice, they may take down barriers, and draw together one new world in peace; through Jesus Christ our Lord. **Amen.**

Let us pray for the work we do.

>   **Silent prayer.**

Manage us, wise God, by your Spirit, so the work we do may serve your purpose, and make this world a good home for all your children; through Jesus Christ our Lord. **Amen.**

Let us pray for the sick.

>   **Silent prayer.**

Merciful God: you bear the hurt of the world. Look with compassion on those who are sick (especially on _____); cheer them by your word, and bring health as a sign that, in your promised kingdom, there will be no more pain or crying; through Jesus Christ our Lord. **Amen.**

Let us pray for those who sorrow.

Silent prayer.

God of comfort: stand with those who sorrow (especially _____); that they may be sure that neither death nor life, nor things present nor things to come, shall separate them from your love; through Jesus Christ our Lord. **Amen.**

Let us pray for friends and families.

Silent prayer.

O God our Father: bless us and those we love, our friends and families; that, drawing close to you, we may be drawn closer to each other; through Jesus Christ our Lord. **Amen.**

God of our fathers: we praise you for all your servants who, having been faithful to you on earth, now live with you in heaven. Keep us in fellowship with them, until we meet with all your children in the joy of the kingdom; through Jesus Christ our Lord. **Amen.**

Mighty God, whose word we trust, whose Spirit prays in our prayers: sort out our requests, and further those which are helpful, and will bring about your purpose for the earth; through Jesus Christ our Lord. **Amen.**

THE PEACE

Let the minister say:

God sent the world his only Son. Since God loved us so much, we too should love one another.

Let us love one another, since love comes from God.

The peace of the Lord Jesus Christ be with you all.

The people may greet one another with a handclasp, saying: "Peace be with you."

It is fitting that the Lord's Supper be celebrated as often as each Lord's Day. If the Lord's Supper is not celebrated, let the service continue on page 38.

OFFERING

The minister shall say:

Let us bring our gifts to God.

As the offerings of the people are gathered, there may be an anthem, or other appropriate music. Then, as the offerings, which may include the bread and the wine, are brought forward, the minister shall say:

Praise God for his goodness.

A hymn or a doxology may be sung.

INVITATION TO THE LORD'S TABLE

Friends: This is the joyful feast of the people of God!

Men will come from east and west, and from north and south, and sit at table in the kingdom of God.

This is the Lord's table. Our Savior invites those who trust him to share the feast which he has prepared.

According to Luke, when our risen Lord was at table with his disciples, he took the bread, and blessed and broke it, and gave it to them. And their eyes were opened and they recognized him.

THE THANKSGIVING

The following may be sung or said:

Lift up your hearts.

We lift them to the Lord.

Give thanks to God, for he is good.

His love is everlasting.

Or,

SERVICE FOR THE LORD'S DAY

Lift up your hearts.

> **We lift them up to the Lord.**

Let us give thanks to the Lord our God.

> **It is right to give him thanks and praise.**

> *Then, the minister may say:*

Holy Lord, Father almighty, everlasting God:
[we thank you for commanding light out of darkness, for dividing the waters into sea and dry land, for creating the whole world and calling it good. We thank you for making us in your image to live with each other in love; for the breath of life, the gift of speech, and freedom to choose your way. You have told us your purpose in commandments to Moses, and called for justice in the cry of the prophets. Through long generations, you have been fair and kind to all your children.]*

Great and wonderful are your works, Lord God almighty. Your ways are just and true. With men of faith from all times and places, we lift our hearts in joyful praise, for you alone are holy:

> *The following may be sung or said:*

> **Holy, holy, holy,**
> **God of power and majesty,**
> **heaven and earth are full of your glory,**
> **O God most high!**

> *Or,*

> **Holy, holy, holy Lord, God of power and might,**
> **heaven and earth are full of your glory.**
> > **Hosanna in the highest.**

> **Blessed is he who comes in the name of the Lord.**
> > **Hosanna in the highest.**

> *Then, the minister may say:*

Holy Father: we thank you for your Son Jesus, who lived with us sharing joy and sorrow. He told your story, healed the sick, and was a friend of sinners. Obeying you, he took up his cross and

---

*According to the church year, some other form may be substituted for this paragraph. See page 40.

was murdered by men he loved. We praise you that he is not dead, but is risen to rule the world; and that he is still the friend of sinners. We trust him to overcome every power to hurt or divide us, so that, when you bring in your promised kingdom, we will celebrate victory with him.

> **Remembering the Lord Jesus, we break bread and share one cup, announcing his death for the sins of the world, and telling his resurrection to all men and nations.**

Great God: give your Holy Spirit in the breaking of bread, so that we may be drawn together, and, joined to Christ the Lord, receive new life, and remain his glad and faithful people until we feast with him in glory.

> **O God, who called us from death to life: we give ourselves to you; and with the church through all ages, we thank you for your saving love in Jesus Christ our Lord. Amen.**

> **Our Father in heaven,**
>   **holy be your name,**
>   **your kingdom come,**
>   **your will be done,**
>   **on earth as in heaven.**
> **Give us today our daily bread.**
> **Forgive us our sins**
>   **as we forgive those who sin against us.**
> **Do not bring us to the test**
>   **but deliver us from evil.**
> **For the kingdom, the power, and the glory are yours**
>   **now and forever. Amen.**

> *The minister shall break bread in the presence of the people, saying:*

The Lord Jesus, on the night of his arrest, took bread, and after giving thanks to God, broke it and said: "This is my body, which is for you; do this, remembering me."

> *The minister shall pour the wine in the presence of the people, saying:*

In the same way, he took the cup after supper, and said: "This cup is the new covenant sealed in my blood. Whenever you drink it, do this, remembering me."

Every time you eat this bread and drink the cup, you proclaim the death of the Lord, until he comes.

> The minister and those assisting him shall themselves partake, and shall distribute the bread and the wine to the people. As the bread and wine are distributed, the people may sing or say psalms, or hymns of praise to Christ.
>
> As the minister gives the bread and the wine, he may say:

Jesus said: I am the bread of life. He who comes to me will never be hungry; he who believes in me will never thirst.

> And,

Jesus said: I am the vine, you are the branches. Cut off from me you can do nothing.

> When all the people have received, the minister shall say:

The grace of the Lord Jesus Christ be with you all. **Amen.**

> Then, the minister and the people shall praise God by singing or saying:

Alleluia! For the Lord our God, the Almighty, has come into his kingdom! Let us rejoice, let us be glad with all our hearts. Let us give him the glory forever and ever. Amen.

> Or,

Bless the Lord, O my soul;

> **And all that is within me, bless his holy name!**

Bless the Lord, O my soul,

> **And forget not all his benefits.**

> Or,

Let us pray.

> **God our help: we thank you for this supper shared in the Spirit with your Son Jesus, who makes us new and strong,**

who brings us life eternal. We praise you for giving us all good gifts in him, and pledge ourselves to serve you, even as in Christ you have served us. Amen.

A hymn may be sung, after which the people shall be dismissed:

Go in peace. Live as free men. Serve the Lord, rejoicing in the power of the Holy Spirit.

Or,

Go out into the world in peace; have courage; hold on to what is good; return no man evil for evil; strengthen the fainthearted; support the weak; help the suffering; honor all men; love and serve the Lord, rejoicing in the power of the Holy Spirit.

And,

The grace of our Lord Jesus Christ and the love of God and the fellowship of the Holy Spirit be with you all.

Let the people say:

Alleluia! Amen.

When the Lord's Supper is omitted, the service shall continue from page 33, and conclude in the following manner:

OFFERING

The minister shall say:

Let us bring our gifts to God.

As the offerings of the people are gathered, an anthem may be sung, or other music provided. When the offerings are brought forward the people may stand to sing a doxology or some other response.

PRAYER OF THANKSGIVING

The following may be sung or said:

Lift up your hearts.

We lift them to the Lord.

Give thanks to God, for he is good.

>**His love is everlasting.**

>*Or,*

Lift up your hearts.

>**We lift them up to the Lord.**

Let us give thanks to the Lord our God.

>**It is right to give him thanks and praise.**

>*Then, the minister may say:*

O God our Father, creator of the world and giver of all good things: we thank you for our home on earth and for the joy of living. We praise you for your love in Jesus Christ, who came to set things right, who died rejected on the cross and rose triumphant from the dead. Because he lives, we live to praise you, Father, Son, and Holy Spirit, our God forever.

>**O God, who called us from death to life: we give ourselves to you; and with the church through all ages, we thank you for your saving love in Jesus Christ our Lord. Amen.**

Let us pray our Lord's Prayer.

>**Our Father in heaven,**
>   **holy be your name,**
>   **your kingdom come,**
>   **your will be done,**
>   **on earth as in heaven.**
>**Give us today our daily bread.**
>**Forgive us our sins**
>   **as we forgive those who sin against us.**
>**Do not bring us to the test**
>   **but deliver us from evil.**
>**For the kingdom, the power, and the glory are yours**
>   **now and forever. Amen.**

A hymn may be sung, after which the people shall be dismissed:

Go in peace. Live as free men. Serve the Lord, rejoicing in the power of the Holy Spirit.

Or,

Go out into the world in peace; have courage; hold on to what is good; return no man evil for evil; strengthen the fainthearted; support the weak; help the suffering; honor all men; love and serve the Lord, rejoicing in the power of the Holy Spirit.

And,

The grace of our Lord Jesus Christ and the love of God and the fellowship of the Holy Spirit be with you all.

Let the people say:

Alleluia! Amen.

SEASONAL VARIATIONS FOR THE THANKSGIVING
(see page 35)

Advent

who made this world a place for Jesus Christ, and, before he was born, promised his coming in the words of the prophets: we thank you for this holy supper, which is for us a sign of his returning to claim his lands and people.

Christmas

we thank you for the gift of your Son Jesus, light in darkness, savior of men, who was born in a poor place, who now rules the world, Lord of lords and King of kings.

Epiphany

who sent a star to guide wise men to where Christ was born, and whose signs and words in every age lead men to him: we thank you for showing us our Lord Jesus, the light of the world, by whom we are saved, and baptized into your service.

Lent
before whose justice no man can stand, yet whose love is so sure we need not hide ourselves: we thank you for your mercy reported by the prophets and shown in Jesus Christ, for the law you give to guide us, and for the promise of new life to live for you and with our neighbors.

Palm Sunday
we thank you for your Son Jesus, who fulfilled the prophets' words, and entered the city of Jerusalem to die for us and all men. We praise you that he enters our world as Savior and King, and calls men to obey him.

Maundy Thursday
who sent Jesus as a servant to wash away our pride, and to feed us with bread of life: we thank you for inviting us to feast with him who died for us, and who teaches us to serve each other in modesty and love.

Good Friday
whose Son Jesus was condemned, forsaken, and hanged on a cross: we are thankful that he obeyed you and died, to show us that we are not forsaken or condemned, but will have a promised paradise with him.

Easter
we thank you for the power which brought our Lord Jesus from death to life, and which is promised to us who believe in him. We praise you that, breaking bread by faith, we know Christ risen, and can trust him to save us from death and from sin.

Ascension
who created this world and raised Christ to rule it: we thank you that because he is lifted in power, he can draw us from weakness into the way of righteousness and truth.

Pentecost
who sent the Holy Spirit to kindle faith and to teach the truth of your Son Jesus: we thank you that you are working in the

church to make us brave disciples who will preach Christ the Lord in every nation.

Trinity

Creator of the world, Savior of men, life-giving Spirit: we thank you for baptizing us in your name, Father, Son, and Holy Spirit, and for welcoming us by faith into one holy church.

World Communion

you have formed the universe in your wisdom, and created all things by your power; and you have set us in families on the earth to live with you in faith. We praise you for good gifts of bread and wine, and for the table you spread in the world as a sign of your love for all men in Christ.

Another Optional Form

we thank you for commanding light to shine out of darkness, for stretching out the heavens, and laying the foundations of the earth; for making all things through your Word. We thank you for creating us in your image and for keeping us in your steadfast love. We praise you for calling us to be your people, for revealing your purpose in the law and the prophets, and for dealing patiently with our pride and disobedience.

ORDER FOR THE
PUBLIC WORSHIP OF GOD

The Sacrament of Baptism*

The service is designed for the baptism of mature believers, or for the baptism of infants. When infants are being baptized, the wording should be changed as indicated in the rubrics.

Ordinarily, baptism is to be administered in the presence of the worshiping congregation, following the preaching of the word and the Apostles' Creed.

Then let the minister say:

Hear the words of our Lord Jesus Christ:
> All authority in heaven and on earth has been given to me. Go therefore and make disciples of all nations, baptizing them in the name of the Father and of the Son and of the Holy Spirit, teaching them to observe all that I have commanded you; and lo, I am with you always, to the close of the age.

Obeying the word of our Lord Jesus, and sure of his presence with us, we baptize those whom he has called to be his own.

In Jesus Christ, God has promised to forgive our sins, and has joined us together in the family of faith which is his church. He has delivered us from darkness and transferred us to the kingdom of his beloved Son. In Jesus Christ, God has promised to be our Father, and to welcome us as brothers and sisters of Christ.

Know that the promises of God are for you. By baptism, God puts his sign on you to show that you belong to him, and gives you Holy Spirit as a guarantee that, sharing Christ's reconciling work, you will also share his victory; that, dying with Christ to sin, you will be raised with him to new life.

---

*This book is for three Churches. Questions asked in this service are those used in The United Presbyterian Church in the United States of America. Other questions may be required in the Cumberland Presbyterian Church and the Presbyterian Church in the United States.

> The minister shall address the person to be baptized, or the parents presenting a child for baptism, saying those words required by the Constitution of his church (see footnote on page 43).

Friend: In presenting yourself for baptism, you announce your faith in Jesus Christ, and show that you want to study him, know him, love him, and serve him as his chosen disciple.

> Or,

Friends: In presenting your *child* for baptism, you announce your faith in Jesus Christ, and show that you want your *child* to study him, know him, love him, and serve him as *his* chosen *disciple*.

> And,

Show your purpose by answering these questions.

Who is your Lord and Savior?

> ***Jesus Christ is my Lord and Savior.***

Do you trust in him?

> *I do.*

Do you intend (your child) to be his disciple, to obey his word and show his love?

> *I do.*

> If the candidate for baptism is to be received as a communicant member of the church, the minister shall ask this additional question:

Will you be a faithful member of this congregation, giving of yourself in every way, and will you seek the fellowship of the church wherever you may be?

> *I will.*

> Let the people stand. An elder representing the session shall address the people (and the parents presenting a child for baptism), saying:

Our Lord Jesus Christ ordered us to teach those who are baptized. Do you, the people of the church, promise to tell this new disciple (*this child*) the good news of the gospel, to help *him*

know all that Christ commands, and, by your fellowship, to strengthen *his* family ties with the household of God?
We do.

> Let the minister say:

Let us pray.

God our Father: we thank you for your faithfulness, promised in this sacrament, and for the hope we have in your Son Jesus. As we baptize with water, baptize us with Holy Spirit, so that what we say may be your word and what we do may be your work. By your power, may we be made one with Christ our Lord in common faith and purpose.

> The minister and the people shall say together:

O God, who called us from death to life: we give ourselves to you, and, with the church through all ages, we thank you for your saving love in Jesus Christ our Lord. Amen.

> Let the minister address the candidate (or the parents presenting a child for baptism), saying:

What is your (child's) name?

> The minister shall baptize the candidate with water, calling him by his given name or names:

_____, I baptize you in the name of the Father and of the Son and of the Holy Spirit. **Amen.**

This child of God is now received into the holy catholic church. See what love the Father has given us, that we should be called children of God; and we are!

> If an infant has been baptized, turn to intercessions on pages 46-47.

> If the baptized person is being received into full communicant membership, let the minister or an elder say those words required by the Constitution of his church (see footnote on page 43).

_____, you are a disciple of Jesus Christ. He has commissioned you. Live in his love, and serve him.

Be filled with gratitude. Let the message of Christ dwell among you in all its richness. Whatever you are doing, whether you speak or act, do everything in the name of the Lord Jesus, giving thanks to God the Father through him.

You are no longer aliens, but fellow citizens with God's people, members of God's household. You are built upon the foundation laid by the apostles and prophets, and Christ Jesus himself is the foundation stone. In him you too are being built with all the rest into a spiritual dwelling for God.

Let a representative of the session lead the people in prayer, saying:

Let us pray.

God our Father: we praise you for calling us to be a servant people, and for gathering us into the body of Christ. We thank you for choosing to add to our number brothers and sisters in faith. Together, may we live in your Spirit and so love one another, that we may have the mind of Jesus Christ our Lord, to whom we give honor and glory forever. Amen.

Let the minister, and the elder representing the session, welcome the baptized member with a handshake, saying:

Welcome to the ministry of Jesus Christ.

The baptized member shall be dismissed:

Go now, and serve the Lord.

The grace of the Lord Jesus Christ, and the love of God, and the fellowship of the Holy Spirit, be with you all. **Amen.**

The following intercessions may be used in the service of baptism:

Let us pray.

Almighty God, giver of life: you have called us by name, and pledged to each of us your faithful love. We pray for your *child*, _____. Watch over *him*. Guide *him* as *he* grows in faith.

Give *him* understanding, and a quick concern for neighbors. Help *him* to be a true disciple of Jesus Christ, who was baptized your Son and servant, who is our risen Lord. **Amen.**

God of grace, Father of us all: we pray for parents, _____ and _____. Help them to know you, to love with your love, to teach your truth, and to tell the story of Jesus to their child, so that your word may be heard, and bring about plans for us you have promised, in Jesus Christ our Lord. **Amen.**

The following prayer may be said in unison:

Holy God: remind us of the promises given in our own baptism, and renew our trust in you. Make us strong to obey your will, and to serve you with joy; for the sake of Jesus Christ our Lord. Amen.

ORDER FOR THE PUBLIC WORSHIP OF GOD

The Commissioning of Baptized Members; the Order for Their Confirmation; and the Reception of Members from Other Churches

Sections I and II of this service may be used separately; or they may be joined as indicated in the rubrics.

I. THE ORDER FOR CONFIRMATION

After the Sermon has been preached, let an elder representing the session invite the candidate(s) for confirmation to stand before the congregation, saying:

_____ *have* been received by the session into the communicant membership of the church. *They have* studied God's word, and *have* learned the belief and practice of his people. *They are* here to declare *their* faith, and to be joined with us in the service of Jesus Christ.

When those to be confirmed have assembled, let the minister say:

Hear the words of our Lord Jesus Christ.

You did not choose me, but I chose you and appointed you that you should go and bear fruit.

Everyone who acknowledges me before men, I also will acknowledge before my Father who is in heaven.

Friends: Jesus Christ has chosen you, and, in baptism, has joined you to himself. He has called you, together with us, into the church, which is his body. Now, he has brought you to this time and place, so you may confess his name before men, and go out to serve him as faithful disciples.

COMMISSIONING BAPTIZED MEMBERS

The minister shall address those to be confirmed, asking questions required by the Constitution of his church (see footnote on page 43).

_____, who is your Lord and Savior?

Jesus Christ is my Lord and Savior.

Do you trust in him?

I do.

Do you intend to be his disciple, to obey his word and to show his love?

I do.

Will you be a faithful member of this congregation, giving of yourself in every way, and will you seek the fellowship of the church wherever you may be?

I will.

Those to be confirmed may kneel. Let the minister or an elder give the following charge:

_____, you are a disciple of Jesus Christ. He has commissioned you. Live in his love, and serve him.

And,

Be filled with gratitude. Let the message of Christ dwell among you in all its richness. Whatever you are doing, whether you speak or act, do everything in the name of the Lord Jesus, giving thanks to God the Father through him.

If there are members who have been received by the session from other Christian churches, they may be recognized and made welcome at this time (see section II). Otherwise, let the minister say:

Let us affirm our faith.

> I believe in God, the Father almighty,
> creator of heaven and earth.
>
> I believe in Jesus Christ, his only Son, our Lord.
> He was conceived by the power of the Holy Spirit
> and born of the Virgin Mary.

> He suffered under Pontius Pilate,
>   was crucified, died, and was buried.
> He descended to the dead.
> On the third day he rose again.
> He ascended into heaven,
>   and is seated at the right hand of the Father.
> He will come again to judge the living and the dead.
>
> I believe in the Holy Spirit,
>   the holy catholic church,
>   the communion of saints,
>   the forgiveness of sins,
>   the resurrection of the body,
>   and the life everlasting. Amen.

Let the representative of the session lead the people in prayer, saying:

Let us pray.

> O God our Father: we praise you for calling us to be a servant people, and for gathering us into the body of Christ. We thank you for choosing to add to our number brothers and sisters in faith. Together, may we live in your Spirit, and so love one another, that we may have the mind of Jesus Christ our Lord, to whom we give honor and glory forever. Amen.

Let the minister and the elder representing the session welcome those confirmed with a handshake, saying:

Welcome to this ministry of Jesus Christ.

Those confirmed shall be dismissed:

Go, and serve the Lord.

The grace of our Lord Jesus Christ, and the love of God, and the fellowship of the Holy Spirit, be with you all. **Amen.**

II. THE RECEPTION OF MEMBERS FROM OTHER CHURCHES

An elder representing the session shall name those who have been received by letter of commendation from other Christian churches, or by reaffirmation of their faith in Jesus Christ. He shall invite them to stand, saying:

_____ *have* been received into the membership of this congregation by letter of commendation from *another* Christian *church*, or by reaffirmation of *their* faith in Jesus Christ.

When those to be received have stood before the congregation, let the minister say:

Friends: As members of the one, holy, catholic, and apostolic church, you do not come to us as strangers, but as brothers and sisters in the Lord. We welcome you to the worship and work of this people of God.

There is one body and one Spirit, one Lord, one faith, one baptism, one God and Father of us all, who is above all, and through all, and in all.

Do you promise to be a faithful member of this congregation, giving of yourself in every way, and so fulfill your calling as a disciple of Jesus Christ the Lord?

I do.

Then, let the minister say:

Let us affirm our faith.

>   **I believe in God, the Father almighty,**
>   **creator of heaven and earth.**
>
>   **I believe in Jesus Christ, his only Son, our Lord.**
>   **He was conceived by the power of the Holy Spirit**
>   **and born of the Virgin Mary.**
>   **He suffered under Pontius Pilate,**
>   **was crucified, died, and was buried.**
>   **He descended to the dead.**
>   **On the third day he rose again.**
>   **He ascended into heaven,**
>   **and is seated at the right hand of the Father.**
>   **He will come again to judge the living and the dead.**

I believe in the Holy Spirit,
   the holy catholic church,
   the communion of saints,
   the forgiveness of sins,
   the resurrection of the body,
   and the life everlasting. Amen.

Let the representative of the session lead the people in prayer, saying:

Let us pray.

O God our Father: we praise you for calling us to be a servant people, and for gathering us into the body of Christ. We thank you for choosing to add to our number brothers and sisters in faith. Together, may we live in your Spirit, and so love one another, that we may have the mind of Jesus Christ our Lord, to whom we give honor and glory forever. Amen.

Let the minister and the elder representing the session welcome the new communicant members with a handshake, saying:

Welcome to this ministry of Jesus Christ.

Then, the new communicant members shall be dismissed:

Go, and serve the Lord.

The grace of our Lord Jesus Christ, and the love of God, and the fellowship of the Holy Spirit, be with you all. **Amen.**

A Brief Order for the Lord's Supper

> This brief order for the Lord's Supper is designed for parish use, but is not intended to be a substitute for the Service for the Lord's Day. The order may be adapted for use with the sick. When the service is used with the sick, the minister should be accompanied by elders and, if possible, by other members of the congregation to show the communal character of the Lord's Supper. With members of the congregation present, the minister or an elder shall say:

Hear what Jesus Christ promises:

Happy are those who hunger and thirst for what is right. They shall be satisfied.

I am the bread of life. He who comes to me will never be hungry; he who believes in me will never thirst.

> A doxology or a psalm may be sung or said. Then, let the minister or the elder say:

This is the word of the Lord: All those whom I love I correct and discipline. Therefore, shake off your complacency and repent. See, I stand knocking at the door. If anyone listens to my voice and opens the door, I will go into his house and dine with him, and he with me.

Let us open our hearts to the Lord.

> **God our Father: we have done wrong, and do not deserve to be called your children. We have turned from your way, and been taken in by our own desires. We have not loved neighbors as you commanded. Have mercy on us, Lord, have mercy on us, and forgive us; for the sake of your Son, our Savior, Jesus Christ. Amen.**

Friends: Hear and believe the good news of the gospel. In Jesus Christ we are forgiven. Let us forgive one another. The peace of the Lord Jesus Christ be with you.

> **Amen.**

A Scripture lesson may be read and briefly interpreted. A psalm or a hymn of thanksgiving may be sung. Then, let the minister say:

According to Luke, when our risen Lord was at table with his disciples, he took the bread, and blessed and broke it, and gave it to them. And their eyes were opened and they recognized him. Remember the Lord Jesus Christ.

We remember and are thankful.

Lift up your hearts.

We lift them to the Lord.

Let us pray.

Mighty God, good Father: we thank you for the gift of life, and for the world our home. We thank you for your loving-kindness to us and all men. Your works are great and wonderful. Your ways are just and true. You alone are holy.

The following response may be sung or said:

Holy, holy, holy
Is the Lord God, the Almighty;
He was, he is and he is to come.

Holy God: we praise you for your Son Jesus, who shared our weakness, and was tempted in every way as we are; who obeyed you, by suffering and dying for us. You have raised him to rule the world, and given him a name above every name—Lord and Christ. We praise him and we glorify you, great God our Father.

Now give us your Spirit in the breaking of bread, so that by your power we may be drawn together and made one with Jesus Christ, who is the way, the truth, and the life.

The following may be said by all the people:

With Christians through all ages, we lift our hearts to you, giving thanks, and trusting you to use us as your people; for the sake of Jesus Christ our Savior.

A BRIEF ORDER FOR THE LORD'S SUPPER

The Lord's Prayer may be said. Then, as the minister breaks bread, let him say:

The Lord Jesus, on the night of his arrest, took bread, and after giving thanks to God, broke it and said: "This is my body, which is for you; do this, remembering me."

As the bread is distributed, the minister may say:

I am the bread of life. He who comes to me will never be hungry; he who believes in me will never thirst.

As the minister lifts the cup, let him say:

In the same way, Jesus took the cup after supper, and said: "This cup is the new covenant sealed in my blood. Whenever you drink it, do this, remembering me."

As the cup is passed, the minister may say:

I am the vine, you are the branches. Cut off from me, you can do nothing.

Then, let the minister or an elder pray, saying:

We thank you, Father, for this supper shared in the Spirit with your Son Jesus, who makes us new and strong, and brings us life eternal. We praise you for giving all good gifts in him, and pledge ourselves to serve you, even as you have served us in Jesus Christ the Lord. **Amen.**

And,

Jesus said: I am the light of the world; anyone who follows me will not be walking in the dark; he will have the light of life.

The grace of the Lord Jesus Christ be with you all. **Amen.**

Morning Prayer

(For Daily Use)

The service shall begin with a Call to Worship:

God said: Let there be light; and there was light. And God saw that the light was good.

This is the day which the Lord has made;

Let us rejoice and be glad in it.

Praise the Lord.

The Lord's name be praised!

Or,

Though you were once all darkness, now as Christians you are light. Live like men who are at home in daylight, for where light is, there all goodness springs up, all justice and truth.

God is light:

In him there is no darkness at all.

Praise the Lord.

The Lord's name be praised!

Or,

God, who said, "Let light shine out of darkness," has shone in our hearts to give the light of the knowledge of the glory of God in the face of Christ.

Glory be to God!

Through Jesus Christ our Lord.

A hymn of praise may be sung, a canticle, or a Gloria. Then, one of the following prayers may be said, or some other appropriate prayer:

Let us pray.

God of light, in whom there is no darkness: look to your wayward children. Forgive our sin, and give us such joy

in Jesus that darkness may be driven from us, and your light shine in our lives by faith; through Jesus Christ our Lord. Amen.

Mighty God, who divided light from darkness, and made the sun to shine: wake us from the night of doubt and fear, and let us live this day, and every day, in the light of the truth taught by your Spirit, and revealed in Jesus Christ our Lord, whom we praise forever. Amen.

New every morning is your love, great God of light, and all day long you are working for good in the world. Stir up in us desire to serve you, to live peacefully with our neighbors, and to devote each day to your Son, our Savior, Jesus Christ the Lord. Amen.

A psalm may be said or sung. Then a Scripture lesson may be read and briefly interpreted.

The following prayer, or other prayers, may be said:

Let us pray.

God our Father: you taught us to pray not only for friends in faith, but for those who do not believe, who also stand before your judgment and live in your love. Answer our prayers according to your great plan for us and for all men.

We pray for peace among men and nations, split by ancient pride and wrongs remembered. Disarm us; break the hold of hate on our hearts, and draw us from every race and nation to live together in brotherhood, as children of one Father.

God of peace, bring peace to the world.

We pray for hungry and poor men, for victims of greed or careless gain. Teach us compassion, so that no one may be kept from a share of the world's richness.

God of love, tell us what to do.

We pray for the friendless, the sick and the fearful, for prisoners, for people who are burdened. May this day not pass without words spoken and gifts given to show that you care.

God of mercy, help us to be helpful.

We pray for leaders who serve in the United Nations, in our nation, and in other lands. May they bow to your power and follow your leading.

God of power, rule your lands and peoples.

We pray for the church, your unworthy servant. Speak commands, and give us the faithfulness to do and say what you want said and done, in the world you love so much.

God of prophets, set your word in our lives.

Hear our prayers, God of grace, and help us to enact them, working for your peace and justice, mercy and purpose, in all we do today; through Jesus Christ our Lord.

Amen.

Our Father . . .

A hymn, or the Doxology, may be sung, after which the people shall be dismissed:

Go in peace.

Serve the Lord.

The grace of our Lord Jesus Christ be with you all. **Amen.**

Evening Prayer

(For Daily Use)

The service shall begin with a Call to Worship:

Lord, your love is better than life itself,

Our lips will recite your praise.

We proclaim your love at daybreak

And your faithfulness all through the night.
Or,

If I asked darkness to cover me,

And light to become night around me,

Darkness would not be dark to you,

Night would be as light as day.

God, examine me and know my heart,

And guide me in the way everlasting.
Or,

God shall come, and there shall be continuous day,

For at evening time there shall be light.

God is light:

In him there is no darkness at all.

Let one of the following prayers be said, or some other appropriate prayer:

Eternal God: you gave your Son Jesus to be light of the world. In his light, help us to face our darkness, to confess our sins, and, trusting your mercy, to rest in peace this night, so that with the coming of the day we may wake in good faith to serve you; through Jesus Christ our Lord. **Amen.**

God our Father: in Jesus Christ you called us to come when we are weary and overburdened. Give us rest from the trials of the day; guard our sleep and speak to our dreaming, so that refreshed we may greet daylight with resolve, and be strong to do your will; through Jesus Christ our Lord. **Amen.**

Morning and evening, for your goodness we praise you, great God of our lives, and pray that awake or asleep we may stay in your care, believing your love for us declared in Jesus Christ your Son, our Lord. **Amen.**

> *A hymn may be sung, or a canticle. Then, Scripture may be read and briefly interpreted.*
>
> *The following prayer, or other prayers, may be said:*

God of mercy: forgive and correct the wrong we have done this day. We have turned from the way of your Son Jesus and have not cared for neighbors. We have permitted pride to blind and anger to burn, and we have failed to live the new life you have given us. We come to you at night with little to offer except our sins, begging mercy in the name of Jesus Christ, who was always faithful to you, and is always faithful to us. **Amen.**

God of power: you hear our prayers before we speak, yet welcome our praying. Work out plans for us and all men as you know best.

> Guide men and nations into peace.
>
> Power the church to be your witness.
>
> Enrich the poor, and show the rich their poverty.
>
> Strengthen those who work nights to make our days brighter.
>
> Watch with the sick who are restless in pain.
>
> Comfort the dying with signs of your presence.
>
> Be close to those who are close to us.

Keep faith with us as you have in the past, and help us to trust your promises, so that we may live expecting goodness and mercy all our days; through Jesus Christ our Lord. **Amen.**

O God our Father, creator of this world and giver of all good things: we thank you for our home on earth and for the joy of living. We praise you for your love in Jesus Christ, who came to set things right, who died rejected on the cross and rose triumphant from the dead; because he lives, we live to praise you, Father, Son, and Holy Spirit, our God forever. Amen.

Our Father . . .

> A hymn may be sung, or the Nunc Dimittis, after which the people shall be dismissed:

Go in peace.

Trust the Lord.

The grace of our Lord Jesus Christ be with you. **Amen.**

Order for an Agape

The Agape, or "love feast," is a fellowship meal that should not be confused with the Lord's Supper. The Agape recalls meals Jesus shared with disciples during his ministry, and is an expression of the fellowship that Christians enjoy when they meet as "the household of God."

The Agape may be held at table, and be conducted by members of the congregation, or by the minister assisted by members of the congregation. Families may bring dishes of food to the table for all to share.

Let the leader say:

Praise to you, O Lord our God, king of the universe, who causes the earth to yield food for all.

Or,

Give thanks to the Lord, for he is good,

His love is everlasting!

Give thanks to the God of gods,

His love is everlasting!

Give thanks to the Lord of lords,

His love is everlasting!

A hymn of praise or thanksgiving may be sung, after which the leader may greet the people, welcoming them as friends in Christ.

Then, let a reader read Luke 9:12–17. The leader shall pray, saying:

Let us pray.

Great God, our Father, whose Son Jesus broke bread to feed a crowd in Galilee: we thank you for the food you give us. May we enjoy your gifts thankfully, and share what we have with brothers on earth who hunger and thirst, giving praise to Jesus Christ, who has shown your perfect love. **Amen.**

Appropriately, there may be five loaves of bread. The leader may break one of them, and, after taking a piece of bread, may pass the broken halves, one to the left and the other to the right. The remaining loaves may be distributed to all the people.

Then, the people shall eat bread, and pass their dishes of food. People may talk together as neighbors in faith; or the leader may direct their conversations by suggesting matters of mutual concern.

When the meal is ended, a reader may read one or more of the following passages, or some other appropriate lesson from Scripture:

>   *Matthew 22:34–40*
>   *Luke 14:16–24*
>   *I Corinthians, ch. 13*
>   *II Corinthians 9:6–15*
>   *Philippians 2:5–11*

Then, let the leader say:

Let us pray.

We praise you, God our creator, for your good gifts to us and all mankind. We thank you for the friendship we have in Christ; and for the promise of your coming kingdom, where there will be no more hunger and thirst, and where men will be satisfied by your love. As this bread was once seed scattered on earth to be gathered into one loaf, so may your church be joined together into one holy people, who praise you for your love made known in Jesus Christ the Lord. **Amen.**

My dear people, we are already children of God. His commandments are these: that we believe in his Son Jesus Christ, and that we love one another. Whoever keeps his commandments lives in God and God lives in him. We know he lives in us by the Spirit he has given us.

>   *Or,*

My dear people, since God loved us so much, we too should love one another. No one has ever seen God; but as long as we love one another God will live in us, and his love will be complete in us.

The people may sing the Doxology.

Then, the leader shall say:

Let us show our love for neighbors.

The leader may wish to announce a particular need to which the people may give. Baskets may be passed around the table, so that the people may contribute. A hymn may be sung as the collection is taken, or after the collection has been taken.

The Lord's Prayer shall be said:

Our Father . . .

The Agape may conclude with a dismissal:

Go in peace. The grace of the Lord Jesus Christ be with you all **Amen.**

ORDER FOR THE
PUBLIC WORSHIP OF GOD

The Marriage Service

The man and the woman to be married may be seated together facing the Lord's table, with their families, friends, and members of the congregation seated with them.

When the people have assembled, let the minister say:

Let us worship God.

There was a marriage at Cana in Galilee; Jesus was invited to the marriage, with his disciples.

Friends: Marriage is established by God. In marriage a man and a woman willingly bind themselves together in love, and become one even as Christ is one with the church, his body.

Let marriage be held in honor among all.

All may join in a hymn of praise and the following prayer:

Let us confess our sin before God.

Almighty God, our Father: you created us for life together. We confess that we have turned from your will. We have not loved one another as you commanded. We have been quick to claim our own rights and careless of the rights of others. We have taken much and given little. Forgive our disobedience, O God, and strengthen us in love, so that we may serve you as a faithful people, and live together in your joy; through Jesus Christ our Lord. Amen.

The minister shall declare God's mercy, saying:

Hear and believe the good news of the gospel.

Nothing can separate us from the love of God in Christ Jesus our Lord!

THE MARRIAGE SERVICE

In Jesus Christ, we are forgiven.

The people may stand to sing a doxology, or some other appropriate response to the good mercy of God.

The minister may offer a Prayer for Illumination.

Before the reading of the Old Testament lesson, the minister shall say:

The lesson is . . .

Listen for the word of God.

The Gloria Patri, or some other response, may be sung.

Before the reading of the New Testament lesson, the minister shall say:

The lesson is . . .

Listen for the word of God.

The minister may deliver a brief Sermon on the lessons from Scripture, concluding with an Ascription of Praise.

Then let the minister address the man and woman, saying:

_____ and _____, you have come together according to God's wonderful plan for creation. Now, before these people, say your vows to each other.

Let the man and the woman stand before the people, facing each other. Then, the minister shall say:

Be subject to one another out of reverence for Christ.

The man shall say to the woman:

_____, I promise with God's help to be your faithful husband, to love and serve you as Christ commands, as long as we both shall live.

The woman shall say to the man:

_____, I promise with God's help to be your faithful wife, to love and serve you as Christ commands, as long as we both shall live.

THE MARRIAGE SERVICE

A ring, or rings, may be given, with the following words:
I give you this ring as a sign of my promise.

The minister shall address the man and the woman, saying:

As God's picked representatives of the new humanity, purified and beloved of God himself, be merciful in action, kindly in heart, humble in mind. Accept life, and be most patient and tolerant with one another. Forgive as freely as the Lord has forgiven you. And, above everything else, be truly loving. Let the peace of Christ rule in your hearts, remembering that as members of the one body you are called to live in harmony, and never forget to be thankful for what God has done for you.

Or,

Love is slow to lose patience—it looks for a way of being constructive. It is not possessive: it is neither anxious to impress nor does it cherish inflated ideas of its own importance. Love has good manners and does not pursue selfish advantage. It is not touchy. It does not keep account of evil or gloat over the wickedness of other people. On the contrary, it is glad with all good men when truth prevails. Love knows no limit to its endurance, no end to its trust, no fading of its hope; it can outlast anything. It still stands when all else has fallen.

The minister shall call the people to prayer, saying:

Praise the Lord.

The Lord's name be praised.

Lift up your hearts.

We lift them to the Lord.

Let us pray.

Eternal God: without your grace no promise is sure. Strengthen _____ and _____ with the gift of your Spirit, so they may fulfill the vows they have taken. Keep them faithful to each other and to you. Fill them with such love and joy that they may build a home where no one is a stranger. And guide them by your word to serve you all the days of their lives; through Jesus Christ our Lord, to whom be honor and glory forever and ever. **Amen.**

The Lord's Prayer shall be said.

Then, the man and the woman having joined hands, the minister shall say:

_____ and _____, you are now husband and wife according to the witness of the holy catholic church, and the law of the state. Become one. Fulfill your promises. Love and serve the Lord.

What God has united, man must not divide.

Here may be sung a hymn of thanksgiving. Then, let the people be dismissed:

Glory be to him who can keep you from falling and bring you safe to his glorious presence, innocent and happy. To God, the only God, who saves us through Jesus Christ our Lord, be the glory, majesty, authority, and power, which he had before time began, now and forever. **Amen.**

Or,

The grace of the Lord Jesus Christ, the love of God, and the fellowship of the Holy Spirit, be with you all. **Amen.**

ORDER FOR THE
PUBLIC WORSHIP OF GOD

A Service for the Recognition of a Marriage

This service may be used to recognize a civil marriage; or with the deletion of the first paragraph, it may be used as a brief marriage service.

The service may be conducted during public worship on the Lord's Day, when the Sacrament is not celebrated, immediately after the preaching of a sermon; or it may be used at other times. Members of the congregation should be present, in addition to the minister.

Let the minister or an elder say:

_____ and _____ have been married by the law of the state, and they have spoken vows pledging loyalty and love. Now, in faith, they come before the witness of the church to acknowledge their marriage covenant and to tell their common purpose in the Lord.

Then, the minister shall say:

Friends: Marriage is God's gift. In marriage a man and a woman bind themselves in love and become one, even as Christ is one with the church, his body.

_____ and _____, be subject to one another out of reverence for Christ.

The man shall say to the woman:

_____, you are my wife. With God's help I promise to be your faithful husband, to love and serve you as Christ commands, as long as we both shall live.

The woman shall say to the man:

_____, *you are my husband. With God's help I promise to be your faithful wife, to love and serve you as Christ commands, as long as we both shall live.*

A ring, or rings, may be given, with the following words:

I give you this ring as a sign of my promise.

Then, let the minister say:

Hear the words of our Lord Jesus Christ:

Remain in my love. If you keep my commandments you will remain in my love, just as I have kept my Father's commandments and remain in his love. I have told you this so that my own joy may be in you and your joy be complete. This is my commandment: love one another, as I have loved you.

Let us pray.

Eternal God: without your grace no promise is sure. Strengthen _____ and _____ with the gift of your Spirit, so they may fulfill the vows they have taken. Keep them faithful to each other and to you. Fill them with such love and joy that they may build a home where no one is a stranger. And guide them by your word to serve you all the days of their lives; through Jesus Christ our Lord, to whom be honor and glory, forever and ever. **Amen.**

The man and the woman having joined hands, the minister shall say:

_____ and _____, you are husband and wife according to the witness of the holy catholic church. Help each other. Be united; live in peace, and the God of love and peace will be with you.

What God has united, man must not divide.

The following benediction may be said:

The grace of the Lord Jesus Christ, the love of God, and the fellowship of the Holy Spirit, be with you all. **Amen.**

ORDER FOR THE PUBLIC WORSHIP OF GOD

Witness to the Resurrection

Funeral Service

The people shall stand, and the minister shall say:

Jesus said: I am the resurrection and the life. If anyone believes in me, even though he die he will live, and whoever lives and believes in me will never die.

Come to me, all you who labor and are overburdened, and I will give you rest.

Our help is in the name of the Lord,

Who made heaven and earth.

Praise the Lord.

The Lord's name be praised.

All may join in a hymn of praise and the following prayer:

Let us confess our sin, trusting God's promised mercy.

The people may kneel and say together:

Eternal Father, guardian of our lives: we confess that we are children of dust, unworthy of your gracious care. We have not loved as we ought to love, nor have we lived as you command, and our years are soon gone. Lord God, have mercy on us. Forgive our sin and raise us to new life, so that as long as we live we may serve you, until, dying, we enter the joy of your presence; through Jesus Christ our Lord. Amen.

Who is in a position to condemn? Only Christ, and Christ died for us, Christ rose for us, Christ reigns in power for us, Christ prays for us.

Hear and believe the good news of the gospel: God is love. In Jesus Christ, we are forgiven. Be reconciled to God our Father. **Amen.**

> *The people may stand to sing a doxology, or some other thankful response to the mercy of God.*
>
> *Then, let the minister say:*

While we live, we are always being given up to death. Lord, to whom shall we go? You have the words of eternal life!

Let us pray.

Almighty God, whose love never fails, and who can turn the shadow of death into daybreak: help us to receive your word with believing hearts, so that, hearing the promises in Scripture, we may have hope and be lifted out of darkness into the light and peace of your presence; through Jesus Christ our Lord. **Amen.**

> *Or,*

Almighty God, our refuge and strength, our present help in trouble: give us such trust in you that, holding on to your word, we may be strong in this and every time of need; through Jesus Christ our Lord. **Amen.**

> *Let the minister say:*

Listen to Scripture read from the Old Testament.

> *Several of the following Old Testament lessons may be read:*

Lord, you have been
our refuge age after age.

Before the mountains were born,
before the earth or the world came to birth,
you were God from all eternity and forever.

You can turn man back into dust
by saying, "Back to what you were, you sons of men!"
To you, a thousand years are a single day,
a yesterday now over, an hour of the night.

You brush men away like waking dreams,
they are like grass
sprouting and flowering in the morning
withered and dry before dusk.

We too are burnt up by your anger
and terrified by your fury;
having summoned up our sins
you inspect our secrets by your own light.

Our days dwindle under your wrath,
our lives are over in a breath
—our life lasts for seventy years,
eighty with good health,

but they all add up to anxiety and trouble—
over in a trice, and then we are gone.

Teach us to count how few days we have
and so gain wisdom of heart.

Let us wake in the morning filled with your love
and sing and be happy all our days;
make our future as happy as our past was sad,
those years when you were punishing us.

Let your servants see what you can do for them,
let their children see your glory.
May the sweetness of the Lord be on us!
Make all we do succeed. *From Psalm 90 (Jerusalem)*

Man, born of woman,
    has a short life yet has his fill of sorrow.
He blossoms, and he withers, like a flower;
    fleeting as a shadow, transient.
Since man's days are measured out,
    since his tale of months depends on you,
    since you assign him bounds he cannot pass,
turn your eyes from him, leave him alone,
    like a hired drudge, to finish his day.
There is always hope for a tree:
    when felled, it can start its life again;
    its shoots continue to sprout.

Its roots may be decayed in the earth,
> its stump withering in the soil,
but let it scent the water, and it buds,
> and puts out branches like a plant new set.
But man? He dies, and lifeless he remains;
> man breathes his last, and then where is he?
>> *From Job, ch. 14 (Jerusalem)*

Lord, you examine me and know me,
you know if I am standing or sitting,
you read my thoughts from far away,
whether I walk or lie down, you are watching,
you know every detail of my conduct.

The word is not even on my tongue,
Lord, before you know all about it;
close behind and close in front you fence me round,
shielding me with your hand.
Such knowledge is beyond my understanding,
a height to which my mind cannot attain.

Where could I go to escape your spirit?
Where could I flee from your presence?
If I climb the heavens, you are there,
there too, if I lie in Sheol.

If I flew to the point of sunrise,
or westward across the sea,
your hand would still be guiding me,
your right hand holding me.

If I asked darkness to cover me,
and light to become night around me,
that darkness would not be dark to you,
night would be as light as day.

It was you who created my inmost self,
and put me together in my mother's womb;
for all these mysteries I thank you:
for the wonder of myself, for the wonder of your works.

You know me through and through,
from having watched my bones take shape
when I was being formed in secret,
knitted together in the limbo of the womb.

You had scrutinized my every action,
all were recorded in your book,
my days listed and determined,
even before the first of them occurred.

God, how hard it is to grasp your thoughts!
How impossible to count them!
I could no more count them than I could the sand,
and suppose I could, you would still be with me.

God, examine me and know my heart,
probe me and know my thoughts;
make sure I do not follow pernicious ways
and guide me in the way that is everlasting.
From Psalm 139 (Jerusalem)

From the depths I call to you,
Lord, listen to my cry for help!
Listen compassionately
    to my pleading!

If you never overlooked our sins,
Lord, could anyone survive?
But you do forgive us:
    and for that we revere you.

I wait for the Lord, my soul waits for him,
    I rely on his promise,
    my soul relies on the Lord
    more than a watchman on the coming of dawn.

Let Israel rely on the Lord
    as much as the watchman on the dawn!
For it is with the Lord that mercy is to be found,
and a generous redemption;
it is he who redeems Israel
    from all their sins.
Psalm 130 (Jerusalem)

Bless the Lord, my soul,
bless his holy name, all that is in me!
Bless the Lord, my soul,
and remember all his kindnesses:

in forgiving all your offenses,
in curing all your diseases,
in redeeming your life from the Pit,
in crowning you with love and tenderness,
in filling your years with prosperity,
in renewing your youth like an eagle's.

The Lord, who does what is right,
is always on the side of the oppressed;
he revealed his intentions to Moses,
his prowess to the sons of Israel.

The Lord is tender and compassionate,
slow to anger, most loving;
his indignation does not last forever,
his resentment exists a short time only;
he never treats us, never punishes us,
as our guilt and our sins deserve.

No less than the height of heaven over earth
is the greatness of his love for those who fear him;
he takes our sins farther away
than the east is from the west.

As tenderly as a father treats his children,
so the Lord treats those who fear him;
he knows what we are made of,
he remembers we are dust.

Man lasts no longer than grass,
no longer than a wild flower he lives,
one gust of wind, and he is gone,
never to be seen there again;

yet the Lord's love for those who fear him
lasts from all eternity and forever,
like his goodness too for their children's children,

as long as they keep his covenant
and remember to obey his precepts.

The Lord has fixed his throne in the heavens,
his empire is over all.
Bless the Lord, all his angels,
heroes mighty to enforce his word,
attentive to his word of command.

Bless the Lord, all his armies,
servants to enforce his will.
Bless the Lord, all his creatures
in every part of his empire!

Bless the Lord, my soul. *Psalm 103 (Jerusalem)*

If I lift up my eyes to the hills,
    where shall I find help?
Help comes only from the Lord,
    maker of heaven and earth.
How could he let your foot stumble?
    How could he, your guardian, sleep?
The guardian of Israel
    never slumbers, never sleeps.
The Lord is your guardian,
    your defense at your right hand;
the sun will not strike you by day
    nor the moon by night.
The Lord will guard you against all evil;
    he will guard you, body and soul.
The Lord will guard your going and your coming,
    now and for evermore. *Psalm 121 (NEB)*

The Lord is my shepherd, I shall not want;
    he makes me lie down in green pastures.
He leads me beside still waters;
    he restores my soul.
He leads me in paths of righteousness
    for his name's sake.

Even though I walk through the valley of the shadow of death,
  I fear no evil;
for you are with me;
  your rod and your staff,
  they comfort me.

You prepare a table before me
  in the presence of my enemies;
you anoint my head with oil,
  my cup overflows.

Surely goodness and mercy shall follow me
  all the days of my life;
and I shall dwell in the house of the Lord
  forever. *Psalm 23 (based on RSV)*

The people may stand and sing the Gloria Patri, or some other appropriate response. Then, let the minister say:

Listen to Scripture read from the New Testament.

Several of the following New Testament lessons may be read:

Two criminals were also led out with him for execution, and when they came to the place called The Skull, they crucified him with the criminals, one on either side of him. But Jesus himself was saying,
"Father, forgive them; they do not know what they are doing."

One of the criminals hanging there covered him with abuse, and said,
"Aren't you Christ? Why don't you save yourself—and us?"
But the other one checked him with the words:
"Aren't you afraid of God even when you're getting the same punishment as he is? And it's fair enough for us, for we've only got what we deserve, but this man never did anything wrong in his life."

Then he said,
"Jesus, remember me when you come into your kingdom."
And Jesus answered,
"I tell you truly, this very day you will be with me in paradise."
From Luke, ch. 23 (Phillips)

Now when Jesus came, he found that Lazarus had already been in the tomb four days. Bethany was near Jerusalem, about two miles off, and many of the Jews had come to Martha and Mary to console them concerning their brother. When Martha heard that Jesus was coming, she went and met him, while Mary sat in the house. Martha said to Jesus, "Lord, if you had been here, my brother would not have died. And even now I know that whatever you ask from God, God will give you." Jesus said to her, "Your brother will rise again." Martha said to him, "I know that he will rise again in the resurrection at the last day." Jesus said to her, "I am the resurrection and the life; he who believes in me, though he die, yet shall he live, and whoever lives and believes in me shall never die. Do you believe this?" She said to him, "Yes, Lord; I believe that you are the Christ, the Son of God." *From John, ch. 11 (RSV)*

"Set your troubled hearts at rest. Trust in God always; trust also in me. There are many dwelling-places in my Father's house; if it were not so, I should have told you; for I am going there on purpose to prepare a place for you. And if I go and prepare a place for you, I shall come again and receive you to myself, so that where I am you may be also; and my way there is known to you." Thomas said, "Lord, we do not know where you are going, so how can we know the way?" Jesus replied, "I am the way; I am the truth and I am life; no one comes to the Father except by me." *From John, ch. 14 (NEB)*

We want you to be quite certain, brothers, about those who have died, to make sure that you do not grieve about them, like the other people who have no hope. We believe that Jesus died and rose again, and that it will be the same for those who have died in Jesus: God will bring them with him.
From I Thessalonians, ch. 4 (Jerusalem)

For I passed on to you—as among the first to hear it, the message I had myself received—that Christ died for our sins, as the scriptures said he would; that he was buried and rose again on the third day, again as the scriptures foretold. He was seen by Cephas, then by the twelve, and subsequently he was seen simultaneously by over five hundred Christians, of whom the majority are still alive, though some have since died. He was then seen by James, then by all the messengers. And last of all, as if to one born abnormally late, he appeared to me!

Now if the rising of Christ from the dead is the very heart of our message, how can some of you deny that there is any resurrection? For if there is no such thing as the resurrection of the dead, then Christ was never raised. And if Christ was not raised, then neither our preaching nor your faith has any meaning at all. Further it would mean that we are lying in our witness for God, for we have given our solemn testimony that he did raise up Christ—and that is utterly false if it should be true that the dead do not, in fact, rise again! For if the dead do not rise, neither did Christ rise, and if Christ did not rise, your faith is futile and your sins have never been forgiven. Moreover, those who have died believing in Christ are utterly dead and gone. Truly, if our hope in Christ were limited to this life only, we should, of all mankind, be the most to be pitied!

But the glorious fact is that Christ *did* rise from the dead!

But perhaps someone will ask: "How is the resurrection achieved? With what sort of body do the dead arrive?" Now that is talking without using your minds! In your own experience you know that a seed does not germinate without itself "dying." When you sow a seed you do not sow the "body" that will eventually be produced, but bare grain, of wheat, for example, or one of the other seeds. God gives the seed a "body" according to his laws—a different "body" to each kind of seed.

There are illustrations here of the raising of the dead. The body is "sown" in corruption; it is raised beyond the reach of corruption. It is "sown" in dishonor; it is raised in splendor. It is sown in weakness; it is raised in power. It is sown a natural body; it is raised a spiritual body. As there is a natural body so will there be a spiritual body. For I assure you, my brothers, it is utterly impossible for flesh and blood to possess the kingdom of God. The transitory could never possess the everlasting.

From I Corinthians, ch. 15 (Phillips)

We are always facing death, but this means that you know more and more of life. And we know for certain that he who raised the Lord Jesus from death shall also raise us with Jesus. We shall all stand together before him.

We wish you could see how all this is working out for your benefit, and how the more grace God gives, the more thanksgiving will redound to his glory. This is the reason that we never collapse. The outward man does indeed suffer wear and tear, but every day the inward man receives fresh strength. These little troubles (which are really so transitory) are winning for us a permanent, glorious and solid reward out of all proportion to our pain. For we are looking all the time not at the visible things but at the invisible. The visible things are transitory: it is the invisible things that are really permanent.

We know, for instance, that if our earthly dwelling were taken down, like a tent, we have a permanent house in Heaven, made, not by man, but by God. In this present frame we sigh with deep longing for the heavenly house, for we do not want to face utter nakedness when death destroys our present dwelling—these bodies of ours. As long as we are clothed in this temporary dwelling we have a painful longing, not because we want just to get rid of these "clothes" but because we want to know the full cover of the permanent house that will be ours. We want our transitory life to be absorbed into the life that is eternal.

Now the power that has planned this experience for us is God, and he has given us his Spirit as a guarantee of its truth. This makes us confident, whatever happens. We realize that being "at home" in the body means that to some extent we are "away" from the Lord, for we have to live by trusting him without seeing him. We are so sure of this that we would really rather be "away" from the body and be "at home" with the Lord.

It is our aim, therefore, to please him, whether we are "at home" or "away."

From II Corinthians, chs. 4 and 5 (Phillips)

In face of all this, what is there left to say? If God is for us, who can be against us? He who did not hesitate to spare his own

Son but gave him up for us all—can we not trust such a God to give us, with him, everything else that we can need?

Who would dare to accuse us, whom God has chosen? The judge himself has declared us free from sin. Who is in a position to condemn? Only Christ, and Christ died for us, Christ rose for us, Christ reigns in power for us, Christ prays for us!

Who can separate us from the love of Christ? Can trouble, pain or persecution? Can lack of clothes and food, danger to life and limb, the threat of force of arms?

No, in all these things we win an overwhelming victory through him who has proved his love for us.

I have become absolutely convinced that neither death nor life, neither messenger of Heaven nor monarch of earth, neither what happens today nor what may happen tomorrow, neither a power from on high nor a power from below, nor anything else in God's whole world has any power to separate us from the love of God in Christ Jesus our Lord!

From Romans, ch. 8 (Phillips)

Then I saw a new Heaven and a new earth, for the first Heaven and the first earth had disappeared, and the sea was no more. I saw the holy city, the new Jerusalem, descending from God out of Heaven, prepared as a bride dressed in beauty for her husband. Then I heard a great voice from the throne crying:

"See! The home of God is with men, and he will live among them. They shall be his people, and God himself shall be with them, and will wipe away every tear from their eyes. Death shall be no more, and never again shall there be sorrow or crying or pain. For all those former things are past and gone."

I could see no Temple in the city, for the Lord, the Almighty God, and the Lamb are themselves its Temple. The city has no need for the light of sun or moon, for the splendor of God fills it with light, and its radiance is the Lamb. The nations will walk by its light, and the kings of the earth will bring their glory into it. The city's gates shall stand open day after day—and there will be no night there.

Nothing that has cursed mankind shall exist any longer; the throne of God and of the Lamb shall be within the city. His servants shall worship him; they shall see his face, and his name will be upon their foreheads. Night shall be no more, they have no more need for either lamplight or sunlight, for the Lord God will shed his light upon them and they shall reign as kings for timeless ages. *From Revelation, chs. 21; 22 (Phillips)*

Blessed be God the Father of our Lord Jesus Christ, who in his great mercy has given us a new birth as his sons, by raising Jesus Christ from the dead, so that we have a sure hope and the promise of an inheritance that can never be spoilt or soiled and never fade away, because it is being kept for you in the heavens. Through your faith, God's power will guard you until the salvation which has been prepared is revealed at the end of time. This is a cause of great joy for you, even though you may for a short time have to bear being plagued by all sorts of trials; so that, when Jesus Christ is revealed, your faith will have been tested and proved like gold—only it is more precious than gold, which is corruptible even though it bears testing by fire—and then you will have praise and glory and honor. You did not see him, yet you love him; and still without seeing him, you are already filled with a joy so glorious that it cannot be described, because you believe; and you are sure of the end to which your faith looks forward, that is, the salvation of your souls.
From I Peter, ch. 1 (Jerusalem)

I kneel in prayer to the Father, from whom every family in heaven and on earth takes its name, that out of the treasures of his glory he may grant you strength and power through his Spirit in your inner being, that through faith Christ may dwell in your hearts in love. With deep roots and firm foundations, may you be strong to grasp, with all God's people, what is the breadth and length and height and depth of the love of Christ, and to know it, though it is beyond knowledge. So may you attain to fullness of being, the fullness of God himself.

Now to him who is able to do immeasurably more than all we can ask or conceive, by the power which is at work among us, to him be glory in the church and in Christ Jesus from generation to generation evermore! Amen.

From Ephesians, ch. 3 (NEB)

After the reading of the Scriptures, the minister may say a prayer:

Eternal God, our Father: we praise you for your word which is our light in darkness. Help us to hear and believe the promises you have spoken; through Jesus Christ our Lord. **Amen.**

A hymn may be sung.

The minister may preach, briefly testifying to the hope that is found in Scripture. He may conclude with an Ascription of Praise.

The people may stand to say a creed of the church, and to pray in unison:

I believe in God, the Father almighty,
    creator of heaven and earth.

I believe in Jesus Christ, his only Son, our Lord.
    He was conceived by the power of the Holy Spirit
        and born of the Virgin Mary.
    He suffered under Pontius Pilate,
        was crucified, died, and was buried.
    He descended to the dead.
    On the third day he rose again.
    He ascended into heaven,
        and is seated at the right hand of the Father.
    He will come again to judge the living and the dead.

I believe in the Holy Spirit,
    the holy catholic church,
    the communion of saints,
    the forgiveness of sins,
    the resurrection of the body,
    and the life everlasting. Amen.

Let us pray.

God of grace: in Jesus Christ you have given a new and living hope. We thank you that by dying he has con-

FUNERAL SERVICE

quered death; and that by rising again he promises eternal life. Help us to know that because he lives, we shall live also; and that neither death, nor life, nor things present, nor things to come, shall be able to separate us from your love; in Jesus Christ our Lord. Amen.

Instead of the Apostles' Creed, the following affirmation may be used:

We believe there is no condemnation for those who are in Christ Jesus: and we know that in everything God works for good with those who love him, who are called according to his purpose. We are sure that neither death, nor life, nor angels, nor principalities, nor things present, nor things to come, nor powers, nor height, nor depth, nor anything else in all creation, will be able to separate us from the love of God in Christ Jesus our Lord. Amen.

Let us pray.

Heavenly Father: in your Son Jesus you have given us a true faith and a sure hope. Help us to live trusting in the communion of saints, the forgiveness of sins, and the resurrection to life eternal. Strengthen this faith and hope in us, all the days of our life; through the love of your Son, Jesus Christ our Savior. Amen.

The minister may say the following prayers, or other appropriate prayers:

O God, before whom generations rise and pass away: we praise you for all your servants who, having lived this life in faith, now live eternally with you. Especially we thank you for your servant _____, for the gift of *his* life, for the grace you have given *him*, for all in *him* that was good and kind and faithful. (*Here mention may be made of characteristics or service.*) We thank you that for *him* death is past, and pain is ended, and *he* has entered the joy you have prepared; through Jesus Christ our Lord. **Amen.**

And,

Almighty God: in Jesus Christ you promised many homes within your house. Give us faith to see beyond touch and sight some sign of your kingdom, and, where vision fails, to trust your love which never fails. Lift heavy sorrow, and give us good hope in Jesus, so we may bravely walk our earthly way, and look forward to glad heavenly reunion; through Jesus Christ our Lord, who was dead but is risen, to whom be honor and praise, now and forever. **Amen.**

Let the minister and people say:

O God, who called us from death to life: we give ourselves to you; and with the church through all ages, we thank you for your saving love in Jesus Christ our Lord. Amen.

A hymn of praise or thanksgiving may be sung, after which the people may be dismissed:

Hear the words of our Lord Jesus Christ:

Peace I leave with you; my peace I give to you; not as the world gives do I give to you. Let not your hearts be troubled, neither let them be afraid.

The grace of the Lord Jesus Christ, and the love of God, and the fellowship of the Holy Spirit, be with you all. **Amen.**

Witness to the Resurrection

Committal Service

When all are assembled, let the minister say:

Thank God, the God and Father of our Lord Jesus Christ, that in his great mercy we men have been born again into a life full of hope, through Christ's rising from the dead.

Do not be afraid. I am the first and the last. I am the living one; for I was dead and now I am alive for evermore.

Because I live, you shall live also.

Almighty God: we commend to you our neighbor _____, trusting your love and mercy; and believing in the promise of a resurrection to eternal life; through our Lord Jesus Christ. **Amen.**

All thanks to God, who gives us the victory through our Lord Jesus Christ!

Then, let the minister say any of the following prayers:

O Lord: support us all the day long, until the shadows lengthen and the evening comes, and the busy world is hushed, and the fever of life is over, and our work is done. Then, in your mercy, grant us a safe lodging, and a holy rest, and peace at the last; through Jesus Christ our Lord. **Amen.**

O God: you have designed this wonderful world, and know all things good for us. Give us such faith that, by day and by night, in all times and in all places, we may without fear trust those who are dear to us to your never-failing love, in this life and in the life to come; through Jesus Christ our Lord. **Amen.**

Eternal God: our days and years are lived in your mercy. Make us know how frail we are, and how brief our time on earth; and lead us by your Holy Spirit, so that, when we have served you in our generation, we may be gathered into your presence, faithful in the church, and loving toward neighbors; through Jesus Christ our Lord. **Amen.**

Father: you gave your own Son Jesus to die on the cross for us, and raised him from death as a sign of your love. Give us faith, so that, though our child has died, we may believe that you welcome *him* and will care for *him*, until, by your mercy, we are together again in the joy of your promised kingdom; through Jesus Christ our Lord. **Amen.**

Almighty God, Father of the whole family in heaven and on earth: stand by those who sorrow; that, as they lean on your strength, they may be upheld, and believe the good news of life beyond life; through Jesus Christ our Lord. **Amen.**

> The Lord's Prayer may be said. Then, the people may be dismissed with a benediction.

ORDER FOR THE PUBLIC WORSHIP OF GOD

A Service for Ordination and Installation*

This service is designed to be used for the ordination of ministers of the word, elders, and deacons; and also for their installation. When a minister of the word is being ordained but not installed, the congregational questions should be omitted.

The service may take place during public worship, following the preaching of a sermon. Let the moderator lead the people, saying:

There are different gifts,

> **But it is the same Spirit who gives them.**

There are different ways of serving God,

> **But it is the same Lord who is served.**

God works through different men in different ways,

> **But it is the same God who achieves his purpose through them all.**

Each one is given a gift by the Spirit,

> **To use it for the common good.**

Together we are the body of Christ,

> **And individually members of him.**

Though we have different gifts, together we are a ministry of reconciliation led by the risen Christ. We work and pray to

---

*This book is for three Churches. The ordination questions in this service are required in The United Presbyterian Church in the United States of America. Other questions may be required in the Cumberland Presbyterian Church and the Presbyterian Church in the United States.

make his church useful in the world, and we call men and women to faith, so that, in the end, every knee shall bow and every tongue confess that Jesus Christ is Lord, to the glory of God the Father.

Within our common ministry, some members are chosen for particular work as ministers of the word, ruling elders, or deacons. In ordination, we recognize these special ministries, remembering that our Lord Jesus said:

Whoever among you wants to be great must become the servant of all, and if he wants to be first among you, he must be the slave of all men!

> **Just as the Son of Man came not to be served, but to serve, and to give his life to set others free.**
>
> Then, let an elder come forward, bringing the candidate(s). Let the elder say to the moderator:

Mr. Moderator, speaking for the people of the church, I bring _____ to be ordained as _____.

> Or,

Mr. Moderator, speaking for the people of the church, I bring _____ to be installed as _____.

> Then, the moderator shall ask those questions required by the Constitution of his church (see footnote on page 89).

_____, God has called you by the voice of the church to serve Jesus Christ in a special way. You know who we are and what we believe, and you understand the work for which you have been chosen.

Do you trust in Jesus Christ your Savior, acknowledge him Lord of the world and head of the church, and through him believe in one God, Father, Son, and Holy Spirit?

> *I do.*

Do you accept the scriptures of the Old and New Testaments to be, by the Holy Spirit, the unique and authoritative witness to Jesus Christ in the church universal, and God's word to you?

> *I do.*

Will you be instructed by the Confessions of our church, and led by them as you lead the people of God?
I will.

Will you be _____ (*a* minister of the word, elder*s*, deacon*s*) in obedience to Jesus Christ, under the authority of Scripture, and continually guided by our Confessions?
I will.

Do you endorse our church's government, and will you honor its discipline? Will you be a friend among your comrades in ministry, working with them, subject to the ordering of God's word and Spirit?
I do and I will.

Will you govern the way you live, by following the Lord Jesus Christ, loving neighbors, and working for the reconciliation of the world?
I will.

Will you seek to serve the people with energy, intelligence, imagination, and love?
I will.

FOR A MINISTER OF THE WORD

> When a minister of the word is being ordained or installed, the following question shall be asked:
>
> Will you be a faithful minister, proclaiming the good news in word and sacrament, teaching faith, and caring for people? Will you be active in government and discipline, serving in courts of the church, and, in your ministry, will you try to show the love and justice of Jesus Christ?

I will

FOR AN ELDER

> When an elder is being ordained, the following question shall be asked:
>
> Will you be a faithful elder, watching over the people, providing for their worship and instruction? Will you

share in government and discipline, serving in courts of the church; and, in your ministry, will you try to show the love and justice of Jesus Christ?

I will.

FOR A DEACON

When a deacon is being ordained, the following question shall be asked:

Will you be a faithful deacon, teaching charity, urging concern, and directing the peoples' help to the friendless and those in need? In your ministry, will you try to show the love and justice of Jesus Christ?

I will.

WHEN ORDAINED ELDERS OR DEACONS ARE AGAIN ELECTED

If there are previously ordained elders or deacons to be installed, let an elder present them to the moderator, saying:

Mr. Moderator: (Elder, Deacon) _____ having been elected again to active service by the vote of this congregation, *he* may now be installed to office.

The moderator shall ask those questions required by the Constitution of his church (see footnote on page 89).

_____, you have been called again to a position of special leadership in the church.

Do you welcome the work for which you have been chosen, and will you serve the people with energy, intelligence, imagination, and love, relying on God's mercy and rejoicing in his promises through Jesus Christ our Lord?

I do and I will.

Then, let a designated elder face the congregation with the candidate(s) being installed, and ask those questions required by the Constitution of his church (see footnote on page 89).

ORDINATION AND INSTALLATION

Do we, members of the church, accept _____ as _____ (*a* minister of the word, elder*s*, deacon*s*), chosen by God through the voice of this congregation, to lead us in the way of Jesus Christ?

We do.

Do we agree to encourage *him*, to respect *his* decisions, and to follow as *he* guides us, serving Jesus Christ, who alone is head of the church?

We do.

FOR A MINISTER OF THE WORD

> When a minister of the word is being installed, the following question may also be asked:

Do we promise to pay *him* fairly and provide for *his* welfare as *he* works among us; to stand by *him* in trouble and share *his* joys? Will we listen to the word *he* preaches, welcome *his* pastoral care, and honor *his* authority, as *he* seeks to honor and obey Jesus Christ our Lord?

We do and we will.

> Candidate(s) for ordination will kneel; ministers of the gospel and elders may come forward for the laying on of hands.

> In an ordination service all of the following prayers, or similar prayers, should be used. When ministers of the word, elders, or deacons, previously ordained, are being installed, only the unison prayer which follows should be said.

Let us pray.

Almighty God: in every age you have chosen servants to speak your word and lead your loyal people. We thank you for *this man* whom you have called to serve you. Give *him* special gifts to do *his* special work; and fill *him* with Holy Spirit, so *he* may have the same mind that was in Christ Jesus, and be *a* faithful *disciple* as long as *he* shall live.

> The candidate(s) may say the following brief prayer, or a similar prayer:

God our Father: you have chosen me. Now give me strength, wisdom, and love to work for the Lord Jesus Christ.

Let all the people join in the following prayer:

God of grace, who called us to a common ministry as ambassadors of Christ, trusting us with the message of reconciliation: give us courage and discipline to follow where your servants rightly lead us; that together we may declare your wonderful deeds and show your love to the world; through Jesus Christ the Lord of all. Amen.

Then, the moderator shall say to the candidate(s):

_____, you are now _____ (*a* minister of the word, elder*s*, deacon*s*) in the church (and for this congregation). Whatever you do, in word or deed, do everything in the name of the Lord Jesus, giving thanks to God the Father through him. **Amen.**

Ministers of the gospel and elders shall welcome the new minister or new elder(s) with a handshake; deacons may join in welcoming the new deacon(s). They shall say:

Welcome to this ministry.

Brief charges may be given. Because the New Testament contains helpful charges, they may be selected and read.

When a minister of the word is ordained or installed, another minister of the word may be appointed to read a passage from Scripture, such as:

II Timothy 4:1–5
II Corinthians 4:1–15

When elders are ordained or installed, another elder may read a passage from Scripture, such as:

I Peter 5:1–4
I Timothy 3:1–7

When deacons are ordained or installed, another deacon may read a passage from Scripture, such as:

I Corinthians, ch. 13
I Timothy 3:8–13

ORDINATION AND INSTALLATION

A charge may be given the congregation by reading a passage from Scripture, such as:

I Peter 5:5–13
I Thessalonians 5:12–23
Philippians 2:1–16
I Corinthians 12:12–26

The service shall conclude with a benediction.

ORDER FOR THE
PUBLIC WORSHIP OF GOD

The Installation of a Commissioned Church Worker

The installation may be conducted during public worship on the Lord's Day, immediately after the preaching of a sermon. Let the moderator say:

Hear what the apostle Paul has written:

Our gifts differ according to the grace given us. If your gift is prophecy, use it as your faith suggests; if administration, then use it for administration; if teaching, then use it for teaching. Let the preachers deliver sermons, the almsgivers give freely, the officials be diligent, and those who do works of mercy do them cheerfully. Do not let your love be pretense, but sincerely prefer good to evil. Work for the Lord with untiring effort and with great earnestness of spirit.

There are different gifts,

>**But it is the same Spirit who gives them.**

Each one is given a gift by the Spirit,

>**To use it for the common good.**

An elder may come forward with the candidate for installation, and say to the moderator:

Mr. Moderator, speaking for the session of this church, I bring _____ to be installed as _____.

Then, let the moderator address the candidate, saying:

_____, you believe yourself called by Jesus Christ to a special work, and you have studied to prepare yourself for a vocation in the church. Presbytery has approved your qualifications and has commissioned you a church worker.

INSTALLATION OF A CHURCH WORKER

Are you willing to be installed as _____?

I am.

Do you welcome this responsibility because you are determined to follow the Lord Jesus, to love neighbors, and to work for the reconciling of the world?

I do.

Will you serve the people with energy, intelligence, imagination, and love, relying on God's mercy and rejoicing in his promises through Jesus Christ our Lord?

I will.

Then, let the elder, standing with the candidate, face the congregation, and say:

Do we, members of _____, accept _____ as _____, chosen of God and appointed by the _____, to guide us in the way of Jesus Christ?

We do.

The candidate may kneel, as the moderator leads the people in prayer, saying:

Let us pray.

God of Grace, who called us to a common ministry as ambassadors of Christ, trusting us with the message of reconciliation: give us courage and discipline to follow where your servants rightly lead us; that together we may declare your wonderful deeds and show your love to the world; through Jesus Christ the Lord of all. Amen.

The moderator shall declare the commissioned church worker installed into office, saying:

_____, you are now installed as _____ in the church. Whatever you do, in word or deed, do everything in the name of the Lord Jesus, giving thanks to God the Father through him.

Amen.

Brief charges may be given the commissioned church worker and the congregation by a minister or another commissioned church worker.

ORDER FOR THE
PUBLIC WORSHIP OF GOD

Recognition of Trustees

The recognition of trustees may take place during public worship on the Lord's Day, following the preaching of a sermon.

Let an elder bring forward the elected trustees, and say to the minister:

Mr. Moderator, _____ *are* elected to serve as *trustees* of the church. We wish to recognize the responsibility *they* have accepted.

The minister shall address the elected trustees, saying:

Friends: God has given you special gifts to serve him, and we have chosen you for a special work. Under the law of the state, you will hold and manage properties and, as authorized, conduct business for the church. By your energy, honesty, and fairness you will demonstrate Christian faith to those you deal with on our behalf.

Let the elder address the elected trustees:

Do you promise to give the business affairs of this congregation your devoted attention, to encourage generosity, and, in all your dealings, work to further our service of Christ in the world?

I do.

Then, standing with the elected trustees, facing the congregation, let the elder say:

Do you receive these persons as your trustees, and do you promise to support them in their work for the church?

We do.

The minister will say:

Let us pray.

Holy God: you made this world and called it good, and appointed us to manage things as agents of your love. Guide your servants as they represent us, and direct our business. Help them to be wise children of light, who show your trust by being trustworthy; through Jesus Christ our Lord. **Amen.**

The minister will say to the trustees:

You are now trustees for this church. Be good and faithful servants, who will enter into the joy of our Lord.

The grace of the Lord Jesus Christ be with you. **Amen.**

ORDER FOR THE
PUBLIC WORSHIP OF GOD

Recognition of Church School Teachers

Those appointed to teach shall stand among or before the congregation. The minister shall say:

Hear, O Israel: The Lord our God is one Lord; and you shall love the Lord your God with all your heart, and with all your soul, and with all your might. And these words which I command you this day shall be upon your heart; and you shall teach them diligently to your children, and shall talk of them when you sit in your house, and when you walk by the way, and when you lie down, and when you rise.

Jesus said to his disciples: I give you a new commandment: Love one another; just as I have loved you.

Go, therefore, make disciples of all the nations; baptize them in the name of the Father and of the Son and of the Holy Spirit, and teach them to observe all the commands I gave you.

> **What we have heard and known for ourselves and what our ancestors have told us must not be withheld from their descendants, but be handed on by us to the next generation; these in their turn will tell their own children so that they too put confidence in God, never forgetting God's achievements, and always keeping his commandments.**

Then, the minister shall address the teachers, saying:

Friends: You have been chosen by the session of this church to serve as teachers. You will announce God's good law to each new generation, and tell of Jesus Christ, so we may know him, love him, and live his truth in the world.

Do you trust Jesus Christ your Savior, and through him believe in one God, Father, Son, and Holy Spirit?

We do.

Do you promise to study the Scriptures and the teachings of the church, so that with imagination and love you may serve the Holy Spirit, by calling men to faith in Christ and training his disciples?

We do.

By the authority of the session, you are commissioned to teach in the church. Be energetic, honest, and faithful to Christ your Lord!

> Let a ruling elder lead the people in prayer:

God of our fathers: in every age you have appointed teachers to tell your power, justice, and love. We thank you for brothers and sisters in faith, who will teach your ways. Give them Holy Spirit, so they may know your Son our Lord, speak his truth, and with us live the new life, serving neighbors, obedient to your commandments; through Jesus Christ our Savior. Amen.

The truth of the Lord Jesus Christ be with you. **Amen.**

Litanies

Litanies

The litany is an ancient form of prayer that predates the New Testament and was in common use among the early Christians.

The litanies that follow are designed for special occasions in the life of the church, but they may be used during public worship on the Lord's Day.

Each of the litanies may be used in entirety, or in separate sections as indicated; or some of the petitions within the litanies may be extended to create brief prayers by adding an "Address" and a "Conclusion."

Litany of the Beatitudes

**For use during Lent,
or in services preparing for the Lord's Supper**

LEADER: Jesus said: Happy are the poor in spirit; theirs is the kingdom of heaven.

God our Father: help us to know that away from you we have nothing. Save us from pride that mistakes your gifts for possessions; and keep us humble enough to see that we are poor sinners who always need you.

PEOPLE: **Happy are the poor in spirit.**

LEADER: Thank you, God, for your Son Jesus, who, though he was rich, became poor to live among us; who had no place for himself on earth. By his weakness we are made strong, and by his poverty, rich.

Happy are the poor in spirit;

PEOPLE: **Theirs is the kingdom of heaven.**

LEADER: Jesus said: Happy are those who mourn; they shall be comforted.

God our Father: we are discouraged by evil and frightened by dying, and have no word of hope within ourselves. Unless you speak to us, O God, we shall be overcome by grieving and despair.

PEOPLE: **Happy are those who mourn.**

LEADER: Thank you, God, for Jesus Christ, who on the cross faced evil, death, and desertion. You raised him in triumph over every dark power to be our Savior. We give thanks for the hope we have in him.

Happy are those who mourn;

PEOPLE: **They shall be comforted.**

LEADER: Jesus said: Happy are the gentle; they shall have the earth.

LITANY OF THE BEATITUDES

God our Father: restrain our arrogance and show us our place on earth. Keep us obedient, for we are your servants, unwise and unworthy, who have no rights and deserve no honors.

PEOPLE: **Happy are the gentle.**

LEADER: Thank you, God, for Jesus Christ our Master, who did not call us slaves, but your true sons. Help us to work with him, ordering all things for joy, according to your will.

Happy are the gentle;

PEOPLE: **They shall have the earth.**

LEADER: Jesus said: Happy are those who hunger and thirst for what is right; they shall be satisfied.

God our Father: stir up in us a desire for justice, and a love of your law. May we never live carelessly or selfishly, but in all our dealing with neighbors may we look for the right and do it.

PEOPLE: **Happy are those who hunger and thirst for what is right.**

LEADER: Thank you, God, for Jesus Christ, who overturned small man-made rules, yet lived your law in perfect love. Give us freedom to live with your Spirit in justice, mercy, and peace.

Happy are those who hunger and thirst for what is right;

PEOPLE: **They shall be satisfied.**

LEADER: Jesus said: Happy are the merciful; they shall have mercy shown them.

God our Father: we do not forgive as you have forgiven us. We nurse old wrongs and let resentments rule us. We tolerate evil in ourselves, yet harshly judge our neighbors. God, forgive us.

PEOPLE: **Happy are the merciful**

LEADER: Thank you, God, for your Son Jesus, who gave his

life for sinners; who on the cross forgave unforgivable things. Receiving his mercy, may we always forgive.

Happy are the merciful;

PEOPLE: **They shall have mercy shown them.**

LEADER: Jesus said: Happy are the pure in heart; they shall see God.

God our Father: we are not pure. We do not live in love. The good we do, we admire too much; we tabulate our virtues. Deliver us, O God, from a divided heart.

PEOPLE: **Happy are the pure in heart.**

LEADER: Thank you, God, for Jesus Christ, whose words and deeds were pure. By his life our lives are justified, and by his death we are redeemed. In him we see you face to face, and praise you for your goodness.

Happy are the pure in heart;

PEOPLE: **They shall see God.**

LEADER: Jesus said: Happy are the peacemakers; they shall be called sons of God.

God our Father: we have not lived in peace. We have spread discord, prejudice, gossip, and fear among neighbors. Help us, for we cannot help ourselves. Show us your way of peace.

PEOPLE: **Happy are the peacemakers.**

LEADER: Thank you, God, for Jesus Christ, who has broken down dividing walls of hate to make one family on earth. As he has reconciled us to you, may we be reconciled to one another, living in peace with all your children everywhere.

Happy are the peacemakers;

PEOPLE: **They shall be called sons of God.**

LEADER: Jesus said: Happy are those who are persecuted in the cause of right; theirs is the kingdom of heaven.

God our Father: we are afraid to risk ourselves for the right. We have grown accustomed to wrong and been silent in the face of injustice. Give us anger without hate, and courage to obey you no matter what may happen.

PEOPLE: **Happy are those who are persecuted in the cause of right.**

LEADER: Thank you, God, for Jesus Christ, who was persecuted for what he said and did; who took the cross upon himself for our sake. May we stand with him in justice and love, and follow where he leads, even to a cross.

Happy are those who are persecuted in the cause of right;

PEOPLE: **Theirs is the kingdom of heaven.**

LEADER: Jesus said: Happy are you when people abuse you and persecute you and speak all kinds of evil against you on my account. Rejoice and be glad, for your reward will be great in heaven.

God our Father: give us a will to live by your commandments. Keep us from slander, cruelty, and mocking talk, so that we may be faithful witnesses to Jesus Christ our Lord.

PEOPLE: **Happy are you when people abuse you and persecute you and speak all kinds of evil against you on my account.**

LEADER: We praise you, O God, for your Son Jesus, who called us to be disciples. Give us grace to confess him before men, and faith to believe he suffered for us. We ask no rewards, only make us brave.

Happy are you when people abuse you and persecute you and speak all kinds of evil against you on my account.

PEOPLE: **Rejoice and be glad, for your reward will be great in heaven.**

LEADER: You are the light of the world. Your light must shine in the sight of men, so that, seeing your good works, they may give praise to your Father in heaven.

PEOPLE: **Amen.**

Litany of Confession

LEADER: Almighty God: you alone are good and holy. Purify our lives and make us brave disciples. We do not ask you to keep us safe, but to keep us loyal, so we may serve Jesus Christ, who, tempted in every way as we are, was faithful to you.

PEOPLE: **Amen.**

LEADER: From lack of reverence for truth and beauty; from a calculating or sentimental mind; from going along with mean and ugly things;

PEOPLE: **O God, deliver us.**

LEADER: From cowardice that dares not face truth; laziness content with half-truth; or arrogance that thinks it knows it all;

PEOPLE: **O God, deliver us.**

LEADER: From artificial life and worship; from all that is hollow or insincere;

PEOPLE: **O God, deliver us.**

LEADER: From trite ideals and cheap pleasures; from mistaking hard vulgarity for humor;

PEOPLE: **O God, deliver us.**

LEADER: From being dull, pompous, or rude; from putting down neighbors;

PEOPLE: **O God, deliver us.**

LEADER: From cynicism about our brothers; from intolerance or cruel indifference;

PEOPLE: **O God, deliver us.**

LEADER: From being satisfied with things as they are, in the church or in the world; from failing to share your indignation;

PEOPLE: **O God, deliver us.**

LEADER: From selfishness, self-indulgence, or self-pity;

PEOPLE: **O God, deliver us.**

LEADER: From token concern for the poor, for lonely or loveless people; from confusing faith with good feeling, or love with a wanting to be loved;

PEOPLE: **O God, deliver us.**

LEADER: For everything in us that may hide your light;

PEOPLE: **O God, light of life, forgive us.**

Litany of Intercession

The Litany of Intercession may be said in entirety, or selectively. The response, "Hear our prayer, O Lord," may be used after each petition instead of the variety of responses provided.

LEADER: Great God our Father: you hear our prayers before we speak, and answer before we know our need. Though we cannot pray, may your Spirit pray in us, drawing us to you and toward our neighbors on earth.

PEOPLE: **Amen.**

LEADER: We pray for the whole creation: may all things work together for good, until, by your design, men inherit the earth and order it wisely.

PEOPLE: **Let the whole creation praise you, Lord and God.**

LEADER: We pray for the church of Jesus Christ; that, begun, maintained, and promoted by your Spirit, it may be true, engaging, glad, and active, doing your will.

PEOPLE: **Let the church be always faithful, Lord and God.**

LEADER: We pray for men and women who serve the church in special ways, preaching, ruling, showing charity; that they may never lose heart, but have all hope encouraged.

PEOPLE: **Let leadership be strong, Lord and God.**

LEADER: We pray for people who do not believe, who are shaken by doubt, or have turned against you. Open their eyes to see beyond our broken fellowship the wonders of your love displayed in Jesus, Jew of Nazareth; and to follow when he calls them.

PEOPLE: **Conquer doubt with faith, O God.**

LEADER: We pray for peace in the world. Disarm weapons, silence guns, and put out ancient hate that smolders still, or flames in sudden conflict. Create goodwill among men of every race and nation.

PEOPLE: **Bring peace to earth, O God.**

LEADER: We pray for men who must go to war, and for those who will not go: may they have conviction, and charity toward one another.

PEOPLE: **Guard brave men everywhere, O God.**

LEADER: We pray for enemies, as Christ commanded; for those who oppose us or scheme against us, who are also children of your love. May we be kept from infectious hate or sick desire for vengeance.

PEOPLE: **Make friends of enemies, O God.**

LEADER: We pray for those involved in world government, in agencies of control or compassion, who work for the reconciling of nations: keep them hopeful, and work with them for peace.

PEOPLE: **Unite our broken world, O God.**

LEADER: We pray for those who govern us, who make, administer, or judge our laws. May this country ever be a land of free and able men, who welcome exiles and work for justice.

PEOPLE: **Govern those who govern us, O God.**

LEADER: We pray for poor people who are hungry, or are housed in cramped places. Increase in us, and all who prosper, concern for the disinherited.

PEOPLE: **Care for the poor, O God.**

LEADER: We pray for social outcasts; for those excluded by their own militance or by the harshness of others. Give us grace to accept those our world names unacceptable, and so show your mighty love.

PEOPLE: **Welcome the alienated, O God.**

LEADER: We pray for sick people who suffer pain, or struggle with demons of the mind, who silently cry out for healing: may they be patient, brave, and trusting.

LITANY OF INTERCESSION

PEOPLE: **Heal sick and troubled men, O God.**

LEADER: We pray for the dying, who face final mystery: may they enjoy light and life intensely, keep dignity, and greet death unafraid, believing in your love.

PEOPLE: **Have mercy on the dying, O God.**

LEADER: We pray for those whose tears are not yet dry, who listen for familiar voices and look for still familiar faces: in loss, may they affirm the gain you promise in Jesus, who prepares a place for us within your spacious love.

PEOPLE: **Comfort those who sorrow, O God.**

LEADER: We pray for people who are alone and lonely, who have no one to call in easy friendship: may they be remembered, befriended, and know your care for them.

PEOPLE: **Visit lonely people, O God.**

LEADER: We pray for families, for parents and children: may they enjoy each other, honor freedoms, and forgive as happily as we are all forgiven in your huge mercy.

PEOPLE: **Keep families in your love, O God.**

LEADER: We pray for young and old: give impatient youth true vision, and experienced age openness to new things. Let both praise your name.

PEOPLE: **Join youth and age together, O God.**

LEADER: We pray for all men everywhere: may they come into their own as sons of God, and inherit the kingdom prepared in Jesus Christ, the Lord of all, and Savior of the world.

PEOPLE: **Hear our prayers, almighty God, in the name of Jesus Christ, who prays with us and for us, to whom be praise forever. Amen.**

Litany of Thanksgiving

LEADER: Give thanks to the Lord, for he is good.

PEOPLE: **His love is everlasting.**

LEADER: Come, let us praise God joyfully.

PEOPLE: **Let us come to him with thanksgiving.**

LEADER: For the good world; for things great and small, beautiful and awesome; for seen and unseen splendors;

PEOPLE: **Thank you, God.**

LEADER: For human life; for talking and moving and thinking together; for common hopes and hardships shared from birth until our dying;

PEOPLE: **Thank you, God.**

LEADER: For work to do and strength to work; for the comradeship of labor; for exchanges of good humor and encouragement;

PEOPLE: **Thank you, God.**

LEADER: For marriage; for the mystery and joy of flesh made one; for mutual forgiveness and burdens shared; for secrets kept in love;

PEOPLE: **Thank you, God.**

LEADER: For family; for living together and eating together; for family amusements and family pleasures;

PEOPLE: **Thank you, God.**

LEADER: For children; for their energy and curiosity; for their brave play and their startling frankness; for their sudden sympathies;

PEOPLE: **Thank you, God.**

LEADER: For the young; for their high hopes; for their irreverence toward worn-out values; their search for freedom; their solemn vows;

LITANY OF THANKSGIVING

PEOPLE: **Thank you, God.**

LEADER: For growing up and growing old; for wisdom deepened by experience; for rest in leisure; and for time made precious by its passing;

PEOPLE: **Thank you, God.**

LEADER: For your help in times of doubt and sorrow; for healing our diseases; for preserving us in temptation and danger;

PEOPLE: **Thank you, God.**

LEADER: For the church into which we have been called; for the good news we receive by word and sacrament; for our life together in the Lord;

PEOPLE: **We praise you, God.**

LEADER: For your Holy Spirit, who guides our steps and brings us gifts of faith and love; who prays in us and prompts our grateful worship;

PEOPLE: **We praise you, God.**

LEADER: Above all, O God, for your Son Jesus Christ, who lived and died and lives again for our salvation; for our hope in him; and for the joy of serving him;

PEOPLE: **We thank and praise you, God our Father, for all your goodness to us.**

LEADER: Give thanks to the Lord, for he is good.

PEOPLE: **His love is everlasting.**

Litany for the Church

A

LEADER: Almighty God: you built your church on the rock of human faith and trust; we praise you for Jesus Christ, the foundation and cornerstone of all we believe.

PEOPLE: **We praise you, God.**

LEADER: For the faith of Abraham, Isaac, and Jacob; and for Moses, who led your people out of slavery, and established the law in their hearts;

PEOPLE: **We praise you, God.**

LEADER: For the prophets who listened for your word and called your people back from disobedience and from the worship of man-made gods;

PEOPLE: **We praise you, God.**

LEADER: For those who foretold the coming of your Son Jesus Christ, and prepared the way for his birth;

PEOPLE: **We praise you, God.**

LEADER: For Mary and Joseph, who taught him to love you and trained him in synagogue and temple to serve you;

PEOPLE: **We praise you, God.**

LEADER: For Christ, our Savior, who loved us and gave himself for us on the cross;

PEOPLE: **We praise you, God.**

LEADER: For the apostles and martyrs of the church, who gave their lives that we, in our day, might receive the good news of grace and forgiveness;

PEOPLE: **We praise you, God.**

LITANY FOR THE CHURCH

LEADER: For the great men of history, whose love for your church made it a willing instrument of your care and mercy; who placed you first in their lives and held to their faith in good times and in bad;

PEOPLE: **We praise you, God.**

B

LEADER: Save us, Father, from living in the past, and from resting on the work of others. Let us find a new beginning and a new vision; that we may know our duty in this place and this world today.

PEOPLE: **O Lord, please hear us.**

LEADER: Keep us from pride that excludes others from the shelter of your love; and from mean prejudice and mass evils that scar the tissues of our common life.

PEOPLE: **O Lord, please hear us.**

LEADER: Spare us from the selfishness that uses your house as a means of getting social position or personal glory, and let us not hold back what we have or what we are when there is so much need.

PEOPLE: **O Lord, please hear us.**

LEADER: Defend us from the ignorance that nourishes injustice and from indifference that causes hearts to break; that, in these times of racial bitterness, we may demonstrate your love and live beyond caste or color as Christ's men and women.

PEOPLE: **O Lord, please hear us.**

LEADER: Help us to avoid isolation in our apartments and our private homes, while others near us do not have a bed of their own or any quiet place; and, as we work to bring a decent life to others, let us know a purer enjoyment of all your blessings.

PEOPLE: **O Lord, please hear us.**

C

LEADER: That we may accept the responsibility of our freedom, the burden of our privilege, and so conduct ourselves as to set an example for those who will follow after;

PEOPLE: **O God, be our strength.**

LEADER: That we may not be content with a secondhand faith, worshiping words rather than the Word;

PEOPLE: **O God, be our strength.**

LEADER: That we may find joy in the study of Scripture, and growth in exposure to new ideas;

PEOPLE: **O God, be our strength.**

LEADER: That we may be part of our presbytery and community, sharing in the great mission which you have set before us, and always seeking the common good;

PEOPLE: **O God, be our strength.**

LEADER: That we may find in your church a prod to our imaginations, a shock to our laziness, and a source of power to do your will;

PEOPLE: **O God, be our strength.**

LEADER: O God, who gave us minds to know you, hearts to love you, and voices to sing your praise: send your Spirit among us; that, confronted by your truth, we may be free to worship you as we should; through Jesus Christ our Lord.

ALL: **Amen.**

Litany for the Unity of Christ's Church

A

LEADER: O God: you have welcomed us by baptism into one holy church, and joined us by faith to Christian men in every place. May your church on earth be a sign of the communion you promise, where we will all be one with Christ, and joyful in your kingdom.

PEOPLE: **Amen.**

LEADER: From a clinging to power that prevents church union; from thinking forms of government perfect, or courts of the church infallible;

PEOPLE: **Good Lord, deliver us.**

LEADER: From mistaken zeal that will not compromise; from worshiping neat doctrines rather than you;

PEOPLE: **Good Lord, deliver us.**

LEADER: From religious pride that belittles faith of others, or claims true wisdom, but will not love;

PEOPLE: **Good Lord, deliver us.**

LEADER: From a worldly mind that drums up party spirit; from divisiveness; from protecting systems that have seen their day;

PEOPLE: **Good Lord, deliver us.**

B

LEADER: As you sent disciples into every land, O God, gather them now, from the ends of the earth, into one fellowship that chooses your purpose and praises your name, in one faith, hope, and love.

PEOPLE: **Amen.**

LEADER: Make us one, Lord, in our eagerness to speak good news and set all captives free.

PEOPLE: **Give us your Holy Spirit.**

LEADER: Make us one, Lord, in concern for the poor, the hurt, and the downtrodden, to show them your love.

PEOPLE: **Give us your Holy Spirit.**

LEADER: Make us one, Lord, in worship, breaking bread together and singing your praise with single voice.

PEOPLE: **Give us your Holy Spirit.**

LEADER: Make us one, Lord, in faithfulness to Jesus Christ, who never fails us, and who will come again in triumph.

PEOPLE: **Give us your Holy Spirit.**

LEADER: Give us your Holy Spirit, God our Father, so we may have among us the same mind that was in Christ Jesus; and proclaim him to the world. May every knee bow down and every tongue confess him Lord, to the glory of your name.

PEOPLE: **Amen.**

Litany of the Names of the Church

> In the New Testament, the church is called by many different names that tell us who we are and what we must be doing for God. This litany uses some of the Scriptural pictures of the church, and urges obedience.

LEADER: God of Abraham and Isaac, of apostles and prophets: in every age you have picked out people to work for you, showing justice, doing mercy, and directing living men. Let the church share Christ's own work as prophet, priest, and king, reconciling the world to your law and your love, and telling your mighty power.

Give thanks to God for the church of Jesus Christ.

PEOPLE: **We are a chosen people.**

LEADER: You have called us out of the world, O God, and chosen us to be a witness to nations. Give us Holy Spirit to show the way, the truth, and the life of our Savior Jesus Christ.

PEOPLE: **Forgive silence and stubbornness. Help us to be your chosen people.**

LEADER: Give thanks to God for the church of Jesus Christ.

PEOPLE: **We are a royal priesthood.**

LEADER: You have appointed us priests, O God, to pray for all men and declare your mercy. Give us Holy Spirit; that, sacrificing ourselves for neighbors in love, they may be drawn to you, and to each other.

PEOPLE: **Forgive hypocrisy and lazy prayers. Help us to be your royal priesthood.**

LEADER: Give thanks to God for the church of Jesus Christ.

PEOPLE: **We are the household of God.**

LEADER: You have baptized us into one family of faith, and named us your children, and brothers of Christ. Give us Holy Spirit to live in peace and serve each other gladly.

PEOPLE: **Forgive pride and unbrotherly divisions. Help us to be your household.**

LEADER: Give thanks to God for the church of Jesus Christ.

PEOPLE: **We are a temple for your Spirit.**

LEADER: You have built us up, O God, into a temple for worship. Give us Holy Spirit to know there is no other foundation for us than Jesus Christ, rock and redeemer.

PEOPLE: **Forgive weakness and lack of reverence. Help us to be a temple for your Spirit.**

LEADER: Give thanks to God for the church of Jesus Christ.

PEOPLE: **We are a colony of heaven.**

LEADER: You have welcomed us as your citizens, O God, to represent our homeland. Give us Holy Spirit to act your laws, speak your language, and to show in life-style your kingdom's courtesy and love.

PEOPLE: **Forgive injustice and going along with the world. Help us to be a colony of heaven.**

LEADER: Give thanks to God for the church of Jesus Christ.

PEOPLE: **We are the body of Christ.**

LEADER: You have joined us in one body, O God, to live for our Lord in the world. Give us Holy Spirit; that, working together without envy or pride, we may serve our Lord and head.

PEOPLE: **Forgive slack faith and separate ways. Help us to be the body of Christ.**

LEADER: O God, we are your church, called, adopted, built up, blessed, and joined to Jesus Christ. Help us to know who we are, and in all we do to be your useful servants.

LITANY OF THE NAMES OF THE CHURCH

PEOPLE: **We are a chosen people**
  a royal priesthood
  a household of God
  a temple for the Spirit
  a colony of heaven
  the body of Christ

LEADER: Give thanks to God.

PEOPLE: **For the church of Jesus Christ.**

LEADER: Give thanks to God.

PEOPLE: **And trust his Holy Spirit. Amen.**

Litany for World Peace

A

LEADER: Remember, O Lord, the peoples of the world divided into many nations and tongues. Deliver us from every evil that gets in the way of your saving purpose; and fulfill the promise of peace on earth among men with whom you are pleased; through Jesus Christ our Lord.

PEOPLE: **Amen.**

LEADER: From the curse of war and the sin of man that causes war;

PEOPLE: **O Lord, deliver us.**

LEADER: From pride that turns its back on you, and from unbelief that will not call you Lord;

PEOPLE: **O Lord, deliver us.**

LEADER: From national vanity that poses as patriotism; from loud-mouthed boasting and blind self-worship that admit no guilt;

PEOPLE: **O Lord, deliver us.**

LEADER: From the self-righteousness that will not compromise, and from selfishness that gains by the oppression of others;

PEOPLE: **O Lord, deliver us.**

LEADER: From the lust for money or power that drives men to kill;

PEOPLE: **O Lord, deliver us.**

LEADER: From trusting in the weapons of war, and mistrusting the councils of peace;

PEOPLE: **O Lord, deliver us.**

LEADER: From hearing, believing, and speaking lies about other nations;

PEOPLE: **O Lord, deliver us.**

LITANY FOR WORLD PEACE

LEADER: From groundless suspicions and fears that stand in the way of reconciliation;

PEOPLE: **O Lord, deliver us.**

LEADER: From words and deeds that encourage discord, prejudice, and hatred; from everything that prevents the human family from fulfilling your promise of peace;

PEOPLE: **O Lord, deliver us.**

B

LEADER: O God our Father: we pray for all your children on earth, of every nation and of every race; that they may be strong to do your will.

We pray for the church in the world.

PEOPLE: **Give peace in our time, O Lord.**

LEADER: For the United Nations;

PEOPLE: **Give peace in our time, O Lord.**

LEADER: For international federations of labor, industry, and commerce;

PEOPLE: **Give peace in our time, O Lord.**

LEADER: For departments of state, ambassadors, diplomats, and statesmen;

PEOPLE: **Give peace in our time, O Lord.**

LEADER: For worldwide agencies of compassion, which bind wounds and feed the hungry;

PEOPLE: **Give peace in our time, O Lord.**

LEADER: For all who in any way work to further the cause of peace and goodwill;

PEOPLE: **Give peace in our time, O Lord.**

LEADER: For common folk in every land who live in peace;

PEOPLE: **Give peace in our time, O Lord.**

LEADER: Eternal God: use us, even our ignorance and weakness, to bring about your holy will. Hurry the day when people shall live together in your love; for yours is the kingdom, the power, and the glory forever.

PEOPLE: **Amen.**

Litany for the Nation

This litany is designed to be used on days of national celebration, or in times of national crisis.

A

LEADER: Mighty God: the earth is yours and nations are your people. Take away our pride and bring to mind your goodness, so that, living together in this land, we may enjoy your gifts and be thankful.

PEOPLE: **Amen.**

LEADER: For clouded mountains, fields and woodland; for shoreline and running streams; for all that makes our nation good and lovely;

PEOPLE: **We thank you, God.**

LEADER: For farms and villages where food is gathered to feed our people;

PEOPLE: **We thank you, God.**

LEADER: For cities where men talk and work together in factories, shops, or schools to shape those things we need for living;

PEOPLE: **We thank you, God.**

LEADER: For explorers, planners, statesmen; for prophets who speak out, and for silent faithful people; for all who love our land and guard freedom;

PEOPLE: **We thank you, God.**

LEADER: For vision to see your purpose hidden in our nation's history, and courage to seek it in brother-love exchanged;

PEOPLE: **We thank you, God.**

B

LEADER: O God: your justice is like rock, and your mercy like pure flowing water. Judge and forgive us. If we have turned from you, return us to your way; for without you we are lost people.

From brassy patriotism and a blind trust in power;

PEOPLE: **Deliver us, O God.**

LEADER: From public deceptions that weaken trust; from self-seeking in high political places;

PEOPLE: **Deliver us, O God.**

LEADER: From divisions among us of class or race; from wealth that will not share, and poverty that feeds on food of bitterness;

PEOPLE: **Deliver us, O God.**

LEADER: From neglecting rights; from overlooking the hurt, the imprisoned, and the needy among us;

PEOPLE: **Deliver us, O God.**

LEADER: From a lack of concern for other lands and peoples; from narrowness of national purpose; from failure to welcome the peace you promise on earth;

PEOPLE: **Deliver us, O God.**

C

LEADER: Eternal God: before you nations rise and fall; they grow strong or wither by your design. Help us to repent our country's wrong, and to choose your right in reunion and renewal.

PEOPLE: **Amen.**

LEADER: Give us a glimpse of the Holy City you are bringing to earth, where death and pain and crying will be gone away; and nations gather in the light of your presence.

PEOPLE: **Great God, renew this nation.**

LITANY FOR THE NATION

LEADER: Teach us peace, so that we may plow up battlefields and pound weapons into building tools, and learn to talk across old boundaries as brothers in your love.

PEOPLE: **Great God, renew this nation.**

LEADER: Talk sense to us, so that we may wisely end all prejudice, and may put a stop to cruelty, which divides or wounds the human family.

PEOPLE: **Great God, renew this nation.**

LEADER: Draw us together as one people who do your will, so that our land may be a light to nations, leading the way to your promised kingdom, which is coming among us.

PEOPLE: **Great God, renew this nation.**

LEADER: Great God, eternal Lord: long years ago you gave our fathers this land as a home for free men. Show us there is no law or liberty apart from you; and let us serve you modestly, as devoted people; through Jesus Christ our Lord.

PEOPLE: **Amen.**

Litany for Those Who Work

LEADER: O Lord God: you are ever at work in the world for us and for all mankind. Guide and protect all who work to get their living.

PEOPLE: **Amen.**

LEADER: For those who plow the earth,
For those who tend machinery;

PEOPLE: **Work with them, O God.**

LEADER: For those who sail deep waters,
For those who venture into space;

PEOPLE: **Work with them, O God.**

LEADER: For those who work in offices and warehouses,
For those who labor in stores or factories;

PEOPLE: **Work with them, O God.**

LEADER: For those who work in mines,
For those who buy and sell;

PEOPLE: **Work with them, O God.**

LEADER: For those who entertain us,
For those who broadcast or publish;

PEOPLE: **Work with them, O God.**

LEADER: For those who keep house,
For those who train children;

PEOPLE: **Work with them, O God.**

LEADER: For all who live by strength of arm,
For all who live by skill of hand;

PEOPLE: **Work with them, O God.**

LEADER: For all who employ or govern;

PEOPLE: **Work with them, O God.**

LITANY FOR THOSE WHO WORK

LEADER: For all who excite our minds with art, science, or learning;

PEOPLE: **Work with them, O God.**

LEADER: For all who instruct,
For writers and teachers;

PEOPLE: **Work with them, O God.**

LEADER: For all who serve the public good in any way by working;

PEOPLE: **Work with them, O God.**

LEADER: For all who labor without hope,
For all who labor without interest;
For those who have too little leisure,
For those who have too much leisure;
For those who are underpaid,
For those who pay small wages;
For those who cannot work,
For those who look in vain for work;
For those who trade on troubles of others,
For profiteers, extortioners, and greedy people;

PEOPLE: **Great God: we pray your mercy, grace, and saving power.**

LEADER: Work through us and help us always to work for you; in Jesus Christ our Lord.

PEOPLE: **Amen.**

The Christian Year

The Christian Year

As they worship, Christians are mindful of the mighty acts of God, especially as they are seen in the birth, the life, the death, and the resurrection of Jesus Christ. The pattern in which worshipers proceed from event to event and from remembrance to remembrance is called the Christian year.

The following prayers and readings are arranged according to the seasons of the Christian year. Calls to worship, readings, and special prayers are provided, as well as collects for each Lord's Day. Congregations are urged to supply Bibles for use in public worship, so that psalms and readings may be sung or said responsively.

For congregations that use color symbolism in connection with the seasons of the Christian year, the following summary of prevailing usage may be helpful:

Advent	Violet
Christmas Eve and Christmastide	White
Epiphany	White
Lent	Violet
Holy Week:	
Monday, Tuesday, Wednesday	Violet
Maundy Thursday	White
Good Friday	Red
Eastertide	White
Pentecost (and week following)	Red
Trinity Sunday (and week following)	White
Sundays After Pentecost (and weekdays)	Green

The Christian Year

ADVENT

CALLS TO WORSHIP

Isaiah 35:3–4 *Mark 1:15* *Romans 13:11–12*
Isaiah 40:9 *Luke 3:4–6* *II Corinthians 6:2*
Matthew 25:31–34 *Luke 12:35–37* *Philippians 4:4–5*

RESPONSIVE READINGS

Psalms 24; 47; 76; 96; 98; Luke 1:46–55 or 68–79

PRAYER OF CONFESSION

God of the future: you are coming in power to bring nations under your rule. We confess that we have not expected your kingdom. We have lived casual lives, and ignored your promised judgment. Judge us, O God, for we have been slow to serve you. Forgive us, for the sake of your faithful servant Jesus, our Savior, whose triumph we want and eagerly wait for. **Amen.**

PRAYER OF THANKSGIVING

God our Father: you go before us, drawing us into the future where you are. We thank you for the hope we have in your word, the good promises of peace, healing, and justice. For signs of your patience, we are grateful. For every call to duty, we give you praise. Help us, O God, to follow where you lead until the day of our Lord Jesus, when the kingdom will come and you rule the world; for the sake of Christ our Savior. **Amen.**

COLLECTS

1st Sunday in Advent

O Lord: keep us awake and alert, watching for your kingdom. Make us strong in faith, so we may greet your Son when he comes, and joyfully give him praise, with you, and with the Holy Spirit. **Amen.**

2d Sunday in Advent

God of prophets: in the wilderness of Jordan you sent a messenger to prepare men's hearts for the coming of your Son. Help us to hear good news, to repent, and be ready to welcome the Lord, our Savior, Jesus Christ. **Amen.**

3d Sunday in Advent

Mighty God: you have made us and all things to serve you; now ready the world for your rule. Come quickly to save us, so that violence and crying shall end, and your children shall live in peace, honoring each other with justice and love; through Jesus Christ, who lives in power with you, and with the Holy Spirit, one God, forever. **Amen.**

4th Sunday in Advent

Eternal God: through long generations you prepared a way in our world for the coming of your Son, and by your Spirit you are still bringing the light of the gospel to darkened lives. Renew us, so that we may welcome Jesus Christ to rule our thoughts and claim our love, as Lord of lords and King of kings, to whom be glory always. **Amen.**

Christmas Eve

Give us, O God, such love and wonder, that with shepherds, and wise men, and pilgrims unknown, we may come to adore the holy child, the promised King; and with our gifts worship him, our Lord and Savior Jesus Christ. **Amen.**

As you came in the stillness of night, great God, enter our lives this night. Overcome darkness with the light of Christ's presence, so that we may clearly see the way to walk, the truth to speak, and the life to live for him, our Lord Jesus Christ. **Amen.**

CHRISTMASTIDE

CALLS TO WORSHIP

Isaiah 9:6　　　　*Luke 2:10–11*　　　*I John 4:9*
Micah 5:2–4　　　*Luke 2:13–14*

RESPONSIVE READINGS

Psalms 67; 85; 113; 148
Isaiah 9:2–7

PRAYER OF CONFESSION

Almighty God, who sent a star to guide men to the holy child Jesus: we confess that we have not followed the light of your word. We have not searched for signs of your love in the world, or trusted good news to be good. We have failed to praise your Son's birth, and refused his peace on earth. We have expected little, and hoped for less. Forgive our doubt, and renew in us all fine desires, so we may watch and wait and once more hear the glad story of our Savior, Jesus Christ the Lord. **Amen.**

PRAYER OF THANKSGIVING

Great God of power: we praise you for Jesus Christ, who came to save us from our sins. We thank you for the prophets' hope, the angels' song, for the birth in Bethlehem. We thank you that in Jesus you joined us, sharing human hurts and pleasures. Glory to you for your wonderful love. Glory to you, eternal God; through Jesus Christ, Lord of lords, and King of kings, forever. **Amen.**

COLLECTS

Christmas Day

All glory to you, great God, for the gift of your Son, light in darkness and hope of the world, whom you sent to save mankind. With singing angels, let us praise your name, and tell the earth his story, so that men may believe, rejoice, and bow down, acknowledging your love; through Jesus Christ our Lord. **Amen.**

Holy Father: you brought peace and goodwill to earth when Christ was born. Fill us with such gladness that, hearing again news of his birth, we may come to worship him, who is Lord of lords, and King of kings, Jesus Christ our Savior. **Amen.**

Almighty God, whose glory angels sang when Christ was born: tell us once more the good news of his coming; that, hearing, we may believe, and live to praise his name, Jesus Christ our Savior. **Amen.**

1st Sunday After Christmas

God our Father: your Son Jesus became a man to claim us men as brothers in faith. Make us one with him, so that we may enjoy your love, and live to serve you as he did, who rules with you and with the Holy Spirit, one God, forever. **Amen.**

2d Sunday After Christmas

Eternal God: to you a thousand years go by as quickly as an evening. You have led us in days past; guide us now and always, that our hearts may turn to choose your will, and new resolves be strengthened; through Jesus Christ our Lord. **Amen.**

EPIPHANY

CALLS TO WORSHIP

Isaiah 60:1–3   *Luke 2:29–32*   *II Corinthians 4:6*
Matthew 2:1–2   *John 1:14*   *Ephesians 2:17–18*

RESPONSIVE READINGS

Psalms 27; 107:1–15
Isaiah 42:1–9
Isaiah, ch. 55

PRAYER OF CONFESSION

Great God our Father: you have given us Jesus, light of the world, but we choose darkness and cling to sins that hide the brightness of your love. We are frightened disciples who are slow to speak your gospel. Immersed in ourselves, we have not risen to new life. Baptize us with Holy Spirit, so that, forgiven and renewed, we may preach your word to nations, and tell your glory shining in the face of Jesus Christ, our Lord and our light forever. **Amen.**

PRAYER OF THANKSGIVING

God of light, Lord of nations: you have shown your glory in Jesus Christ to all mankind. We thank you for the power in him that has drawn us together, and baptized us into one holy church. We praise you for the work you have asked us to do in the world, going before you with good news, so that all people shall know your truth, and praise you; through Jesus Christ the Lord of all. **Amen.**

COLLECTS

Epiphany

God our Father, who by a star led men from far away to see the child Jesus: draw us and all men to him, so that, praising you now, we may in life to come meet you face to face; through Christ our Lord. **Amen.**

God of hope, who sent a star to guide men to where Christ was born: guide us by the light of your word, so we may come to him offering the gift of our lives, and go out into the world glorifying and praising you, for our Savior Jesus Christ. **Amen.**

1st Sunday After Epiphany

Holy God: you sent your Son to be baptized among sinners, to seek and save the lost. May we, who have been baptized in his name, never turn away from the world, but reach out in love to rescue wayward men; by the mercy of Christ our Lord. **Amen.**

2d Sunday After Epiphany

Great God: your mercy is an unexpected miracle. Help us to believe and obey, so that we may be free from the worry of sin, and be filled with the wine of new life, promised in the power of Jesus Christ our Savior. **Amen.**

3d Sunday After Epiphany

Almighty God: your Son our Lord called men to serve him as disciples. May we who have also heard his call rise up to follow where he leads, obedient to your perfect will; through Jesus Christ our Lord. **Amen.**

4th Sunday After Epiphany

Give us, O God, patience to speak good news to those who oppose us, and to help those who may rage against us, so that, following in the way of your Son, we may rejoice even when rejected, trusting in your perfect love which never fails; through Jesus Christ our Lord. **Amen.**

5th Sunday After Epiphany

God our Father: you have appointed us witnesses, to be a light that shines in the world. Let us not hide the bright hope you have given us, but tell all men your love, revealed in Jesus Christ the Lord. **Amen.**

6th Sunday After Epiphany

Almighty God: you gave the law as a good guide for our lives. May we never shrink from your commandments, but, as we are taught by your Son Jesus, fulfill the law in perfect love; through Christ our Lord and Master. **Amen.**

7th Sunday After Epiphany

Almighty God: you have commanded us to love our enemies, and to do good to those who hate us. May we never be content with affection for our friends, but reach out in love to all your children; through Jesus Christ our Lord. **Amen.**

8th Sunday After Epiphany

Gracious God: you know that we are apt to bring back the troubles of yesterday, and to forecast the cares of tomorrow. Give us grace to throw off fears and anxieties, as our Lord commanded, so that today and every day we may live in peace; through Jesus Christ our Lord. **Amen.**

LENT

CALLS TO WORSHIP

Psalm 139:23–24 *Luke 15:18* *I John 1:8–9*
Isaiah 1:18 *I Corinthians 10:13*
Isaiah 53:6 *Hebrews 4:14–16*

RESPONSIVE READINGS

Psalms 1; 6; 14; 32; 39; 51; 73; 130

PRAYER OF CONFESSION

O God of mercy: you sent Jesus Christ to save lost men. Judge us with love, and lift the burden of our sins. We confess that we are twisted by pride. We see ourselves pure when we are stained, and great when we are small. We have failed in love, forgotten to be just, and have turned away from your truth. Have mercy, O God, and forgive our sin, for the sake of Jesus your Son, our Savior. **Amen.**

PRAYER OF THANKSGIVING

We give thanks to you, God our Father, for mercy that reaches out, for patience that waits our returning, and for your love that is ever ready to welcome sinners. We praise you that in Jesus Christ you came to us with forgiveness, and that, by your Holy Spirit, you move us to repent and receive your love. Though we are sinners, you are faithful and worthy of all praise. We praise you, great God, in Jesus Christ our Lord. **Amen.**

COLLECTS

Ash Wednesday

Almighty God: you love all your children, and do not hate them for their sins. Help us to face up to ourselves, admit we are in the wrong, and reach with confidence for your mercy; in Jesus Christ the Lord. **Amen.**

1st Sunday in Lent

Almighty God: you know that in this world we are under great pressure, so that, at times, we cannot stand. Stiffen our resolve and make faith strong, so we may dig in against temptation and, by your power, overcome; through Jesus Christ the Lord. **Amen.**

2d Sunday in Lent

O God, who revealed glory in Jesus Christ to disciples: help us to listen to your word, so that, seeing the wonders of Christ's love, we may descend with him to a sick and wanting world, and minister as he ministered with compassion for all; for the sake of Jesus, your Son, our Lord. **Amen.**

3d Sunday in Lent

God of holy love: you have poured out living water in the gift of your Son Jesus. Keep us close to him, and loyal to his leading, so that we may never thirst for righteousness, but live eternal life; through our Savior, Christ the Lord. **Amen.**

4th Sunday in Lent

Almighty God, merciful Father: we do not deserve to be called your children, for we have left you, and wasted our gifts. Help us to know that when we repent and turn to you, you are forgiving, and are coming with joy to welcome us; through Jesus Christ our Lord. **Amen.**

5th Sunday in Lent

Great God, whose Son Jesus came as a servant among us: control our wants and restrain our ambitions, so that we may serve you faithfully and fulfill our lives; in Jesus Christ our Lord. **Amen.**

O God: your Son Jesus set his face toward Jerusalem, and did not turn from the cross. Save us from timid minds that shrink from duty, and prepare us to take up our cross, and to follow in the way of Jesus Christ our Lord. **Amen.**

PALM SUNDAY AND HOLY WEEK

CALLS TO WORSHIP

Psalm 24:9–10; Zechariah 9:9; Mark 11:9–10; Revelation 11:15b

RESPONSIVE READINGS

Psalms 24; 118:19–29; 150

PRAYER OF CONFESSION

Eternal God: in Jesus Christ you entered Jerusalem to die for our sins. We confess we have not hailed you as king, or gone before you in the world with praise. For brief faith that fades in trouble, for enthusiasms that fizzle out, for hopes we parade but do not pursue, have mercy on us. Forgive us, God, and give us such trust in your power that, in every city, we may live for justice and tell your loving-kindness; for the sake of our Savior, the Lord Jesus Christ. **Amen.**

PRAYER OF THANKSGIVING

Great God of power: you sent the Lord Jesus to enter our world and save men from sins. We thank you for glad disciples, who greeted him with praise and spread branches in his pathway. We thank you that he comes again to enter our lives by faith, and that, as his new disciples, we too may shout Hosanna, and welcome him, the King of love, Jesus Christ our Savior. **Amen.**

COLLECTS

Palm Sunday

Almighty God: you gave your Son to be the leader of men. As he entered Jerusalem, may we enter our world to follow him, obeying you and trusting your power, willing to suffer or die; through Jesus Christ the Lord. **Amen.**

Monday

Great God: cleanse your church of fake piety, overturn our greed, and let us be a holy people, repentant, prayerful, and ready to worship you in Spirit and in truth; through Jesus Christ our Lord. **Amen.**

Tuesday

Holy Father, whose mercy never ends: even as Jesus came not to judge but to save men, so may we, his believing people, seek to reach men everywhere with your saving word; through Jesus Christ our Lord. **Amen.**

Wednesday

Everlasting God, who delivered the Children of Israel from cruel captivity: may we be delivered from sin and death by your mighty power, and celebrate the hope of life eternal within your promised kingdom; through Jesus Christ our Savior. **Amen.**

MAUNDY THURSDAY

CALLS TO WORSHIP

Luke 22:15–16   *John 6:9*   *I Corinthians 5:7–8*

RESPONSIVE READINGS

Psalms 23; 42; 59:1–4, 14–17; 63:1–9

PRAYER OF CONFESSION

Eternal God, whose covenant with us is never broken: we confess that we have failed to fulfill your will for us. We betray our neighbors and desert our friends, and run in fear when we should be loyal. Though you have bound yourself to us, we will not bind ourselves to you. God, have mercy on us, weak and willful people. Lead us once more to table, and, once more, unite us to Christ, who is bread of life and the vine from which we grow in grace, to whom be praise forever. **Amen.**

PRAYER OF THANKSGIVING

God of grace: you welcome us to the table of our Lord Jesus and give gifts more than we deserve or desire. We are grateful for Christ, who feeds our faith and renews your covenant with us, who by his death gives life to all who trust in him. How can we thank you for his love? Give us a willingness to serve as he has served us, our Lord and Savior, Jesus Christ your Son. **Amen.**

COLLECT

O God: your love lived in Jesus Christ, who washed disciples' feet on the night of his betrayal. Wash from us the stain of sin, so that, in hours of danger, we may not fail, but follow your Son through every trial, and praise him to the world as Lord and Christ, to whom be glory now and forever. **Amen.**

GOOD FRIDAY

CALLS TO WORSHIP

Psalm 22:1; Isaiah 53:4; Lamentations 1:12; I Peter 2:24–25

RESPONSIVE READINGS

Psalms 13; 22:1–11; 88; 89:38–52

PRAYER OF CONFESSION

Holy God, Father of our Lord Jesus Christ: your mercy is more than our minds can measure; your love outlasts our sin. Forgive our guilt and fear and angers. We pass by neighbors in distress, and are cruel to needy men. We are quick to blame others, slow making up, and our resentments fester. Have mercy on us, God, have mercy on us, who blindly live our lives, for we do not know what we are doing. Destroy sin and sick pride, and renew us by the love of Christ, who was crucified, and died for us. **Amen.**

PRAYER OF THANKSGIVING

Great God: we thank you for Jesus, who was punished for our sins, and suffered shameful death to rescue us. We praise you for the trust we have in him, for mercy undeserved, and for love you pour out on us and all men. Give us gratitude, O God, and a great desire to serve you, by taking our cross, and following in the way of Jesus Christ the Savior. **Amen.**

COLLECTS

Merciful Father: you gave your Son to suffer the shame of the cross. Save us from hardness of heart, so that, seeing him who died for us, we may repent, confess our sin, and receive your overflowing love, in Jesus Christ our Lord. **Amen.**

How great is your love, O God, for sending Jesus to take up a cross and lay down his life for the world. Work in us such true remorse that we may cast out sin, welcome mercy, and live in wonder, praising the perfect sacrifice of Jesus Christ the Savior. **Amen.**

EASTERTIDE

CALLS TO WORSHIP

John 11:25 *I Corinthians 15:55* *I Peter 1:3–4*
I Corinthians 15:20–21 *Colossians 3:1–4*

RESPONSIVE READINGS

Psalms 30; 66; 103; 111; 116; 150

PRAYER OF CONFESSION

Mighty God: by your power is Christ raised from death to rule this world with love. We confess that we have not believed in him, but fall into doubt and fear. Gladness has no home in our hearts, and gratitude is slight. Forgive our dread of dying, our hopelessness, and set us free for joy in the victory of Jesus Christ, who was dead but lives, and will put down every power to hurt or destroy, when your promised kingdom comes. **Amen.**

PRAYER OF THANKSGIVING

We give you thanks, great God, for the hope we have in Jesus, who died but is risen, and rules over all. We praise you for his presence with us. Because he lives, we look for eternal life, knowing that nothing past, present, or yet to come can separate us from your great love made known in Jesus Christ our Lord. **Amen.**

COLLECTS

Easter

Almighty God: through the rising of Jesus Christ from the dead you have given us a living hope. Keep us joyful in all our trials, and guard faith, so we may receive the wonderful inheritance of life eternal, which you have prepared for us; through Jesus Christ the Lord. **Amen.**

Mighty God: you raised up Jesus from death to life. Give us such trust in your power that, all our days, we may be glad, looking to that perfect day when we celebrate your victory with Christ the Lord, to whom be praise and glory. **Amen.**

2d Sunday in Eastertide

Mighty God, whose Son Jesus broke bonds of death and scattered the powers of darkness: arm us with such faith in him that, facing evil and death, we may overcome as he overcame, Jesus Christ, our hope and our redeemer. **Amen.**

3d Sunday in Eastertide

Tell us, O God, the mystery of your plans for the world, and show us the power of our risen Lord, so that day by day obeying you, we may look forward to a feast with him within your promised kingdom; by the grace of our Lord Jesus Christ. **Amen.**

4th Sunday in Eastertide

Almighty God, who sent Jesus, the good shepherd, to gather us together: may we not wander from his flock, but follow where he leads us, knowing his voice and staying near him, until we are safely in your fold, to live with you forever; through Jesus Christ our Lord. **Amen.**

5th Sunday in Eastertide

God of hope: you promise many homes within your house where Christ now lives in glory. Help us to take you at your word, so our hearts may not be troubled or afraid, but trust your fatherly love, for this life, and the life to come; through Jesus Christ our Lord. **Amen.**

6th Sunday in Eastertide

O God: your Son Jesus prayed for his disciples, and sent them into the world to preach good news. Hold the church in unity by your Holy Spirit, and keep the church close to your word, so that, breaking bread together, disciples may be one with Christ in faith and love and service. **Amen.**

ASCENSION DAY

CALLS TO WORSHIP

John 17:1–3 *Acts 1:11* *Hebrews 4:14*
John 20:17 *Colossians 3:1–2*

RESPONSIVE READINGS

Psalms 47; 93; 95:1–7; 97; 113

PRAYER OF CONFESSION

Almighty God: you have lifted up our Lord Jesus from death into life eternal, and set him over men and nations. We confess that we have not bowed before him, or acknowledged his rule in our lives. We have gone along with the way of the world, and been careless of fellowmen. Forgive us, O God, and lift us out of sin. Make us men who live to praise you, and to obey the commands of our Lord Jesus Christ, who is King of the world and head of the church his body. **Amen.**

PRAYER OF THANKSGIVING

Great God, mighty God: by your power is Jesus raised to be Savior of men and ruler of nations. We thank you that he commands our lives, lifts our aims, and leads us into faith. We praise you for his love which embraces the world, and works compassion in us. Glory to you for the gift of his life. Glory to you for his loving death. Glory to you for Jesus Christ, the master of us all. **Amen.**

COLLECTS

Ascension Day

Almighty God: your Son Jesus promised that if he was lifted up, he would draw all men to himself. Draw us to him by faith, so that we may live to serve you, and look toward life eternal; through Jesus Christ the Lord. **Amen.**

7th Sunday in Eastertide

Lord of all times and places: your thoughts are not our thoughts, your ways are not our ways, and you are lifted high above our little lives. Rule our minds, and renew our ways, so that, in mercy, we may be drawn near you; through Jesus Christ our Lord and Master. **Amen.**

PENTECOST

CALLS TO WORSHIP

Joel 2:28
Matthew 9:37–38
John 3:6–8

John 14:15–17
Acts 1:8
Romans 5:3–5

I Corinthians 12:4–7
I John 4:13

RESPONSIVE READINGS

Psalms 19; 29; 84; 139

PRAYER OF CONFESSION

Almighty God, who sent the promised power of the Holy Spirit to fill disciples with willing faith: we confess that we have held back the force of your Spirit among us; that we have been slow to serve you, and reluctant to spread the good news of your love. God, have mercy on us. Forgive our divisions, and by your Spirit draw us together. Fill us with flaming desire to do your will, and be a faithful people; for the sake of your Son, our Lord, Jesus Christ. **Amen.**

PRAYER OF THANKSGIVING

Mighty God: you have called us together, and, by your Holy Spirit, made us one with your Son our Lord. We thank you for the church, for the power of the word and the sacraments. We praise you for apostles, martyrs, and brave men who have witnessed for you. We are glad you have joined us in friendship with all Christian men, and that you sent us into the world full of Holy Spirit to say that you are love; through Jesus Christ our Lord. **Amen.**

COLLECTS

Pentecost (Whitsunday)

O God: you sent the promised fire of your Spirit to make saints of common men. Once more, as we are waiting and together, may we be enflamed with such love for you that we may speak boldly in your name, and show your wonderful power to the world; through Jesus Christ our Lord. **Amen.**

Mighty God: by the fire of your Spirit you have welded disciples into one holy church. Help us to show the power of your love to all men, so they may turn, and, with one voice in one faith, call you Lord and Father; through Jesus Christ. **Amen.**

1st Sunday After Pentecost (Trinity Sunday)

Almighty God, Father of our Lord Jesus Christ and giver of the Holy Spirit: keep our minds searching your mystery, and our faith strong to declare that you are one eternal God and Father, revealed by the Spirit, through our Lord Jesus Christ. **Amen.**

2d Sunday After Pentecost

Almighty God: you have commanded us to rise up and walk in righteousness. Help us not only to hear you, but to do what you require; through Jesus Christ, our rock and our redeemer. **Amen.**

3d Sunday After Pentecost

God of power: you work for good in the world, and you want us to work with you. Keep us from being divided, so that when you call, we may follow single-mindedly in the way of Jesus Christ, our Lord and Master. **Amen.**

4th Sunday After Pentecost

Mighty God: your kingdom has come in Jesus of Nazareth, and grows among us day by day. Send us into the world to preach good news, so that men may believe, be rescued from sin, and become your faithful people; through Jesus Christ our Savior. **Amen.**

5th Sunday After Pentecost

Great God: you guard our lives, and put down powers that could overturn us. Help us to trust you, to acknowledge you before men, and to live for Jesus Christ, the Lord of all. **Amen.**

6th Sunday After Pentecost

Holy God: your Son demands complete devotion. Give us courage to take up our cross, and, without turning back, to follow where he leads us, Christ our Lord and Master. **Amen.**

7th Sunday After Pentecost

Almighty God: you have disclosed your purpose in Jesus of Nazareth. May we never reject him, but, hearing his message with childlike faith, praise him, our Lord and Master. **Amen.**

8th Sunday After Pentecost

Great God: your word is seed from which faith grows. As we receive good news, may your love take root in our lives, and bear fruit of compassion; through Jesus Christ our Lord. **Amen.**

9th Sunday After Pentecost

God of compassion: you are patient with evil, and you care for lost men. Teach us to obey you, and to live our lives following the good shepherd, Jesus Christ our Lord. **Amen.**

10th Sunday After Pentecost

Help us to seek you, God of our lives, so that in seeking, we may find the hidden treasure of your love, and rejoice in serving you; through Jesus Christ our Lord. **Amen.**

11th Sunday After Pentecost

God of grace: your Son Jesus fed hungry men with loaves of borrowed bread. May we never hoard what we have, but gratefully share with others good things you provide; through Jesus Christ, the bread of life. **Amen.**

12th Sunday After Pentecost

Mighty God: your Son Jesus came to comfort fearful men. May we never be afraid, but, knowing you are with us, take heart, and faithfully serve Christ the Lord. **Amen.**

13th Sunday After Pentecost

Holy God: we do not deserve crumbs from your table, for we are sinful, dying men. May we have grace to praise you for the bread of life you give in Jesus Christ, the Lord of love, and the Savior of us all. **Amen.**

14th Sunday After Pentecost

God our Father: you sent your Son to be our Savior. Help us to confess his name, to serve him without getting in the way, and to hear words of eternal life through him, Jesus Christ our Lord. **Amen.**

15th Sunday After Pentecost

Holy God: you welcome men who are modest and loving. Help us to give up pride, serve neighbors, and humbly walk with your Son, our Lord, Jesus Christ. **Amen.**

16th Sunday After Pentecost

God our Father: you have promised the Holy Spirit whenever we gather in the name of your Son. Be with us now, so we may hear your word, and believe in Christ, our Lord and Savior. **Amen.**

17th Sunday After Pentecost

Loving Father: whenever we wander, in mercy you find us. Help us to forgive without pride or ill will, as you forgive us, so that your joy may be ours; through Jesus Christ the Lord. **Amen.**

18th Sunday After Pentecost

Almighty God: you call men to serve you, and count desire more than deeds. Keep us from measuring ourselves against neighbors who are slow to serve you; and make us glad whenever men turn to you in faith; through Jesus Christ our Lord. **Amen.**

19th Sunday After Pentecost

Great God, Father of us all: you send us into the world to do your work. May we not only promise to serve you, but do what you command, loving neighbors, and telling the good news of Jesus Christ our Lord. **Amen.**

20th Sunday After Pentecost

Great God: you have put us to work in the world, reaping the harvest of your word. May we be modest servants, who follow orders willingly, in the name of Jesus Christ, your faithful Son, our Lord. **Amen.**

21st Sunday After Pentecost

Gracious God: you have invited us to feast in your promised kingdom. May we never be so busy taking care of things that we cannot turn to you, and thankfully celebrate the power of your Son, our Lord, Jesus Christ. **Amen.**

22d Sunday After Pentecost

Almighty God: in your kingdom the last shall be first, and the least shall be honored. Help us to live with courtesy and love, trusting the wisdom of your rewards, made known in Jesus Christ our Lord. **Amen.**

23d Sunday After Pentecost

Eternal God: you taught us that we shall live, if we love you and our neighbor. Help us to know who our neighbor is, and to serve him, so that we may truly love you; through Jesus Christ our Lord. **Amen.**

24th Sunday After Pentecost

Lord God: open our eyes to see wonderful things in your law, and open our hearts to receive the gift of your saving love; through Jesus Christ the Lord. **Amen.**

25th Sunday After Pentecost

Eternal God: help us to watch and wait for the coming of your Son, so that when he comes, we may be found living in light, ready to celebrate the victory of Jesus Christ the Lord. **Amen.**

26th Sunday After Pentecost

God our Father: you have given us a measure of faith, and told us to be good workmen. Keep us busy, brave, and unashamed, ever ready to greet your Son Jesus Christ, our judge and our redeemer. **Amen.**

27th Sunday After Pentecost

Eternal God: in Jesus Christ you judge the nations. Give us a heart to love the loveless, the lonely, the hungry, and the hurt, without pride or a calculating spirit, so that at last we may bow before you, and be welcomed into joy; through Jesus Christ, King of ages and Lord of all creation. **Amen.**

Special Days

NEW YEAR'S EVE OR DAY

CALLS TO WORSHIP

Isaiah 40:31 *II Peter 3:8–9* *Revelation 4:8b*

RESPONSIVE READINGS

Psalms 60; 121; 150
Isaiah 65:17–25

PRAYER OF CONFESSION

Eternal God: you make all things new, and forgive old wrongs we can't forget. We confess we have spent time without loving, and years without purpose; and the calendar condemns us. Daily we have done wrong, and failed to do what you demand. Forgive the past; do not let evil cripple or shame us. Lead us into the future, free from sin, free to love, and ready to work for your Son, our Savior, Jesus Christ the Lord. **Amen.**

PRAYER OF THANKSGIVING

God of our lives: you will be faithful in time to come, as in years gone by. We praise you for goodness undeserved, and gifts received we cannot number. For life and health and loving friends; for work and leisure; for all grand things you give, we thank you, Lord and God. Above all, we praise you for Jesus Christ, who lifts our hopes, and leads us in your way. Praise and reverence, honor and glory, to you, great God; through Jesus Christ the Lord. **Amen.**

COLLECT

Judge eternal: in your purpose our lives are lived, and by your grace our hopes are bright. Be with us in the coming year, forgiving, leading, and saving; so that we may walk without fear, in the way of Jesus Christ our Lord. **Amen.**

CHRISTIAN UNITY

(*See also Litany for the Unity of Christ's Church*)

CALLS TO WORSHIP

Matthew 18:19–20   *Ephesians 2:13–15*   *Ephesians 4:4–6*
Romans 15:5–6

RESPONSIVE READINGS

Psalms 81; 84; 96; 100; 111; 122

PRAYER OF CONFESSION

Great God: your Son called disciples, and prayed for their unity. Forgive divisions. Help us to confess our lack of charity toward people whose customs are different, or whose creeds conflict with what we believe. Forgive arrogance that claims God's truth; that will not listen or learn new ways. Heal broken fellowship in your mercy, and draw the church together in one faith, loyal to one Lord and Savior, Jesus Christ. **Amen.**

PRAYER OF THANKSGIVING

God of prophets and apostles, whose Spirit is working peace among us: you have called us to be your holy people, and invited us to break bread in common faith. We thank you for every word or act that makes unity in the church; for open minds and hearts; for patient understanding. Above all, we thank you for your Son, who prays for us; that we may be one in charity toward each other, serving him who is our head, Christ the Lord and Savior. **Amen.**

COLLECT

Eternal God: you have called us to be members of one body. Bind us to those who in all times and places have called on your name, so that, with one heart and mind, we may display the unity.of the church, and bring glory to your Son, our Savior, Jesus Christ. **Amen.**

WORLD COMMUNION

(*See also Litany for the Church, and Litany of the Names of the Church*)

CALLS TO WORSHIP

I Corinthians 10:16–17; II Corinthians 5:17–18; Ephesians 4:4–6

RESPONSIVE READINGS

Psalms 23; 65; 84; 116; 130

PRAYER OF CONFESSION

Almighty God: from the ends of the earth you have gathered us around Christ's holy table. Forgive our separate ways. Forgive everything that keeps us apart; the prides that prevent our proper reunion. O God, have mercy on your church, troubled and divided. Renew in us true unity of purpose; that we may break bread together, and, with one voice, praise Jesus Christ our Lord. **Amen.**

PRAYER OF THANKSGIVING

God our Father: we thank you for setting a table before us, and for calling disciples from every place to feast together. We praise you for love that binds, and for faith that makes us brothers. We glorify you for your Spirit at work, building one holy church in the world, to serve Jesus Christ, the true vine and the bread of life, our Lord and living Savior. **Amen.**

COLLECT

O God: your Son prayed for his disciples; that they might be one. Draw us to you, so that we may be united in fellowship with your Spirit, loving one another as in Jesus Christ you have loved us. **Amen.**

REFORMATION SUNDAY

CALLS TO WORSHIP

Psalm 27:4 *Hebrews 12:1–2*

RESPONSIVE READINGS

Psalms 85; 145; 150

PRAYER OF CONFESSION

God of our Fathers: you raised up brave and able men to reform the church. We confess that we have lost our way again, and need new reformation. We are content with easy religion, with too much money and too little charity; we cultivate indifference. Lord, let your word shake us up, and your Spirit renew us, so that we may repent, have better faith, and never shrink from sacrifice; in the name of Jesus Christ our only Lord and Savior. **Amen.**

PRAYER OF THANKSGIVING

Holy God: you have chosen us to serve you, and appointed us the agents of your love. We thank you for prophets who recall us to your will. We are grateful for every impulse to confess and correct wrongs, to keep faith pure and purposes faithful. We praise you for your Holy Spirit always reforming the church, so we may better serve as disciples of your Son, Jesus Christ the Lord. **Amen.**

COLLECT

God of Abraham, Isaac, and Jacob; God of prophets and martyrs: give us courage to obey your word, and power to renew your church, so that we may live in the Spirit, sharing faith with Jesus Christ our Lord. **Amen.**

THANKSGIVING DAY

(*See also Litany of Thanksgiving*)

CALLS TO WORSHIP

Psalm 24:1 *Psalm 100:4–5* *Psalm 107:1*
Psalm 72:18–19

RESPONSIVE READINGS

Psalms 67; 103; 107; 136; 138; 148

PRAYER OF CONFESSION

Almighty God: in love you spread good gifts before us, more than we need or deserve. You feed, heal, teach, and save us. We confess that we always want more; that we never share as freely as you give. We resent what we lack, and are jealous of neighbors. We misuse what you intend for joy. God, forgive our stubborn greed, and our destructiveness. In mercy, help us to take such pleasure in your goodness that we will always be thanking you; through Jesus Christ our Lord. **Amen.**

PRAYER OF THANKSGIVING

Gracious God: by your providence we live and work and join in families; and from your hand receive those things we need, gift on gift, all free. We thank you for the harvest of goodness you supply: for food and shelter, for words and gestures, for all our human friendships. Above all, we praise you for your Son, who came to show mercy, and who names us his own brothers. Glory to you for great kindness to us and all your children; through Jesus Christ our Lord. **Amen.**

COLLECT

Heavenly Father: you have filled the world with beauty. Open our eyes to see love in all your works, so that, enjoying the whole creation, we may serve you with gladness; through Jesus Christ our Lord. **Amen.**

DAY OF CIVIC OR NATIONAL SIGNIFICANCE

(*See also Litany for the Nation*)

CALLS TO WORSHIP

Psalm 29:11   *Psalm 62:8*   *Matthew 5:9*
Psalm 33:12

RESPONSIVE READINGS

Psalms 2; 33; 46; 47; 98
Isaiah 9:2–7

PRAYER OF CONFESSION

God our Father: you led men to this land, and, out of conflict, created in us a love of peace and liberty. We have failed you by neglecting rights and restricting freedoms. Forgive pride that overlooks national wrong, or justifies injustice. Forgive divisions caused by prejudice or greed. Have mercy, God, on the heart of this land. Make us compassionate, fair, and helpful to each other. Raise up in us a right patriotism, that sees and seeks this nation's good; through Jesus Christ the Lord. **Amen.**

PRAYER OF THANKSGIVING

Great God: we thank you for this land so fair and free; for its worthy aims and charities. We are grateful for people who have come to our shores, with customs and accents to enrich our lives. You have led us in the past, forgiven evil, and will lead us in time to come. Give us a voice to praise your goodness in this land of living men, and a will to serve you, now and always; through Jesus Christ our Lord. **Amen.**

COLLECT

Almighty God, judge of nations: make us brave to seek your will in the land you have given us, lest in our political actions, we neglect those things which belong to your glory; through Jesus Christ our Lord. **Amen.**

Lectionary
for the Christian Year

Lectionary for the Christian Year

A lectionary is a list of Scripture lessons, each lesson assigned to be helpful on a particular Lord's Day within the Christian year. Presbyterian churches seek to be obedient to Holy Scripture. A lectionary not only aids worshipers in the remembering of the events of God but also assures the reading and the hearing of the Old Testament and the New Testament in their fullness.

This lectionary provides readings for a cycle of three years. The designations A, B, and C are used for the first, second, and third years. Each Christian year in the three-year cycle begins, of course, at Advent of one year and continues to the Lord's Day just before the beginning of Advent in the next year.

Because other Christian churches are using this lectionary, congregations may wish to follow the cycle in the same pattern as the others. The general practice is such that those years whose last two digits are divisible by three are years in which the lessons designated B are employed, beginning at Advent. This arithmetical rule is usable from 1969 to 1999. For example: the year 1981 has as its last two digits 81. They are divisible by 3, with the result being 27, and no fraction. Thus a congregation using the lectionary, and wanting to read the Scriptures concurrently with its neighbors, would begin to use the readings for year B at Advent 1981 and would conclude year B just before Advent 1982. Year C would immediately follow and would be followed by Year A.

Lectionary for the Christian Year

ADVENT

A four-week period in which the church joyfully remembers the coming of Christ and eagerly looks forward to his coming again. Beginning with the Sunday nearest November 30, the season is observed for the four Sundays prior to Christmas.

Sunday or Festival	Year	First Lesson	Second Lesson	Gospel
1st Sunday in Advent	A	Isa. 2:1–5	Rom. 13:11–14	Matt. 24:36–44
	B	Isa. 63:16 to 64:4	I Cor. 1:3–9	Mark 13:32–37
	C	Jer. 33:14–16	I Thess. 5:1–6	Luke 21:25–36
2d Sunday in Advent	A	Isa. 11:1–10	Rom. 15:4–9	Matt. 3:1–12
	B	Isa. 40:1–5, 9–11	II Peter 3:8–14	Mark 1:1–8
	C	Isa. 9:2, 6–7	Phil. 1:3–11	Luke 3:1–6
3d Sunday in Advent	A	Isa. 35:1–6, 10	James 5:7–10	Matt. 11:2–11
	B	Isa. 61:1–4, 8–11	I Thess. 5:16–24	John 1:6–8, 19–28
	C	Zeph. 3:14–18	Phil. 4:4–9	Luke 3:10–18
4th Sunday in Advent	A	Isa. 7:10–15	Rom. 1:1–7	Matt. 1:18–25
	B	II Sam. 7:8–16	Rom. 16:25–27	Luke 1:26–38
	C	Micah 5:1–4	Heb. 10:5–10	Luke 1:39–47
Christmas Eve	A	Isa. 62:1–4	Col. 1:15–20	Luke 2:1–14
	B	Isa. 52:7–10	Heb. 1:1–9	John 1:1–14
	C	Zech. 2:10–13	Phil. 4:4–7	Luke 2:15–20

CHRISTMASTIDE

The festival of the birth of Christ, the celebration of the incarnation. A twelve-day period from December 25 to January 5, which may include either one or two Sundays after Christmas.

Sunday or Festival	Year	First Lesson	Second Lesson	Gospel
Christmas Day	A	Isa. 9:2, 6–7	Titus 2:11–15	Luke 2:1–14
	B	Isa. 62:6–12	Col. 1:15–20	Matt. 1:18–25
	C	Isa. 52:6–10	Eph. 1:3–10	John 1:1–14

CHRISTMASTIDE—Continued

Sunday or Festival	Year	First Lesson	Second Lesson	Gospel
1st Sunday After Christmas	A	Eccl. 3:1–9, 14–17	Col. 3:12–17	Matt. 2:13–15, 19–23
	B	Jer. 31:10–13	Heb. 2:10–18	Luke 2:25–35
	C	Isa. 45:18–22	Rom. 11:33 to 12:2	Luke 2:41–52
2d Sunday After Christmas	A	Prov. 8:22–31	Eph. 1:15–23	John 1:1–5, 9–14
	B	Isa. 60:1–5	Rev. 21:22 to 22:2	Luke 2:21–24
	C	Job 28:20–28	I Cor. 1:18–25	Luke 2:36–40

EPIPHANY

A season marking the revelation of God's gift of himself to all men. Beginning with the day of Epiphany (January 6), this season continues until Ash Wednesday, and can include from four to nine Sundays.

Sunday or Festival	Year	First Lesson	Second Lesson	Gospel
Epiphany		Isa. 60:1–6	Eph. 3:1–6	Matt. 2:1–12
1st Sunday After Epiphany	A	Isa. 42:1–7	Acts 10:34–43	Matt. 3:13–17
	B	Isa. 61:1–4	Acts 11:4–18	Mark 1:4–11
	C	Gen. 1:1–5	Eph. 2:11–18	Luke 3:15–17, 21–22

(or the readings for the day of Epiphany, if observed on Sunday)

Sunday or Festival	Year	First Lesson	Second Lesson	Gospel
2d Sunday After Epiphany	A	Isa. 49:3–6	I Cor. 1:1–9	John 1:29–34
	B	I Sam. 3:1–10	I Cor. 6:12–20	John 1:35–42
	C	Isa. 62:2–5	I Cor. 12:4–11	John 2:1–12
3d Sunday After Epiphany	A	Isa. 9:1–4	I Cor. 1:10–17	Matt. 4:12–23
	B	Jonah 3:1–5, 10	I Cor. 7:29–31	Mark 1:14–22
	C	Neh. 8:1–3, 5–6, 8–10	I Cor. 12:12–30	Luke 4:14–21
4th Sunday After Epiphany	A	Zeph. 2:3; 3:11–13	I Cor. 1:26–31	Matt. 5:1–12
	B	Deut. 18:15–22	I Cor. 7:32–35	Mark 1:21–28
	C	Jer. 1:4–10	I Cor. 13:1–13	Luke 4:22–30
5th Sunday After Epiphany	A	Isa. 58:7–10	I Cor. 2:1–5	Matt. 5:13–16
	B	Job 7:1–7	I Cor. 9:16–19, 22–23	Mark 1:29–39
	C	Isa. 6:1–8	I Cor. 15:1–11	Luke 5:1–11

EPIPHANY—Continued

Sunday or Festival	Year	First Lesson	Second Lesson	Gospel
6th Sunday After Epiphany	A	Deut. 30:15–20	I Cor. 2:6–10	Matt. 5:27–37
	B	Lev. 13:1–2, 44–46	I Cor. 10:31 to 11:1	Mark 1:40–45
	C	Jer. 17:5–8	I Cor. 15:12–20	Luke 6:17–26
7th Sunday After Epiphany	A	Lev. 19:1–2, 17–18	I Cor. 3:16–23	Matt. 5:38–48
	B	Isa. 43:18–25	II Cor. 1:18–22	Mark 2:1–12
	C	I Sam. 26:6–12	I Cor. 15:42–50	Luke 6:27–36
8th Sunday After Epiphany	A	Isa. 49:14–18	I Cor. 4:1–5	Matt. 6:24–34
	B	Hos. 2:14–20	II Cor. 3:17 to 4:2	Mark 2:18–22
	C	Job 23:1–7	I Cor. 15:54–58	Luke 6:39–45
9th Sunday After Epiphany		Use readings listed for 27th Sunday after Pentecost.		

LENT

A period of forty weekdays and six Sundays, beginning on Ash Wednesday and culminating in Holy Week. In joy and sorrow during this season, the church proclaims, remembers, and responds to the atoning death of Christ.

Sunday or Day	Year	First Lesson	Second Lesson	Gospel
Ash Wednesday	A	Joel 2:12–18	II Cor. 5:20 to 6:2	Matt. 6:1–6, 16–18
	B	Isa. 58:3–12	James 1:12–18	Mark 2:15–20
	C	Zech. 7:4–10	I Cor. 9:19–27	Luke 5:29–35
1st Sunday in Lent	A	Gen. 2:7–9; 3:1–7	Rom. 5:12–19	Matt. 4:1–11
	B	Gen. 9:8–15	I Peter 3:18–22	Mark 1:12–15
	C	Deut. 26:5–11	Rom. 10:8–13	Luke 4:1–13
2d Sunday in Lent	A	Gen. 12:1–7	II Tim. 1:8–14	Matt. 17:1–9
	B	Gen. 22:1–2, 9–13	Rom. 8:31–39	Mark 9:1–9
	C	Gen. 15:5–12, 17–18	Phil. 3:17 to 4:1	Luke 9:28–36

LENT—Continued

Sunday	Year	First Lesson	Second Lesson	Gospel
3d Sunday in Lent	A	Ex. 24:12–18	Rom. 5:1–5	John 2:13–25
	B	Ex. 20:1–3, 7–8, 12–17	I Cor. 1:22–25	John 4:19–26
	C	Ex. 3:1–8, 13–15	I Cor. 10:1–12	Luke 13:1–9
4th Sunday in Lent	A	II Sam. 5:1–5	Eph. 5:8–14	John 9:1–11
	B	II Chron. 36:14–21	Eph. 2:1–10	John 3:14–21
	C	Josh. 5:9–12	II Cor. 5:16–21	Luke 15:11–32
5th Sunday in Lent	A	Ezek. 37:11–14	Rom. 8:6–11	John 11:1–4, 17, 34–44
	B	Jer. 31:31–34	Heb. 5:7–10	John 12:20–33
	C	Isa. 43:16–21	Phil. 3:8–14	Luke 22:14–30
Palm Sunday	A	Isa. 50:4–7	Phil. 2:5–11	Matt. 21:1–11
	B	Zech. 9:9–12	Heb. 12:1–6	Mark 11:1–11
	C	Isa. 59:14–20	I Tim. 1:12–17	Luke 19:28–40

HOLY WEEK

The week prior to Easter, during which the church gratefully commemorates the passion and death of Jesus Christ.

Day of Holy Week	Year	First Lesson	Second Lesson	Gospel
Monday		Isa. 50:4–10	Heb. 9:11–15	Luke 19:41–48
Tuesday		Isa. 42:1–9	I Tim. 6:11–16	John 12:37–50
Wednesday		Isa. 52:13 to 53:12	Rom. 5:6–11	Luke 22:1–16
Maundy Thursday	A	Ex. 12:1–8, 11–14	I Cor. 11:23–32	John 13:1–15
	B	Deut. 16:1–8	Rev. 1:4–8	Matt. 26:17–30
	C	Num. 9:1–3, 11–12	I Cor. 5:6–8	Mark 14:12–26
Good Friday	A	Isa. 52:13 to 53:12	Heb. 4:14–16; 5:7–9	John 19:17–30
	B	Lam. 1:7–12	Heb. 10:4–18	Luke 23:33–46
	C	Hos. 6:1–6	Rev. 5:6–14	Matt. 27:31–50

EASTERTIDE

A fifty-day period of seven Sundays, beginning with Easter, the festival of Christ's resurrection. Ascension Day, forty days after Easter, is celebrated to affirm that Jesus Christ is Lord of all times and places.

Sunday or Festival	Year	First Lesson	Second Lesson	Gospel
Easter	A	Acts 10:34–43	Col. 3:1–11	John 20:1–9
	B	Isa. 25:6–9	I Peter 1:3–9	Mark 16:1–8
	C	Ex. 15:1–11	I Cor. 15:20–26	Luke 24:13–35
2d Sunday in Eastertide	A	Acts 2:42–47	I Peter 1:3–9	John 20:19–31
	B	Acts 4:32–35	I John 5:1–6	Matt. 28:11–20
	C	Acts 5:12–16	Rev. 1:9–13, 17–19	John 21:1–14
3d Sunday in Eastertide	A	Acts 2:22–28	I Peter 1:17–21	Luke 24:13–35
	B	Acts 3:13–15, 17–19	I John 2:1–6	Luke 24:36–49
	C	Acts 5:27–32	Rev. 5:11–14	John 21:15–19
4th Sunday in Eastertide	A	Acts 2:36–41	I Peter 2:19–25	John 10:1–10
	B	Acts 4:8–12	I John 3:1–3	John 10:11–18
	C	Acts 13:44–52	Rev. 7:9–17	John 10:22–30
5th Sunday in Eastertide	A	Acts 6:1–7	I Peter 2:4–10	John 14:1–12
	B	Acts 9:26–31	I John 3:18–24	John 15:1–8
	C	Acts 14:19–28	Rev. 21:1–5	John 13:31–35
6th Sunday in Eastertide	A	Acts 8:4–8, 14–17	I Peter 3:13–18	John 14:15–21
	B	Acts 10:34–48	I John 4:1–7	John 15:9–17
	C	Acts 15:1–2, 22–29	Rev. 21:10–14, 22–23	John 14:23–29
Ascension Day		Acts 1:1–11	Eph. 1:16–23	Luke 24:44–53
7th Sunday in Eastertide	A	Acts 1:12–14	I Peter 4:12–19	John 17:1–11
	B	Acts 1:15–17, 21–26	I John 4:11–16	John 17:11–19
	C	Acts 7:55–60	Rev. 22:12–14, 16–17, 20	John 17:20–26

(or the readings for Ascension Day, if observed on Sunday)

PENTECOST

The festival commemorating the gift of the Holy Spirit to the church, and an extended season for reflecting on how God's people live under the guidance of his Spirit. The season extends from the seventh Sunday after Easter to the beginning of Advent.

Sunday	Year	First Lesson	Second Lesson	Gospel
Pentecost (Whitsunday)	A	I Cor. 12:4–13	Acts 2:1–13	John 14:15–26
	B	Joel 2:28–32	Acts 2:1–13	John 16:5–15
	C	Isa. 65:17–25	Acts 2:1–13	John 14:25–31
1st Sunday After Pentecost (Trinity Sunday)	A	Ezek. 37:1–4	II Cor. 13:5–13	Matt. 28:16–20
	B	Isa. 6:1–8	Rom. 8:12–17	John 3:1–8
	C	Prov. 8:22–31	I Peter 1:1–9	John 20:19–23
2d Sunday After Pentecost	A	Deut. 11:18–21	Rom. 3:21–28	Matt. 7:21–29
	B	Deut. 5:12–15	II Cor. 4:6–11	Mark 2:23 to 3:6
	C	I Kings 8:41–43	Gal. 1:1–10	Luke 7:1–10
3d Sunday After Pentecost	A	Hos. 6:1–6	Rom. 4:13–25	Matt. 9:9–13
	B	Gen. 3:9–15	II Cor. 4:13 to 5:1	Mark 3:20–35
	C	I Kings 17:17–24	Gal. 1:11–19	Luke 7:11–17
4th Sunday After Pentecost	A	Ex. 19:2–6	Rom. 5:6–11	Matt. 9:36 to 10:8
	B	Ezek. 17:22–24	II Cor. 5:6–10	Mark 4:26–34
	C	II Sam. 12:1–7a	Gal. 2:15–21	Luke 7:36–50
5th Sunday After Pentecost	A	Jer. 20:10–13	Rom. 5:12–15	Matt. 10:26–33
	B	Job 38:1–11	II Cor. 5:16–21	Mark 4:35–41
	C	Zech. 12:7–10	Gal. 3:23–29	Luke 9:18–24
6th Sunday After Pentecost	A	II Kings 4:8–16	Rom. 6:1–11	Matt. 10:37–42
	B	Gen. 4:3–10	II Cor. 8:7–15	Mark 5:21–43
	C	I Kings 19:15–21	Gal. 5:1, 13–18	Luke 9:51–62
7th Sunday After Pentecost	A	Zech. 9:9–13	Rom. 8:6–11	Matt. 11:25–30
	B	Ezek. 2:1–5	II Cor. 12:7–10	Mark 6:1–6
	C	Isa. 66:10–14	Gal. 6:11–18	Luke 10:1–9
8th Sunday After Pentecost	A	Isa. 55:10–13	Rom. 8:12–17	Matt. 13:1–17
	B	Amos 7:12–17	Eph. 1:3–10	Mark 6:7–13
	C	Deut. 30:9–14	Col. 1:15–20	Luke 10:25–37
9th Sunday After Pentecost	A	II Sam. 7:18–22	Rom. 8:18–25	Matt. 13:24–35
	B	Jer. 23:1–6	Eph. 2:11–18	Mark 6:30–34
	C	Gen. 18:1–11	Col. 1:24–28	Luke 10:38–42

PENTECOST—Continued

Sunday	Year	First Lesson	Second Lesson	Gospel
10th Sunday After Pentecost	A	I Kings 3:5–12	Rom. 8:26–30	Matt. 13:44–52
	B	II Kings 4:42–44	Eph. 4:1–6, 11–16	John 6:1–15
	C	Gen. 18:20–33	Col. 2:8–15	Luke 11:1–13
11th Sunday After Pentecost	A	Isa. 55:1–3	Rom. 8:31–39	Matt. 14:13–21
	B	Ex. 16:2–4, 12–15	Eph. 4:17–24	John 6:24–35
	C	Eccl. 2:18–23	Col. 3:1–11	Luke 12:13–21
12th Sunday After Pentecost	A	I Kings 19:9–16	Rom. 9:1–5	Matt. 14:22–33
	B	I Kings 19:4–8	Eph. 4:30 to 5:2	John 6:41–51
	C	II Kings 17:33–40	Heb. 11:1–3, 8–12	Luke 12:35–40
13th Sunday After Pentecost	A	Isa. 56:1–7	Rom. 11:13–16, 29–32	Matt. 15:21–28
	B	Prov. 9:1–6	Eph. 5:15–20	John 6:51–59
	C	Jer. 38:1b–13	Heb. 12:1–6	Luke 12:49–53
14th Sunday After Pentecost	A	Isa. 22:19–23	Rom. 11:33–36	Matt. 16:13–20
	B	Josh. 24:14–18	Eph. 5:21–33	John 6:60–69
	C	Isa. 66:18–23	Heb. 12:7–13	Luke 13:22–30
15th Sunday After Pentecost	A	Jer. 20:7–9	Rom. 12:1–7	Matt. 16:21–28
	B	Deut. 4:1–8	James 1:19–25	Mark 7:1–8, 14–15, 21–23
	C	Prov. 22:1–9	Heb. 12:18–24	Luke 14:1, 7–14
16th Sunday After Pentecost	A	Ezek. 33:7–9	Rom. 13:8–10	Matt. 18:15–20
	B	Isa. 35:4–7	James 2:1–5	Mark 7:31–37
	C	Prov. 9:8–12	Philemon 8–17	Luke 14:25–33
17th Sunday After Pentecost	A	Gen. 4:13–16	Rom. 14:5–9	Matt. 18:21–35
	B	Isa. 50:4–9	James 2:14–18	Mark 8:27–35
	C	Ex. 32:7–14	I Tim. 1:12–17	Luke 15:1–32
18th Sunday After Pentecost	A	Isa. 55:6–11	Phil. 1:21–27	Matt. 20:1–16
	B	Jer. 11:18–20	James 3:13 to 4:3	Mark 9:30–37
	C	Amos 8:4–8	I Tim. 2:1–8	Luke 16:1–13
19th Sunday After Pentecost	A	Ezek. 18:25–29	Phil. 2:1–11	Matt. 21:28–32
	B	Num. 11:24–30	James 5:1–6	Mark 9:38–48
	C	Amos 6:1, 4–7	I Tim. 6:11–16	Luke 16:19–31
20th Sunday After Pentecost	A	Isa. 5:1–7	Phil. 4:4–9	Matt. 21:33–43
	B	Gen. 2:18–24	Heb. 2:9–13	Mark 10:2–16
	C	Hab. 1:1–3; 2:1–4	II Tim. 1:3–12	Luke 17:5–10

PENTECOST—Continued

Sunday	Year	First Lesson	Second Lesson	Gospel
21st Sunday After Pentecost	A B C	Isa. 25:6–9 Prov. 3:13–18 II Kings 5:9–17	Phil. 4:12–20 Heb. 4:12–16 II Tim. 2:8–13	Matt. 22:1–14 Mark 10:17–27 Luke 17:11–19
22d Sunday After Pentecost	A B C	Isa. 45:1–6 Isa. 53:10–12 Ex. 17:8–13	I Thess. 1:1–5 Heb. 5:1–10 II Tim. 3:14 to 4:2	Matt. 22:15–22 Mark 10:35–45 Luke 18:1–8
23d Sunday After Pentecost	A B C	Ex. 22:21–27 Jer. 31:7–9 Deut. 10:16–22	I Thess. 1:2–10 Heb. 5:1–6 II Tim. 4:6–8, 16–18	Matt. 22:34–40 Mark 10:46–52 Luke 18:9–14
24th Sunday After Pentecost	A B C	Mal. 2:1–10 Deut. 6:1–9 Ex. 34:5–9	I Thess. 2:7–13 Heb. 7:23–28 II Thess. 1:11 to 2:2	Matt. 23:1–12 Mark 12:28–34 Luke 19:1–10
25th Sunday After Pentecost	A B C	S. of Sol. 3:1–5 I Kings 17:8–16 I Chron. 29:10–13	I Thess. 4:13–18 Heb. 9:24–28 II Thess. 2:16 to 3:5	Matt. 25:1–13 Mark 12:38–44 Luke 20:27–38
26th Sunday After Pentecost	A B C	Prov. 31:10–13, 19–20, 30–31 Dan. 12:1–4 Mal. 3:16 to 4:2	I Thess. 5:1–6 Heb. 10:11–18 II Thess. 3:6–13	Matt. 25:14–30 Mark 13:24–32 Luke 21:5–19
27th Sunday After Pentecost	A B C	Ezek. 34:11–17 Dan. 7:13–14 II Sam. 5:1–4	I Cor. 15:20–28 Rev. 1:4–8 Col. 1:11–20	Matt. 25:31–46 John 18:33–37 Luke 23:35–43
28th Sunday After Pentecost		Use readings listed for 8th Sunday after Epiphany.		

LECTIONARY

SPECIAL DAYS

"It is also fitting that congregations celebrate such other days as recall the heritage of the reformed church, proclaim its mission, and forward its work; and such days as recognize the civic responsibilities of the people." (*Directory for Worship*, 19.04c.)

Special Day	Year	First Lesson	Second Lesson	Gospel
New Year's Eve or Day	A	Deut. 8:1–10	Rev. 21:1–7	Matt. 25:31–46
	B	Eccl. 3:1–13	Col. 2:1–7	Matt. 9:14–17
	C	Isa. 49:1–10	Eph. 3:1–10	Luke 14:16–24
Christian Unity	A	Isa. 11:1–9	Eph. 4:1–16	John 15:1–8
	B	Isa. 35:3–10	I Cor. 3:1–11	Matt. 28:16–20
	C	Isa. 55:1–5	Rev. 5:11–14	John 17:1–11
World Communion	A	Isa. 49:18–23	Rev. 3:17–22	John 10:11–18
	B	Isa. 25:6–9	Rev. 7:9–17	Luke 24:13–35
	C	I Chron. 16:23–34	Acts 2:42–47	Matt. 8:5–13
Reformation Sunday	A	Hab. 2:1–4	Rom. 3:21–28	John 8:31–36
	B	Gen. 12:1–4	II Cor. 5:16–21	Matt. 21:17–22
	C	Ex. 33:12–17	Heb. 11:1–10	Luke 18:9–14
Thanksgiving Day	A	Isa. 61:10–11	I Tim. 2:1–8	Luke 12:22–31
	B	Deut. 26:1–11	Gal. 6:6–10	Luke 17:11–19
	C	Deut. 8:6–17	II Cor. 9:6–15	John 6:24–35
Day of civic or national significance	A	Deut. 28:1–9	Rom. 13:1–8	Luke 1:68–79
	B	Isa. 26:1–8	I Thess. 5:12–23	Mark 12:13–17
	C	Dan. 9:3–10	I Peter 2:11–17	Luke 20:21–26

Other Prayers for Christian Worship

Other Prayers for Christian Worship

In a Time of International Crisis

Eternal God, our only hope, our help in times of trouble: get nations to work out differences. Do not let threats multiply or power be used without compassion. May your word rule the words of men, so that they may agree and settle claims peacefully. Hold back impulsive persons, lest desire for vengeance overwhelm our common welfare. Bring peace to earth right now, through Jesus Christ, the Prince of peace and Savior of us all. **Amen.**

For World Community

God our Father: in Jesus Christ you have ordered us to live as loving neighbors. Though we are scattered in different places, speak different words, or descend from different races, give us brotherly concern, so that we may be one people, who share the governing of the world under your guiding purpose. May greed, war, and lust for power be curbed, and all men enter the community of love promised in Jesus Christ our Lord. **Amen.**

For Racial Peace

Great God and Father of us all: destroy prejudice that turns us against our brothers. Teach us that we are all children of your love, whether we are black or red or white or yellow. Encourage us to live together, loving one another in peace, so that someday a golden race of men may have the world, giving praise to Jesus Christ our Lord. **Amen.**

When There Has Been a Natural Disaster

God of earthquake, wind, and fire: tame natural forces that defy control, or shock us by their fury. Keep us from calling disaster your justice; and help us, in good times or in calamity, to trust your mercy, which never ends, and your power, which in Jesus Christ stilled storms, raised the dead, and put down demonic powers. **Amen.**

In a Time of Social Change

All things are new in your grace, Lord God, and old things pass away. Break our hold on familiar things that you discard, and give us forward-looking courage to reach toward wiser ways. Lead us beyond ourselves to the new life promised in Jesus Christ, who is first and last, the beginning and the end. **Amen.**

During a National Crisis

God of ages, eternal Father: in your sight nations rise and fall, and pass through times of peril. Now when our land is troubled, be near to judge and save. May leaders be led by your wisdom; may they search your will and see it clearly. If we have turned from your way, reverse our ways and help us to repent. Give us your light and your truth; let them guide us; through Jesus Christ, who is Lord of this world, and our Savior. **Amen.**

For a Right Use of Nature's Power

Mighty God: your power fills heaven and earth, is hidden in atoms and flung from the sun. Control us so that we may never turn natural forces to destruction, or arm nations with cosmic energy; but guide us with wisdom and love, so that we may tame power to good purpose, for the building of human brotherhood and the bettering of our common lives; through Jesus Christ the Lord. **Amen.**

During an Election

Under your law we live, great God, and by your will we govern ourselves. Help us as good citizens to respect neighbors whose views differ from ours, so that without partisan anger, we may work out issues that divide us, and elect candidates to serve the welfare of mankind in freedom; through Jesus Christ the Lord. **Amen.**

For Conserving Natural Resources

Almighty God: you made the world and named it good and gave it to our management. Make us wise enough to keep air clear and water pure and natural beauty beautiful. Prevent us from destroying land and fouling streams. Let us treat lovely things with love and courtesy, so that all men may enjoy the earth; through Jesus Christ our Lord. **Amen.**

When There Is Tragedy

God of compassion: you watch the ways of men, and weave out of terrible happenings wonders of goodness and grace. Surround those who have been shaken by tragedy with a sense of your present love, and hold them in faith. Though they are lost in grief, may they find you and be comforted; through Jesus Christ, who was dead, but lives, and rules this world with you. **Amen.**

For Victims of Oppression

Great God: with justice you watch over the ways of men, and in love know each one by name. Lift those who are put down by poverty, hurt by war, or scorned by neighbors. Do not let us forget people you remember. Prevent us from oppressing, and make us do something to show helpful love; for the sake of Jesus Christ, a victim of cruelty, who is now our Lord and Savior. **Amen.**

For the Handicapped

God of compassion: in Jesus Christ you cared for men who were blind or deaf, crippled or slow to learn. Though all of us need help, give special attention to those who are handicapped. Make us care, so they may know the great regard you have for them, and believe in your love; through Jesus Christ our Lord. **Amen.**

For Those in Mental Distress

Mighty God: in Jesus Christ you dealt with spirits that darken minds or set men against themselves. Give peace to people who are torn by conflict, are cast down, or dream deceiving dreams. By your power, drive from our minds demons that shake confidence and wreck love. Tame unruly forces in us, and bring us to your truth, so that we may accept ourselves as good, glad children of your love, known in Jesus Christ. **Amen.**

For the Lonely

God of comfort, companion of the lonely: be with those who by neglect or willful separation are left alone. Fill empty places with present love, and long times of solitude with lively thoughts of you. Encourage us to visit lonely men and women, so they may be cheered by the Spirit of Jesus Christ, who walked among us as a friend, and is our Lord forever. **Amen.**

For Prisoners

God our Father: your Son Jesus was condemned to death, held captive, and hung on a cross with criminals. Never let us forget that our laws are not your law, that those we punish are still children of your love. Keep us from condemning men whose crimes are seen, in order to cover up our unseen sins. Move us to care for prisoners, and to visit them in unpleasant places, so they may know they are still loved brothers of Jesus Christ your Son. **Amen.**

For Social Misfits

In Jesus Christ, O God, you were despised and rejected by men. Watch over people who are different, who cannot copy well-worn customs, or put on popular styles of life. If they are left out because narrow men fear different ways, help us to welcome them into the wider love of Jesus Christ, brother of us all. **Amen.**

For Addicts

Faithful God: you have power to set men free from harmful habits and weakness of the will. May those who are hooked on drugs, or gripped by cravings too strong to control, be given freedom. Keep us from condemning the weakness of others while we overlook our own ungoverned desires. Enable us to help those who can no longer help themselves, so that they may see your power and believe in Jesus Christ, the liberator. **Amen.**

For the Unemployed

Lord God: you have made us co-workers with you in the world. May we never neglect the unemployed, or name them lazy if they have no work. Help us to help them, to train them, and to open doors, so that they may find employment. Working together with one another and with you, may we shape a world in which no child goes hungry, and every man contributes to the good of all; through Jesus Christ our Lord. **Amen.**

For Travelers

The world is yours, mighty God, and all men live by your faithfulness. Watch over people who are traveling, who drive or fly, or speed through space. May they be careful, but not afraid, and safely reach their destinations. Wherever we wander in your spacious world, teach us that we never journey beyond your loving care, revealed in Jesus Christ our Lord. **Amen.**

For Healing

By your power, great God, our Lord Jesus healed the sick and gave new hope to hopeless men. Though we cannot command or possess your power, we pray for those who want to be healed (especially for _____). Close wounds, cure sickness, make broken people whole again, so they may live to rejoice in your love. Help us to welcome every healing as a sign that, though death is against us, you are for us, and have promised renewed and risen life in Jesus Christ the Lord. **Amen.**

For Rejoicing in Childbirth

Mighty God: by your love we are given children through the miracle of birth. May we greet each new son and daughter with joy, and surround them all with faith, so they may know who you are and want to be your disciples. Never let us neglect children, but help us to enjoy them, showing them the welcome you have shown us all; through Jesus Christ the Lord. **Amen.**

For Little Children

Great God our Father, Father of families: guard the laughter of children. Bring them safely through injury and illness, so they may live the promises you give. Do not let us be so preoccupied with our purposes that we fail to hear their voices, or pay attention to their special vision of the truth; but keep us with them, ready to listen and to love, even as in Jesus Christ you have loved us, your grown-up, wayward children. **Amen.**

For the Young

Almighty God: again and again you have called on young people to force change or fire human hopes. Never let us be so set in our ways that we refuse to hear young voices, or so firm in our grip on power that we reject them. Let the young be candid, but not cruel. Keep them dreaming dreams that you approve, and living in the Spirit of the young man Jesus, who was crucified, who now rules the world. **Amen.**

For Graduates

Father: in your will our lives are lived, and by your wisdom truth is found. We pray for graduates who finish a course of study, and now move on to something new. Take away anxiety, or confusion of purpose; and give them a confidence in the future you plan, where energies may be gathered up and given to neighbors in love; for the sake of Jesus Christ our Lord. **Amen.**

For Those Engaged to Marry

Almighty God: in the beginning you made man and woman to join themselves in shared affection. May those who engage to marry be filled with joy. Let them be so sure of each other that no fear or disrespect may shake their vows. Though their eyes may be bright with love for each other, keep in sight a wider world, where neighbors want and strangers beg, and where service is a joyful duty; through Jesus Christ the Lord. **Amen.**

For the Newly Married

God of grace: in your wisdom you made man and woman to be one flesh in love. As in Jesus Christ you came to serve us, let newlyweds serve each other, putting aside selfishness and separate rights. May they build homes where there is free welcome. At work or in leisure, let them enjoy each other, forgive each other, and embrace each other faithfully, serving the Lord of love, Jesus Christ. **Amen.**

For Those in Middle Years

Eternal God: you have led us through our days and years, made wisdom ripe and faith mature. Show men and women your purpose for them, so that, when youth is spent, they may not find life empty or labor stale, but may devote themselves to dear loves and worthy tasks, with undiminished strength; for the sake of Jesus Christ the Lord. **Amen.**

For Retired People

Your love for us never ends, eternal God, even when by age or weakness we can no longer work. When we retire, keep us awake to your will for us. Give us energy to enjoy the world, to attend to neighbors busy men neglect, and to contribute wisely to the life of the church. If we can offer nothing but our prayers, remind us that our prayers are a useful work you want, so that we may live always serving Jesus Christ, our hope and our true joy. **Amen.**

For the Dying

Almighty God: by your power Jesus Christ was raised from death. Watch over dying men and women. Fill eyes with light, to see beyond human sight a home within your love, where pain is gone and frail flesh turns to glory. Banish fear. Brush tears away. Let death be gentle as nightfall, promising a day when songs of joy shall make us glad to be together with Jesus Christ, who lives in triumph, the Lord of life eternal. **Amen.**

For Those Who Suffer Sexual Confusion

God of creation: you made men and women to find in love fulfillment as your creatures. We pray for those who deny love between man and woman, who are repelled by flesh, or frightened by their daydreams. Straighten us all out, O Lord, and show us who we are, so that we may affirm each other bodily in covenants of love, approved by Jesus Christ our Lord. **Amen**

For Those in Marital Difficulty

Lord God, who set us in families, where we learn to live together in charity and truth: strengthen weak bonds of love. Where separation threatens, move in with forgiving power. Melt hard hearts, free fixed minds, break the hold of stubborn pride. Lay claim on us, so that our separate claims may be set aside in love; through Jesus Christ our Lord. **Amen.**

For the Divorced or Separated

God of grace: you are always working to hold us together, to heal division, and make love strong. Help men and women whose marriages break up to know that you are faithful. Restore confidence, bring understanding, and ease the hurt of separation. If they marry others, instruct them in better love, so that vows may be said and kept with new resolve; through Jesus Christ our Lord. **Amen.**

For Families Where There is Only One Parent

God our Father: we are never away from your care, and what we lack you give in love. Watch over families where, by death or separation, a parent is left alone with children. Lift bitterness, or too great a sense of lonely obligation. Show them that they live under your protection, so that they have not less love, but more; through Jesus Christ, your Son and our eternal brother.
Amen.

For Orphans

Gracious God: you care for all your children. Pay attention to orphans. May they be free from unprotected fears or secret bitterness. Enroll them in the human family as special children of your love. By our concern, may we welcome them into the brotherhood of your church, showing them by word and deed your great concern for them; through Jesus Christ our Lord. **Amen.**

For City People

Eternal God: you are bringing your holy city to earth, where death and pain shall be no more, and men shall live together in your light. We pray for cities, where, in high towers or close-built houses, people work and live. Ease tensions and break down separation, so that every stranger may know himself to be a citizen among citizens, governed by Jesus Christ, who came to Jerusalem as a Savior. **Amen.**

For People in Rural Areas

O God, your Son Jesus grew up in a small town and walked the hills of Galilee. We pray for people who live on farms or in little villages. May they take pleasure in nature's natural beauty, and watch over growing things with love. Help them to keep neighborhoods wide open to your world, so that they may be in touch with the whole human family; through Jesus Christ the Lord. **Amen.**

For Agreement Between Labor and Management

O God: you have made a world where men may join to get things done according to your will. Bring understanding between those who labor and those who manage. Do not let greed blind us to basic needs, or make men careless of one another. May wages be fair and work be worthy. Where there are grievances, help us to talk them out, so that name-calling may end, and we may work together as comrades; through Jesus Christ our Master. **Amen.**

For Those in Military Service

Righteous God: you rule the nations. Guard brave men who risk themselves in battle for their country. Give them compassion for enemies who also fight for patriotic causes. Keep our sons from hate that hardens, or from scorekeeping with human lives. Though they must be men of war, let them live for peace, as eager for agreement as for victory. Encourage them as they encourage one another, and never let hard duty separate them from loyalty to your Son, our Lord, Jesus Christ. **Amen.**

For Those Who Refuse Military Service

God of peace, whose Son Jesus Christ came preaching goodwill among men: guard brave people among us who refuse military service because of conviction. May they never confuse conscience with cowardice, but, in good faith, withstand all public opposition. Save them from self-righteousness. Give them charity to love brothers who fight, but courage to speak the call to peace, heard in Jesus Christ, your Son our Lord. **Amen.**

For Play

God our Father: you made the world for sane and cheerful pleasures. Show us how to live free from false restraint or the terror of aimless craving, so that we may enjoy good times together, like guiltless children who play within the safety of your love, known in Jesus Christ, who set us free for joy. **Amen.**

For Those Who Do Not Believe

God of love, who sent Jesus Christ to seek and save lost men: may we who have been found by him value those who do not believe, and never shun neighbors who reject you. Remembering how our faith was given, may we preach good news with goodwill, trusting you to follow up your word, so that men may hear and believe and come to you; through Jesus Christ our Lord. **Amen.**

For Those We May Forget in Prayer

We do not know how to pray, O God, unless your Spirit guides us. Help us to pray for neighbors on earth, who wait for us to care, whose needs we have neglected, whose names we do not know. Make us want to know and name and care. Through our prayers draw us toward forgotten men and women, who are children of your love and our brothers in Jesus Christ, the Lord of all. **Amen.**

For Criminals and Racketeers

Holy God, your Son Jesus visited a crooked tax collector, and died between criminals. Never let us pretend to be pure while neglecting those who live in evil, but send us out with the friendliness of Christ to those our world condemns, so they may turn to you, restored and forgiven, to live as loyal children by your law, revealed in Jesus Christ our Lord. **Amen.**

For Prostitutes

God of compassion: your Son Jesus showed mercy to a woman condemned by harsh judgment, and gave her new life. We pray for prostitutes, who are victims of lovelessness, or of a craving to be loved. Keep us from easy blame or cruel dismissal. May our church seek them out, and show such genuine friendship that they may know your welcome, and live among us, as sisters of Jesus Christ our Lord. **Amen.**

For Those Who Work in International Government

High God, holy God: you rule the ways of men, and govern every earthly government. Work with those who work for peace. Make every diplomat an agent of your reconciliation, and every statesman an ambassador of hope. Bring peace and goodwill among men, fulfilling among us the promise made in Jesus Christ, who was born to save the world. **Amen.**

For Those Who Fight for Social Justice

You give us prophets, holy God, to cry out for justice and mercy. Open our ears to hear them, and to follow the truth they speak, lest we support injustice to secure our own well-being. Give prophets the fire of your word, but love as well. Though they speak for you, may they know that they stand with us before you, and have no Messiah other than your Son, Jesus Christ, the Lord of all. **Amen.**

For Scientists

God of wisdom: you have given us a world filled with hidden holy meaning. Thank you for scientists who search for truth, who use their minds to better life on earth. Give them patience, moral judgment, and curiosity to grope through great mysteries. May their work be constructive, building community among men and nations; through Jesus Christ our Lord. **Amen.**

For Those Who Grow, Prepare, and Distribute Food

God of grace: in your world there are fields to seed and harvest. We thank you for men who farm the land, and for workers who prepare or distribute food. Give them joy in the miracle of growth, and trust in your provision. May no one starve because of greed, but let men hunger for righteousness alone; through Jesus Christ the Lord. **Amen.**

For Migrant Workers

Eternal God: your Son Jesus had no place to lay his head, and no home to call his own. We pray for men and women who follow seasons and go where the work is, who harvest crops or do part-time jobs. Follow them around with love, so they may believe in you, and be pilgrim people, trusting Jesus Christ the Lord. **Amen.**

For Communication Workers

God of grace: you have taught us that faith comes from hearing the good news, and that we fulfill our lives by sending messages of love. Thank you for those who work to speed words between us, who enable us to converse with neighbors. May their skill draw close ties between us all, so that in our words your word may sound; through Jesus Christ our Lord and living Master. **Amen.**

For Transportation Workers

God almighty: you scattered us throughout the earth, yet bound us in a brotherhood of need and service. Thank you for those who move us through the world, who speed deliveries, or take us to and from our homes. May they see themselves as workmen who help us to share ourselves with neighbors; through Jesus Christ the Lord. **Amen.**

For Those Who Manufacture and Sell

Great God: you keep us going and give us energy to get things done. Thank you for men and women in industry, who work in factories and offices, or cover territories. Though they may do routine tasks or run machines, keep them free and thoughtful, so that their work may contribute to a better world, where neighbors will take time to love one another; through Jesus Christ, who lived and worked among us. **Amen.**

For Those in Business or Commerce

God of the covenant: you give love without return, and lavish gifts without looking for gain. Watch over the ways of business, so that those who buy or sell, get or lend, may live justly and show mercy and walk in your ways. May profits be fair and contracts kept. In our dealings with each other may we display true charity; through Jesus Christ, who has loved us with mercy. **Amen.**

For Those in Medical Services

Merciful God: by your power people are healed. Give strength to doctors, nurses, and technicians, who staff hospitals and homes for the sick. Make them brave to battle our last enemy, trusting your power to overcome death and pain and crying. May they be thankful for every sign of health you give, and humble before the mystery of mending grace; through Jesus Christ our Lord. **Amen.**

For Journalists, Publishers, and Printers

By your word, Lord God, the earth was created, and by our words we serve your will. Thank you for men and women who write, print, and publish, who bring us news and help us to think things out. Keep them in touch with all that you are doing in the world, so that their printed words may tell good news, to reconcile nations and renew the minds of men; through Jesus Christ the Lord. **Amen.**

For Janitors, Maintenance Men, and Refuse Collectors

Great God: you have made the world a home for us, and surrounded us with beauty. Thank you for those who take pride in keeping air fresh and streets clean; who make corridors and working spaces clear and safe for us. May they labor faithfully to maintain your world; for the sake of Jesus Christ our Lord.
Amen.

For Those in Legal Work

God of justice: you gave us law by Moses, and in Jesus Christ interpreted the law in selfless love. Give to those who make, administer, or defend our laws love for mercy and truth. May we never confuse our paper laws with the tablets of your eternal will, but have courage to repeal wrong rules. May our laws set men free for righteousness, revealed in Jesus Christ, the Judge and Savior of us all. **Amen.**

For Secretaries and Clerical Workers

Almighty God: your word has come to us copied by scribes with loving care. Guard those who record words, and keep files, without whose work we would lose track of ourselves, or slip into sad confusion. Help them to be alert and accurate; to rule machines they use and not be run by them. May they know that they are your servants, who speed messages within the broken world you love; through Jesus Christ our Lord. **Amen.**

For Architects, Builders, and Decorators

Great God: you gave Jesus Christ to be the foundation on which our lives are built. Thank you for men and women who build shelters, order space, and decorate rooms where our lives are lived. Help them to provide hospitable places where men may be free for one another, in the love of Jesus Christ our Lord. **Amen.**

For Entertainers

God our Father: you have made us for each other, to live by glad exchanges of love and skill. Thank you for men and women who work to entertain us, who deepen understanding, make laughter, or give us songs to sing. May they desire truth more than profit, and art more than applause. In all they do, may they celebrate good humanity, revealed in your man Jesus Christ, the Lord of all creation. **Amen.**

For Those in the Arts

God of life: you filled the world with beauty. Thank you for artists who see clearly, who with trained skill can paint, shape, or sing your truth to us. Keep them attentive, and ready to applaud the wonder of your works, finding in the world signs of the love revealed in Jesus Christ our Lord. **Amen.**

For Counselors

God of wisdom, God of love: when we are perplexed you give light to go by. Thank you for those who work out problems with us. May they have respect for our struggles, and never fail to marvel at the mystery of human minds. Guide them with your Holy Spirit, so they may guide us into the way of Jesus Christ, our truth and our new life. **Amen.**

For Government Workers

Almighty God: you have plans for us, and power to make them happen. Give legislators, executives, and government workers a knowledge of your will for the world. Let them remember that they serve a public trust, beyond personal gain or glory. May they see that no nation lives for itself alone, but is responsible to you for peace, and for the well-being of all your children; through Jesus Christ our Lord. **Amen.**

For Those Who Wait on Others

Great God and Father of mankind: you have taught us that if we want to be great, we must be servants of all. We thank you for those who help with household chores or wait on tables, whose work gives ease and comfort to others. Help them to know that their work is specially valued by Jesus Christ, who came as a servant with humility and love. **Amen.**

For Those Who Work in Education

Holy Father: you have led us in each new generation to discoveries of the truth. Thank you for men and women who teach, administer, and work in schools and colleges. Make them eager to explore your world, searching mysteries. Never let them neglect students who are slow to learn. Keep teachers young in mind, resilient, exciting, and devoted to human welfare; through the love of Jesus Christ our Lord. **Amen.**

For Students

Eternal God: your wisdom is greater than our small minds can contain, and your truth shows up our little learning. To those who study, give curiosity, imagination, and patience enough to wait and work for insight. Help them to doubt with courage, but to hold all their doubts in the larger faith of Jesus Christ our Lord. **Amen.**

For Those Who Work in Social Service or Charitable Agencies

As you have given yourself to us, O God, help us to give ourselves to one another in perfect charity. Thank you for men and women who work for the welfare of others. Fill them with energetic love to show friendship and compassion with no strings attached, so that men may believe you care; through Jesus Christ our Lord. **Amen.**

For Mechanics, Repairmen, and Those in Skilled Trades

Almighty God: you have given us intelligence, and skillful hands to work with. Thank you for those who provide, maintain, and repair things we use. Help them to know that neighbors depend on them, and to be worthy workmen; for the sake of Jesus Christ our Lord. **Amen.**

For Those in Dangerous Occupations

God of earth and air, height and depth: we pray for those who work in danger above, below, or on the earth. Give them caution and a concern for one another, so that in safety they may do what must be done, under your watchful love, in Jesus Christ our Lord. **Amen.**

For the Mission of the Church

The whole world lives in your love, holy God, and we are your people. Send us out in faith to tell your story and to demonstrate your truth to men of every race and nation, so that, won by your powerful word, the world of men may join together giving you praise, and living to serve you in Jesus Christ the Lord. **Amen.**

For a Particular Mission of the Church

By your will, O God, we go out into the world with good news of your undying love, and minister among men to show wonders of your grace. We pray for _____, where there are men and women who minister for you. May they be strengthened by our concern, and supported by our gifts. Do not let them be discouraged, but make them brave and glad and hopeful in your word; through Jesus Christ the Lord. **Amen.**

For Evangelists and Fraternal Workers

Great God: in every age you have picked out people to spread good news, and to light your light in darkness. Guard those who witness to you in far-off places, in crowded cities or in open fields. Keep them sure of your power, so that they may work without fear of failure. Help them tell your wonderful story until all men turn to you, even as you have turned to us with love, in Jesus Christ our Savior. **Amen.**

For Teachers in the Church

Almighty God: you have given your law to lead us in a life of love, and you have appointed teachers to interpret your will. Create in those who instruct your people a mind to study your word, and good understanding, so that we may learn your truth and do it gladly; for the sake of Jesus Christ our Master. **Amen.**

For Ministers of the Word

In every age, O God, you have appointed spokesmen, prophets and priests, to lead your faithful people. May ministers of the gospel tell the truth in love. Keep them from mouthing pieties they do not mean. Make them humble men and women without pretense or pride, who bring light to darkness, showing the way of Jesus Christ, to whom be praise forever. **Amen.**

For Chaplains

O God: you have ordered men and women to serve the church, and given them special gifts by your Spirit. May those who serve as chaplains be strong in faith. Keep them from being discouraged. Let us bring them hope and friendship wherever they may serve; through Jesus Christ our Lord and Savior. **Amen.**

For a Moderator

Almighty God: you called us into the church, and from among us chose leaders to direct us in your way. We thank you for _____, our Moderator. Enlarge *his* gifts and help *him* to obey you, so that we may enjoy good work under *his* guidance, loyally serving Jesus Christ the Lord. **Amen.**

For Those Who Intend Christian Service

God of prophets and apostles: you have chosen leaders to train your people in the way of Jesus Christ. We thank you that in our day you are still claiming men and women for special work within the church. As _____ has dedicated *himself* to you, let us pledge ourselves to *him*, so that, surrounded by affection and hope, *he* may grow in wisdom, mature in love, and become a faithful worker, approved by Jesus Christ our Lord. **Amen.**

For Church Workers

How many are the ways we serve within your church, O God. Watch over those who work for boards or in agencies of the church, who promote the gospel. Do not let them think themselves lesser or greater than those who preach or teach; but show them that their gifts are needed in the one ministry of the Lord Jesus Christ, who is head of the church. **Amen.**

When a Minister Is Leaving or Retiring

You have bound us together in the church, great God, and built up the Spirit of love among us. Though we must go separate ways in working for your kingdom, help us to know that we are joined forever in your loving care. We thank you for years together, for mutual support and mutual forgiveness. Never let friendship fade, but keep us remembering one another, and grateful for the life we have shared, in Jesus Christ our Lord. **Amen.**

For a Meeting of the General Assembly, Synod, or Presbytery

Almighty God: in Jesus Christ you called disciples and, by the Holy Spirit, made them one church to serve you. Be with members of our *General Assembly*. Help them to welcome new things you are doing in the world, and to respect old things you keep and use. Save them from empty slogans or senseless controversy. In their deciding, determine what is good for us and all men. As the *General Assembly* meets, let your Spirit rule, so that our church may be joined in love and service to Jesus Christ, who, having gone before us, is coming to meet us in the promise of your kingdom. **Amen.**

For Church Schools and Colleges

God of light: your truth makes every dark place bright, and sets men free from foolishness to live in wisdom. Build up schools and colleges where men and women may grow in the knowledge of your Son. Keep them from becoming sheltered groves away from human agony. Draw faculty, staff, and students together in your Spirit, so they may know that you alone are good and true; through Jesus Christ our Lord. **Amen.**

For Seminaries

Almighty God: in Jesus Christ you called ordinary men to be disciples and sent them out to teach and preach your truth. Bring to seminaries men and women who are honest and eager to serve you. Give them tender hearts to care for fellowmen, and tough minds to wrestle with your word, so that, as they speak and act for you, men may repent and return to love, believing in Jesus Christ, who is our Lord and Master. **Amen.**

For a Church Meeting

Eternal God: you called us to be a special people, to preach the gospel and show mercy. Keep your Spirit with us as we meet together, so that in everything we may do your will. Guide us lest we stumble or be misguided by our own desires. May all we do be done for the reconciling of the world, for the upbuilding of the church, and for the greater glory of Jesus Christ our Lord. **Amen.**

For a Church Supper

God our companion: in Jesus Christ you ate and drank with sinners, broke bread with disciples, and joined your Spirit with

Christian men at table. As we meet and eat together, be among us to bring love, so that as we go out into the world, your Spirit may go with us, spreading the fellow-feeling we find at table here; through Jesus Christ our Lord. **Amen.**

When New Members Are Received by the Session

Almighty God: by the love of Jesus Christ you draw men to faith, and welcome them into the church family. May we show your joy by embracing new brothers and sisters, who with us believe and with us will work to serve you. Keep us close together in your Spirit, breaking bread in faith and love, one with Jesus Christ our Lord and Master. **Amen.**

For Founders and Previous Leaders of a Congregation

We thank you, Lord God, for brave and believing men who brought your message to this place. Let us not forget them (*names may be named*). By their energies this church was gathered, given order, and continued. Remembering all those Christians who have gone before us, may we follow as they followed in the way, truth, and life of Jesus Christ, the head of the church. **Amen.**

For the Acknowledgment of Special Gifts

God of goodness: from your love we have received all that we need or can rightly desire, and by your grace we are prompted to grateful generosity. Thank you for the special gift we now receive. May we use everything to spread word of your deeds and proclaim your faithful love. Let those who have given this gift live in our affection. With them, may we do all things to honor your name; through Jesus Christ our Lord. **Amen.**

For a New Church Building

Eternal God, high and holy: no building can contain your glory or display the wonders of your love. May this space be used as a gathering place for men of goodwill. If we worship, let us worship gladly; if we study, let us learn your truth. May every meeting held here meet with your approval, so that this building may stand as a sign of your Spirit at work in the world, and as a witness to our Lord and Savior, Jesus Christ. **Amen.**

For a Right Use of Church Money and Property

Righteous God: you have taught us that the poor shall have your kingdom, and that the gentle-minded shall inherit the earth. Keep the church poor enough to preach to poor people, and humble enough to walk with the despised. Never weigh us down with real estate or too much cash on hand. Save your church from vain display or lavish comforts, so that, traveling light, we may move through the world showing your generous love, made known in Jesus Christ our Lord. **Amen.**

When the Church Faces a Decision

O God: you are always forcing us to face decisions, so that in choosing, we will choose your will. Now that we must decide what to do, guide us with your word and Spirit. Prevent us from clinging to old strategies, and show new ways for us to follow and obey; through Jesus Christ, the pioneer of faith. **Amen.**

For the Authority of Scripture in the Church

We thank you, Lord God, for men of old who preserved your word for us, who recorded your law, copied the prophets, and remembered the gospel message. May your church never neglect the study of Scripture, but with lively and persistent interest read, recite, interpret, and teach the news declared in Jesus Christ your living Word, and the Savior of us all. **Amen.**

For the Holy Spirit in the Church

Almighty God: you poured out the Holy Spirit on believers at Pentecost, drawing them together in the mission of the church. Give us great enthusiasm for your work, and keep your Spirit with us, so that, united and in peace with one another, we may live new lives as ambassadors of Jesus Christ, who is head of the church, our Savior and our strength. **Amen.**

For Worship in the Church

Holy God: you call us to worship, and by your Spirit prompt prayers and praise. Keep us from saying words or singing hymns with ritual disinterest. Fill us with such wonder that we may worship you, grateful for the mystery of your unfailing love for us, in Jesus Christ the Lord. **Amen.**

For an Inclusive Church

How great is your love, Lord God, how wide is your mercy! Never let us board up the narrow gate that leads to life with rules or doctrines that you dismiss; but give us a Spirit to welcome all people with brotherly affection, so that your church may never exclude secret friends of yours, who are included in the love of Jesus Christ, who came to save us all. **Amen.**

For Peace in the Church

God of our lives: by the power of your Holy Spirit, we have been drawn together by one baptism into one faith, serving one Lord and Savior. Do not let us tear away from one another through division or hard argument. May your peace embrace our differences, preserving us in unity, as one body of Jesus Christ our Lord. **Amen.**

When There Is Division in the Church

Holy God, giver of peace, author of truth: we confess that we are divided and at odds with one another, that a bad spirit has risen among us, and set us against your Holy Spirit of peace and love. Take from this congregation mistrust, party spirit, contention, and all evil that now divides us. Work in us a desire for reconciliation, so that, putting aside personal grievances, we may go about your business with a single mind, devoted to our Lord and Savior, Jesus Christ. **Amen.**

For Courage by the Church

Strong God of truth: your Son Jesus was arrested and killed for outspoken faith. Save us from shrinking back in the face of opposition or from trembling when conflicts flare. Do not let us fall in love with martyrdom, but make us brave to speak your word and do your truth with courage, obeying Jesus Christ, whose disciples we are, whose commands we serve. **Amen.**

For Jewish Friends of the Church

God of Abraham, Isaac, and Jacob, Father of us all, whose Son Jesus was born a Jew, was circumcised, and was dedicated in the Temple: thank you for patriarchs and prophets and righteous rabbis, whose teaching we revere, whose law is our law fulfilled in Jesus Christ. Never let us forget that we, who are your people, are by faith children of Abraham, bound in one family with Jewish brothers, who also serve your purpose; through Jesus Christ, our Master and Messiah. **Amen.**

For Other Christian Churches

Almighty God: in Jesus Christ you called disciples and prayed for them to be joined in faith. We pray for Christian churches from which we are separated. Never let us be so sure of ourselves that we condemn the faith of others or refuse reunion with them, but make us ever ready to reach out for more truth, so that your church may be one in the Spirit; through Jesus Christ our Lord. **Amen.**

By Women in the Church

God of love: you chose the woman Mary to bring your Son to the world, and on Easter Day sent women from his empty tomb with news of resurrection. Show us the special work you have for us. Give us a desire to follow worthy women who, in every age, brought life to earth, spread your word, and witnessed to the risen power of Jesus Christ, a woman's child, who is now the Lord of all. **Amen.**

By Men in the Church

Mighty God: your Son Jesus picked out disciples from ordinary men, and told them to follow him. Keep us, who are his disciples now, unafraid and faithful, so that, with manly courage, we may say and do what you want said and done in the world; through Jesus Christ, a man among men, who is the Lord forever. **Amen.**

For Families of the Church

Lord God, holy Father: you set us in families to teach one another and practice ways of love. Oversee families in the church, so that, fed by your word and held in your Spirit, they may forgive one another, and give one another gifts of joy and courage. Join families day by day to the wider family of mankind as friends and neighbors in Jesus Christ, the Lord of all. **Amen.**

For Enemies of the Church

Strong God, God of love: your Son Jesus told us that his church would be persecuted as he was persecuted. If we should suffer for righteousness' sake, save us from self-righteousness. Give us grace to pray for enemies, and to forgive them, even as you have forgiven us; through Jesus Christ, who was crucified but is risen, whom we praise forever. **Amen.**

For Those Who Write Prayers

Almighty God: you have no patience with solemn assemblies, or heaped-up prayers to be heard by men. Forgive those who have written prayers for congregations. Remind them that their foolish words will pass away, but that your word will last and be fulfilled, in Jesus Christ our Lord. **Amen.**

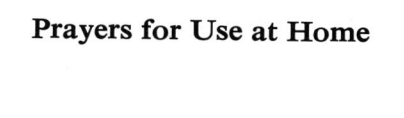

Prayers for Use at Home

Prayers for Use at Home

Parents' Prayer

God our Father: you have brought children out of our love, and put us in charge of them for a little while. Keep us from doing damage. May love be strong, but not possessive; liberating, but never careless. Help us to remember that we are also your children, willful and foolish, in need of patient grace; through Jesus Christ our Lord. **Amen.**

A Family Prayer

Our Father: we are your children. You know us better than we know ourselves, or can know each other. Help us to love, so that we can learn to love our neighbors. May we forgive, hold no grudges, and put up with being hurt. Let there be laughter as we enjoy each other. Serving, may we practice serving you; through Jesus Christ our Lord. **Amen.**

Morning Prayers

God: be with us all day, in streets or buildings where we work, so that everything we do may be for you, and your Son, our Lord, Jesus Christ. **Amen.**

May we wake thinking of your love, great God, and trusting your plans for us. Give us your Spirit today, so we may do what you want done in the world; through Jesus Christ our Lord. **Amen.**

Evening Prayers

As darkness comes, Father, forgive wrong things we have said or done. Renew our love for one another, and give us quiet minds to sleep, so when morning comes, we may be glad to serve you; for the sake of Jesus Christ. **Amen.**

Strong God: you made day and night. As we sleep, tell us your love, so that when light comes we may wake happy, forgiven, and ready to live for you; through Jesus Christ our Lord. **Amen.**

Grace at Table

Father: we thank you for good things you give us. May we enjoy, share, and give thanks; through Jesus Christ our Lord. **Amen.**

> FATHER: Praise the Lord.
> FAMILY: **The Lord's name be praised.**
> FATHER: Let us thank God.
> FAMILY: **For he is good.**

God: we thank you for home, family, and friends. May your love be with us as we break bread in Jesus' name. **Amen.**

Thank you, God, for food, and all your gifts; through Jesus Christ our Lord. **Amen.**

When a Family Is Separated

Lord God: watch over us while we are apart. Keep us in your love, and bring us together again to praise you; through Jesus Christ our Lord. **Amen.**

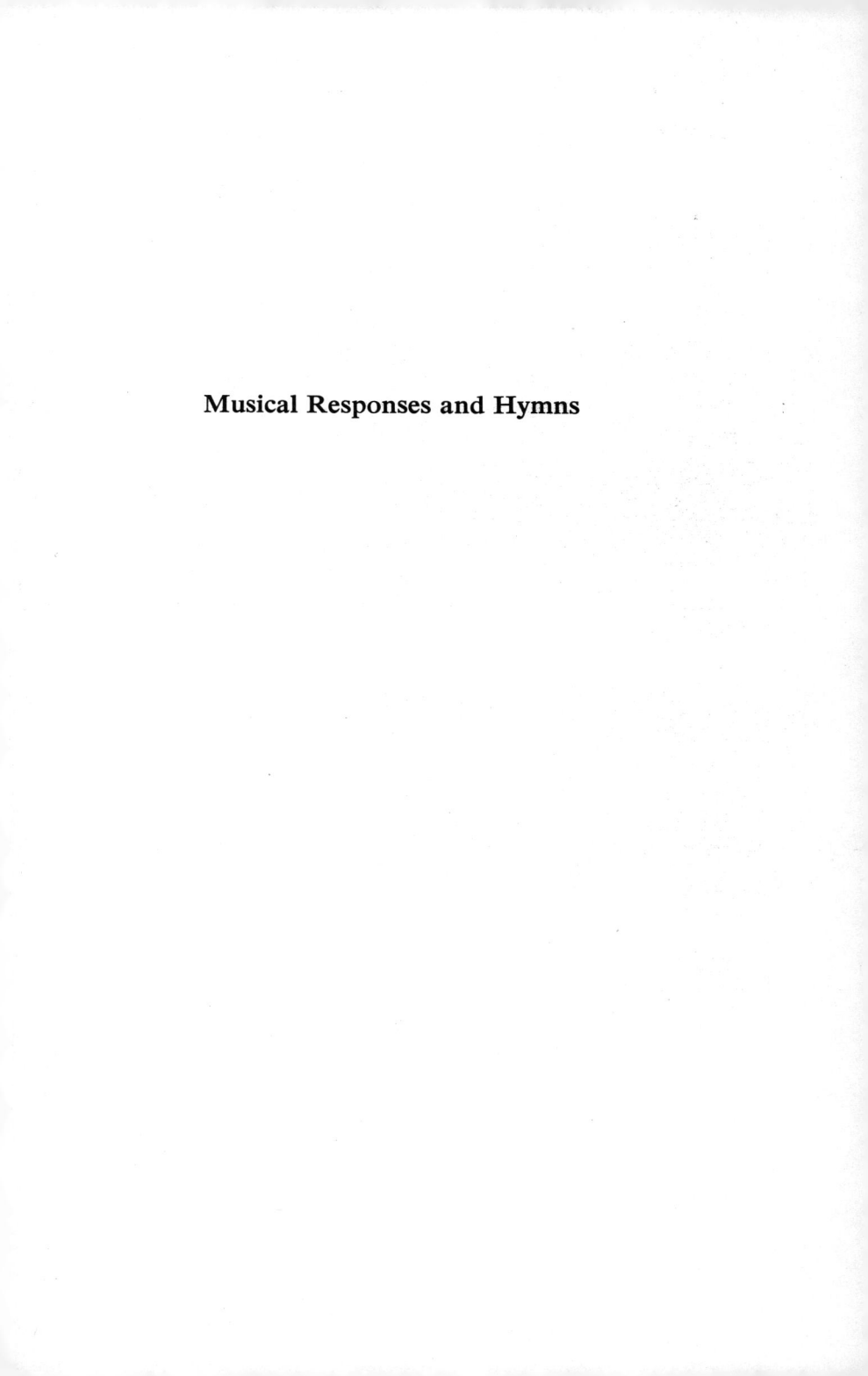

Musical Responses and Hymns

Musical Responses—Contents

Each musical response is listed by its first line. The numbers in parentheses refer to the page or pages in the Service for the Lord's Day on which the words appear. The numbers that follow are page numbers of the several musical settings included in this book. A number in brackets indicates a page in the Service for the Lord's Day on which the given response does not appear, but where its use would be appropriate. Further guidance will be found in the outlines for the Service, pp. 21–23.

    Setting One . . . . . David N. Johnson 211–233
    Setting Two . . . . . Joseph Goodman 234–252
    Setting Three . . . . . Richard D. Wetzel 253–271
    Traditional Setting 272

Praise the Lord (25), 211, 234, 253
You are the Lord, giver of mercy! (27), 212, 234, 253
    Or, Lord, have mercy upon us [27], 213, 235
Glory to the Father (Gloria Patri) [27], 214, 236, 254, 272
Glory to God in the highest (Gloria in Excelsis) [27], 215, 237, 255
I believe in God, the Father almighty (30), 259
This is the good news (30), 219, 241, 263
The Lord is risen (31), 223, 243, 265
Praise God, from whom all blessings flow! (Doxology) [34, 38], 224, 244,
    266, 272; *also hymn* 292, *stanza* 4
Lift up your hearts (first) (34, 38), 225, 245, 267
Lift up your hearts (second) (35, 39), 226, 246, 268
Holy, holy, holy, God of power and majesty (35), 227, 247, 268
Holy, holy, holy, Lord, God of power and might (35), 228, 248, 269
Alleluia! For the Lord our God (37), 230, 250, 270
Bless the Lord, O my soul (37), 232, 252, 271

Preface to the Musical Responses and Hymns

The musical responses and hymns on the following pages complete *The Worshipbook—Services and Hymns*. This volume provides Presbyterian churches in North America with precisely the sort of liturgical book that was first produced at the time, and under the influence, of the Protestant Reformation of the sixteenth century. It is a *people's* book, including texts and music for song, spoken prayer, and proclamation. This book is in harmony with the Reformed tradition in that it envisions a high level of vocal participation as well as personal comprehension of public worship. Its provision for the careful integration of liturgical and musical materials follows the best theology and practice of Reformed worship. The latter point may require explanation, and a brief description of the structure and use of this book is offered here.

As stated in the general Preface, page 7, the Joint Committee on Worship, in planning for the compilation of musical responses and hymns, did not have as its intention "to create a general hymnal." Rather, through The Committee on Selection of Hymns, it sought to provide musical materials which, when thoughtfully chosen, would complete and fulfill the structure and style of worship embodied in the services here, especially the Service for the Lord's Day. The Joint Committee envisioned a style of worship marked by a careful integration of varied elements, among them musical responses and hymns. Hence the fitness of the aphorism, "Music is a part of worship, not apart from worship."

In order to provide adequate resources for the kind of worship envisioned here, the compilers of the musical section have drawn material from many traditions. The quality, variety, and organization of this musical material will facilitate more frequent celebration of the Lord's Supper, regular observance of the Christian year, and the employment of texts which originate from, and apply to, the contemporary situation. Congregations will wish to supplement these musical materials with some of their own. To do so is recommended and is in accordance with the familiar Reformed principle of freedom in all things liturgical.

Underlying the unity of *The Worshipbook* is the Bible, the basic source and resource for worship. The Lectionary for the Christian Year, a three-year cycle of Bible readings, is the cornerstone of this Scriptural foundation. The **Index of Scripture and Scriptural Allusions** can be used to locate related prayers, hymns, and liturgical materials for completion of the structure of a service. The **Guide for the Use of Prayers** and the **Guide for the Use of Hymns** will assist the worship planner in selection by topic or by worship-related category. The usual alphabetical index of first lines has been omitted, since the hymns in this book are arranged in *alphabetical order*. An **Index of Familiar Hymns with Unfamiliar First Lines** has been prepared to help the user find hymns whose first lines have been extensively altered.

In keeping with the general use of modern translations of the Bible in the services and modern expression in the prayers, changes have been made where possible in the language of song. Thus in some familiar hymns, the contemporary familiar form *you* rather than the archaic familiar form *thee* is used in address to the Deity. Because the music in this book is meant to be an integral part of corporate worship, some hymns that refer to the people, the singers, now use *we* rather than *I*. An asterisk (*) before a stanza indicates that the stanza may be omitted without impairing the remaining text, if the situation so requires. Chord symbols for guitar and other folk-type instruments have been added above the music of appropriate hymns and responses to encourage the use of a diversity of instruments for accompaniment of the singing.

Reformed worship can be described as bringing together the people of God and the Word of God. This book is intended to provide a context for that encounter, in its structure and in its content, in word and in music.

Musical Responses—Setting One
by David N. Johnson

211

Praise the Lord

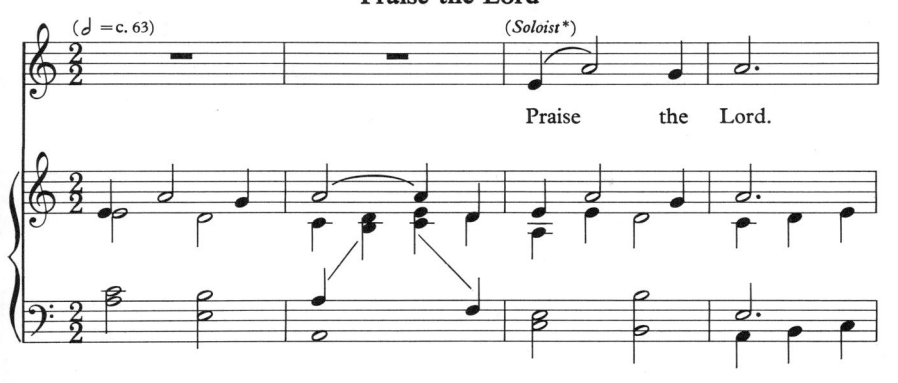

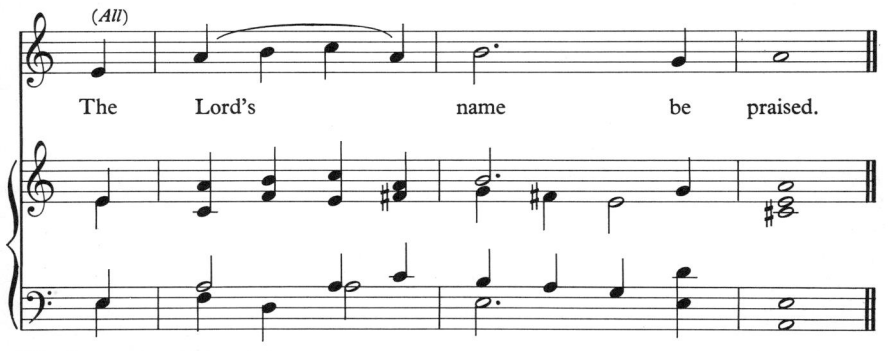

*May be sung by minister, choir, or everyone.

Words copyright 1970, music copyright 1972 by The Westminster Press.

212   You Are the Lord, Giver of Mercy!

You are the Lord, giver of mercy! You are the Christ, giver of mercy! You are the Lord, giver of mercy!

Setting One (cont.)

Lord, Have Mercy Upon Us 213

Lord, have mer-cy up-on us.

Christ, have mer-cy up-on us.

Lord, have mer-cy up-on us.

Setting One (cont.)

214 Glory to the Father

Glo-ry to the Fa-ther, and to the Son, and to the Ho-ly Spir-it: as in the be-gin-ning, so now, and for-ev-er. A-men.

Setting One (cont.)

Glory to God in the Highest 215

See following page.
Setting One (cont.)

216   **Glory to God in the Highest** (cont.)

give you thanks, we praise you for your glo - ry. Lord Je-sus Christ, on-ly Son of the Fa - ther, Lord God, Lamb of God, you take a-way the sin of the world: Have

p subdued

Setting One (cont.)

Glory to God in the Highest (cont.) 217

Glory to God in the Highest (cont.)

lone are the Most High, Je-sus Christ, with the Ho-ly Spir-it, in the glo-ry of God the Fa-ther. A-men, A-men.

slower

Setting One (cont.)

This Is the Good News 219

Moderately fast ($\quarternote$ = c. 63)

This is the good news which we re-ceived, in which we stand, and by which we are saved: that Christ died for our sins, that Christ died ac-cord-ing to the

See following page.
Setting One (cont.)

220 This Is the Good News (cont.)

Scrip-tures, that he was bur-ied and that he was raised, that he was rais-ed on the third day; and that he ap-peared to Pe-ter, then to the Twelve and to

Setting One (cont.)

This Is the Good News (cont.) 221

many faithful witnesses. We believe he is the Christ, the Son of the living God.

He is the first and the last, the beginning and the end,

See following page.
Setting One (cont.)

222 This Is the Good News (cont.)

he is our Lord and our God. He is our Lord and our God. A — — men.

Setting One (cont.)

The Lord Is Risen 223

Fast (♩ = c. 76)

The Lord is risen.

He is risen indeed.

*May be sung by minister, choir, or everyone.

Setting One (cont.)

224 Praise God, from Whom All Blessings Flow

Thomas Ken, 1693, 1709

Praise God, from whom all bless-ings flow; Praise him, all crea-tures here be-low; Praise him a-bove, ye heav-enly host: Praise Fa-ther, Son, and Ho-ly Ghost. A - men, A - men.

Setting One (cont.)

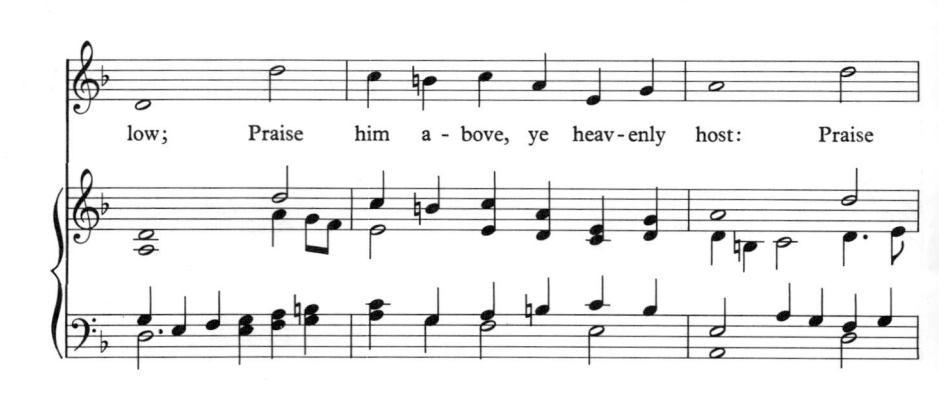

Lift Up Your Hearts (1)   225

Lift up your hearts. **We lift them to the Lord.** *Give thanks to God, for he is good.* **His love is everlasting.**

*May be sung by minister, choir, or everyone.

Setting One (cont.)

226 Lift Up Your Hearts (2)

($\quarternote$ = c. 120)

(Soloist*) Lift up your hearts. *(All)* We lift them up to the Lord. *(Soloist*)* Let us give thanks to the Lord our God. *(All)* It is right to give him thanks and praise.

*May be sung by minister, choir, or everyone.

Setting One (cont.)

Holy, Holy, Holy

227

Moderate ($\quarternote$ = c. 100)

Ho - ly, ho - ly, ho - ly,

faster ($\quarternote$ = c. 112)

God of power and maj - es - ty, heaven and earth are full of your glo - ry, O God most high!

Setting One (cont.)

228 Holy, Holy, Holy Lord

Ho - ly, ho - ly, ho - ly Lord, God of power and might, heaven and earth are full of your glo - ry. Ho - san - na in the

Setting One (cont.)

Holy, Holy, Holy Lord (cont.) 229

high-est. Bless-ed is he who comes in the name of the Lord. Ho-san-na in the high-est. Ho-san-na in the high-est!

Setting One (cont.)

230 Alleluia!

Fast and lively ($\quarternote$ = c. 132)

Alleluia! For the Lord our God, the Almighty, has come into his kingdom! Let us rejoice,

Setting One (cont.)

Alleluia! (cont.) 231

let us be glad with all our hearts. Let us give him the glory for-ev-er and ev - er. A - men, A - men, A - men!

Setting One (cont.)

232. Bless the Lord, O My Soul

Moderately slowly (♩ = c. 80)

Bless the Lord, O my soul; And all that is with-in me, bless his ho-ly name! Bless the Lord, O my soul, And for-get not all his

Setting One (cont.)

Bless the Lord, O My Soul (cont.)

ben - e - fits, his ben - e - fits.

Bless the Lord, O my soul.

Setting One (cont.)

234

Musical Responses—Setting Two
by Joseph Goodman

Praise the Lord

Praise the Lord. The Lord's name be praised.

*May be sung by minister, choir, or everyone.

You Are the Lord, Giver of Mercy!

You are the Lord, giv-er of mer-cy! You are the Christ, giv-er of mer-cy! You are the Lord, giv-er of mer-cy!

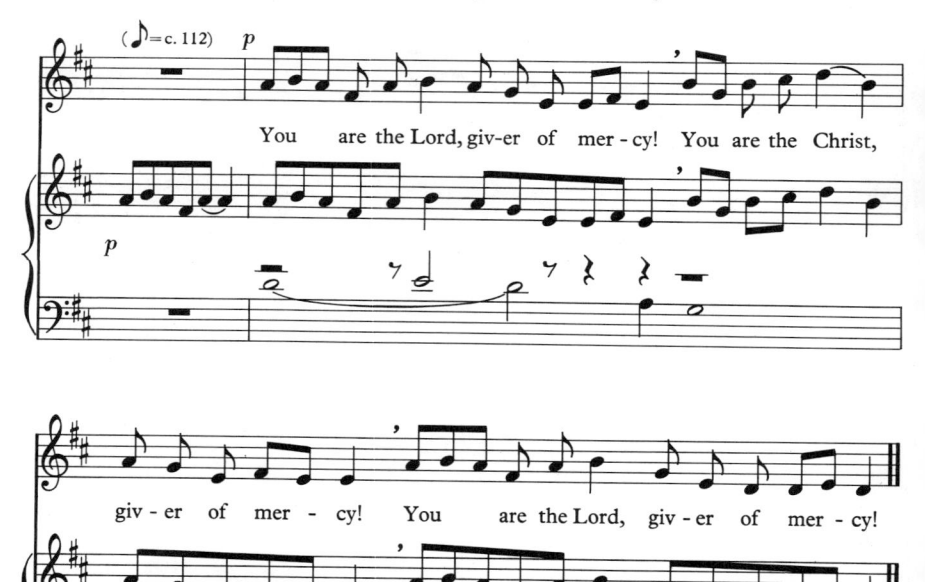

Words copyright 1970, music copyright 1972 by The Westminster Press.

Lord, Have Mercy Upon Us   235

Setting Two (cont.)

236 Glory to the Father

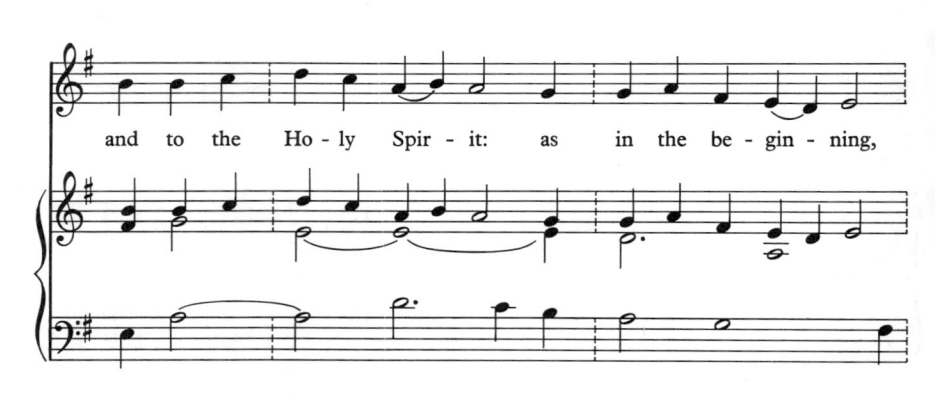

Glory to the Father, and to the Son, and to the Holy Spirit: as in the beginning, so now, and forever. Amen.

Setting Two (cont.)

Glory to God in the Highest 237

Glo - ry to God in the high - est, and peace to his peo - ple on earth. Lord God, heav - enly King, al - might - y God and Fa - ther, we wor - ship you, we give you

See following page.
Setting Two (cont.)

238 Glory to God in the Highest (cont.)

thanks, we praise you for your glo-ry. Lord Je-sus Christ, on-ly Son of the Fa-ther, Lord God, Lamb of God, you take a-way the sin of the

Setting Two (cont.)

Glory to God in the Highest (cont.) 239

world: have mer-cy on us; you are seat-ed at the right hand of the Fa-ther: re-ceive our prayer. For you a-lone are the Ho-ly One, you a-lone

See following page.
Setting Two (cont.)

240 — Glory to God in the Highest (cont.)

are the Lord, you a-lone are the Most High, Je-sus Christ, with the Holy Spir-it, in the glo-ry of God the Fa-ther. A-men.

Setting Two (cont.)

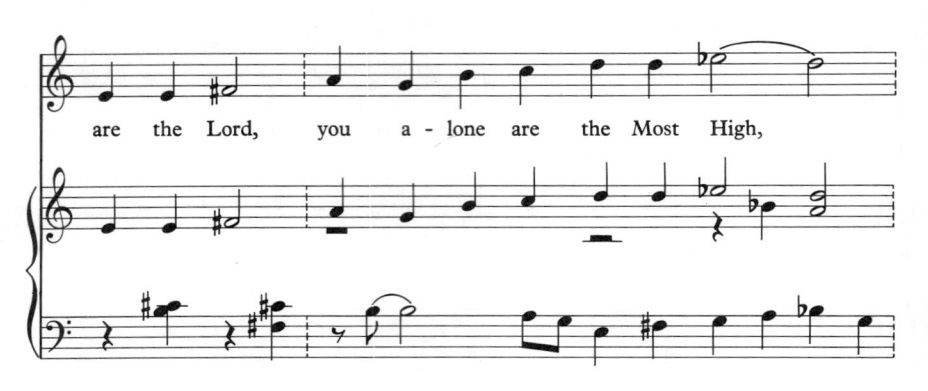

This Is the Good News   241

This is the good news which we re-ceived; in which we stand, and by which we are saved: that Christ died for our sins ac-cord-ing to the Scrip-tures, that he was bur-ied,

See following page.
Setting Two (cont.)

This Is the Good News (cont.)

that he was raised on the third day; and that he appeared to Peter, then to the Twelve and to many faithful witnesses.

We believe he is the Christ, the Son of the living God.

Setting Two (cont.)

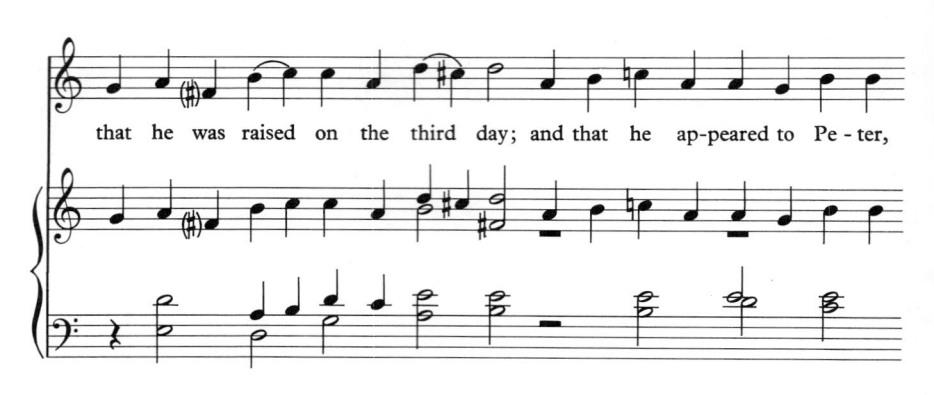

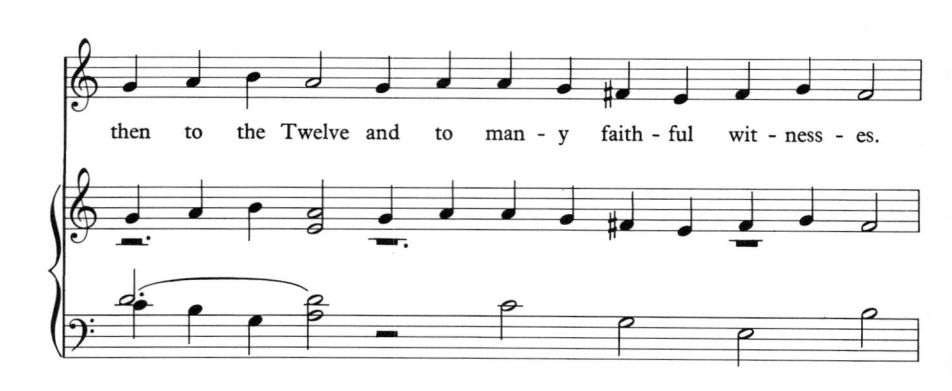

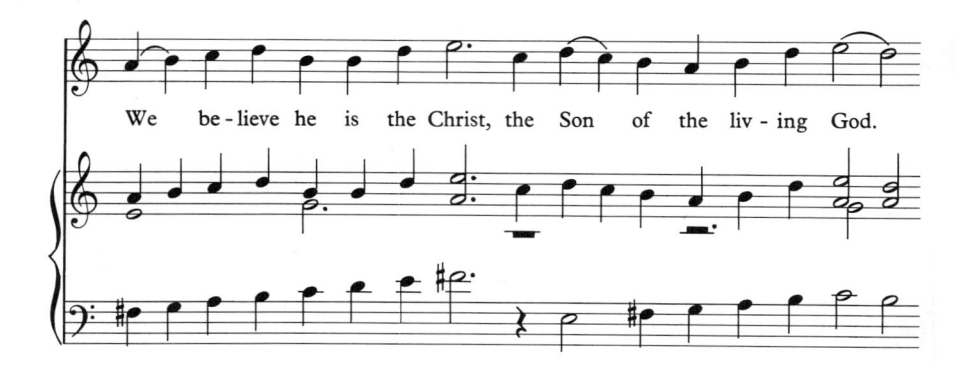

This Is the Good News (cont.) 243

He is the first and the last, the be-gin-ning and the end,

f poco rit.

he is our Lord and our God. A-men.

The Lord Is Risen

($\quarternote$ = 92)

f (Soloist*) (All)

The Lord is ris-en. He is ris-en in-deed.

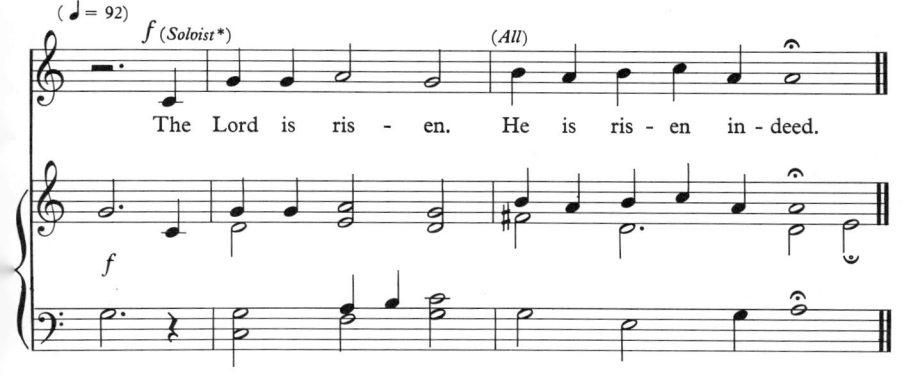

*May be sung by minister, choir, or everyone.

Setting Two (cont.)

244 Praise God, from Whom All Blessings Flow!

Thomas Ken, 1693, 1709

Praise God, from whom all bless-ings flow! Praise him, all crea-tures here be-low! Praise him a-bove, ye heav-enly host! Praise Fa-ther, Son, and Ho-ly Ghost. A-men.

Setting Two (cont.)

Lift Up Your Hearts (1) 245

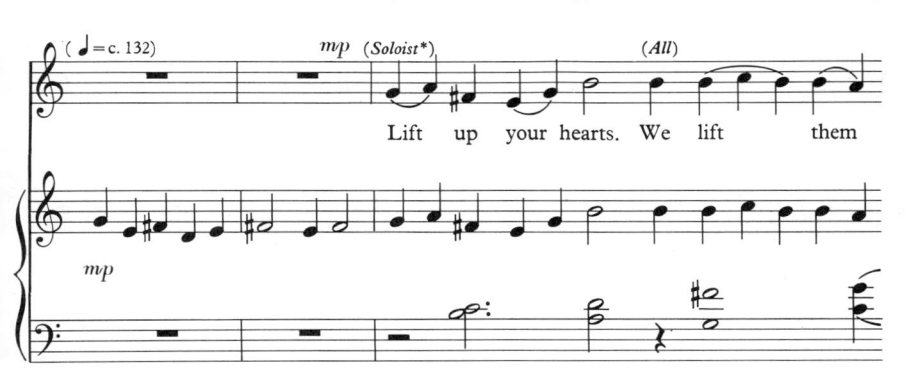

Lift up your hearts. We lift them to the Lord. Give thanks to God, for he is good. His love is everlasting.

*May be sung by minister, choir, or everyone.

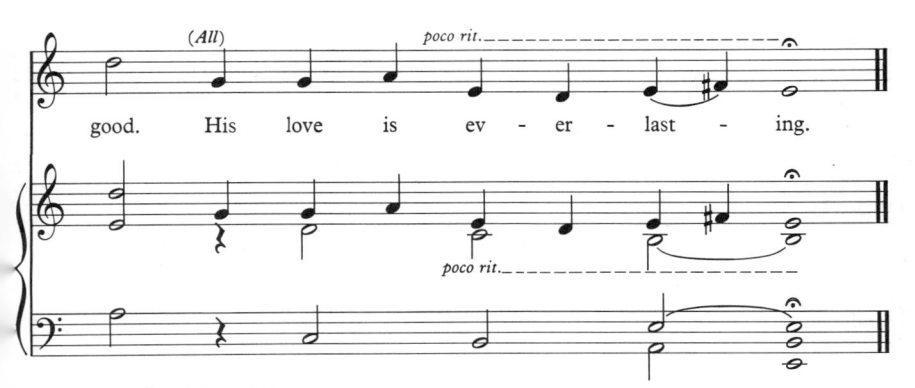

Setting Two (cont.)

246 Lift Up Your Hearts (2)

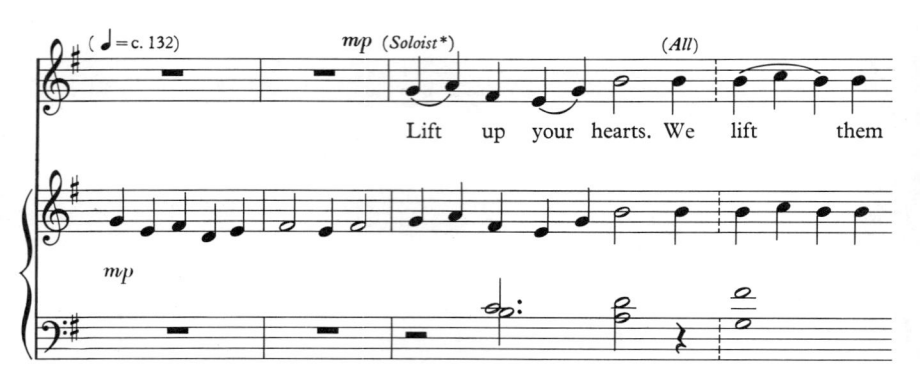

(♩=c. 132)

mp (Soloist*) (All)
Lift up your hearts. We lift them up to the Lord. Let us give thanks to the Lord our God. It is right to give him thanks and praise.

*May be sung by minister, choir, or everyone.

Setting Two (cont.)

Holy, Holy, Holy 247

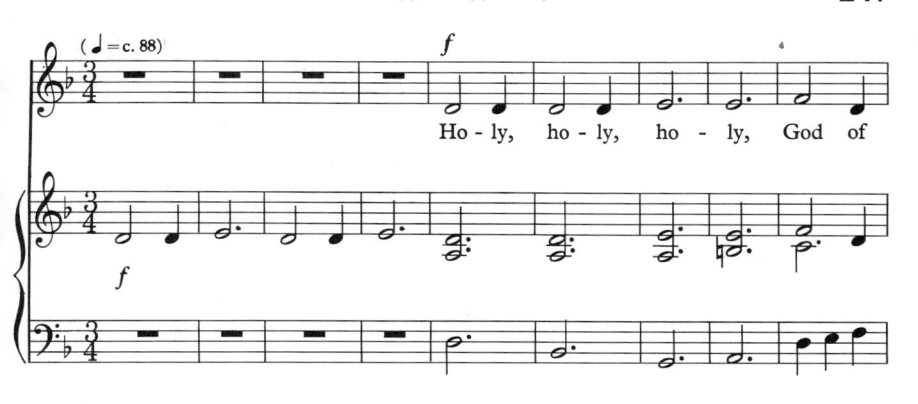

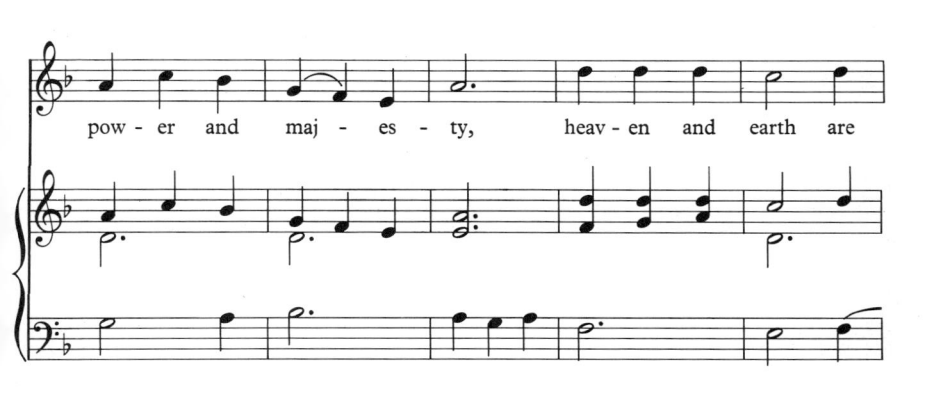

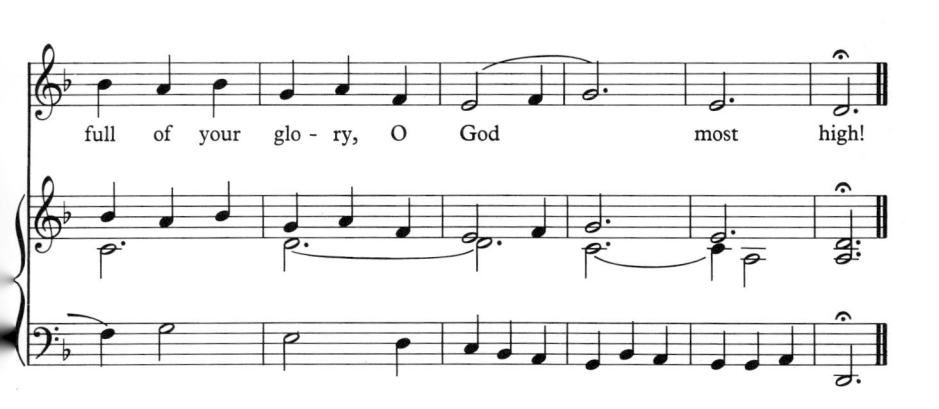

Holy, holy, holy, God of power and majesty, heaven and earth are full of your glory, O God most high!

Setting Two (cont.)

248 Holy, Holy, Holy Lord

Holy, holy, holy Lord, God of power and might, heaven and earth are full of your glory. Hosanna in the highest.

Setting Two (cont.)

Holy, Holy, Holy Lord (cont.) 249

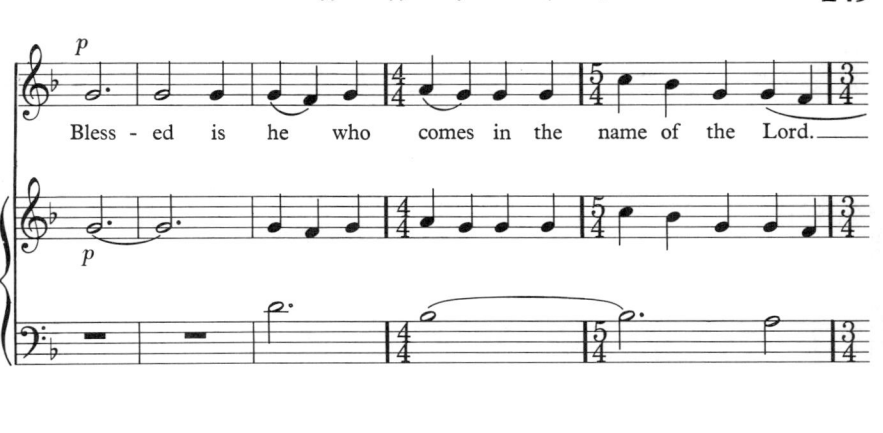

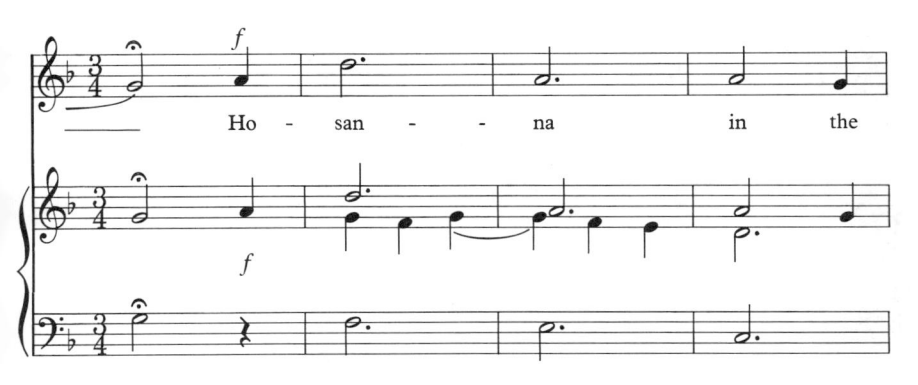

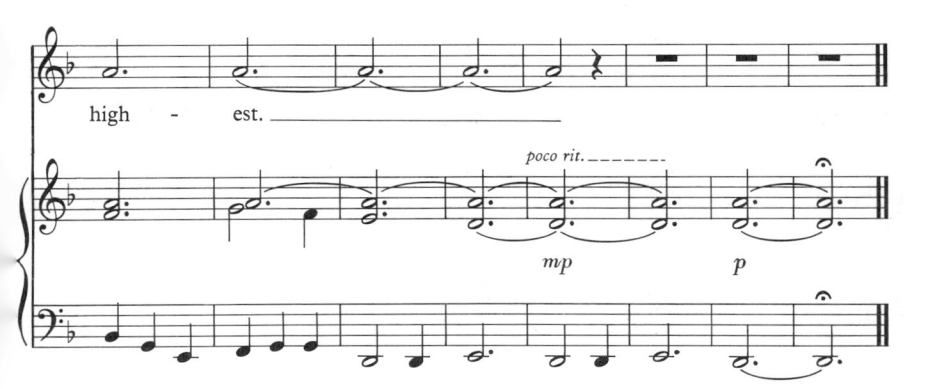

Bless-ed is he who comes in the name of the Lord. Ho-san-na in the high-est.

Setting Two (cont.)

250 Alleluia!

Alleluia! For the Lord our God, the Almighty, has come into his kingdom!

Setting Two (cont.)

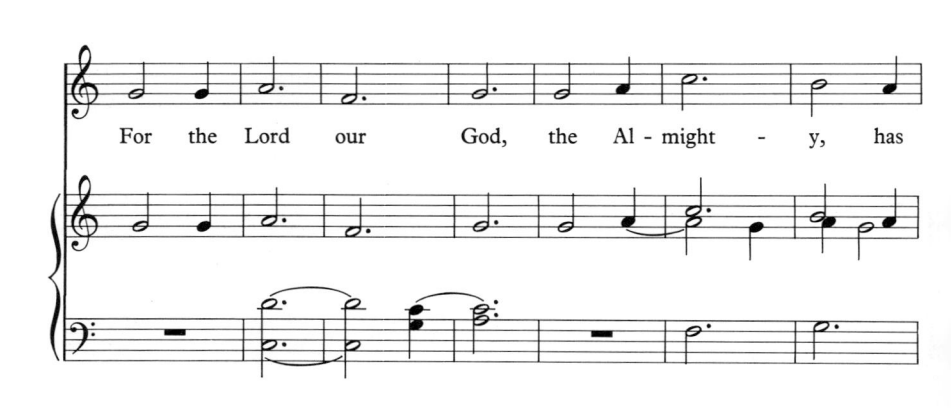

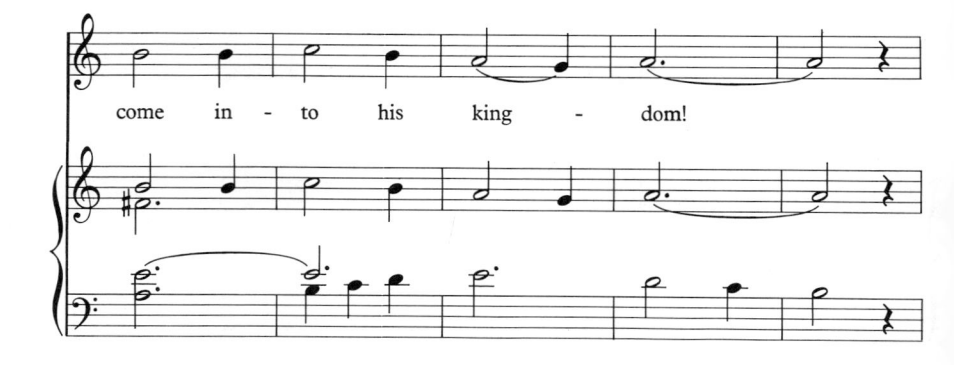

Alleluia! (cont.)

Let us rejoice, let us be glad with all our hearts. Let us give him the glory for ever and ever. Amen.

Setting Two (cont.)

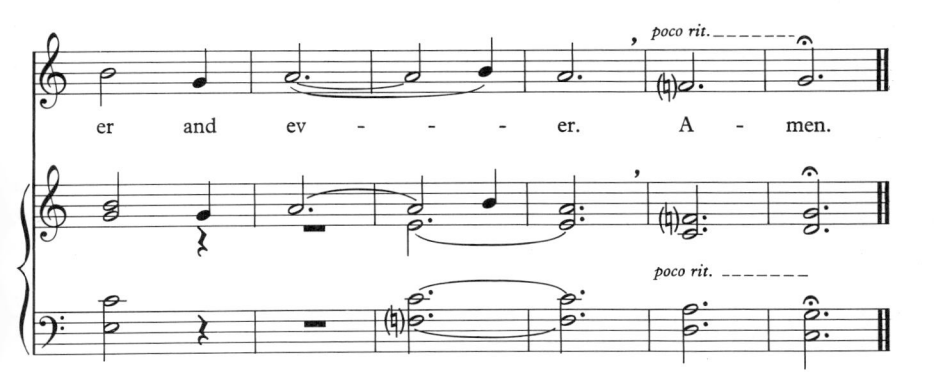

252   Bless the Lord, O My Soul

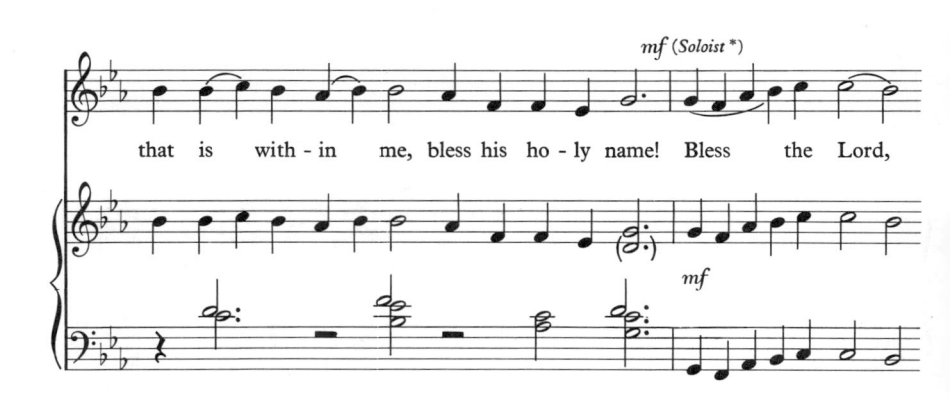

Bless the Lord, O my soul; And all that is with-in me, bless his ho-ly name! Bless the Lord, O my soul, And for-get not all his ben-e-fits.

*May be sung by minister, choir, or everyone.

Setting Two (cont.)

Musical Responses—Setting Three (Folk Style) 253
Arranged or Composed by Richard D. Wetzel

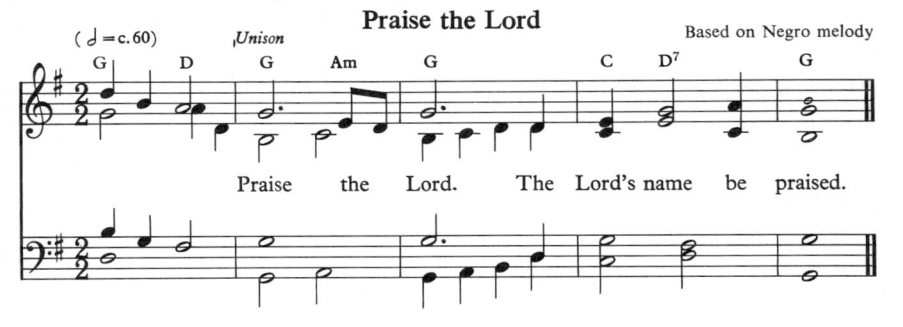

Praise the Lord
Based on Negro melody

Praise the Lord. The Lord's name be praised.

You Are the Lord, Giver of Mercy!
Based on Appalachian folk melody

You are the Lord, giv-er of mer-cy!

You are the Christ, giv-er of mer-cy!

You are the Lord, giv-er of mer-cy!

Words copyright 1970, music copyright 1972 by The Westminster Press.

254 Glory to the Father

Glo-ry to the Fa-ther, and to the Son, and to the Ho-ly Spir-it: as in the be-gin-ning, so now, and for-ev-er. A-men.

Setting Three (cont.)

Glory to God in the Highest 255

(♩ = 112)

Glo-ry to God in the high-est, and peace to his peo-ple on earth. Lord God, heav-en-ly King, al-might-y God and Fa-ther, we wor-ship

See following page.
Setting Three (cont.)

256 Glory to God in the Highest (cont.)

you, we give you thanks, we praise you for your glo-ry.

Lord Je-sus Christ, on-ly Son of the Fa-ther,

Lord God, Lamb of God, you take a-way the sin of the

Setting Three (cont.)

Glory to God in the Highest (cont.) 257

world: have mercy upon us; you are seated at the right hand of the Father: receive our prayer. For you alone are the Holy One, you alone are the

See following page.
Setting Three (cont.)

258 Glory to God in the Highest (cont.)

Lord, you alone are the Most High, Jesus Christ, with the Holy Spirit, in the glory of God the Father. A- - men.

Setting Three (cont.)

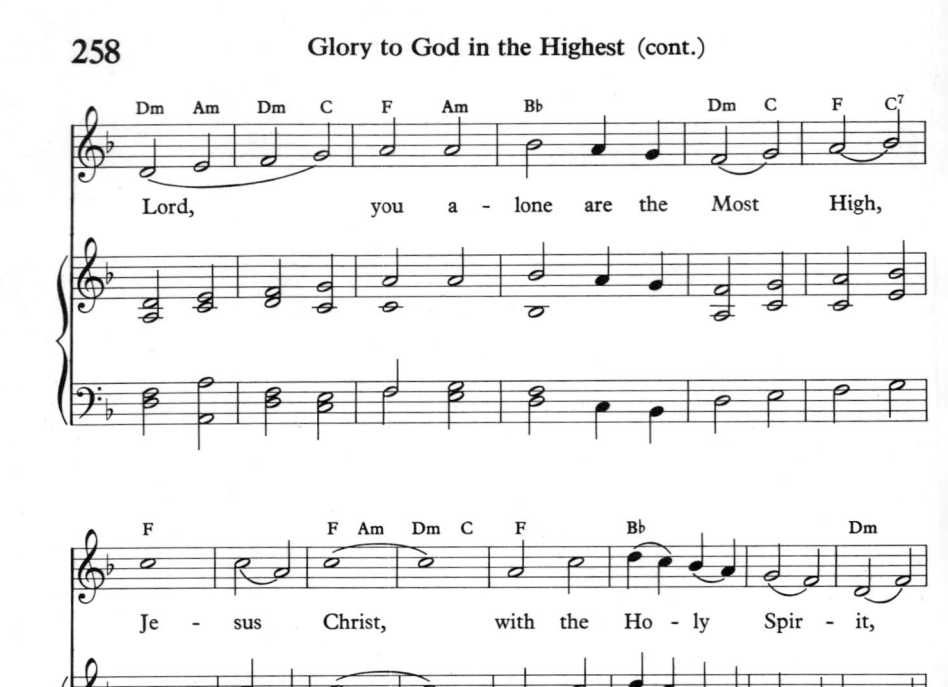

I Believe in God   259

I believe in God, the Father almighty, creator of heaven and earth.

I believe in Jesus Christ, his only Son, our Lord.

See following page.
Setting Three (cont.)

260   I Believe in God (cont.)

He was conceived by the power of the Holy Spirit and born of the Virgin Mary. He suffered under Pontius Pilate, was crucified, died, and was buried. He descended to the dead.

Setting Three (cont.)

… I Believe in God (cont.) **261**

On the third day he rose again. He ascended into heaven, and is seated at the right hand of the Father. He will come again to judge the living and the dead. I believe in the Holy

See following page.
Setting Three (cont.)

262 I Believe in God (cont.)

Spirit, the holy catholic church, the communion of saints, the forgiveness of sins, the resurrection of the body, and the life everlasting. Amen.

Setting Three (cont.)

This Is the Good News   263

Based on Dakota Indian melody

This is the good news which we received, in which we stand, and by which we are saved: that Christ died for our sins according to the Scriptures, that he was buried, that he was

See following page.
Setting Three (cont.)

264 This Is the Good News (cont.)

raised on the third day; and that he appeared to Peter, then to the Twelve and to many faithful witnesses.

We believe he is the Christ, the Son of the living God. He is the first and the

Setting Three (cont.)

This Is the Good News (cont.)

last, the be-gin-ning and the end, he is our Lord and our God. A-men.

The Lord Is Risen

($\quarter = c.72$)

The Lord is ris-en. He is risen in-deed.

*May be sung by minister, choir, or everyone.

Setting Three (cont.)

266. Praise God, from Whom All Blessings Flow

Thomas Ken, 1693, 1709

Unison ($\quarternote$ = c. 72)

Praise God, from whom all bless-ings flow;
Praise him, all crea-tures here be-low;
Praise him a-bove, ye heav-enly host:
Praise Fa-ther, Son, and Ho-ly Ghost. A-men.

Setting Three (cont.)

Lift Up Your Hearts (1)   267

Based on Southern mountain melody

Lift up your hearts. We lift them to the Lord. Give thanks to God, for he is good. His love is ev-er-last-ing.

Setting Three (cont.)

268 Lift Up Your Hearts (2)

Lift up your hearts. We lift them up to the Lord. Let us give thanks to the Lord our God. It is right to give him thanks and praise.

Holy, Holy, Holy

Based on Russian folk melody

Holy, holy, holy, God of power and majesty, heaven and earth are full of your glory, O God most high!

Setting Three (cont.)

Holy, Holy, Holy Lord 269

(♩ = 60) Unison

Based on Russian folk melody

Ho-ly, ho-ly, ho-ly Lord, God of power and might, heaven and earth are full of your glo-ry. Ho-san-na in the high-est. Bless-ed is he who comes in the name of the Lord. Ho-san-na in the high-est.

Setting Three (cont.)

270 Alleluia!

Alleluia! For the Lord our God, the Almighty, has come into his kingdom! Let us rejoice, let us be glad with all our hearts. Let us give him the glory forever and ever. Amen.

Setting Three (cont.)

Bless the Lord, O My Soul   271

(Play in Em—capo on II) *(Soloist*)* Based on Appalachian folk melody

Bless the Lord, O my soul;
And all that is with-in me, bless his ho-ly name! Bless the Lord, O my soul, And for-get not all his ben-e-fits.

*May be sung by minister, choir, or everyone.

Setting Three (cont.)

272 Musical Responses—Traditional Settings

Glory to the Father

Old Scottish chant

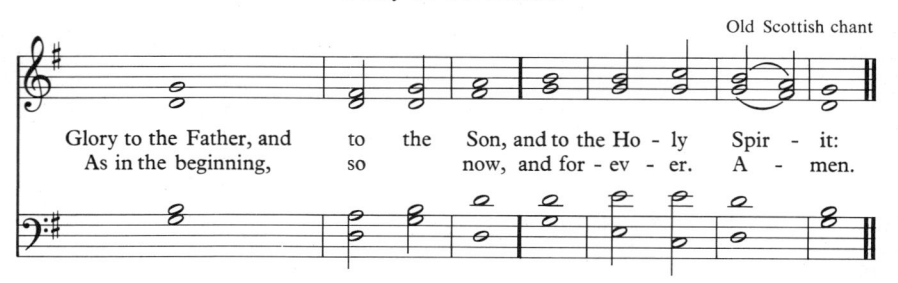

Glory to the Father, and to the Son, and to the Ho-ly Spir-it:
As in the beginning, so now, and for-ev-er. A-men.

Praise God, from Whom All Blessings Flow
OLD HUNDREDTH L.M.

Thomas Ken, 1693, 1709 — Comp. or adapted by Louis Bourgeois, 1551

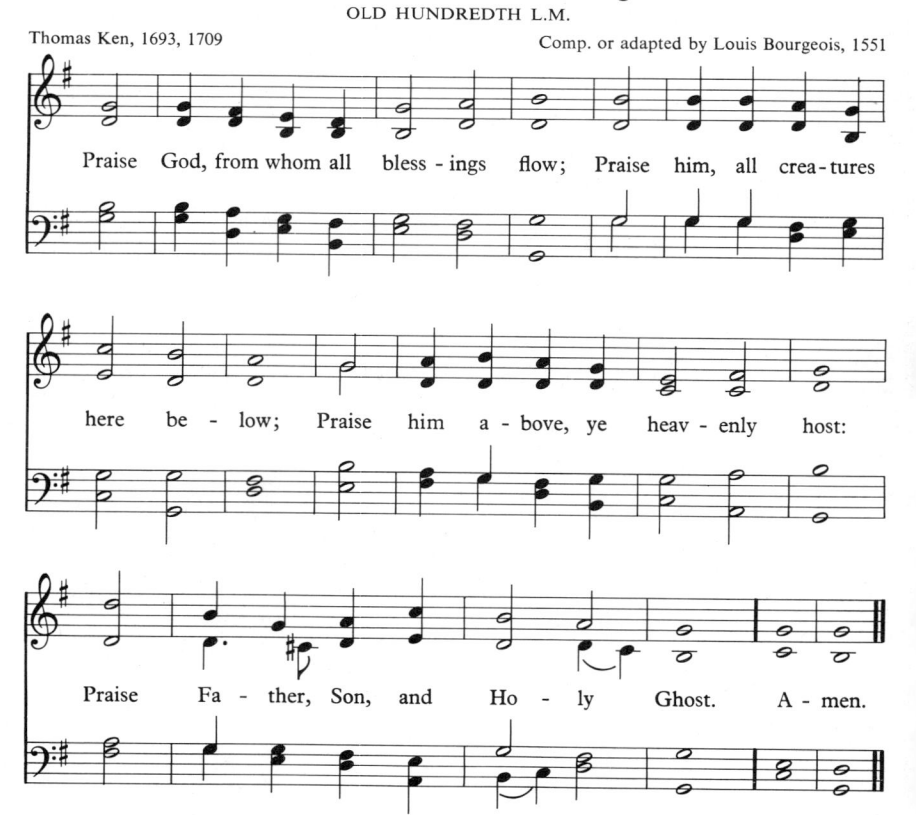

Praise God, from whom all bless-ings flow; Praise him, all crea-tures here be-low; Praise him a-bove, ye heav-enly host: Praise Fa-ther, Son, and Ho-ly Ghost. A-men.

A Hymn of Glory Let Us Sing

273

DEO GRACIAS L.M.

The Venerable Bede (ca. 672-735)
Sts. 1, 2 trans. by Elizabeth Rundle Charles,
1858; alt., 1972
St. 3 trans. by Benjamin Webb, 1854; alt., 1972

"The Agincourt Song," England, ca. 1415
Arr. in *Hymnal for Colleges and Schools*, 1956

1. A hymn of glory let us sing, New hymns throughout the world shall ring; By a new way none ever trod Christ takes his place—the throne of God!
2. You are a present joy, O Lord; You will be ever our reward; And great the light in you we see To guide us to eternity.
3. O risen Christ, ascended Lord, All praise to you let earth accord, Who are, while endless ages run, With Father and with Spirit, One. A-men.

Music from *Hymnal for Colleges and Schools*, edited by E. Harold Geer; used by permission of Yale University Press.

274 A Mighty Fortress Is Our God
EIN' FESTE BURG P.M.

Martin Luther, 1529
Trans. by Frederick H. Hedge, 1853; alt., 1972

Martin Luther, 1529

1. A mighty fortress is our God, A bulwark never failing; Our helper he amid the flood Of mortal ills prevailing: For still our ancient foe Does
2. Did we in our own strength confide, Our striving would be losing, Were not the right Man on our side, The Man of God's own choosing: You ask who that may be? Christ
3. And though this world, with devils filled, Should threaten to undo us, We will not fear, for God has willed His truth to triumph through us: The prince of darkness grim, We
4. That word above all earthly powers, No thanks to them, is standing; The Spirit and his gifts are ours— We answer his commanding. Let goods and kindred go, This

A Mighty Fortress Is Our God (cont.)

seek to work us woe; His craft and power are great, And
armed with cru-el hate, On earth is not his e-qual.

Je-sus, it is he; The Lord of Hosts his name, From
age to age the same, And he must win the bat-tle.

trem-ble not for him; His rage we can en-dure, For
lo! his doom is sure, One lit-tle word shall fell him.

mor-tal life al-so; The bod-y they may kill: God's
truth is rul-ing still— His king-dom is for-ev-er! A-men.

276 A Mighty Fortress Is Our God
EIN' FESTE BURG P.M.

Based on Psalm 46
J. Clifford Evers, 1964
Lines 1, 2, Martin Luther, 1529; trans.
by Frederick H. Hedge, 1853

Martin Luther, 1529

1. A mighty fortress is our God, A bulwark never failing, Protecting us with staff and rod, His power all-prevailing. What if the nations
2. The waters of his goodness flow Throughout his holy city, And gladden hearts of those who know His tenderness and pity. Though nations stand un-
3. Behold his wondrous deeds of peace, The God of our salvation; He knows our wars and makes them cease In every land and nation. The warrior's spear and

Words reprinted by permission of World Library Publications, Inc., Cincinnati, Ohio. Harmonization from *The Lutheran Hymnal*, copyright 1941 by Concordia Publishing House; used by permission.

A Mighty Fortress Is Our God (cont.)   277

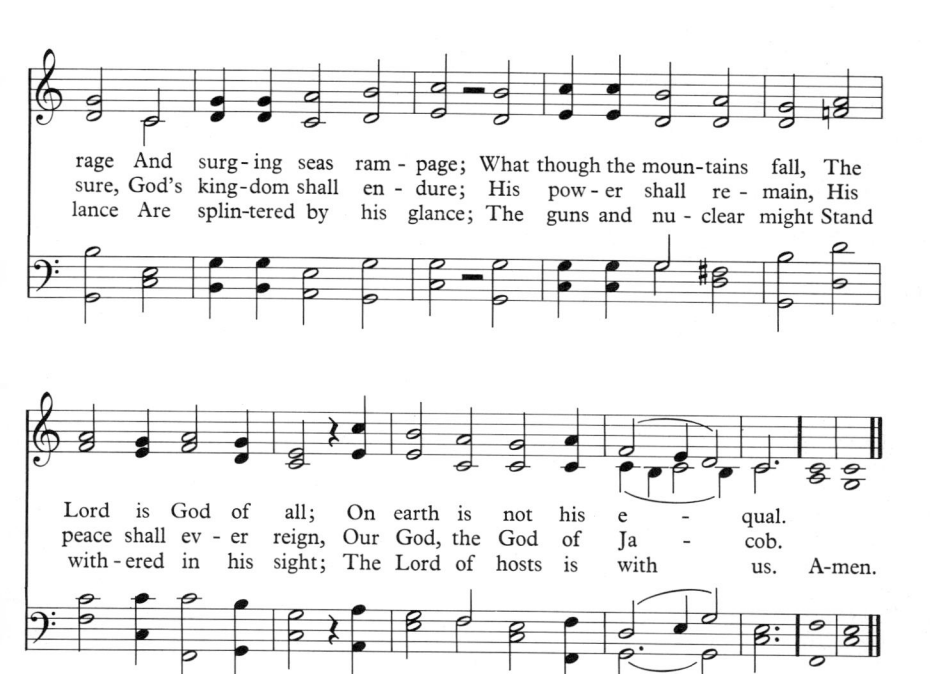

rage And surg-ing seas ram-page; What though the moun-tains fall, The Lord is God of all; On earth is not his e-qual.

sure, God's king-dom shall en-dure; His pow-er shall re-main, His peace shall ev-er reign, Our God, the God of Ja-cob.

lance Are splin-tered by his glance; The guns and nu-clear might Stand with-ered in his sight; The Lord of hosts is with us. A-men.

278 Abide with Me: Fast Falls the Eventide
EVENTIDE 10.10.10.10.

Henry Francis Lyte, 1847; alt.
William Henry Monk, 1861

1. A-bide with me: fast falls the e-ven-tide;
2. I need your pres-ence ev-ery pass-ing hour.
3. I fear no foe, with you at hand to bless;
4. Hold now the cross be-fore my clos-ing eyes;

The dark-ness deep-ens; Lord, with me a-bide.
What but your grace can foil the tempt-er's power?
Ills have no weight, and tears no bit-ter-ness.
Shine through the gloom, and point me to the skies:

When oth-er help-ers fail and com-forts flee,
Who like your-self my guide and stay can be?
Where is death's sting? Where, grave, your vic-to-ry?
Heaven's morn-ing breaks, and earth's vain shad-ows flee:

Help of the help-less, O a-bide with me.
Through cloud and sun-shine, O a-bide with me.
I tri-umph still, if you a-bide with me.
In life, in death, O Lord, a-bide with me. A-men.

Ah, Dearest Jesus, Holy Child
VOM HIMMEL HOCH L.M.

279

Martin Luther, 1535
Trans. by Catherine Winkworth, 1855; alt.

Geystliche Lieder, Leipzig, 1539

1. Ah, dearest Jesus, holy Child, Make thee a bed, soft, undefiled, Within our hearts, that they may be All quiet chambers kept for thee.
2. Our hearts for very joy do leap, Our lips no more can silence keep; We, too, must sing with joyful tongue That sweetest ancient cradle song.
3. Glory to God in highest heaven, Who unto man his Son hath given, While angels sing with tender mirth A glad new year to all the earth. Amen.

280 Ah, Holy Jesus, How Have You Offended
HERZLIEBSTER JESU 11.11.11.5.

Latin, attr. to Jean de Fécamp (d. 1078)
Para. by Johann Heermann, 1630
Repara. by Robert Bridges, 1899; alt., 1972

Johann Crüger, 1640

1. Ah, holy Jesus, how have you offended, That man to judge you has in hate pretended, By foes derided, by your own rejected, O most afflicted!

2. Who was the guilty? Who brought this upon you? Alas, my treason, Jesus, has undone you! 'Twas I, Lord Jesus, I it was denied you; I crucified you.

3. For me, kind Jesus, was your incarnation, Your mortal sorrow, and your life's oblation; Your death of anguish and your bitter passion, For my salvation.

4. Therefore, kind Jesus, since I cannot pay you, I do adore you, and will ever pray you, Think on your pity and your love unswerving, Not my deserving. A-men.

Words altered from *The Yattendon Hymnal*; used by permission of Oxford University Press.

All Beautiful the March of Days 281
FOREST GREEN C.M.D.

Frances Whitmarsh Wile, 1911; alt., 1972

Traditional English melody, collected and harm. by Ralph Vaughan Williams, 1906

1. All beau-ti-ful the march of days, As sea-sons come and go;
   The hand that shaped the rose has wrought The crys-tal of the snow,
   Has sent the hoar-y frost of heaven, The flow-ing wa-ters sealed,
   And laid a si-lent love-li-ness On hill and wood and field.

2. O'er white ex-pans-es spar-kling pure The ra-diant morns un-fold;
   The sol-emn splen-dors of the night Burn bright-er through the cold.
   Life mounts in ev-ery throb-bing vein, Love deep-ens round the hearth,
   And clear-er sounds the an-gel hymn, "Good will to men on earth."

3. O God, from whose un-fath-omed law The year in beau-ty flows,
   Your-self the vi-sion pass-ing by In crys-tal and in rose,
   Day un-to day does ut-ter speech, And night to night pro-claim,
   In ev-er-chang-ing words of light, The won-der of your name. A-men.

Music from *The English Hymnal*; used by permission of Oxford University Press.

282 All Creatures of Our God and King

LASST UNS ERFREUEN 8.8.8.8.8.6. with Alleluias

Francis of Assisi, ca. 1225
Para. by William H. Draper (1855-1933)

Geistliche Kirchengesäng, Cologne, 1623
Arr. and harm. by Ralph Vaughan Williams, 1906

For lower key, see "From All That Dwell Below the Skies."

All Glory Be to God on High 283

ALLEIN GOTT IN DER HÖH' 8.7.8.7.8.8.7.

Based on Gloria in excelsis
Attr. to Nikolaus Decius, 1525
Trans. by Catherine Winkworth, 1863; alt.

Based on plainsong melody
Attr. to Nikolaus Decius, 1539
As in *Service Book and Hymnal*, 1958

1. All glory be to God on high, Who has our race befriended!
To us no harm shall now come nigh, The strife at last is ended;
God his good-will displays to men, And peace shall reign on earth again;
O thank him for his goodness!

2. We praise, we worship you, we trust And give you thanks forever,
O Father, that your rule is just And wise, and changes never;
Your boundless power o'er all things reigns, You do whate'er your will ordains;
'Tis well you are our ruler!

3. O Jesus Christ, our God and Lord, Begotten of the Father,
O Savior, who our peace restored, And who lost sheep did gather,
O Lamb of God, enthroned on high, Behold our need and hear our cry;
Have mercy on us, Jesus!

4. O Holy Spirit, precious gift, O Comforter unfailing,
Do you our troubled souls uplift, Against the foe prevailing;
Avert our woes and calm our dread: For us the Savior's blood was shed;
Do you in faith sustain us! A-men.

Used by permission of the Commission on the Liturgy and Hymnal.

284 All Glory, Laud, and Honor
ST. THEODULPH 7.6.7.6.D.

Theodulph of Orleans, ca. 820
Trans. by John Mason Neale, 1851; alt., 1859

Melchior Teschner, 1615

1. All glory, laud, and honor To thee, Redeemer, King,
To whom the lips of children Made sweet hosannas ring!
The people of the Hebrews With palms before thee went;
Our praise and prayer and anthems Before thee we present.

2. Thou art the King of Israel, Thou David's royal son,
Who in the Lord's name comest, The King and blessed One;
To thee, before thy passion, They sang their hymns of praise;
To thee, now high exalted, Our melody we raise.

3. Thou didst accept their praises; Accept the prayers we bring,
Who in all good delightest, Thou good and gracious King.
All glory, laud, and honor To thee, Redeemer, King,
To whom the lips of children Made sweet hosannas ring! A-men.

All Hail the Power of Jesus' Name! 285

CORONATION C.M.
(First Tune)

Sts. 1,2, Edward Perronet, 1779, 1780; alt.
Sts. 3,4, John Rippon, 1787

Oliver Holden, 1793

1. All hail the power of Jesus' name! Let angels prostrate fall;
2. Hail him, the heir of David's line, Whom David Lord did call;
3. Let ev-ery kin-dred, ev-ery tribe, On this ter-res-trial ball
4. O that with yon-der sa-cred throng We at his feet may fall!

Bring forth the roy-al di-a-dem,
The God in-car-nate, man di-vine,
To him all maj-es-ty as-cribe,
We'll join the ev-er-last-ing song,

And crown him Lord of all! Bring forth the roy-al
And crown him Lord of all! The God in-car-nate,
And crown him Lord of all! To him all maj-es-
And crown him Lord of all! We'll join the ev-er-

di-a-dem, And crown him Lord of all!
man di-vine, And crown him Lord of all!
ty as-cribe, And crown him Lord of all!
last-ing song, And crown him Lord of all! A-men.

286 All Hail the Power of Jesus' Name!

MILES LANE C.M.
(Second Tune)

Sts. 1,2, Edward Perronet, 1779, 1780; alt.
Sts. 3,4, John Rippon, 1787

William Shrubsole, 1779
Melody alt., ca. 1861

1. All hail the power of Jesus' name! Let angels prostrate fall; Bring forth the royal diadem, And crown him, crown him, crown him, crown him Lord of all! A-men.
2. Hail him, the heir of David's line, Whom David Lord did call; The God incarnate, man divine, And crown him, crown him, crown him, crown him Lord of all!
3. Let every kindred, every tribe, On this terrestrial ball To him all majesty ascribe, And crown him, crown him, crown him, crown him Lord of all!
4. O that with yonder sacred throng We at his feet may fall! We'll join the everlasting song, And crown him, crown him, crown him, crown him Lord of all!

All My Heart Today Rejoices

287

WARUM SOLLT ICH (EBELING) 8.3.3.6.D.

Paul Gerhardt, 1653
Trans. by Catherine Winkworth, 1858; alt.

Johann Georg Ebeling, 1666

1. All my heart to-day re-joic-es, As I hear,
Far and near, Sweet-est an-gel voic-es:
"Christ is born," their choirs are sing-ing,
Till the air, Ev-ery-where, Now with joy is ring-ing.

2. Hark! a voice from yon-der man-ger, Soft and sweet,
Does en-treat: "Flee from woe and dan-ger;
Broth-ers, come; from all that grieves you
You are freed; All you need I will sure-ly give you."

3. Come, then, let us has-ten yon-der; Here let all,
Great and small, Kneel in awe and won-der;
Love him, who with love is yearn-ing;
Hail the star That from far Bright with hope is burn-ing!

4. You, dear Lord, with heed I'll cher-ish; Live to you,
And, with you Dy-ing, shall not per-ish;
But shall dwell with you for-ev-er,
Far on high, In the joy That shall al-ter nev-er. A-men.

288. All People That on Earth Do Dwell

OLD HUNDREDTH L.M.

Psalm 100
Para. by William Kethe, 1561; alt., 1650

Comp. or adapted by Louis Bourgeois, 1551
Rhythm, English Psalters

1. All people that on earth do dwell, Sing to the Lord with cheerful voice; Him serve with mirth, His praise forth tell, Come ye before him and rejoice.
2. Know that the Lord is God indeed; Without our aid he did us make; We are his folk, he doth us feed, And for his sheep he doth us take.
3. O enter then his gates with praise, Approach with joy his courts unto; Praise, laud, and bless his name always, For it is seemly so to do.
4. For why? the Lord our God is good, His mercy is forever sure; His truth at all times firmly stood, And shall from age to age endure. A-men.

All Poor Men and Humble

OLWEN 6.6.8.D.

289

Welsh carol
Para. by Katherine E. Roberts, 1928

Welsh carol
Arr. by Caradog Roberts (1879-1935)

1. All poor men and humble, All lame men who stumble, Come haste ye, nor feel ye afraid; And Jesus in beauty Accepted their duty; Contented in manger he lay.

2. Though Wise Men who found him Laid rich gifts around him, Yet oxen they gave him their hay: For Jesus, our treasure, With love past all measure, In lowly poor manger was laid.

3. Then haste we to show him The praises we owe him; Our service he ne'er can despise: Whose love still is able To show us that stable Where softly in manger he lies.

Words from *The Oxford Book of Carols*; used by permission of Oxford University Press. Music used by permission of the Union of Welsh Independents.

290 All Praise Be Yours; for You, O King Divine
NATIONAL CITY 10.10.10. with Alleluia

F. Bland Tucker, 1938, 1972
Lawrence P. Schreiber, 1967

1. All praise be yours; for you, O King divine, Your rightful glory freely did resign, That in our darkened hearts your grace might shine.
2. You came to us in lowliness of thought; By you the outcast and the poor were sought; And by your death was God's salvation wrought.
3. O Jesus, let your mind within us be; For you were servant that we might be free, And humbly stooped to death on Calvary. Alleluia!
4. Therefore you are, by God's eternal vow, Most high exalted o'er all creatures now, And given the name to which all knees shall bow.
5. Let every tongue confess with one accord In heaven and earth that Jesus Christ is Lord; And God the Father be by all adored. A-men.

Words used by permission of The Church Pension Fund. Music copyright © 1967 by The Bethany Press; from *Hymnbook for Christian Worship*; used by permission.

All Praise to God in Highest Heaven

291

GELOBT SEI GOTT 8.8.8. with Alleluias

Michael Weisse, 1531
Sts. 1,2,4-6 trans. by Margaret Barclay, 1950; alt., 1972
St. 3 trans. by Dalton E. McDonald, 1972

Attr. to Melchior Vulpius, 1609
As in *Pilgrim Hymnal*, 1958

1. All praise to God in highest heaven And his incarnate Son be given, Who gloriously for us has striven.
2. On the third morn at break of day, While still the stone above him lay, Free he arose, to go his way.
3. Three women came their grief to share And, frightened, saw an angel there— A heavenly light shone everywhere!
4. Then spoke the angel, "O fear naught! I know why you are thus distraught: You cannot find the Lord you sought."
5. "He is arisen from the dead, And all travail has conquered. Lo, where he lay, his shroud is spread."
6. Savior and Lord, grant us to see You in your risen majesty; Grant us to live right blessedly.

Alleluia! Alleluia! Alleluia! Amen.

Words of stanzas 1, 2, 4-6 altered from *Cantate Domino*; used by permission of the World Student Christian Federation.
Words of stanza 3 copyright 1972 by The Westminster Press.

292 All Praise to Thee, Our God, This Night
TALLIS' CANON L.M.

Thomas Ken, 1693, 1709; alt., 1972
Thomas Tallis, ca. 1567

1. All praise to thee, our God, this night, For all the blessings of the light; Keep us, O keep us, King of kings, Beneath thine own almighty wings.
2. Forgive us, Lord, for thy dear Son, The ill that we this day have done; That with the world, ourselves, and thee We, ere we sleep, at peace may be.
3. O may our souls on thee repose, And with sweet sleep our eyelids close; Sleep that may us more vigorous make To serve our God when we awake.
4. Praise God, from whom all blessings flow; Praise him, all creatures here below; Praise him above, ye heavenly host: Praise Father, Son, and Holy Ghost. Amen.

*May be sung as a canon.

All Who Love and Serve Your City   293

CHARLESTOWN 8.7.8.7.

Erik Routley, 1967

The United States Sacred Harmony, 1799
Harm. by Carlton R. Young, 1965

1. All who love and serve your cit-y, All who bear its dai-ly stress, All who cry for peace and jus-tice, All who curse and all who bless.
2. In your day of loss and sor-row, In your day of help-less strife, Hon-or, peace, and love re-treat-ing, Seek the Lord, who is your life.
3. In your day of wealth and plen-ty, Wast-ed work and wast-ed play, Call to mind the word of Je-sus, "Work ye yet while it is day."
4. For all days are days of judg-ment, And the Lord is wait-ing still, Draw-ing near to men who spurn him, Of-fering peace from Cal-vary's hill.
5. Ris-en Lord, shall yet the cit-y Be the cit-y of de-spair? Come to-day, our Judge, our Glo-ry, Be its name "The Lord is there!" A-men.

Words © copyright 1969 by Galliard, Ltd. All rights reserved. Used by permission of Galaxy Music Corp., N.Y., sole U.S. agent. Harmonization copyright © 1965 by Abingdon Press; from *The Methodist Hymnal*; used by permission.

294 Alone You Journey Forth, O Lord
BANGOR C.M.

Peter Abelard (1079-1142)
Trans. by F. Bland Tucker, 1938, 1972

Comp. or arr. by William Tans'ur, 1734

1. A-lone you jour-ney forth, O Lord, In sac-ri-fice to die; Is this your sor-row naught to us Who pass un-heed-ing by?
2. Our sins, not yours, O Lord, you bear; Make us your sor-row feel, Till through our pit-y and our shame Love an-swers love's ap-peal.
3. This is earth's dark-est hour, but you Both light and life re-store; Then let all praise to you be given Who live for-ev-er-more.
4. Give us com-pas-sion for you, Lord, That, as we share this hour, Your cross may bring us to your joy And res-ur-rec-tion power. A-men.

Words used by permission of The Church Pension Fund.

"Am I My Brother's Keeper?"

WHITFORD 7.6.7.6.D.

Ian Ferguson, 1967

John Ambrose Lloyd, Sr., 1870

1. "Am I my brother's keeper?" The muttered cry was drowned
By Abel's life-blood shouting In silence from the ground.
For no man is an island Divided from the main—
The bell which tolled for Abel Tolled equally for Cain.

2. The ruler called for water And thought his hands were clean.
Christ counted less than order, The man than the machine.
The crowd cried, "Crucify him," Their malice wouldn't budge,
So Pilate called for water, And history's his judge.

3. As long as people hunger, As long as people thirst,
And ignorance and illness And warfare do their worst,
As long as there's injustice In any of God's lands,
I am my brother's keeper, I dare not wash my hands. A-men.

Words © copyright 1969 by Galliard, Ltd. All rights reserved. Used by permission of Galaxy Music Corp., N.Y., sole U.S. agent.

296 Amazing Grace! How Sweet the Sound

AMAZING GRACE C.M.

John Newton, 1779

American folk hymn
Arr. by Edwin O. Excell, 1900

1. A-mazing grace! How sweet the sound That saved a wretch like me! I once was lost, but now am found, Was blind, but now I see.
2. 'Twas grace that taught my heart to fear, And grace my fears relieved; How precious did that grace appear The hour I first believed!
3. Through many dangers, toils, and snares I have already come; 'Tis grace has brought me safe thus far, And grace will lead me home.
4. The Lord has promised good to me, His word my hope secures; He will my shield and portion be As long as life endures. A-men.

Ancient of Days, Who Sit Enthroned in Glory 297

L'OMNIPOTENT 11.10.11.10.

William C. Doane, 1886; alt., 1972

Comp. or adapted by Louis Bourgeois, 1551
As in *Pilgrim Hymnal*, 1958

1. Ancient of Days, who sit enthroned in glory,
To you all knees are bent, all voices pray;
Your love has blest the wide world's wondrous story
With light and life since Eden's dawning day.

2. O Holy Father, you have led your children
In all the ages, with the fire and cloud,
Through seas dry-shod, through weary wastes bewildering;
To you, in reverent love, our hearts are bowed.

3. O Holy Jesus, Prince of Peace and Savior,
To you we owe the peace that still prevails,
Stilling the rude wills of men's wild behavior,
And calming passion's fierce and stormy gales.

4. O Holy Ghost, the Lord and the Life-giver,
Yours is the quickening power that gives increase;
From you have flowed, as from a pleasant river,
Our heritage, our blessings, and our peace.

5. O Triune God, with heart and voice adoring,
Praise we the goodness that does crown our days;
Pray we that you will hear us, still imploring
Your love and favor, given to us always. A-men.

298. Angels, from the Realms of Glory

REGENT SQUARE 8.7.8.7.8.7.

James Montgomery, 1816, 1825; alt., 1972

Henry Smart, 1867

1. Angels, from the realms of glory, Wing your flight o'er all the earth; As you sang creation's story, Now proclaim Messiah's birth: Come and worship, Come and worship, Worship Christ, the new-born King! A-men.

2. Shepherds, in the fields abiding, Watching o'er your flocks by night, God with man is now residing, Yonder shines the infant Light: Come and worship, Come and worship, Worship Christ, the new-born King!

3. Sages, leave your contemplations, Brighter visions beam afar; Seek the great Desire of nations; You have seen his natal star: Come and worship, Come and worship, Worship Christ, the new-born King!

4. Saints, before the altar bending, Watching long in hope and fear, Suddenly the Lord, descending, In his temple shall appear: Come and worship, Come and worship, Worship Christ, the new-born King!

Angels We Have Heard on High   299
GLORIA 7.7.7.7. with Refrain

French carol
Trans. in *Crown of Jesus*, 1862; alt.
Adapted by Earl Marlatt, 1937

French carol
As in *Pilgrim Hymnal*, 1958

1. An-gels we have heard on high, Sing-ing sweet-ly through the night,
2. Shep-herds, why this ju - bi - lee? Why these songs of hap - py cheer?
3. Come to Beth - le - hem and see Him whose birth the an - gels sing;
4. See him in a man - ger laid Whom the an - gels praise a - bove;

And the moun-tains in re - ply Ech - o - ing their brave de - light.
What great bright-ness did you see? What glad ti - dings did you hear?
Come, a - dore on bend - ed knee Christ, the Lord, the new - born King.
Mar - y, Jo - seph, lend your aid, While we raise our hearts in love.

Glo - - - - - ri - a

Words from *The New Church Hymnal*; used by permission of Fleming H. Revell Company, publisher.

See following page.

Angels We Have Heard on High (cont.)

As Men of Old Their Firstfruits Brought 301
HIGH POPPLES C.M.D.

Frank von Christierson, 1960, 1972 — Samuel Walter, 1964

1. As men of old their first-fruits brought Of or-chard, flock, and field To God, the giv-er of all good, The source of boun-teous yield; So we to-day first-fruits would bring, The wealth of this good land, Of farm and mar-ket, shop and home, Of mind and heart and hand.
2. A world in need now sum-mons us To la-bor, love, and give; To make our life an of-fer-ing To God, that man may live; The church of Christ is call-ing us To make the dream come true: A world re-deemed by Christ-like love, All life in Christ made new.
3. In grat-i-tude and hum-ble trust We bring our best to-day, To serve your cause and share your love With all a-long life's way. O God, who gave your-self to us In Christ, your on-ly Son, Teach us to give our-selves each day Un-til life's work is done. A-men.

Words copyright 1961 by The Hymn Society of America; altered from *Ten New Stewardship Hymns*; used by permission. Music copyright © 1964 by Abingdon Press; from *The Methodist Hymnal*; used by permission.

Alternative Tune: FOREST GREEN

302 As with Gladness Men of Old
DIX 7.7.7.7.7.7.

William Chatterton Dix, ca. 1858

Conrad Kocher, 1838
Abr. by William Henry Monk, 1861

1. As with glad-ness men of old Did the guid-ing star be-hold; As with joy they hailed its light, Lead-ing on-ward, beam-ing bright; So, most gra-cious Lord, may we Ev-er-more be led to thee.
2. As with joy-ful steps they sped To that low-ly man-ger bed, There to bend the knee be-fore Him whom heaven and earth a-dore, So may we with will-ing feet Ev-er seek thy mer-cy seat.
3. As they of-fered gifts most rare At that man-ger rude and bare, So may we with ho-ly joy, Pure, and free from sin's al-loy, All our cost-liest trea-sures bring, Christ, to thee, our heav-enly King.
4. Ho-ly Je-sus, ev-ery day Keep us in the nar-row way; And, when earth-ly things are past, Bring our ran-somed souls at last Where they need no star to guide, Where no clouds thy glo-ry hide. A-men.

At the Name of Jesus
KING'S WESTON 6.5.6.5.D.

Caroline Maria Noel, 1870; alt., 1931

Ralph Vaughan Williams, 1925
Arr. for *The Hymnbook*, 1955

1. At the name of Jesus Every knee shall bow,
Every tongue confess him King of glory now:
'Tis the Father's pleasure We should call him Lord,
Who from the beginning Was the mighty Word.

2. Humbled for a season, To receive a name
From the lips of sinners, Unto whom he came,
Faithfully he bore it Spotless to the last,
Brought it back victorious, When from death he passed;

3. Bore it up triumphant, With its human light,
Through all ranks of creatures, To the central height,
To the throne of Godhead, To the Father's breast;
Filled it with the glory Of that perfect rest.

4. Brothers, this Lord Jesus Shall return again,
With his Father's glory O'er the earth to reign;
For all wreaths of empire Meet upon his brow,
And our hearts confess him King of glory now. A-men.

Music arranged from *Songs of Praise*, Enlarged Edition; used by permission of Oxford University Press.

304 Be Thou My Vision
SLANE 10.10.9.10.

Ancient Irish
Trans. by Mary Byrne, 1905
Versified by Eleanor Hull, 1912; alt.

Traditional Irish melody
Harm. by David Evans, 1927

1. Be thou my vision, O Lord of my heart;
   Naught be all else to me, save that thou art—
   Thou my best thought, by day or by night,
   Waking or sleeping, thy presence my light.

2. Be thou my wisdom, and thou my true word;
   I ever with thee and thou with me, Lord;
   Thou my great Father, I thy true son;
   Thou in me dwelling, and I with thee one.

3. Riches I heed not, nor man's empty praise,
   Thou mine inheritance, now and always;
   Thou and thou only, first in my heart,
   High King of heaven, my treasure thou art.

4. High King of heaven, my victory won,
   May I reach heaven's joys, O bright heaven's Sun!
   Heart of my own heart, whatever befall,
   Still be my vision, O Ruler of all. A-men.

Words used by permission of Eleanor Hull's Estate and Chatto & Windus, Ltd. Music altered from *The Church Hymnary*, Revised Edition, 1927; used by permission of Oxford University Press.

Become to Us the Living Bread

305

O FILII ET FILIAE 8.8.8. with Alleluia

Miriam Drury, 1970

Probably French, ca. 15th century
As in *Pilgrim Hymnal*, 1958

1. Be-come to us the liv-ing bread By which the Chris-tian life is fed, Re-newed, and great-ly com-fort-ed, Al-le-lu-ia!
2. Be-come the nev-er-fail-ing wine, The spring of joy that shall in-cline Our hearts to bear the cov-e-nant sign, Al-le-lu-ia!
3. May Chris-tians all with one ac-cord U-nite a-round the sa-cred board To praise your ho-ly name, O Lord, Al-le-lu-ia! A-men.

Words copyright 1972 by The Westminster Press.

306 Before the Lord Jehovah's Throne
PARK STREET L.M.

Based on Psalm 100
Isaac Watts, 1719
Alt. by John Wesley, 1737, and others

Frédéric M.-A. Venua, ca. 1810

1. Be-fore the Lord Je-ho-vah's throne, All na-tions, bow with sa-cred joy; Know that the Lord is God a-lone, He can cre-ate, and he de-stroy; He can cre-ate, and he de-stroy.
2. His sov-ereign power, with-out our aid, Made us of clay, and formed us men; And when like wan-dering sheep we strayed, He brought us to his fold a-gain, He brought us to his fold a-gain.
3. We'll crowd his gates with thank-ful songs, High as the heavens our voic-es raise; And earth, with her ten thou-sand tongues, Shall fill his courts with sound-ing praise, Shall fill his courts with sound-ing praise.
4. Wide as the world is his com-mand, Vast as e-ter-ni-ty his love; Firm as a rock his truth shall stand, When roll-ing years shall cease to move, When roll-ing years shall cease to move. A-men.

Behold the Lamb of God! 307

WIGAN 6.6.6.4.8.8.4.

Matthew Bridges, 1848; alt.
Samuel S. Wesley, 1872

1. Be-hold the Lamb of God! O thou for sin-ners slain,
Let it not be in vain That thou hast died.
Thee for my Sav-ior let me take. My on-ly ref-uge
let me make Thy pierc-ed side!

2. Be-hold the Lamb of God! All hail, in-car-nate Word!
Thou ev-er-last-ing Lord, Sav-ior most blest!
Fill us with love that nev-er faints. Grant us, with all thy
bless-ed saints, E-ter-nal rest.

3. Be-hold the Lamb of God! Wor-thy is he a-lone
To sit up-on the throne Of God a-bove,
One with the An-cient of all days, One with the Com-fort-
er in praise, All Light, all Love! A-men.

308 Beneath the Cross of Jesus
ST. CHRISTOPHER 7.6.8.6.8.6.8.6.

Sts. 1,2, Elizabeth C. Clephane, 1872
St. 3, Dalton E. McDonald
and Donald D. Kettring, 1972

Frederick C. Maker, 1881

1. Be-neath the cross of Je-sus I fain would take my stand—
The shad-ow of a might-y rock With-in a wea-ry land;
A home with-in the wil-der-ness, A rest up-on the way,
From the burn-ing of the noon-tide heat, And the bur-den of the day.

2. Up-on the cross of Je-sus Mine eye at times can see
The ver-y dy-ing form of one Who suf-fered there for me:
And from my strick-en heart with tears Two won-ders I con-fess—
The won-ders of re-deem-ing love And my un-worth-i-ness.

3. "Take up your cross," said Je-sus, "And fol-low af-ter me."
I take your cross to learn your will, What-e'er the cost may be;
We share the vi-sion of a world Which puts an end to strife,
And work that all man-kind shall know Your way, your truth, your life. A-men.

Stanza 3 copyright 1972 by The Westminster Press. Music copyright; used by permission of the Psalms and Hymns Trust.

Blessed Jesus, at Your Word

309

LIEBSTER JESU 7.8.7.8.8.8.

Tobias Clausnitzer, 1663
Trans. by Catherine Winkworth, 1858; alt., 1972

Johann Rudolph Ahle, 1664
Arr. by J. S. Bach, 1769

1. Blessed Jesus, at your word
We are gathered all to hear you;
Let our hearts and souls be stirred
Now to seek and love and fear you;
By your teachings true and holy,
Drawn from earth to love you solely.

2. All our knowledge, sense, and sight
Lie in deepest darkness shrouded,
Till your Spirit breaks our night
With the beams of truth unclouded;
You alone to God can win us,
You must work all good within us.

3. Glorious Lord, yourself impart!
Light of light, from God proceeding,
Open now our ears and heart,
Help us by your Spirit's pleading;
Hear the cry that we are raising;
Hear, and bless our prayers and praising. A-men.

310. Blessed Jesus, We Are Here
LIEBSTER JESU 7.8.7.8.8.8.

Benjamin Schmolck, 1706
Trans. by C. Winfred Douglas, 1939; alt., 1972

Johann Rudolph Ahle, 1664
Arr. by J. S. Bach, 1769

Bless-ed Jesus, we are here, Your be-lov-ed word o-bey-ing. With {these chil-dren we / this child we now} draw near As you bid us in your say-ing, "Let the lit-tle ones be giv-en Un-to me; of such is heav-en." A-men.

Words used by permission of The Church Pension Fund.

Blessing and Honor and Glory and Power   311
O QUANTA QUALIA 10.10.10.10.

Horatius Bonar, 1866; alt., 1972
Paris Antiphoner, 1681
Harm. by David Evans, 1927

1. Bless-ing and hon-or and glo-ry and power,
   Wis-dom and rich-es and strength ev-er-more,
   Give we to him who our bat-tle has won,
   Whose are the king-dom, the crown, and the throne.

2. Hear through the heav-ens the sound of his name,
   While rings the earth with his glo-ry and fame;
   O-cean and moun-tain, stream, for-est, and flower
   Ech-o his prais-es and tell of his power.

3. Ev-er as-cend-ing the song and the prayer;
   Ev-er de-scend-ing the love that we share;
   Bless-ing and hon-or and glo-ry and praise—
   This is the theme of the hymns that we raise.

4. Give we the glo-ry and praise to the Lamb;
   Take we the robe and the harp and the palm;
   Sing we the song of the Lamb that was slain,
   Dy-ing in weak-ness, but ris-ing to reign. A-men.

Music from *The Church Hymnary*, Revised Edition, 1927; used by permission of Oxford University Press.

312 Born in the Night, Mary's Child
(Mary's Child)

Geoffrey Ainger, 1964
Harm. by Richard D. Wetzel, 1972

Geoffrey Ainger, 1964

1. Born in the night, Mary's Child, A long way from your home; Coming in need, Mary's Child, Born in a borrowed room.
2. Clear shining light, Mary's Child, Your face lights up our way; Light of the world, Mary's Child, Dawn on our darkened day.
3. Truth of our life, Mary's Child, You tell us God is good; Prove it is true, Mary's Child, Go to your cross of wood.
4. Hope of the world, Mary's Child, You're coming soon to reign; King of the earth, Mary's Child, Walk in our streets again.

Words and music © copyright 1964 by Geoffrey Ainger; assigned to Galliard, Ltd. All rights reserved. Reprinted by permission of Galaxy Music Corp., N.Y., sole U.S. agent.

Bread of Heaven, on Thee We Feed 313

ARFON 7.7.7.7.7.7.

Josiah Conder, 1824; alt.

Traditional melody, France and Wales
Adapted by Hugh Davies, ca. 1906

1. Bread of heaven, on thee we feed, For thou art our food indeed; Ever may our souls be fed With this true and living Bread, Day by day with strength supplied Through the life of him who died.

2. Vine of heaven, thy love supplies This blest cup of sacrifice; 'Tis thy wounds our healing give; To thy cross we look and live: Thou our life! O let us be Rooted, grafted, built on thee. A-men.

314 Break Forth, O Beauteous Heavenly Light

ERMUNTRE DICH 8.7.8.7.8.8.7.7

St. 1, Johann von Rist, 1641;
trans. by John Troutbeck, 1873; alt., 1972
St. 2, Dalton E. McDonald, 1972

Johann Schop, 1641
Alt. by Johann Crüger, 1648
Harm. by J. S. Bach, 1734

1. Break forth, O beauteous heavenly light, And usher in the morning. You shepherds, shrink not with affright, But hear the angel's warning. This child, now weak in

2. He comes to reconcile all men, And men to God forever; He comes to mend the cords of love Wherever sin does sever. He is the light up-

Stanza 2 copyright 1972 by The Westminster Press.

Break Forth, O Beauteous Heavenly Light (cont.) 315

in - fan - cy, Our con - fi - dence and joy shall be, The power of Sa - tan break - ing, Our peace e - ter - nal mak - ing.
on our way To bring us to the prom-ised day—This child, God's in - car - na - tion, Our hope and our sal - va - tion! A-men.

316 Break Forth, O Living Light of God
ST. PETER C.M.

Frank von Christierson, 1952; alt., 1972
Alexander R. Reinagle, ca. 1836

1. Break forth, O living light of God, Upon the world's dark hour! Show us the way the Master trod; Reveal his saving power.
2. Remove the veil of ancient words, With message long obscure; Restore to us your truth, O God, And make its meaning sure.
*3. Show us the prophets and the priests, The kings, the common men, Who kept the faith and walked with you; O make them live again!
4. O let your Word be light anew To every nation's life; Unite us in your will, O Lord, And end all sinful strife.
5. O may one Lord, one faith, one Word, One Spirit lead us still: And one great church go forth in might To work God's perfect will. A-men.

Words copyright 1953 by The Hymn Society of America; altered from *Ten New Hymns on the Bible*; used by permission.

Break Thou the Bread of Life   317

BREAD OF LIFE 6.4.6.4.D.

Mary Ann Lathbury, 1877 — William F. Sherwin, 1877

1. Break thou the bread of life, Dear Lord, to me,
As thou didst break the loaves Beside the sea.
Beyond the sacred page I seek thee, Lord;
My spirit pants for thee, O living Word.

2. Bless thou the truth, dear Lord, To me— to me,
As thou didst bless the bread By Galilee.
Then shall all bondage cease, All fetters fall,
And I shall find my peace, My all in all. A-men.

318 Brightest and Best of the Sons of the Morning
WALKER 11.10.11.10.

Reginald Heber, 1811; alt., 1972

Southern Harmony, 1835
Harm. by Richard M. Peek, 1972

1. Brightest and best of the sons of the morning,
Dawn on our darkness and lend us your aid;
Star of the East, the horizon adorning,
Guide where our infant Redeemer is laid.

2. Cold on his cradle the dewdrops are shining;
Low lies his head with the beasts of the stall;
Angels adore him in slumber reclining,
Maker and Monarch and Savior of all.

3. Say, shall we yield him, in costly devotion,
Odors of Edom and offerings divine,
Gems of the mountain and pearls of the ocean,
Myrrh from the forest, or gold from the mine?

4. Vainly we offer each ample oblation,
Vainly with gifts would his favor secure;
Richer by far is the heart's adoration,
Dearer to God are the prayers of the poor. A-men.

Music copyright 1972 by The Westminster Press.

Bring a Torch, Jeannette, Isabella 319

BRING A TORCH Irregular

Traditional French carol (?)
Trans. by E. Cuthbert Nunn (1868-1914); alt., 1972

Traditional French carol (?)
Harm. by E. Cuthbert Nunn (1868-1914)
Alt. in *Pilgrim Hymnal*, 1958

1. Bring a torch, Jean-nette, Is - a - bel - la! Bring a torch, to the cra - dle run! It is Je - sus, good folk of the vil - lage; Christ is born and Mar - y's call - ing. Ah! ah! beau - ti - ful is the moth - er! Ah! ah! beau - ti - ful is her Son!

2. It is wrong when the child is sleep - ing, It is wrong to talk so loud; Si - lence, all, as you gath - er a - round, Lest your noise should wak - en Je - sus. Hush! hush! see how fast he slum - bers; Hush! hush! see how fast he sleeps!

3. Soft - ly to the lit - tle sta - ble, Soft - ly for a mo - ment come; Look and see how charm - ing is Je - sus, How he is warm, his cheeks are ros - y. Hush! hush! see how the child is sleep - ing; Hush! hush! see how he smiles in dreams.

Words and music used by permission of Frank Distributing Corp.

320 Built on the Rock

KIRKEN (BUILT ON THE ROCK) 8.8.8.8.8.8.8.8.

Nicolai F. S. Grundtvig, 1837
Trans. by Carl Döving, 1909; alt., 1972

Ludvig M. Lindeman, 1840

1. Built on the rock the church does stand, E-ven when stee-ples are fall-ing; Crum-bled have spires in ev-ery land, Bells still are chim-ing and call-ing; Call-ing the young and old to rest, But a-bove all the soul dis-tressed, Long-ing for rest ev-er last-ing.

2. Sure-ly in tem-ples made with hands God, the most high, is not dwell-ing; High a-bove earth his tem-ple stands, All earth-ly tem-ples ex-cell-ing; Yet he whom heavens can-not con-tain Chose to a-bide on earth with men, Built in our bod-ies his tem-ple.

3. We are God's house of liv-ing stones, Build-ed for his hab-i-ta-tion; He through bap-tis-mal grace us owns, Heirs of his won-drous sal-va-tion; Were we but two his name to tell, Yet he would deign with us to dwell, With all his grace and his fa-vor.

4. Now we may gath-er with our King, E'en in the low-li-est dwell-ing; Prais-es to him we there may bring, His won-drous mer-cy forth-tell-ing; Je-sus his grace to us ac-cords, Spir-it and life are all his words, His truth does hal-low the tem-ple. A-men.

NOTE: Stanza 3 may be used for Baptism.

By the Babylonian Rivers

(Hymn for Those in Captivity)

Based on Psalm 137:1-4
Ewald Bash, 1964

Latvian melody
Arr. by Ewald Bash, 1964
Harm. by Paul Abels, 1966

321

1. By the Babylonian rivers We sat down in grief and wept; Hanged our harps upon a willow, Mourned for Zion when we slept.
2. There our captors in derision Did require of us a song; So we sat with staring vision, And the days were hard and long.
3. How shall we sing the Lord's song In a strange and bitter land? Can our voices veil the sorrow? Lord God, help thy holy band.
4. Let thy cross be benediction For men bound in tyranny; By the power of resurrection Loose them from captivity.

Words and arrangement of music copyright 1964 by The Youth Department of The American Lutheran Church; from *Songs for Today*; used by permission. Harmonization from *Risk*, Vol. II, No. 3, 1966, published by World Council of Churches; used by permission.

322 Call Jehovah Your Salvation

HYFRYDOL 8.7.8.7.D.

Based on Psalm 91
James Montgomery, 1822; alt., 1972

Rowland Hugh Prichard, 1855

1. Call Jehovah your salvation, Rest beneath th' Almighty's shade, In his secret habitation Dwell, nor ever be dismayed: There no tumult can alarm you, You shall dread no hidden snare; Guile nor violence can harm you, In eternal safeguard there.

2. From the sword at noon-day wasting, From the noisome pestilence, In the depth of midnight blasting, God shall be your sure defense: He shall charge his angel legions Watch and ward o'er you to keep; Though you walk through hostile regions, Though in desert wilds you sleep.

3. Since, with pure and firm affection, You on God have set your love, With the wings of his protection He will shield you from above: You shall call on him in trouble, He will hearken, he will save; Here for grief reward you double, Crown with life beyond the grave. A-men.

Cast Your Burden on the Lord 323
SAVANNAH 7.7.7.7.

Based on Psalm 55:22
Rowland Hill's Psalms and Hymns, 1783; alt., 1972

Foundery Collection, 1742

1. Cast your bur-den on the Lord; On-ly lean up-on his word. You will soon have cause to bless His e-ter-nal faith-ful-ness.
2. He sus-tains you by his hand; He en-a-bles you to stand. Those whom Je-sus once has loved From his grace are nev-er moved.
3. Hu-man coun-sels come to naught; That shall stand which God has wrought. His com-pas-sion, love, and power Are the same for-ev-er-more.
4. Heaven and earth may pass a-way; God's free grace shall not de-cay. He has prom-ised to ful-fill All the plea-sure of his will.
5. Je-sus, guard-ian of your flock, Be your-self our con-stant rock. Make us, by your power-ful hand, Strong as Zi-on's moun-tain stand. A-men.

324. Christ, Above All Glory Seated

IN BABILONE 8.7.8.7.D.

Latin hymn, ca. 9th century
Trans. by James Russell Woodford, 1852; alt., 1972

Traditional Dutch melody
Harm. by Julius Röntgen, ca. 1906

1. Christ, a-bove all glo-ry seat-ed! King e-ter-nal, strong to save!
Dy-ing, you have death de-feat-ed, Bur-ied, you have doomed the grave.
You are gone, where now is giv-en What no mor-tal might could gain:
On th'e-ter-nal throne of heav-en, In your Fa-ther's power to reign.

2. There your king-doms all a-dore you, Heaven a-bove and earth be-low,
While the depths of hell be-fore you, Trem-bling and de-feat they know.
We, O Lord! with hearts a-dor-ing, Fol-low you a-bove the sky:
Hear our prayers your grace im-plor-ing, Lift our souls to you on high.

3. So when you a-gain in glo-ry On the clouds of heaven ap-pear,
We, your flock, may stand be-fore you, Faith-ful fol-lowers, with-out fear.
Hail! all hail! In you con-fid-ing, Je-sus, all shall you a-dore,
In your Fa-ther's might a-bid-ing With one spir-it ev-er-more! A-men.

Words copyright 1972 by The Westminster Press. Music used by permission of F. E. Röntgen.

Christ Is Made the Sure Foundation   325
REGENT SQUARE 8.7.8.7.8.7.

Latin hymn, ca. 7th century
Trans. by John Mason Neale, 1851; alt., 1861, 1972

Henry Smart, 1867

1. Christ is made the sure foun-da-tion, Christ the head and cor-ner-stone,
Cho-sen of the Lord and pre-cious, Bind-ing all the church in one;
Ho-ly Zi-on's help for-ev-er, And her con-fi-dence a-lone.

2. To this tem-ple, where we call you, Come, O Lord of Hosts, to-day!
With your wont-ed lov-ing-kind-ness Hear your peo-ple as they pray,
And your full-est ben-e-dic-tion Shed with-in its walls al-way.

3. Here be-stow on all your serv-ants What they ask of you to gain:
What they gain from you for-ev-er With the bless-ed to re-tain,
And here-af-ter in your glo-ry Ev-er-more with you to reign.

4. Laud and hon-or to the Fa-ther, Laud and hon-or to the Son,
Laud and hon-or to the Spir-it, Ev-er Three and ev-er One;
One in might, and One in glo-ry, While un-end-ing ag-es run. A-men.

326. Christ Is the World's True Light
ST. JOAN 6.7.6.7.6.6.6.6.

George Wallace Briggs, 1931; alt., 1972

Percy E. B. Coller, 1941

1. Christ is the world's true Light, Its Captain of salvation, The Day-star clear and bright Of every man and nation. New life, new hope, awakes Wher-e'er men own his sway: Freedom her bondage breaks, And night is turned to day.

2. In Christ all races meet, Their ancient feuds forgetting, The whole round world complete, From sunrise to its setting. When Christ is throned as Lord, Men shall forsake their fear, To plow-share beat the sword, To pruning hook the spear.

3. One Lord, in one great name, Unite us all who own you; Cast out our pride and shame That hinder to enthrone you. The world has waited long, Has travailed long in pain; To heal its ancient wrong, Come, Prince of Peace, and reign. A-men.

Words altered from *Songs of Praise*, Enlarged Edition; used by permission of Oxford University Press. Music used by permission of The Church Pension Fund.

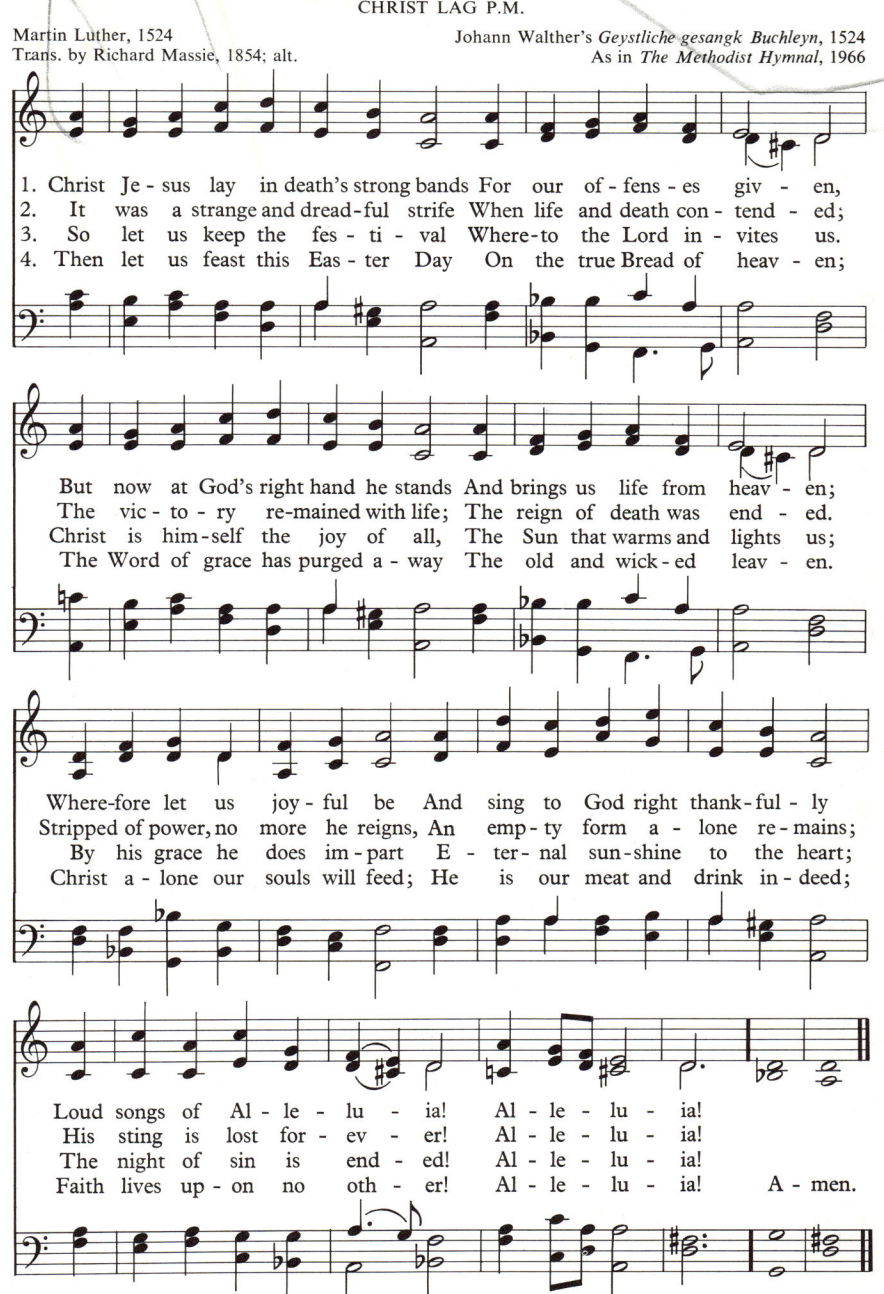

Christ Jesus Lay in Death's Strong Bands   327
CHRIST LAG P.M.

Martin Luther, 1524
Trans. by Richard Massie, 1854; alt.

Johann Walther's *Geystliche gesangk Buchleyn*, 1524
As in *The Methodist Hymnal*, 1966

1. Christ Jesus lay in death's strong bands For our offenses given,
2. It was a strange and dreadful strife When life and death contended;
3. So let us keep the festival Whereto the Lord invites us.
4. Then let us feast this Easter Day On the true Bread of heaven;

But now at God's right hand he stands And brings us life from heaven;
The victory remained with life; The reign of death was ended.
Christ is himself the joy of all, The Sun that warms and lights us;
The Word of grace has purged away The old and wicked leaven.

Wherefore let us joyful be And sing to God right thankfully
Stripped of power, no more he reigns, An empty form alone remains;
By his grace he does impart Eternal sunshine to the heart;
Christ alone our souls will feed; He is our meat and drink indeed;

Loud songs of Alleluia! Alleluia!
His sting is lost forever! Alleluia!
The night of sin is ended! Alleluia!
Faith lives upon no other! Alleluia! Amen.

328 Christ the Lord Is Risen Again
CHRIST IST ERSTANDEN 7.7.7.7. with Alleluias

Michael Weisse, 1531
Trans. by Catherine Winkworth, 1858

German folk hymn, 12th century
Arr. by Ethel Porter, 1958

1. Christ the Lord is risen a-gain, Christ has bro-ken ev-ery chain.
2. He who bore all pain and loss, Com-fort-less up-on the cross,
3. He who slum-bered in the grave Is ex-alt-ed now to save;

Hark, the an-gels shout for joy, Sing-ing ev-er-more on high:
Lives in glo-ry now on high, Pleads for us and hears our cry:
Now through Chris-ten-dom it rings That the Lamb is King of kings:

Al - le - lu - ia! Al - le - lu - ia! Al - le -

Christ the Lord Is Risen Again (cont.) 329

lu - ia! Al - le - lu - ia! Hark, the an - gels shout for joy,
Lives in glo - ry now on high,
Now through Chris-ten - dom it rings

Sing - ing ev - er - more on high:
Pleads for us and hears our cry: Al - le - lu - ia!
That the Lamb is King of kings: A - men.

330 "Christ the Lord Is Risen Today"

LLANFAIR 7.7.7.7. with Alleluias

Charles Wesley, 1739; alt., 1760, 1972
Robert Williams, 1817
Harm. by David Evans, 1927

May be sung in unison

1. "Christ the Lord is risen to-day," Sons of men and an-gels say; Raise your joys and tri-umphs high; Sing, you heavens, and earth re-ply, Alleluia!
2. Vain the stone, the watch, the seal; Christ has burst the gates of hell; Death in vain for-bids his rise; Christ has o-pened par-a-dise. Alleluia!
3. Lives a-gain our glo-rious King; Where, O death, is now your sting? Once he died, our souls to save; Where your vic-to-ry, O grave? Alleluia!
4. Soar we now where Christ has led, Fol-lowing our ex-alt-ed Head; Made like him, like him we rise; Ours the cross, the grave, the skies. Alleluia!
5. Hail, the Lord of earth and heaven! Praise to thee by both be given; You we greet tri-um-phant now; Hail, the res-ur-rec-tion Thou! A-men.

Music from *The Church Hymnary*, Revised Edition, 1927;
used by permission of Oxford University Press.

Alternative Tune: EASTER HYMN

Christ Was the Word

CLAY COURT 7.7.7.7.

Attr. to Elizabeth I (1533-1603)
Richard Hillert, 1969

Christ was the Word who spake it: He took the bread and brake it: And what his word doth make it, That I believe and take it.

Music copyright 1972 by The Westminster Press.

332   Christ, Whose Glory Fills the Skies

RATISBON 7.7.7.7.7.7.

Charles Wesley, 1740

German melody, adapted in J. G. Werner's *Choralbuch*, 1815

1. Christ, whose glory fills the skies, Christ, the true, the only light, Sun of righteousness, arise, Triumph o'er the shades of night; Day-spring from on high, be near; Day-star, in my heart appear.

2. Dark and cheerless is the morn Unaccompanied by thee; Joyless is the day's return, Till thy mercy's beams I see, Till they inward light impart, Glad my eyes and warm my heart.

3. Visit, then, this soul of mine; Pierce the gloom of sin and grief; Fill me, Radiancy divine, Scatter all my unbelief; More and more thyself display, Shining to the perfect day. A-men.

Come, Christians, Join to Sing

MADRID 6.6.6.6.D.

Christian Henry Bateman, 1843; alt.

Source unknown
Harm. by David Evans, 1927

1. Come, Christians, join to sing Loud praise to Christ our King; Let all, with heart and voice, Before his throne rejoice; Praise is his gracious choice. Alleluia! Amen!
2. Come, lift your hearts on high; Let praises fill the sky; He is our guide and friend; To us he'll condescend; His love shall never end. Alleluia! Amen!
3. Praise yet our Christ again; Life shall not end the strain; On heaven's blissful shore His goodness we'll adore, Singing forevermore, Alleluia! Amen!

A-men.

Music used by permission of the Executors of the late Professor Evans.

334 Come Down, O Love Divine
DOWN AMPNEY 6.6.11.D.

Bianco da Siena, ca. 1367
Trans. by Richard F. Littledale, 1867; alt., 1972

Ralph Vaughan Williams, 1906

1. Come down, O Love divine, Seek out this soul of mine, And visit it with your own ardor glowing; O Comforter, draw near, Within my heart appear, And kindle it, your holy flame bestowing.
2. O let it freely burn, Till earthly passions turn To dust and ashes in its heat consuming; And let your glorious light Shine ever on my sight, And clothe me round, the while my path illuming.
3. And so the yearning strong With which the soul will long Shall far outpass the power of human telling; For none can guess its grace Till he become the place Wherein the Holy Spirit makes his dwelling. A-men.

Music from *The English Hymnal*; used by permission of Oxford University Press.

Come, Holy Ghost, Our Souls Inspire

VENI CREATOR SPIRITUS L.M.

Latin hymn, ca. 9th century
Trans. by John Cosin, 1627

Plainsong melody, Mechlin form
As in *Pilgrim Hymnal*, 1958

335

1. Come, Holy Ghost, our souls inspire And lighten with celestial fire; Thou the anointing Spirit art Who dost thy seven-fold gifts impart.
2. Thy blessed unction from above Is comfort, life, and fire of love; Enable with perpetual light The dullness of our blinded sight.
3. Anoint and cheer our soiled face With the abundance of thy grace; Keep far our foes, give peace at home; Where thou art guide no ill can come.
4. Teach us to know the Father, Son, And thee, of both, to be but One; That through the ages all along This may be our endless song: Praise to thy eternal merit, Father, Son, and Holy Spirit. Amen.

After last stanza

336 Come, Holy Spirit, God and Lord!
DAS NEUGEBORNE KINDELEIN L.M.

Based on medieval Latin antiphon
Martin Luther, 1524
Trans. by Catherine Winkworth, 1855, and others

Melchior Vulpius, 1609
Harm. by J. S. Bach, 1724

1. Come, Holy Spirit, God and Lord! Let all your graces be outpoured On each believer's mind and heart; Your fervent love to us impart.
2. Lord, by the brightness of your light, You in the faith do men unite Of every land and every tongue; This to your praise, O Lord, be sung.
3. From every error keep us free; Let none but Christ our Master be, That we in living faith abide, In him with all our might confide.
4. Lord, by your power prepare each heart And to our weakness strength impart, That bravely here we may contend, Through life and death to you ascend. A-men.

Come, My Soul, You Must Be Waking

MEINE ARMUTH 8.4.7.D.

337

Friedrich R. L. von Canitz (1654-1699)
Trans. attr. to Thomas Arnold
and Henry J. Buckoll, 1838, 1841; alt.

Freylinghausen's *Geistreiches Gesangbuch*, 1704
As in *Songs of Syon*, 1910

1. Come, my soul, you must be waking. Now is breaking O'er the earth another day. Come to him who made this splendor; May you render All your feeble strength can pay.
2. Gladly hail the sun returning; Ready burning Be the incense of your powers. For the night is safely ended; God has tended With his care your helpless hours.
3. Pray that he may prosper ever Each endeavor When your aim is good and true; But that he may ever thwart you, And convert you, When you evil would pursue.
4. Only God's free gifts abuse not, Light refuse not, But his Spirit's voice obey; You with him shall dwell, beholding Light enfolding All things in unclouded day. A-men.

Music used by permission of Mrs. J. Meredith Tatton.

338 Come, O Come, Great Quickening Spirit
KOMM, O KOMM, DU GEIST DES LEBENS 8.7.8.7.7.7.

Heinrich Held, ca. 1658
Trans. by Edward Traill Horn III, 1958; alt., 1972

Attr. to Johann Christoph Bach, ca. 1680
Arr. by Ulrich S. Leupold, 1958

1. Come, O come, great quick-ening Spir-it, God be-fore the dawn of time! Fire our hearts with ho-ly ar-dor, Bless-ed Com-fort-er sub-lime! Let your ra-diance fill our night, Turn-ing dark-ness in-to light.

2. May your will and your de-sir-ing Be our ob-ject; with your hand Lead our ev-ery thought and ac-tion That they be what you com-mand. All our sin-ful-ness e-rase With the in-crease of your grace.

3. Bless-ed Spir-it, bring re-new-al To all dwell-ing on the earth, When the e-vil one as-sails us Help us prove our heav-enly birth; Arm us with your might-y sword In the le-gions of the Lord.

4. Help us keep the faith for-ev-er; Let not Sa-tan, death, or shame Draw us from you, or de-prive us Of the hon-or of your name. With your Word and sac-ra-ments Be, our God, the sure de-fense. A-men.

Words and music from *Service Book and Hymnal*; used by permission of the Commission on the Liturgy and Hymnal.

Come, O Thou God of Grace

TRINITY (ITALIAN HYMN) 6.6.4.6.6.6.4.

William E. Evans, 1886

Felice de Giardini, 1769
Arr. by Robert Carwithen, 1972

1. Come, O thou God of grace, Dwell in this ho-ly place, E'en now de-scend! This tem-ple, reared to thee, O may it ev-er be Filled with thy maj-es-ty, Till time shall end!
2. Be in each song of praise Which here thy peo-ple raise With hearts a-flame! Let ev-ery an-them rise Like in-cense to the skies, A joy-ful sac-ri-fice, To thy blest name!
3. Speak, O e-ter-nal Lord, Out of thy liv-ing Word, O give suc-cess! Do thou the truth im-part Un-to each wait-ing heart; Source of all strength thou art, Thy gos-pel bless!
4. To the great One in Three Glo-ry and prais-es be In love now given! Glad songs to thee we sing, Glad hearts to thee we bring, Till we our God and King Shall praise in heaven! A-men.

Music copyright 1972 by The Westminster Press.

340 Come, Risen Lord, and Deign to Be Our Guest

SURSUM CORDA (Smith) 10.10.10.10.

George Wallace Briggs, 1931 — Alfred M. Smith, 1941

1. Come, ris-en Lord, and deign to be our guest; Nay, let us be thy guests; the feast is thine; Thy-self at thine own board make man-i-fest In this our Sac-ra-ment of bread and wine.
2. We meet, as in that up-per room they met, Thou at the ta-ble, bless-ing, yet dost stand; "This is my bod-y"; so thou giv-est yet: Faith still re-ceives the cup as from thy hand.
3. One bod-y we, one bod-y who par-take, One church u-nit-ed in com-mu-nion blest; One name we bear, one bread of life we break, With all thy saints on earth and saints at rest.
4. One with each oth-er, Lord, for one in thee, Who art one Sav-ior and one liv-ing Head; Then o-pen thou our eyes, that we may see; Be known to us in break-ing of the bread. A-men.

Words from *Songs of Praise*, Enlarged Edition; used by permission of Oxford University Press. Music used by permission of Alfred M. Smith.

Come, Thou Fount of Every Blessing 341
NETTLETON 8.7.8.7.D.

Robert Robinson, 1758

American folk hymn
Wyeth's *A Repository of Sacred Music*, 2d part, 1813

1. Come, thou fount of ev-ery bless-ing, Tune my heart to sing thy grace;
Streams of mer-cy, nev-er ceas-ing, Call for songs of loud-est praise.
Teach me some me-lo-dious son-net, Sung by flam-ing tongues a-bove;
Praise the mount! I'm fixed up-on it, Mount of God's un-chang-ing love.

2. Je-sus sought me when a stran-ger, Wan-dering from the fold of God:
He, to res-cue me from dan-ger, In-ter-posed his pre-cious blood.
O to grace how great a debt-or Dai-ly I'm con-strained to be!
Let that grace now, like a fet-ter, Bind my wan-dering heart to thee. A-men.

342 Come, Thou Long-expected Jesus
STUTTGART 8.7.8.7.

Charles Wesley, 1744

Psalmodia Sacra, 1715
Adapted in *Hymns Ancient & Modern*, 1861

1. Come, thou long-expected Jesus, Born to set thy people free; From our fears and sins release us; Let us find our rest in thee.
2. Israel's Strength and Consolation, Hope of all the earth thou art; Dear Desire of every nation, Joy of every longing heart.
3. Born thy people to deliver, Born a child, and yet a King, Born to reign in us forever, Now thy gracious kingdom bring.
4. By thine own eternal Spirit Rule in all our hearts alone; By thine all-sufficient merit Raise us to thy glorious throne. Amen.

Alternative Tune: HYFRYDOL

Come to Us, Mighty King

343

TRINITY (ITALIAN HYMN) 6.6.4.6.6.6.4.

Anonymous tract, 1757; alt., 1972

Felice de Giardini, 1769
Arr. by Robert Carwithen, 1972

1. Come to us, mighty King, Help us your name to sing, Help us to praise: Father, all-glorious, O'er all victorious, Come, and reign over us, Ancient of Days.
2. Come now, Incarnate Word, Gird on your mighty sword, Our prayer attend: Come, and your people bless, And give your word success; Spirit of holiness, On us descend.
3. Come, Holy Comforter, Your sacred witness bear In this glad hour: To all your grace impart, Now rule in every heart, And never from us part, Spirit of power.
4. To the great One in Three The highest praises be, For evermore! His sovereign majesty May we in glory see, And to eternity Love and adore. A-men.

Music copyright 1972 by The Westminster Press.

344 Come, You Faithful, Raise the Strain
AVE VIRGO VIRGINUM 7.6.7.6.D.

Attr. to John of Damascus (675?-749?)
Trans. by John Mason Neale, 1859; alt., 1972

Bohemian Brethren Hymnal, 1544
As in *Pilgrim Hymnal*, 1958

1. Come, you faithful, raise the strain Of triumphant gladness;
   God has brought his Israel Into joy from sadness;
   Loosed from Pharaoh's bitter yoke Jacob's sons and daughters;
   Led them with unmoistened foot Through the Red Sea waters.

2. 'Tis the spring of souls today; Christ has burst his prison,
   And from three days' sleep in death As a sun has risen;
   All the winter of our sins, Long and dark, is flying
   From his light, to whom we give Laud and praise undying.

3. Now the queen of seasons, bright With the day of splendor,
   With the royal feast of feasts, Comes its joy to render;
   Comes to glad Jerusalem Who with true affection
   Welcomes in unwearied strains Jesus' resurrection.

4. Neither might the gates of death, Nor the tomb's dark portal,
   Nor the watchers, nor the seal Hold you as a mortal;
   But today amid the twelve You did stand, bestowing
   That your peace which evermore Passes human knowing.

*5. "Alleluia!" now we cry To our King immortal,
   Who, triumphant, burst the bars Of the tomb's dark portal;
   "Alleluia," with the Son God the Father praising;
   "Alleluia!" yet again To the Spirit raising. A-men.

Come, You People, Rise and Sing 345

BOUNDLESS MERCY 7.6.7.6.D.

Cyril A. Alington (1872-1955); alt., 1972

Southern folk hymn
Harm. by Donald D. Kettring, 1965

1. Come, you people, rise and sing Hymns of adoration,
And to heaven's eternal King Offer dedication;
Bring your praise for mercies past, All his love confessing,
And on life, while life shall last, Ask your Father's blessing.

2. Praise we God the Father's name For our world's creation,
And his saving health proclaim Unto every nation;
Till, his name by all confessed, Every heart enthrone him,
And from farthest east and west All his children own him.

3. Praise we God the only Son, Who in mercy sought us;
Born to save a world undone, Out of death he brought us;
Here awhile he showed his love, Suffered uncomplaining,
Now he pleads for us above, Risen, ascended, reigning!

4. Grant us, Holy Ghost, we pray, More and more to know him,
More and more and every day In our lives to show him,
That with hearts by you made brave, Strong and wise and tender,
We, with all the powers we have, Service fit may render. A-men.

Words used by permission of the family of the late Dean Alington. Music copyright 1968 by The Westminster Press.

346. Come, You Thankful People, Come

ST. GEORGE'S, WINDSOR 7.7.7.7.D.

Henry Alford, 1844, 1865; alt., 1972
George J. Elvey, 1859

1. Come, you thankful people, come, Raise the song of harvest home:
All is safely gathered in, Ere the winter storms begin;
God, our maker, does provide For our wants to be supplied:
Come to God's own temple, come, Raise the song of harvest home.

2. All the world is God's own field, Fruit unto his praise to yield;
Wheat and tares together sown, Unto joy or sorrow grown;
First the blade, and then the ear, Then the full corn shall appear:
Lord of harvest, grant that we Wholesome grain and pure may be.

3. For the Lord our God shall come, And shall take his harvest home,
From his field shall in that day All offenses purge away,
Give his angels charge at last In the fire the tares to cast,
But the fruitful ears to store In his garner evermore.

4. Even so, Lord, quickly come To your final harvest home;
Gather all your people in, Free from sorrow, free from sin;
There, forever purified, In your presence to abide:
Come, with all your angels, come, Raise the glorious harvest home. Amen.

Comfort, Comfort You My People

347

PSALM 42 8.7.8.7.7.7.8.8.

Isaiah 40:1-8
Para. by Johannes Olearius, 1671
Trans. by Catherine Winkworth, 1863; alt.

Comp. or adapted by Louis Bourgeois, 1551
As in *Pilgrim Hymnal*, 1958

1. Com-fort, com-fort you my peo-ple, Tell of peace, thus says our God;
2. Hark, the her-ald voice is cry-ing In the des-ert far and near,
3. Make you straight what long was crook-ed, Make the rough-er plac-es plain;

Com-fort those who sit in dark-ness Mourn-ing 'neath their sor-rows' load.
Bid-ding all men to re-pent-ance Since the king-dom now is here.
Let your hearts be true and hum-ble, As be-fits his ho-ly reign.

Speak you to Je-ru-sa-lem Of the peace that waits for them;
Oh, that warn-ing cry o-bey! Now pre-pare for God a way;
For the glo-ry of the Lord Now o'er earth is shed a-broad;

Tell her that her sins I cov-er, And her war-fare now is o-ver.
Let the val-leys rise to meet him And the hills bow down to greet him.
And all flesh shall see the to-ken That his word is nev-er bro-ken. A-men.

348   Creator of the Stars of Night
CONDITOR ALME L.M.

Medieval Latin hymn
Trans. by John Mason Neale, 1851
The Hymnal 1940 version; alt., 1972

Plainsong, Mode IV, Sarum form
Harm. by C. Winfred Douglas, 1940

1. Creator of the stars of night, The people's everlasting light, O Christ, the Savior of us all, We pray now, hear us when we call.
2. At the great name of Jesus, now All knees must bend, all hearts must bow; And things celestial him shall own, And things terrestrial, Lord alone.
3. Come in all holy might, we pray; Redeem us for eternal day From every power of darkness, when Your judgment comes for sons of men.
4. To God the Father, God the Son, And God the Spirit, Three in One, Laud, honor, might, and glory be From age to age eternally. Amen.

Words and music used by permission of The Church Pension Fund.

Crown Him with Many Crowns

349

DIADEMATA S.M.D.

Sts. 1, 2, 4, Matthew Bridges, 1851; alt., 1972
St. 3, Godfrey Thring, 1874

George J. Elvey, 1868; alt.

1. Crown him with many crowns, The Lamb upon his throne;
Hark! how the heavenly anthem drowns All music but its own!
Awake, my soul, and sing Of him who died for you,
And hail him as your matchless King With worship as his due.

2. Crown him the Lord of peace, Whose power a scepter sways
From pole to pole, that wars may cease, Absorbed in prayer and praise.
His reign shall know no end; And round his piercèd feet
Fair flowers of paradise extend Their fragrance ever sweet.

3. Crown him the Lord of life, Who triumphed o'er the grave,
And rose victorious in the strife For those he came to save.
His glories now we sing Who died and rose on high,
Who died, eternal life to bring, And lives that death may die.

4. Crown him the Lord of years, The Potentate of time,
Creator of the rolling spheres, Ineffably sublime.
All hail, Redeemer, hail! For you have died for me;
Your praise shall never, never fail Throughout eternity. A-men.

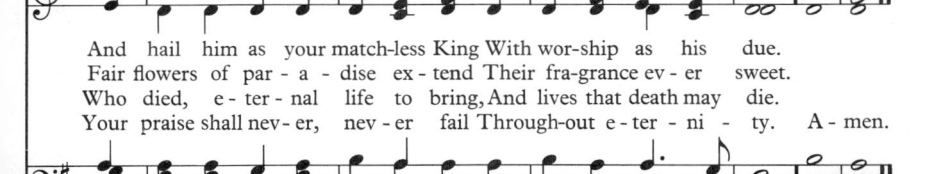

350 Dear Lord and Father of Mankind

REST 8.6.8.8.6.

John Greenleaf Whittier, 1872

Frederick C. Maker, 1887

1. Dear Lord and Father of mankind, Forgive our foolish ways; Reclothe us in our rightful mind, In purer lives thy service find, In deeper reverence, praise.
2. In simple trust like theirs who heard, Beside the Syrian sea, The gracious calling of the Lord, Let us, like them, without a word Rise up and follow thee.
3. O Sabbath rest by Galilee! O calm of hills above, Where Jesus knelt to share with thee The silence of eternity, Interpreted by love!
4. Drop thy still dews of quietness, Till all our strivings cease; Take from our souls the strain and stress, And let our ordered lives confess The beauty of thy peace.
5. Breathe through the heats of our desire Thy coolness and thy balm; Let sense be dumb, let flesh retire; Speak through the earthquake, wind, and fire, O still, small voice of calm! A-men.

Music copyright; used by permission of the Psalms and Hymns Trust.

Deck Yourself, My Soul, with Gladness
SCHMÜCKE DICH L.M.D.

351

Johann Franck, 1649, 1653
Trans. by Catherine Winkworth, 1863; alt.;
and John Caspar Mattes, 1913
Composite alt., 1972

Johann Crüger, 1649
Harm. by J. S. Bach, 1724

1. Deck your-self, my soul, with glad-ness, Leave be-hind all gloom and sad-ness; Come in-to the day-light's splen-dor, There with joy your prais-es ren-der Un-to him whose grace un-bound-
2. Sun, who all my life does bright-en; Light, who does my soul en-light-en; Joy, your won-drous gift be-stow-ing; Fount, from which all good is flow-ing: At your feet I cry, my Mak-
*3. Je-sus, source of life and plea-sure, Tru-est friend and dear-est trea-sure, By your love I am in-vit-ed, Be your love with love re-quit-ed. From this ban-quet let me mea-

See following page.

352 Deck Yourself, My Soul, with Gladness (cont.)

ed Has this won-drous ban-quet found-ed; Come, for now the King most ho-ly Stoops to you in like-ness low-ly.
er, Let me be a fit par-tak-er Of this bless-ed food from heav-en, For our good, your glo-ry, giv-en.
sure, Lord, how vast and deep its trea-sure; Through the gifts that here you give me, As your guest in heaven re-ceive me. A-men.

Descend, O Spirit, Purging Flame

LLEF L.M.

Scott Francis Brenner, 1969

Griffith Hugh Jones, 1890
Arr. by Donald D. Kettring, 1972

1. De-scend, O Spir-it, purg-ing flame, Brand us this day with Jesus' name! Con-firm our faith, con-sume our doubt; Sign us as Christ's, with-in, with-out.
2. Wash us with wa-ter, make us pure; Thrust us in mis-sion to en-dure. Let now your heal-ing wa-ters win New life, new hope, re-lease from sin.
3. For-bid us not this sec-ond birth; Grant un-to us the great-er worth! Con-script us in your serv-ice, Lord; Bap-tize all na-tions with your Word. A-men.

Words and music copyright 1972 by The Westminster Press.

354 Earth and All Stars

Herbert Brokering, 1968
David N. Johnson, 1968

1. Earth and all stars, Loud rushing planets
2. Steel and machines, Loud pounding hammers
3. Class-rooms and labs, Loud boiling test tubes
4. Knowl-edge and truth, Loud sounding wisdom

Sing to the Lord a new song!
Sing to the Lord a new song!
Sing to the Lord a new song!
Sing to the Lord a new song!

Hail, wind, and rain, Loud blowing snowstorm
Lime-stone and beams, Loud building workmen
Ath-lete and band, Loud cheering people
Daugh-ter and son, Loud praying members

Words and music reprinted from *Twelve Folksongs and Spirituals*, compiled and arranged by David N. Johnson, 1968; used by permission of Augsburg Publishing House, Minneapolis, Minnesota, copyright owner.

Earth and All Stars (cont.) 355

Sing to the Lord a new song!
Sing to the Lord a new song!
Sing to the Lord a new song!
Sing to the Lord a new song!

He hath done mar - - - vel - ous things.

I, too, will praise him with a new song! A - men.

356 Eternal Father, Strong to Save
MELITA 8.8.8.8.8.8.

Sts. 1, 4, William Whiting, 1860; alt., 1861, 1937, 1972
Sts. 2, 3, Robert Nelson Spencer, 1937; alt., 1972

John B. Dykes, 1861

1. E-ter-nal Fa-ther, strong to save, Whose arm has bound the rest-less wave, Who bids the might-y o-cean deep Its own ap-point-ed lim-its keep: To you we pray most ear-nest-ly For those in per-il on the sea.

2. O Christ, the Lord of hill and plain O'er which our traf-fic runs a-main By moun-tain pass or val-ley low; Wher-ev-er, Lord, your peo-ple go, Pro-tect them by your guard-ing hand From ev-ery per-il on the land.

3. O Spir-it, whom the Fa-ther sent To spread a-broad the fir-ma-ment; O Wind of heav-en, by your might Save all who dare the ea-gle's flight, And keep them by your watch-ful care From ev-ery per-il in the air.

4. O Trin-i-ty of love and power, Our broth-ers shield in dan-ger's hour; From rock and tem-pest, fire and foe, Pro-tect them where-so-e'er they go; Thus ev-er-more with thanks shall we Give praise from air and land and sea. A-men.

Stanzas 2 and 3 used by permission of The Church Pension Fund.

Eternal God, Whose Power Upholds 357
FOREST GREEN C.M.D.

Henry Hallam Tweedy, 1929; alt., 1972
Traditional English melody, collected and harm. by Ralph Vaughan Williams, 1906

1. E-ter-nal God, whose power up-holds Both flower and flam-ing star, To whom there is no here nor there, No time, no near nor far, No a-lien race, no for-eign shore, No child un-sought, un-known: O send us forth, your proph-ets true, To make all lands your own!

2. O God of truth, whom sci-ence seeks And rev-erent souls a-dore, Il-lu-mine ev-ery ear-nest mind Of ev-ery clime and shore: Dis-pel the gloom of er-ror's night, Of ig-no-rance and fear, Un-til true wis-dom from a-bove Shall make life's path-way clear!

3. O God of beau-ty, oft re-vealed In dreams of hu-man art, In speech that flows to mel-o-dy, In ho-li-ness of heart: Teach us to ban all ug-li-ness, And all dis-har-mo-ny, Till all shall know the love-li-ness Of lives made fair and free!

4. O God of righ-teous-ness and grace, Seen in the Christ, your Son, Whose life and death re-veal your face, By whom your will was done; Help us to spread your gra-cious reign Till greed and hate shall cease, And kind-ness dwell in hu-man hearts, And all the earth find peace! A-men.

Words copyright 1929 by The Hymn Society of America; used by permission. Music from *The English Hymnal*; used by permission of Oxford University Press.

358 Eternal Ruler of the Ceaseless Round
SONG 1 10.10.10.10.10.10.

John W. Chadwick, 1864 — Orlando Gibbons, 1623

1. Eternal Ruler of the ceaseless round Of circling planets singing on their way, Guide of the nations from the night profound Into the glory of the perfect day, Rule in our hearts, that we may ever be Guided and strengthened and upheld by thee.

2. We are of thee, the children of thy love, The brothers of thy well-beloved Son; Descend, O Holy Spirit, like a dove Into our hearts, that we may be as one: As one with thee, to whom we ever tend; As one with him our brother and our friend.

*3. We would be one in hatred of all wrong, One in our love of all things sweet and fair, One with the joy that breaketh into song, One with the grief that trembleth into prayer, One in the power that makes thy children free To follow truth, and thus to follow thee.

4. O clothe us with thy heavenly armor, Lord, Thy trusty shield, thy sword of love divine; Our inspiration be thy constant word; We ask no victories that are not thine; Give or withhold, let pain or pleasure be, Enough to know that we are serving thee. Amen.

Every Star Shall Sing a Carol 359

Sydney Carter, 1961
Arr. by Richard D. Wetzel, 1972

1. Ev - ery star shall sing a car - ol,
2. When the King of all cre - a - tion
3. Who can tell what oth - er cra - dle
4. Who can count how man - y cross - es
5. Who can tell what oth - er bod - y
6. Ev - ery star and ev - ery plan - et,

Ev - ery crea - ture, high or low, Come and praise the
Had a cra - dle on the earth, Ho - ly was the
High a - bove the milk - y way Still may rock the
Still to come or long a - go, Cru - ci - fy the
He will hal - low for his own? I will praise the
Ev - ery crea - ture high and low, Come and praise the

King of heav - en By what - ev - er name you know.
hu - man bod - y, Ho - ly was the hu - man birth.
King of heav - en On an - oth - er Christ - mas Day?
King of heav - en? Ho - ly is the name I know.
son of Mar - y, Broth - er of my blood and bone.
King of heav - en By what - ev - er name you know.

God a - bove, Man be - low, Ho - ly is the name I know.

Words and music © copyright 1961 by Galliard, Ltd. All rights reserved. Reprinted by permission of Galaxy Music Corp., N.Y., sole U.S. agent.

360 Fairest Lord Jesus
CRUSADERS' HYMN 5.6.8.5.5.8.

MS., Münster, 1662; alt.
Sts. 1-3 trans. in *Church Chorals and Choir Studies*, 1850
St. 4 trans. by Joseph A. Seiss, 1873

Silesian folk melody
In *Schlesische Volkslieder*, 1842

1. Fairest Lord Jesus, Ruler of all nature, O thou of God and man the Son, Thee will I cherish, Thee will I honor, Thou, my soul's glory, joy, and crown.
2. Fair are the meadows, Fairer still the woodlands, Robed in the blooming garb of spring: Jesus is fairer, Jesus is purer, Who makes the woeful heart to sing.
3. Fair is the sunshine, Fairer still the moonlight, And all the twinkling, starry host: Jesus shines brighter, Jesus shines purer, Than all the angels heaven can boast.
4. Beautiful Savior, Lord of the nations, Son of God and Son of Man! Glory and honor, Praise, adoration, Now and forevermore be thine! Amen.

Faith of Our Fathers

361

ST. CATHERINE 8.8.8.8.8.8.

Frederick W. Faber, 1849; alt.

Henri F. Hemy, 1864
Refrain, James G. Walton, 1874

1. Faith of our fathers! living still In spite of dungeon, fire, and sword, O how our hearts beat high with joy When-e'er we hear that glorious word: Faith of our fathers, holy faith! We will be true to thee till death. A-men.
2. Faith of our fathers! God's great power Shall win all nations unto thee; And through the truth that comes from God Mankind shall then be truly free:
3. Faith of our fathers! we will love Both friend and foe in all our strife, And preach thee, too, as love knows how, By kindly words and virtuous life:

362 Father Eternal, Ruler of Creation
LANGHAM 11.10.11.10.10.

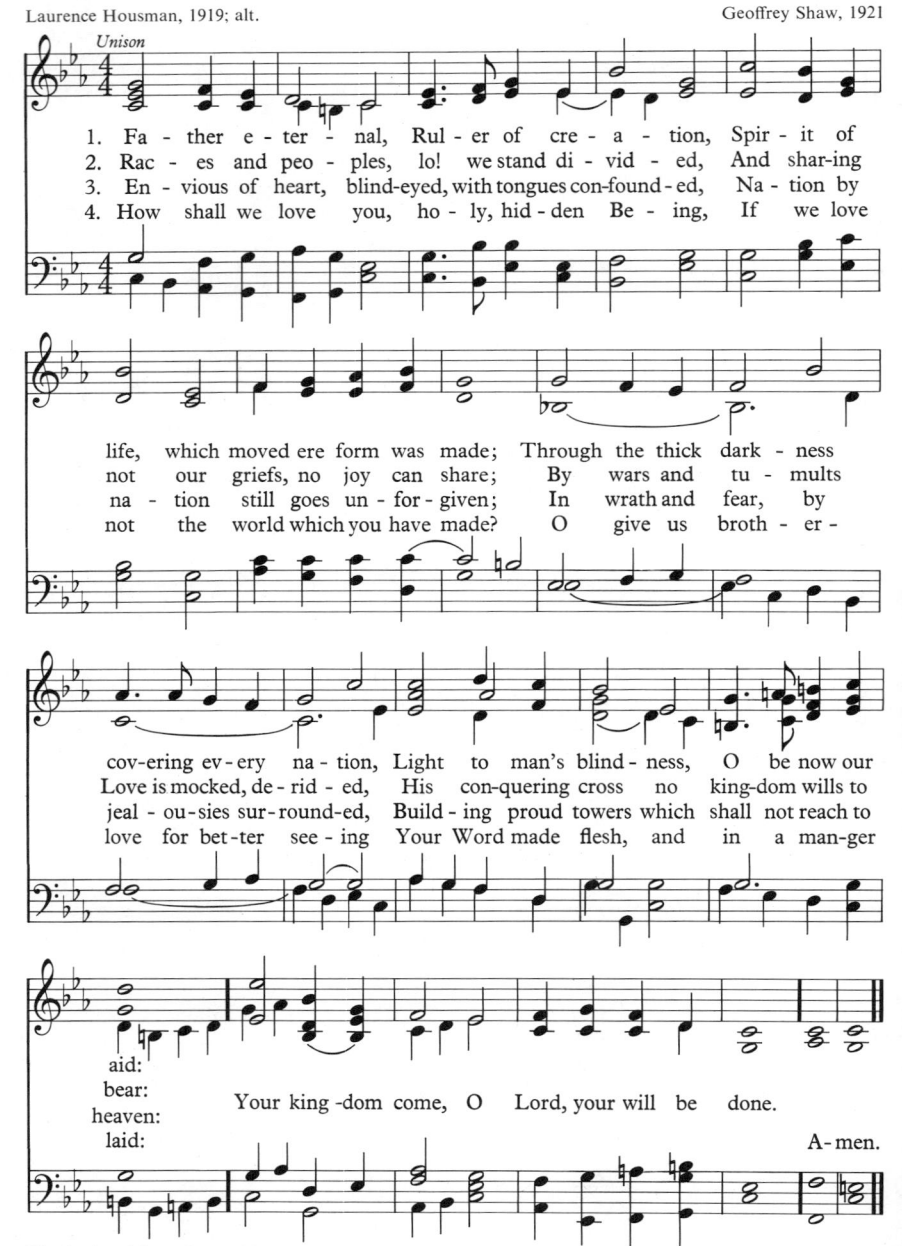

Laurence Housman, 1919; alt.
Geoffrey Shaw, 1921

1. Father eternal, Ruler of creation, Spirit of life, which moved ere form was made; Through the thick darkness covering every nation, Light to man's blindness, O be now our aid: Your kingdom come, O Lord, your will be done.

2. Races and peoples, lo! we stand divided, And sharing not our griefs, no joy can share; By wars and tumults Love is mocked, derided, His conquering cross no kingdom wills to bear: Your kingdom come, O Lord, your will be done.

3. Envious of heart, blind-eyed, with tongues confounded, Nation by nation still goes unforgiven; In wrath and fear, by jealousies surrounded, Building proud towers which shall not reach to heaven: Your kingdom come, O Lord, your will be done.

4. How shall we love you, holy, hidden Being, If we love not the world which you have made? O give us brotherlove for better seeing Your Word made flesh, and in a manger laid: Your kingdom come, O Lord, your will be done.

A-men.

Words altered from *Songs of Praise*, Enlarged Edition; used by permission of Oxford University Press. Music used by permission of the League of Nations Union.

Father, in Your Mysterious Presence 363
DONNE SECOURS 11.10.11.10.

Samuel Johnson, 1846; alt., 1972
Comp. or adapted by Louis Bourgeois, 1551

1. Fa - ther, in your mys - te - rious pres - ence kneel - ing,
   Now would our souls feel all your kin - dling
   love, For we are weak and need some deep re - veal - ing
   Of trust and strength and calm - ness from a - bove.

2. Lord, we have wan - dered forth through doubt and sor - row,
   And you have made each step an on - ward
   one, And we will ev - er trust each un - known mor - row;
   You will sus - tain us till its work is done.

3. Now, Fa - ther, now, in your dear pres - ence kneel - ing,
   Our spir - its yearn to feel your kin - dling
   love; Now make us strong, we need your deep re - veal - ing
   Of trust and strength and calm - ness from a - bove. A - men.

364. Father, We Greet You

DONNE SECOURS 11.10.11.10.

James G. Adderley, 1924; alt., 1972

Comp. or adapted by Louis Bourgeois, 1551

1. Father, we greet you, God of love, whose glory
   Shines mirrored in the face of Jesus
   Christ, Who by his perfect life of love and labor
   And in his perfect death was sacrificed.

2. Father, we dare, by our great Brother bidden,
   Take up the cross and humbly follow
   him: Send out your light and truth that they may lead us;
   Show us the way amid the darkness dim.

3. Here we present ourselves, our souls and bodies,
   Strengthened with bread, the food of every man,
   Ready to love and work, but yet confessing
   Lonely we cannot, by his grace we can.

4. Friends at his table, priests around his altar,
   Soldiers of Christ, disciples of your Son,
   Father, we stand, prepared to do your bidding;
   Come, God's own kingdom, and God's will be done. Amen.

Words used by permission of the author's heir.

Father, We Praise You 365
CHRISTE SANCTORUM 11.11.11.5.

Attr. to Gregory I (540-604)
Trans. by Percy Dearmer, 1906; alt., 1972

Paris Antiphoner, 1681
Harm. by David Evans, 1927

1. Father, we praise you, now the night is over;
   Active and watchful, stand we all before you;
   Singing, we offer prayer and meditation: Thus we adore you.

2. Monarch of all things, fit us for your mansions;
   Banish our weakness, health and wholeness sending;
   Bring us to heaven, where your saints united
   Joy without ending.

3. All-holy Father, Son, and equal Spirit,
   Trinity blessed, send us your salvation;
   Yours is the glory, gleaming and resounding
   Through all creation. Amen.

Words altered from *The English Hymnal*; music from *The Church Hymnary*, Revised Edition, 1927; used by permission of Oxford University Press.

366 Father, We Thank You that You Planted
RENDEZ À DIEU 9.8.9.8.D.

Greek, 1st or 2d century
Para. by F. Bland Tucker, 1939; alt., 1972

Comp. or adapted by Louis Bourgeois, 1543, 1551

1. Father, we thank you that you planted Your holy name within our hearts. Knowledge and faith and life immortal Jesus your Son to us imparts. You, Lord, have made all for your

2. Watch o'er the church, O Lord, in mercy, Save it from evil, guard it still; Perfect it in your love, unite it, Cleansed and conformed unto your will. As grain, once scattered on the

Words used by permission of The Church Pension Fund.

Father, We Thank You that You Planted (cont.) 367

plea - sure And given man food for all his days, Giv - ing in
hill - sides, Was in this bro - ken bread made one, So from all

Christ the Bread e - ter - nal; Yours is the power, be yours the praise.
lands your church be gath - ered In - to your king - dom by your Son. A - men.

368. Father, Whose Will Is Life and Good

NUN DANKET ALL' (GRÄFENBERG) C.M.

Hardwicke D. Rawnsley, 1922; alt.
Crüger's *Praxis Pietatis Melica*, 1653

1. Father, whose will is life and good For all of mortal breath, Bind strong the bond of brotherhood Of those who fight with death.
2. Empower the hands and hearts and wills Of friends both near and far, Who battle with the body's ills And wage your holy war.
3. Where'er they heal the maimed and blind, Let love of Christ attend: Proclaim the good Physician's mind, And prove the Savior friend.
4. O Father, look from heaven and bless What e'er your servants do, Their works of pure unselfishness, Made consecrate to you. Amen.

For All the Saints

369

SINE NOMINE 10.10.10. with Alleluias

William Walsham How, 1864; alt.
Ralph Vaughan Williams, 1906; alt., 1927

Unison (Harmony for stanzas 3, 4, next page)

1. For all the saints who from their la-bors rest, All who by faith be-fore the world con-fessed, Your name, O Je - sus, be for - ev - er blest.
2. You were their rock, their for - tress, and their might; Je - sus, their cap - tain in the well-fought fight; You in the dark - ness drear, their one true Light.
3. O may your sol - diers, faith - ful, true, and bold, Fight as the saints who no - bly fought of old, And win with them the vic - tor's crown of gold.
4. O blest com - mu - nion, fel - low - ship di - vine! We fee - bly strug - gle, they in glo - ry shine; Yet all are one with - in your great de - sign.
5. And when the strife is fierce, the war - fare long, Steals on the ear the dis - tant tri - umph song, And hearts are brave a - gain, and arms are strong.
6. From earth's wide bounds, from o - cean's far - thest coast, Through gates of pearl streams in the count - less host, Sing - ing to Fa - ther, Son, and Ho - ly Ghost,

Music from *The English Hymnal Service Book*;
used by permission of Oxford University Press.

See following page.

370 For All the Saints (cont.)

Al - le - lu - ia! Al - le - lu - ia!

Harmony
A - men.

Harmony, stanzas 3, 4

3. O may your sol-diers, faith-ful, true, and bold, Fight as the saints who no-bly fought of old, And win with them the vic-tor's crown of gold.
4. O blest com-mu-nion, fel-low-ship di-vine! We fee-bly strug-gle, they in glo-ry shine; Yet all are one with-in your great de-sign.

D.C. for stanza 5

Al - le - lu - ia! Al - le - lu - ia!

For Perfect Love So Freely Spent 371
CHESHIRE C.M.

Louise Marshall McDowell, 1965

Este's Psalter, 1592
As in *Songs of Syon*, 1910

1. For perfect love so freely spent, For fellowship restored, We celebrate the sacrament And sing your praise, O Lord.

2. We come, by sin disquieted, And find our lives made whole; Around this table we are fed Refreshment for the soul.

3. Abide with us; in all our ways Your saving love be shown. So may our lives be hymns of praise, O Christ, to you alone. A-men.

Words copyright 1972 by The Westminster Press. Music used by permission of Mrs. J. Meredith Tatton.

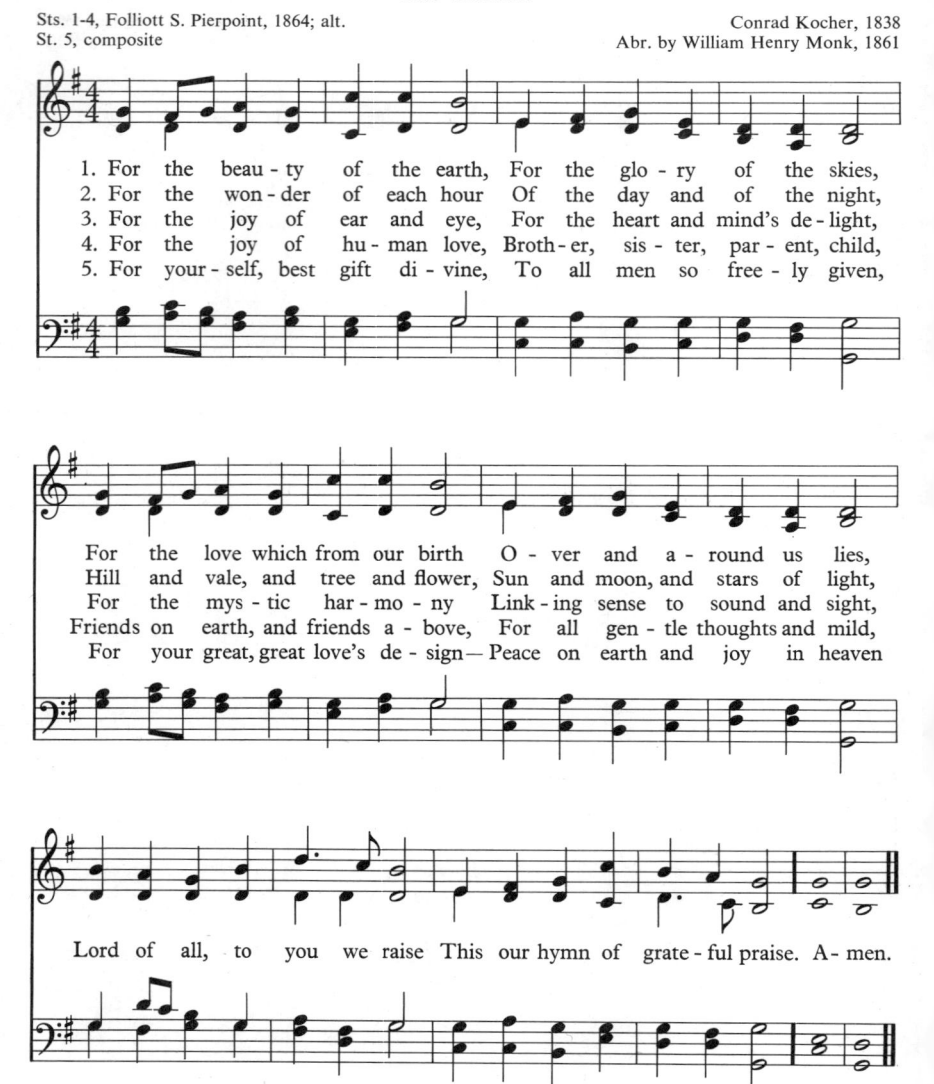

372 For the Beauty of the Earth
DIX 7.7.7.7.7.7.

Sts. 1-4, Folliott S. Pierpoint, 1864; alt.
St. 5, composite

Conrad Kocher, 1838
Abr. by William Henry Monk, 1861

1. For the beau-ty of the earth, For the glo-ry of the skies,
2. For the won-der of each hour Of the day and of the night,
3. For the joy of ear and eye, For the heart and mind's de-light,
4. For the joy of hu-man love, Broth-er, sis-ter, par-ent, child,
5. For your-self, best gift di-vine, To all men so free-ly given,

For the love which from our birth O-ver and a-round us lies,
Hill and vale, and tree and flower, Sun and moon, and stars of light,
For the mys-tic har-mo-ny Link-ing sense to sound and sight,
Friends on earth, and friends a-bove, For all gen-tle thoughts and mild,
For your great, great love's de-sign— Peace on earth and joy in heaven

Lord of all, to you we raise This our hymn of grate-ful praise. A-men.

From All That Dwell Below the Skies 373

LASST UNS ERFREUEN L.M. with Alleluias

Based on Psalm 117
Isaac Watts, 1719

Geistliche Kirchengesäng, Cologne, 1623
Arr. and harm. by Ralph Vaughan Williams, 1906

1. From all that dwell be-low the skies Let the Cre-a-tor's praise a-rise: Al-le-lu-ia! Al-le-lu-ia! Let the Re-deem-er's name be sung Through ev-ery land, in ev-ery tongue. Al-le-lu-ia! Al-le-lu-ia! Al-le-lu-ia! Al-le-lu-ia! A-men.
2. In ev-ery land be-gin the song, To ev-ery land the strains be-long: Al-le-lu-ia! Al-le-lu-ia! In cheer-ful sound all voic-es raise And fill the world with joy-ful praise.
3. E-ter-nal are your mer-cies, Lord; E-ter-nal truth at-tends your word: Al-le-lu-ia! Al-le-lu-ia! Your praise shall sound from shore to shore, Till suns shall rise and set no more.

Music from *The English Hymnal*;
used by permission of Oxford University Press.

For higher key, see "All Creatures of Our God and King."

374 From Shepherding of Stars
SHEPHERDING C.M.

F. Samuel Janzow, 1963
Richard Hillert, 1963

1. From shep-herd-ing of stars that gaze Toward heav-enly fields of light, I come with ti-dings to a-maze You watch-ers in the night, You watch-ers in the night.
2. Your Shep-herd-King from star-lit hall Bends down to wea-ry lands, Lies man-gered low in cat-tle stall. Go touch his in-fant hands, Go touch his in-fant hands.
3. This night your King brings from a-far The Vir-gin's lull-a-by, The Wise Men's faith, a guid-ing star, And love from God most high, And love from God most high.
4. He shep-herds from the this-tled place The flock by thick-ets torn, His pierc-ed hand heals all your race— Sore wound-ed by the thorn, Sore wound-ed by the thorn.
5. Cra-dle the Christ-child, and with songs Bind up the hearts of men: To Shep-herd-Heal-er-King let throngs Sing glo-ri-as a-gain, Sing glo-ri-as a-gain.

Words and music copyright 1963, 1967 by Concordia Publishing House; from *A New Song*; used by permission.

Gentle Mary Laid Her Child 375
TEMPUS ADEST FLORIDUM 7.6.7.6.D.

Joseph Simpson Cook, 1919

Piae Cantiones, 1582
Harm. by Ernest MacMillan, 1930

1. Gentle Mary laid her child Lowly in a manger;
   There he lay, the undefiled, To the world a stranger.
   Such a babe in such a place, Can he be the Savior?
   Ask the saved of all the race Who have found his favor.

2. Angels sang about his birth; Wise Men sought and found him;
   Heaven's star shone brightly forth, Glory all around him.
   Shepherds saw the won-drous sight, Heard the angels singing;
   All the plains were lit that night; All the hills were ringing.

3. Gentle Mary laid her child Lowly in a manger;
   He is still the undefiled, But no more a stranger.
   Son of God, of humble birth, Beautiful the story;
   Praise his name in all the earth; Hail the King of glory! A-men.

Words copyright © 1956, 1958, by Gordon V. Thompson, Ltd., Toronto, Canada; International Copyright secured; used by permission of Carl Fischer, Inc., U.S.A., agents on behalf of Alta Lind Cook and Gordon V. Thompson, Ltd. Music used by permission of Ernest MacMillan.

376 Give to Our God Immortal Praise
ELTON L.M.

Isaac Watts, 1719 — Lowell Mason, 1854

1. Give to our God immortal praise; Mercy and truth are all his ways; Wonders of grace to God belong, Repeat his mercies in your song. Amen.
2. He built the earth, he spread the sky, And fixed the starry lights on high; Wonders of grace to God belong, Repeat his mercies in your song. Amen.
3. He sent his Son with power to save From guilt and darkness and the grave; Wonders of grace to God belong, Repeat his mercies in your song. Amen.

Give to the Winds Your Fears
ST. BRIDE S.M.

377

Paul Gerhardt, 1653
Trans. by John Wesley, 1739; alt.

Samuel Howard, 1762

1. Give to the winds your fears; In hope be un-dis-mayed: God hears your sighs and counts your tears, God shall lift up your head.
2. To him com-mit your griefs; Your ways put in his hands— To his sure truth and ten-der care Who earth and heaven com-mands.
3. O put your trust in God; In du-ty's path go on. Walk in his strength with faith and hope, So shall your work be done.
4. Leave to his sov-ereign sway To choose and to com-mand; So you shall, faith-ful, seek his way— How wise, how strong his hand! A-men.

378 Glorious Is Your Name, Most Holy

AUSTRIAN HYMN 8.7.8.7.D.

Ruth Elliot, 1960; alt., 1972
Franz Joseph Haydn, 1797

1. Glorious is your name, Most Holy, God and Father of us all;
We, your servants, bow before you, Strive to answer every call.
You with life's great good have blest us, Cared for us from earliest years;
Unto you our thanks we render; Your deep love o'ercomes all fears.

2. For our world of need and anguish We would lift to you our prayer.
Faithful stewards of your bounty, May we with our brothers share.
In the name of Christ our Savior, Who redeems and sets us free,
Gifts we bring of heart and treasure, That our lives may worthier be.

3. In the midst of time we journey; From your hand comes each new day:
We would use it in your service, Humbly, wisely, while we may.
So to you, Lord and Creator, Praise and honor we accord!
Yours the earth and yours the heavens, Through all time the eternal Word. A-men.

Words copyright 1961 by The Hymn Society of America; altered from *Ten New Stewardship Hymns*; used by permission.

Glorious Things of You Are Spoken 379
AUSTRIAN HYMN 8.7.8.7.D.

John Newton, 1779; alt., 1972
Franz Joseph Haydn, 1797

1. Glo-rious things of you are spo-ken, Zi-on, cit-y of our God;
2. See, the streams of liv-ing wa-ters, Spring-ing from e-ter-nal Love,
3. Round each hab-i-ta-tion hov-ering, See the cloud and fire ap-pear

He whose word can-not be bro-ken Formed you for his own a-bode.
Well sup-ply your sons and daugh-ters, And all fears of want re-move:
For a glo-ry and a cov-ering, Show-ing that the Lord is near:

On the Rock of Ag-es found-ed, What can shake your sure re-pose?
Who can faint, while such a riv-er Flows their thirst to sat-is-fy?
Thus de-riv-ing from their ban-ner Light by night and shade by day,

With sal-va-tion's walls sur-round-ed, You may smile at all your foes.
Grace, which, like the Lord the giv-er, Nev-er fails; he does sup-ply.
Safe they feed up-on the man-na Which he gives them when they pray. A-men.

380. Go, Tell It on the Mountain

GO TELL IT P.M.

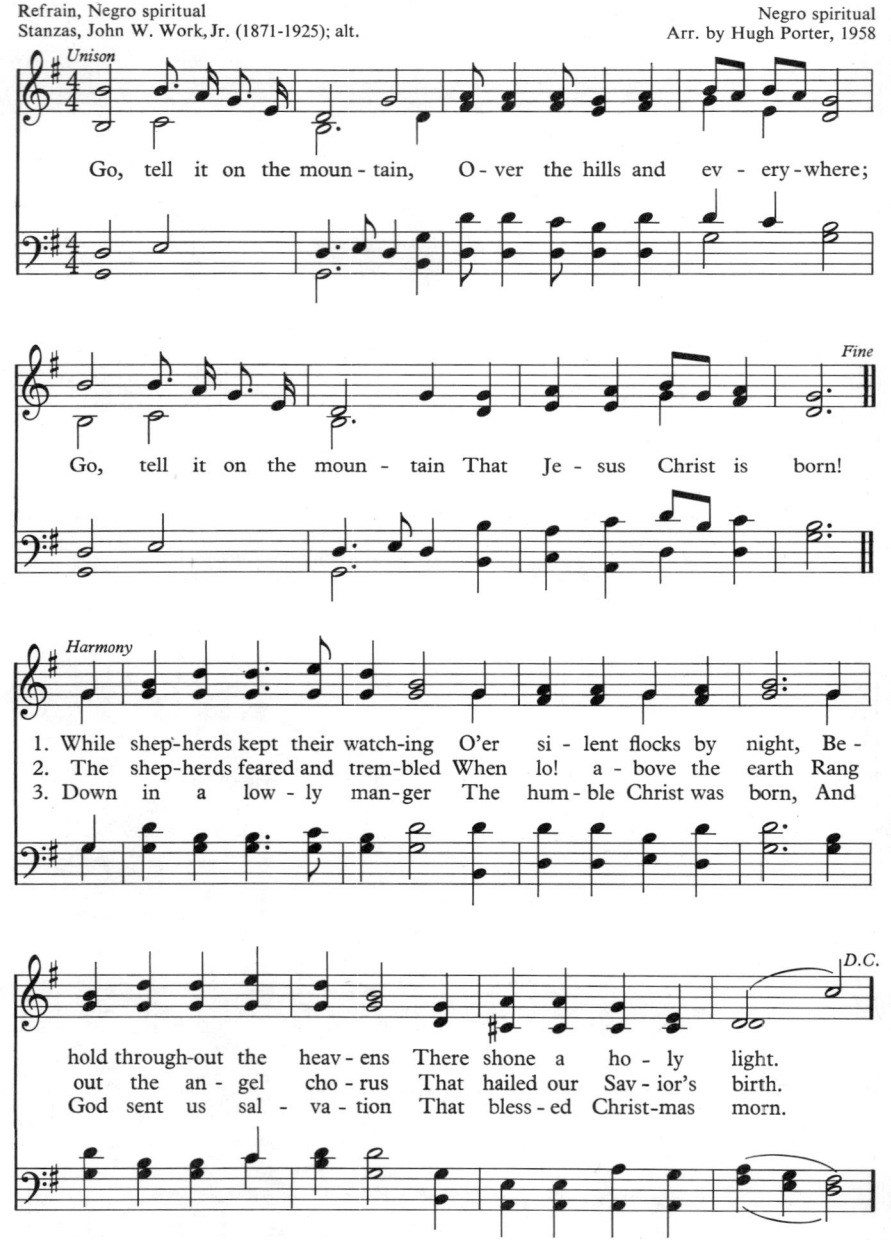

Refrain, Negro spiritual
Stanzas, John W. Work, Jr. (1871-1925); alt.

Negro spiritual
Arr. by Hugh Porter, 1958

Go, tell it on the mountain, O-ver the hills and ev-erywhere;

Go, tell it on the mountain That Jesus Christ is born!

1. While shepherds kept their watching O'er silent flocks by night, Behold through-out the heavens There shone a holy light.
2. The shepherds feared and trembled When lo! above the earth Rang out the angel chorus That hailed our Savior's birth.
3. Down in a lowly manger The humble Christ was born, And God sent us salvation That blessed Christmas morn.

Words and music altered from *American Negro Songs and Spirituals*, by John W. Work III, copyright 1940 by John W. Work III; used by permission.

God Gives His People Strength   381

Miriam Therese Winter, 1965
Arr. by Richard D. Wetzel, 1972

Miriam Therese Winter, 1965

Unison

1. God gives his peo-ple strength. If we be-lieve in his way, He's swift to re-pay All those who bear the bur-den of the day. God gives his peo-ple strength.
2. God gives his peo-ple hope. If we but trust in his word, Our prayers are al-ways heard. He warm-ly wel-comes an-y-one who's erred. God gives his peo-ple hope.
3. God gives his peo-ple love. If we but o-pen wide our heart, He's sure to do his part; He's al-ways the first to make a start. God gives his peo-ple love.
4. God gives his peo-ple peace. When sor-row fills us to the brim, And cour-age grows dim, He lays to rest our rest-less-ness in him. God gives his peo-ple peace.

Words and music © MCMLXV by Medical Mission Sisters, Philadelphia, Pa. Sole selling agent Vanguard Music Corp., 250 W. 57th St., New York, N.Y. 10019. All rights reserved. Permission to reprint granted by Vanguard Music Corp. Arrangement copyright 1972 by The Westminster Press.

382 God Has Spoken—by His Prophets

EBENEZER (TON-Y-BOTEL) 8.7.8.7.D.

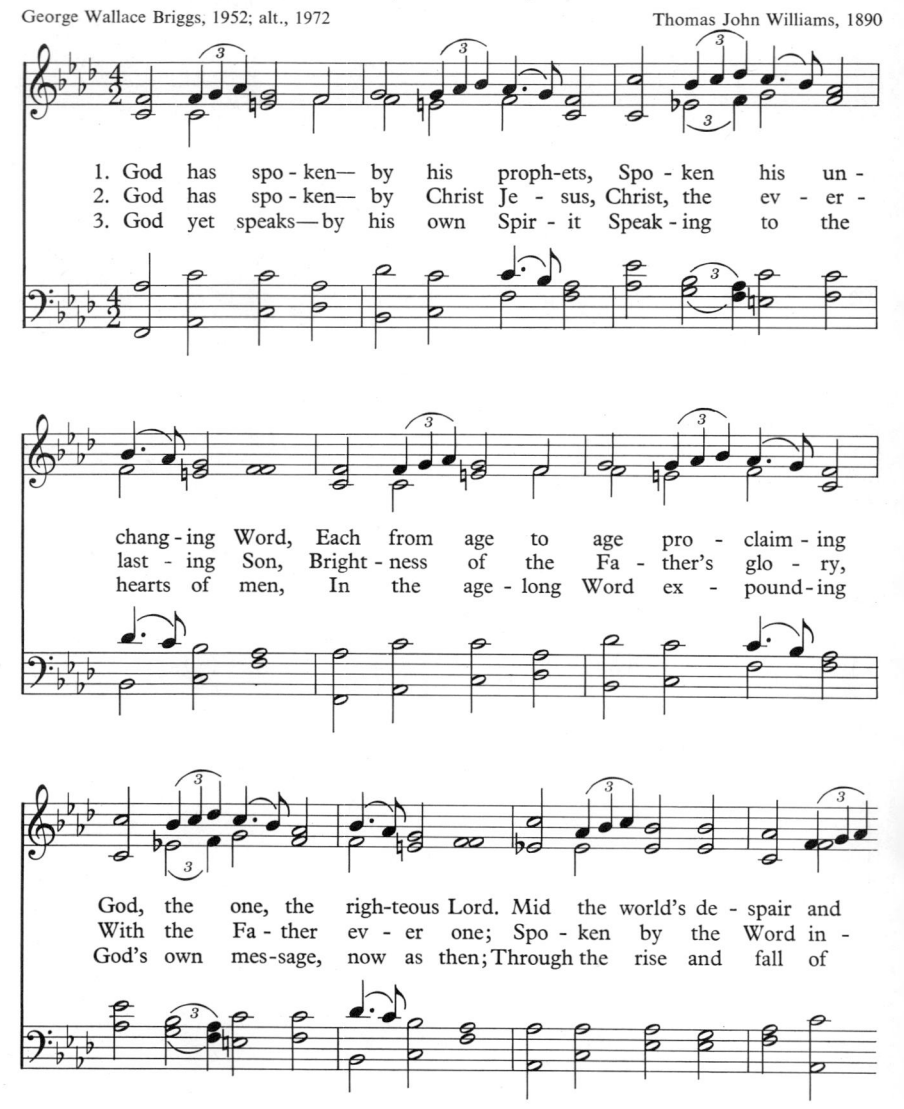

George Wallace Briggs, 1952; alt., 1972　　　　　　　　　　　　　　　Thomas John Williams, 1890

1. God has spo-ken— by his proph-ets, Spo-ken his un-chang-ing Word, Each from age to age pro-claim-ing God, the one, the right-teous Lord. Mid the world's de-spair and
2. God has spo-ken— by Christ Je-sus, Christ, the ev-er-last-ing Son, Bright-ness of the Fa-ther's glo-ry, With the Fa-ther ev-er one; Spo-ken by the Word in-
3. God yet speaks— by his own Spir-it Speak-ing to the hearts of men, In the age-long Word ex-pound-ing God's own mes-sage, now as then;Through the rise and fall of

Words copyright 1953 by The Hymn Society of America; altered from *Ten New Hymns on the Bible*; used by permission.
Music copyright by Gwenlyn Evans, Ltd.; used by permission.

God Has Spoken—by His Prophets (cont.) 383

tur - moil, One firm an - chor hold - ing fast; God is King, his throne e - ter - nal, God the first, and God the last.
car - nate, God of God, ere time be - gan, Light of Light, to earth de - scend-ing, Man, re - veal - ing God to man.
na - tions One sure faith yet stand - ing fast, God is King, his Word un - chang-ing, God the first, and God the last. A - men.

384 God Himself Is with Us
ARNSBERG P.M.

Gerhard Tersteegen, 1729
Trans. composite, as in *The Hymnal*, 1941; alt., 1972

Attr. to Joachim Neander, 1680
Harm. by David Evans, 1927

1. God himself is with us: Let us now adore him
   And with awe appear before him. God is in his
   temple, All within keep silence, And before him

2. God himself is with us: Whom angelic legions
   Serve with awe in heavenly regions. "Holy, Holy,
   Holy," Sing the hosts of heaven, Praise to God be

3. Lord, come dwell within us, While on earth we tarry;
   Make us your blest sanctuary. Grant us now your
   presence, Unto us draw nearer, And reveal your-

Music from *The Church Hymnary*, Revised Edition, 1927; used by permission of Oxford University Press.

God Himself Is with Us (cont.) — 385

bow with rev - erence. Him a - lone, God we own;
ev - er giv - en. O give ear To us here:
self still clear - er. Where we are, Near or far,

To our Lord and Sav - ior Prais - es sing for - ev - er.
Hear, O Christ, the prais - es That your church now rais - es.
Let us see your pow - er, Ev - ery day and hour. A-men.

386 God Is Love: Let Heaven Adore Him

ABBOT'S LEIGH 8.7.8.7.D.

Timothy Rees (1874-1939); alt.
Cyril V. Taylor, 1951

1. God is love: let heaven adore him; God is love: let earth rejoice; Let creation sing before him, And exalt him with one voice. He who laid the
2. God is love: he is enfolding All the world in one embrace; With unfailing grasp he's holding Every child of every race. And when human
3. God is love: and though with blindness Sin afflicts the souls of men, God's eternal lovingkindness Holds and guides them even then. Sin and death and

Words altered from *Sermons and Hymns*, by Timothy Rees; used by permission of A. R. Mowbray & Co. Limited. Music from *The BBC Hymn Book*; used by permission of Oxford University Press.

God Is Love: Let Heaven Adore Him (cont.) 387

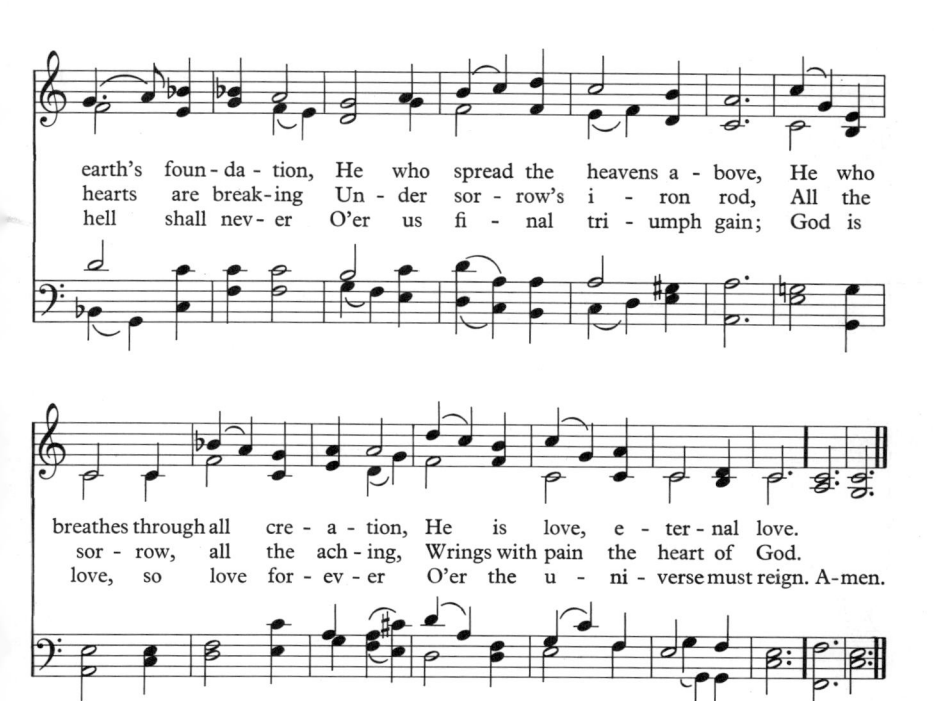

earth's foun-da-tion, He who spread the heavens a-bove, He who
hearts are break-ing Un-der sor-row's i-ron rod, All the
hell shall nev-er O'er us fi-nal tri-umph gain; God is

breathes through all cre-a-tion, He is love, e-ter-nal love.
sor-row, all the ach-ing, Wrings with pain the heart of God.
love, so love for-ev-er O'er the u-ni-verse must reign. A-men.

388 God Is Our Strong Salvation

WEDLOCK 7.6.7.6.D.

From Psalm 27
Para. by James Montgomery, 1822; alt., 1972

Folk song melody
Collected by Cecil J. Sharp, 1918
Harm. by Richard D. Wetzel, 1972

1. God is our strong sal-va-tion; What foe have we to fear?
In dark-ness and temp-ta-tion Our light, our help is near.
Though hosts en-camp a-round us, Firm to the fight we stand;
What ter-ror can con-found us, With God at our right hand?

2. Place on the Lord re-li-ance; Have faith, with cour-age wait;
His truth be your af-fi-ance, When faint and des-o-late.
His might your heart shall strength-en, His love your joy in-crease;
Your days shall mer-cy length-en; The Lord will give you peace. A-men.

Melody from *English Folk Songs from the Southern Appalachians*; used by permission of Oxford University Press. Harmonization copyright 1972 by The Westminster Press.

God Is Working His Purpose Out

PURPOSE Irregular

Arthur Campbell Ainger, 1894
Martin Shaw, 1931

1. God is work-ing his pur-pose out As year suc-ceeds to year: God is work-ing his pur-pose out, And the time is draw-ing near; Near-er and near-er draws the time, The time that shall sure-ly be,
2. What can we do to work God's work, To pros-per and in-crease The broth-er-hood of all man-kind, The reign of the Prince of Peace? What can we do to has-ten the time, The time that shall sure-ly be,
3. March we forth in the strength of God, With the ban-ner of Christ un-furled, That the light of the glo-rious gos-pel of truth May shine through-out the world: Fight we the fight with sor-row and sin To set their cap-tives free,
4. All we can do is noth-ing worth Un-less God bless-es the deed; Vain-ly we hope for the har-vest-tide Till God gives life to the seed; Yet near-er and near-er draws the time, The time that shall sure-ly be,

Octaves to the end

Music from *Songs of Praise*, Enlarged Edition; used by permission of Oxford University Press.   *See following page.*

390 God Is Working His Purpose Out (cont.)

When the earth shall be filled with the glo-ry of God
When the earth shall be filled with the glo-ry of God
That the earth shall be filled with the glo-ry of God
When the earth shall be filled with the glo-ry of God

As the wa-ters cov-er the sea.
As the wa-ters cov-er the sea.
As the wa-ters cov-er the sea.
As the wa-ters cov-er the sea. A-men.

God Moves in a Mysterious Way   391
DUNDEE (FRENCH) C.M.

William Cowper, 1774; alt., 1972
Scottish Psalter, 1615

1. God moves in a mys-te-rious way His wonders to per-form; He plants his foot-steps in the sea, And rides up-on the storm.
2. Deep in un-fath-om-a-ble mines Of nev-er-fail-ing skill He trea-sures up his bright de-signs, And works his sov-ereign will.
3. You fear-ful saints, fresh cour-age take; The clouds you so much dread Are big with mer-cy, and shall break In bless-ings on your head.
4. Blind un-be-lief is sure to err, And scan his work in vain; God is his own In-ter-pret-er, And he will make it plain. A-men.

392 God of Compassion, in Mercy Befriend Us
O QUANTA QUALIA 11.11.11.11.

John J. Moment, 1933(?); alt., 1972

Paris Antiphoner, 1681
Harm. by David Evans, 1927

1. God of compassion, in mercy befriend us;
   Giver of grace for our needs all-availing.
   Wisdom and strength for each day you will send us,
   Patience untiring and courage unfailing.

2. Wandering and lost, you have sought us and found us,
   Stilled our rude hearts with your word of consoling;
   Wrap now your peace, like a mantle, around us,
   Guarding our thoughts and our passions controlling.

3. How shall we stray, with the hand to direct us
   That all the stars in their courses is guiding?
   What shall we fear, with your power to protect us,
   We who walk forth in your greatness confiding? A-men.

Music from *The Church Hymnary*, Revised Edition, 1927; used by permission of Oxford University Press.

God of Grace and God of Glory

393

CWM RHONDDA 8.7.8.7.8.7.

Harry Emerson Fosdick, 1930; alt., 1972

John Hughes, 1907

1. God of grace and God of glory, On your people pour your power; Crown the ancient church's story; Bring her bud to glorious flower. Grant us wisdom, grant us courage, For the facing of this hour, For the facing of this hour.

2. Lo! the hosts of evil round us Scorn the Christ, assail his ways! From the fears that long have bound us, Free our hearts to faith and praise. Grant us wisdom, grant us courage, For the living of these days, For the living of these days.

3. Cure your children's warring madness, Bend our pride to your control; Shame our wanton, selfish gladness, Rich in things and poor in soul. Grant us wisdom, grant us courage, Lest we miss the kingdom's goal, Lest we miss the kingdom's goal.

4. Save us from weak resignation To the evils we deplore; Let the search for your salvation Be our glory evermore. Grant us wisdom, grant us courage, Serving God whom we adore, Serving God whom we adore. A-men.

Words used by permission of Elinor F. Downs. Music © by Mrs. Dilys Webb, c/o Mechanical-Copyright Protection Society Ltd., and reproduced by permission of the legal representatives of the composer who reserve all rights therein.

394 God of Our Fathers, Whose Almighty Hand

NATIONAL HYMN 10.10.10.10.

Daniel C. Roberts, 1876 — George William Warren, 1892

Trumpets (with each stanza)

1. God of our fathers, whose almighty hand
Leads forth in beauty all the starry band
Of shining worlds in splendor through the skies,
Our grateful songs before thy throne arise.

2. Thy love divine hath led us in the past;
In this free land by thee our lot is cast;
Be thou our ruler, guardian, guide, and stay;
Thy word our law, thy paths our chosen way.

3. From war's alarms, from deadly pestilence,
Be thy strong arm our ever sure defense;
Thy true religion in our hearts increase;
Thy bounteous goodness nourish us in peace.

4. Refresh thy people on their toilsome way,
Lead us from night to never-ending day;
Fill all our lives with love and grace divine,
And glory, laud, and praise be ever thine. A-men.

God of Our Life, Through All the Circling Years 395
WITMER 10.4.10.4.10.10.

Hugh T. Kerr, 1916; alt., 1928, 1972

Richard D. Wetzel, 1969

1. God of our life, through all the cir-cling years, We trust in you;
In all the past, through all our hopes and fears, Your hand we view.
With each new day, when morn-ing lifts the veil,
We own your mer-cies, Lord, which nev-er fail.

2. God of the past, our times are in your hand; With us a-bide.
Lead us by faith to hope's true Prom-ised Land; Be now our guide.
With you to bless, the dark-ness shines as light,
And faith's fair vi-sion chang-es in-to sight.

3. God of the com-ing years, through paths un-known We fol-low you;
When we are strong, Lord, leave us not a-lone; Our faith re-new.
Be now for us in life our dai-ly bread,
Our heart's true home when all our years have sped. A-men.

Words from *The Church School Hymnal for Youth,* copyright 1928; renewed 1956 by Board of Christian Education of the Presbyterian Church in the U.S.A. Music copyright 1972 by The Westminster Press.

396. God of the Ages, by Whose Hand

GOD OF THE AGES L.M.

Elisabeth Burrowes, 1956, 1971
David N. Johnson, 1964

1. God of the ag-es, by whose hand Through years long past our lives were led, Give us new cour-age now to stand, New faith to find the paths a-head.
2. You are the thought be-yond all thought, The gift be-yond our ut-most prayer; No far-thest reach where you are not, No height but we may find you there.
3. Lift up our hearts and set us free From wild a-larms and trem-bling fears; In your strong hand e-ter-nal-ly Rests the un-fold-ing of the years.
4. Though there be dark, un-chart-ed space With worlds on worlds be-yond our sight, Still may we trust your love and grace And wait your word, "Let there be light." A-men.

Words copyright 1958 by The Hymn Society of America; revised from *Twelve New World Order Hymns*; used by permission. Music reprinted from *Instruction Book for Beginning Organist*, by David N. Johnson, 1964; used by permission of Augsburg Publishing House, Minneapolis, Minnesota, copyright owner.

God of the Living, in Whose Eyes 397

GOTTLOB, ES GEHT 8.8.8.8.8.8.

John Ellerton, 1859, 1862; alt., 1972
Comp. or arr. by J. S. Bach, 1769
As in *The Harvard University Hymn Book*, 1926

1. God of the liv-ing, in whose eyes Un-veiled your whole cre-a-tion lies, All souls are yours; we must not say That those are dead who pass a-way; From this our world of flesh set free, We know they live e-ter-nal-ly.

2. Re-leased from earth-ly toil and strife, With you is hid-den still their life; Yours are their thoughts, their works, their powers, All yours, and yet most tru-ly ours, For well we know, wher-e'er they be, Our dead now live e-ter-nal-ly.

3. Your word is true, your will is just; To you we leave them, Lord, in trust, And bless you for the love which gave Your Son to fill a hu-man grave, That none might fear that world to see Where all do live e-ter-nal-ly. A-men.

Music from *The Harvard University Hymn Book*; copyright 1926 by Harvard University Press, renewed 1954 by Archibald T. Davison; used by permission.

398 God of the Prophets! Bless the Prophets' Sons
TOULON 10.10.10.10.

Denis Wortman, 1884; alt.

Comp. or adapted by Louis Bourgeois, 1551
Abr. in English Psalters

1. God of the prophets! Bless the prophets' sons,
   Elijah's mantle o'er Elisha cast;
   Each age its solemn task may claim but once;
   Make each one nobler, stronger, than the last.

2. Anoint them prophets! Make their ears attent
   To your divinest speech; their hearts awake
   To human need; their lips make eloquent
   To gird the right and every evil break.

3. Anoint them priests! Strong intercessors they
   For pardon, and for charity and peace!
   O that with them might pass the world, astray,
   Into the dear Christ's life of sacrifice!

4. Make them apostles! Heralds of the cross,
   Forth may they go to tell all realms your grace;
   Inspired of God, may they count all but loss,
   And stand at last with joy before your face. A-men.

God Our Father, You Our Maker 399

BAKER 8.9.8.9.D.

Robert W. McClellan, 1950, 1969
Mary Elizabeth Caldwell, 1950, 1969

1. God our Father, you our Maker, We your people heed your sov-ereign call; Bow before you, paying homage, Owning you alone as Lord of all. May your wisdom be our portion,
2. Christ our Leader, Lord and Savior, You the only Way and Truth and Life; Make your presence known among us, Giving peace to each and settling strife. May we learn from you our Teacher,
3. Holy Spirit, good companion, You the loving Guide the Father sends; Gently urge us; ever stir us To uphold the Truth toward holy ends. Light of God, dispel our darkness,
4. Church of Jesus, church with vision, Built with living faith and hope to stand; May your people, now rejoicing, Raise your song of praise throughout the land. May your walls be strong and sturdy;

Words and music copyright 1951 by Robert W. McClellan and Mary Elizabeth Caldwell; used by permission.

See following page.

400 God Our Father, You Our Maker (cont.)

And with-in our hearts your love in-still.
God-ly du-ty as your love de-mands.
And to wait-ing hearts make par-don known.
And your tow-er point to God on high.

Lead us for-ward, ev-er up-ward.
Live with-in us, gra-cious Mas-ter;
Grant your com-fort, now be-friend us;
Let these sym-bols, ev-er pres-ent,

Give us grace to do your ho-ly will.
Grant us strength to fol-low your com-mands.
Then shall qui-et cour-age be our own.
Help us know that God is al-ways nigh. A-men.

God Rest You Merry, Gentlemen   401

GOD REST YOU MERRY Irregular with Refrain

English carol, 18th century

English carol, 18th century
Harm. by John Stainer, 1871

May be sung in unison

1. God rest you mer-ry, gen-tle-men, Let noth-ing you dis-may;
2. From God, our heav-enly Fa-ther, A bless-ed an-gel came;
3. "Fear not, then," said the an-gel, "Let noth-ing you af-fright;
4. Now to the Lord sing prais-es, All you with-in this place,

Re-mem-ber Christ, our Sav-ior, Was born on Christ-mas Day,
And un-to cer-tain shep-herds Brought ti-dings of the same:
This day is born a Sav-ior, Of a pure vir-gin bright,
And with true love and broth-er-hood Each oth-er now em-brace;

To save us all from Sa-tan's power When we were gone a-stray.
How that in Beth-le-hem was born The Son of God by name.
To free all those who trust in him From Sa-tan's power and might."
This ho-ly tide of Christ-mas Doth bring re-deem-ing grace.

See following page.

God Rest You Merry, Gentlemen (cont.)

O tidings of comfort and joy, comfort and joy;
O tidings of comfort and joy! A-men.

God, the Lord, a King Remaineth 403
BRYN CALFARIA 8.7.8.7.4.7.

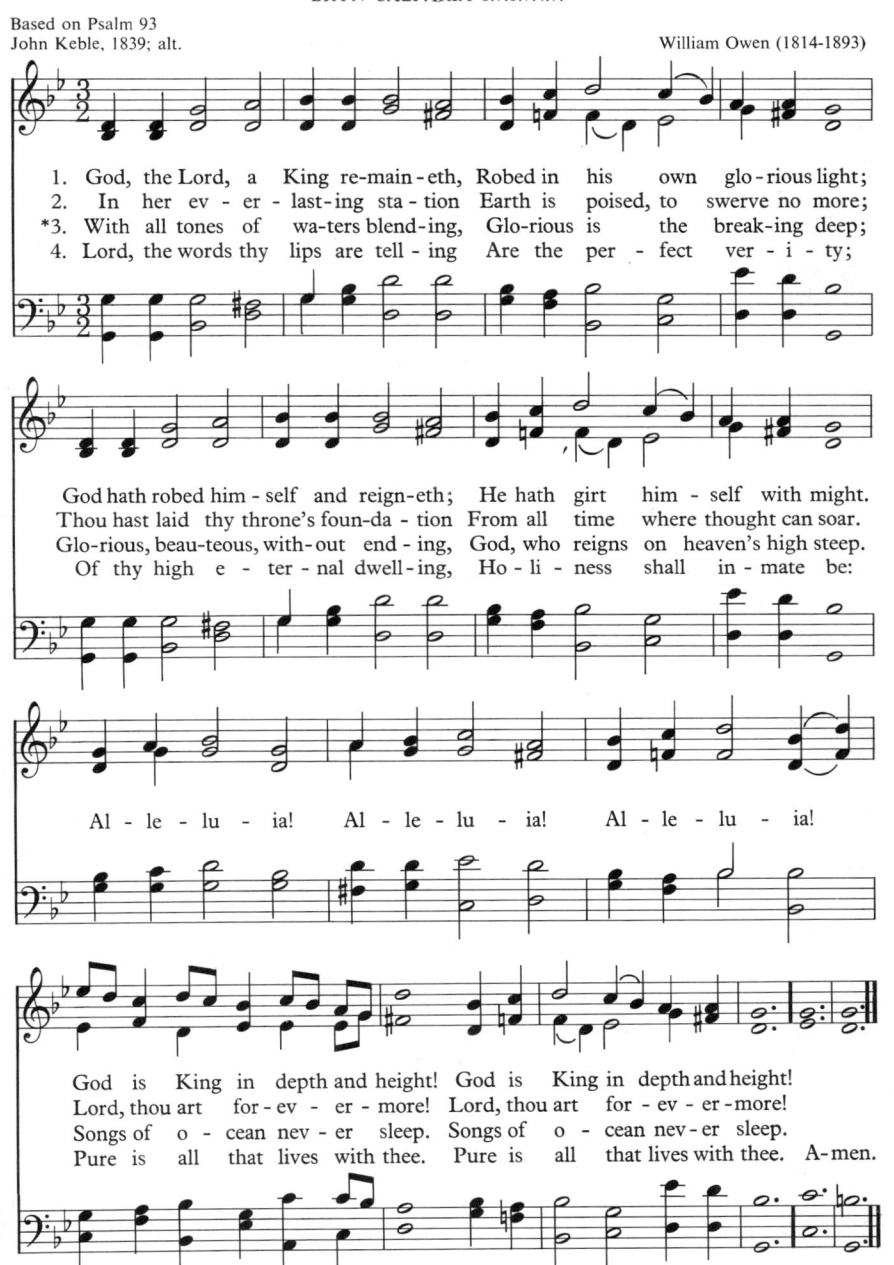

Based on Psalm 93
John Keble, 1839; alt.

William Owen (1814-1893)

1. God, the Lord, a King re-main-eth, Robed in his own glo-rious light;
2. In her ev-er-last-ing sta-tion Earth is poised, to swerve no more;
*3. With all tones of wa-ters blend-ing, Glo-rious is the break-ing deep;
4. Lord, the words thy lips are tell-ing Are the per-fect ver-i-ty;

God hath robed him-self and reign-eth; He hath girt him-self with might.
Thou hast laid thy throne's foun-da-tion From all time where thought can soar.
Glo-rious, beau-teous, with-out end-ing, God, who reigns on heaven's high steep.
Of thy high e-ter-nal dwell-ing, Ho-li-ness shall in-mate be:

Al-le-lu-ia! Al-le-lu-ia! Al-le-lu-ia!

God is King in depth and height! God is King in depth and height!
Lord, thou art for-ev-er-more! Lord, thou art for-ev-er-more!
Songs of o-cean nev-er sleep. Songs of o-cean nev-er sleep.
Pure is all that lives with thee. Pure is all that lives with thee. A-men.

404 God, Who Made the Earth and Heaven
AR HYD Y NOS 8.4.8.4.8.8.8.4.

St. 1, Reginald Heber, 1827; alt., 1972
St. 2, Frederick Lucian Hosmer, 1912; alt., 1972

Traditional Welsh melody
Harm. attr. to L. O. Emerson, 1906

1. God, who made the earth and heav-en, Dark-ness and light,
2. When the con-stant sun re-turn-ing Un-seals our eyes,

Who the day for toil has giv-en, For rest the night,
May we, re-born like the morn-ing, To la-bor rise;

May your lov-ing care de-fend us, Slum-ber sweet your mer-cy send us;
Gird us for the tasks that call us, Let not ease and self en-thrall us.

Ho-ly dreams and hopes at-tend us, This live-long night.
Make us strong what-e'er be-fall us, O God most wise! A-men.

God's Word Is like a Flaming Sword   405
OLD 107th C.M.D.

Carl Bernhard Garve, 1825
Trans. by Catherine Winkworth, 1855; alt., 1972

Comp. or adapted by Louis Bourgeois, 1543
As in Scottish Psalter, 1635

1. God's word is like a flaming sword, A wedge that cleaves the stone;
   Keen as a fire, so burns his word, And pierces flesh and bone.
   Let it go forth o'er all the earth To cleanse our hearts within,
   To show God's power in Satan's hour, And break the might of sin.

2. God's word, a wondrous guiding star, On pilgrim hearts does rise,
   Leads those to God who dwell afar, And makes the simple wise.
   Let not its light e'er sink in night, But in each spirit shine,
   That none may miss heaven's final bliss, Led by God's light divine. A-men.

406 Good Christian Men, Rejoice
IN DULCI JUBILO P.M.

Based on medieval carol
John Mason Neale, 1853

German carol, 14th century
Harm. by John Stainer, 1871

1. Good Christian men, rejoice With heart, and soul, and voice;
Give ye heed to what we say: News! news! Jesus Christ is born today.
Ox and ass before him bow, And he is in the manger now.
Christ is born today! Christ is born today!

2. Good Christian men, rejoice With heart, and soul, and voice;
Now ye hear of endless bliss: Joy! joy! Jesus Christ was born for this!
He has oped the heavenly door, And man is blessed evermore.
Christ was born for this! Christ was born for this!

3. Good Christian men, rejoice With heart, and soul, and voice;
Now ye need not fear the grave: Peace! peace! Jesus Christ was born to save!
Calls you one and calls you all, To gain his everlasting hall.
Christ was born to save! Christ was born to save! A-men.

Good Christian Men, Rejoice and Sing   407

GELOBT SEI GOTT 8.8.8. with Alleluias

Cyril A. Alington, 1931; alt., 1972

Attr. to Melchior Vulpius, 1609
As in *Pilgrim Hymnal*, 1958

1. Good Christian men, rejoice and sing! Now is the triumph of our King! To all the world glad news we bring: Alleluia! Alleluia! Alleluia! Amen.
2. The Lord of life is risen today! Sing songs of praise along his way; Let all mankind rejoice and say: Alleluia! Alleluia! Alleluia! Amen.
3. Praise we in songs of victory That love, that life which cannot die, And sing with hearts uplifted high: Alleluia! Alleluia! Alleluia! Amen.
4. Your name we bless, O risen Lord, And sing today with one accord The life laid down, the life restored: Alleluia! Alleluia! Alleluia! Amen.

Words used by permission of the Proprietors of *Hymns Ancient & Modern*.

408 Great God, We Sing That Mighty Hand
WAREHAM L.M.

Philip Doddridge, 1755; alt., 1972
William Knapp, 1738

1. Great God, we sing that mighty hand
By which supported still we stand;
The opening year your mercy shows;
That mercy crowns it till it close.

2. By day, by night, at home, abroad,
Still are we guarded by our God;
By his incessant bounty fed,
By his unerring counsel led.

3. With grateful hearts the past we own;
The future, all to us unknown,
We to your guardian care commit,
And peaceful leave before your feet.

4. In scenes exalted or depressed,
You are our joy, and you our rest;
Your goodness all our hopes shall raise,
Adored through all our changing days. A-men.

Guide Me, O Thou Great Jehovah 409

CWM RHONDDA 8.7.8.7.8.7.

William Williams, 1745
St. 1 trans. by Peter Williams, 1771
Sts. 2, 3 trans. by William or John Williams, ca. 1772

John Hughes, 1907

1. Guide me, O thou great Jehovah, Pilgrim through this barren land; I am weak, but thou art mighty; Hold me with thy powerful hand; Bread of heaven, Bread of heaven, Feed me till I want no more, Feed me till I want no more.

2. Open now the crystal fountain, Whence the healing stream doth flow; Let the fire and cloudy pillar Lead me all my journey through; Strong Deliverer, strong Deliverer, Be thou still my strength and shield, Be thou still my strength and shield.

3. When I tread the verge of Jordan, Bid my anxious fears subside; Death of deaths, and hell's Destruction, Land me safe on Canaan's side; Songs of praises, songs of praises I will ever give to thee, I will ever give to thee. A-men.

Music © by Mrs. Dilys Webb, c/o Mechanical-Copyright Protection Society Ltd., and reproduced by permission of the legal representatives of the composer who reserve all rights therein.

410. Hark! the Glad Sound, the Savior Comes
RICHMOND C.M.

Based on Luke 4: 18-19
Philip Doddridge, 1735; alt., 1972

Thomas Haweis, 1792
Abr. by Samuel Webbe, Jr, (ca.1770-1843)

1. Hark! the glad sound, the Savior comes, The Savior promised long! Let every heart prepare a throne, And every voice a song.

2. He comes the prisoners to release In Satan's bondage held; The gates of brass before him burst, The iron fetters yield.

3. He comes the broken heart to bind, The bleeding soul to cure; And with the treasures of his grace To enrich the humble poor.

4. Our glad hosannas, Prince of Peace, Your welcome shall proclaim; And heaven's eternal arches ring With your beloved name. A-men.

Hark! the Herald Angels Sing   411

MENDELSSOHN 7.7.7.7.D. with Refrain

Charles Wesley, 1739; alt.
Felix Mendelssohn, 1840
Arr. by William H. Cummings, 1855

1. Hark! the her-ald an-gels sing, "Glo-ry to the new-born King;
Peace on earth, and mer-cy mild, God and sin-ners rec-on-ciled!"
Joy-ful, all ye na-tions, rise, Join the tri-umph of the skies;
With th'an-gel-ic host pro-claim, "Christ is born in Beth-le-hem!"
Hark! the her-ald an-gels sing, "Glo-ry to the new-born King!" A-men.

2. Christ, by high-est heaven a-dored; Christ, the ev-er-last-ing Lord!
Late in time be-hold him come, Off-spring of the Vir-gin's womb:
Veiled in flesh the God-head see; Hail th'in-car-nate De-i-ty,
Pleased as man with men to dwell, Je-sus, our Em-man-u-el.

3. Hail the heaven-born Prince of Peace! Hail the Sun of Right-eous-ness!
Light and life to all he brings, Risen with heal-ing in his wings.
Mild he lays his glo-ry by, Born that man no more may die,
Born to raise the sons of earth, Born to give them sec-ond birth.

412. He Did Not Want to Be Far

Huub Oosterhuis
Trans. by C. Michael de Vries, 1966; alt., 1972

Bernard Huijbers; alt; 1972
Harm. by Richard D. Wetzel, 1972

1. He did not want to be far, Nearness he intended,
Therefore into what we are Christ the Lord descended.
A-mong you is standing He whom you don't know.
A-mong you is standing He whom you don't know.

2. Ev-erywhere he's at our side, Human 'mongst the human;
Nowhere is he recognized, No one sees the New Man.
A-mong you is standing He whom you don't know.
A-mong you is standing He whom you don't know.

3. God of God and Light of Light, Keeper of creation,
He assumed the human plight, Joined our generation.
A-mong you is standing He whom you don't know.
A-mong you is standing He whom you don't know.

4. Therefore, that the world may know, Christ became our brother;
No man anything we owe But to love each other.
A-mong you is standing He whom you don't know.
A-mong you is standing He whom you don't know.

5. Let's rejoice and sing and cheer: God, to whom be given
Praise, is infinitely near, Dwells where we are living.
A-mong you is standing He whom you don't know.
A-mong you is standing He whom you don't know.

Words and melody from *Risk*, Vol. II, No. 3, 1966, published by World Council of Churches; used by permission.
Harmonization copyright 1972 by The Westminster Press.

He Is the Way

413

NEW DANCE P.M.

W. H. Auden, 1944
Richard D. Wetzel, 1972

1. He is the Way. Follow him through the Land of Unlikeness; You will see rare beasts, and have unique adventures.
2. He is the Truth. Seek him in the Kingdom of Anxiety; You will come to a great city that has expected your return for years.
3. He is the Life. Love him in the World of the Flesh; And at your marriage all its occasions shall dance for joy. A-men.

Words copyright © 1944 by W. H. Auden; reprinted by permission of Curtis Brown, Ltd. Music copyright 1972 by The Westminster Press.

414. He Who Would Valiant Be

ST. DUNSTAN'S 6.5.6.5.6.6.6.5.

John Bunyan, 1684
Adapted by Percy Dearmer, 1906

C. Winfred Douglas, 1917

1. He who would valiant be 'Gainst all disaster,
Let him in constancy Follow the Master.
There's no discouragement Shall make him once relent
His first avowed intent To be a pilgrim.

2. Who so beset him round With dismal stories
Do but themselves confound— His strength the more is.
No foes shall stay his might; Though he with giants fight,
He will make good his right To be a pilgrim.

3. Since, Lord, thou dost defend Us with thy Spirit,
We know we at the end Shall life inherit.
Then, fancies, flee away! I'll fear not what men say,
I'll labor night and day To be a pilgrim. Amen.

Words from *The English Hymnal*; used by permission of Oxford University Press. Music used by permission of The Church Pension Fund.

Heaven and Earth, and Sea and Air

415

GOTT SEI DANK 7.7.7.7.

Joachim Neander, 1680
Trans. composite; *Church Book*, 1868

Freylinghausen's *Geistreiches Gesangbuch*, 1704; alt.

1. Heaven and earth, and sea and air, All their Maker's praise declare; Wake, my soul, awake and sing: Now thy grateful praises bring.
2. See the glorious orb of day Breaking through the clouds his way; Moon and stars with silvery light Praise him through the silent night.
3. See how he hath everywhere Made this earth so rich and fair; Hill and vale and fruitful land, All things living, show his hand.
4. Lord, great wonders workest thou! To thy sway all creatures bow; Write thou deeply in my heart What I am, and what thou art. A-men.

416 Heralds of Christ, Who Bear the King's Commands
NATIONAL HYMN 10.10.10.10.

Laura S. Copenhaver, 1894; alt., 1972
George William Warren, 1892

Trumpets (with each stanza)

1. Heralds of Christ, who bear the King's commands,
Immortal tidings in your mortal hands,
Pass on and carry swift the news you bring:
Make straight, make straight the highway of the King.

2. Through desert ways, dark fen, and deep morass,
Through jungles, sluggish seas, and mountain pass,
Build you the road, and falter not, nor stay;
Prepare across the earth the King's highway.

3. Where once the crooked trail in darkness wound,
Let marching feet and joyous song resound,
Where burn the funeral pyres, and censers swing,
Make straight, make straight the highway of the King.

4. Lord, give us faith and strength the road to build,
To see the promise of the day fulfilled,
When war shall be no more and strife shall cease
Upon the highway of the Prince of Peace. A-men.

Here, O Lord, Your Servants Gather

417

TŌKYŌ 7.5.7.5.D.

Tokuo Yamaguchi, 1958
Para. by Everett M. Stowe, 1958; alt., 1972

Japanese gagaku mode
Isau Koizumi, 1958

1. Here, O Lord, your serv-ants gath-er, Hand we link with hand;
   Look-ing toward our Sav-ior's cross, Joined in love we stand.
   As we seek the realm of God, We u-nite to pray:
   Je-sus, Sav-ior, guide our steps, For you are the Way.

2. Man-y are the tongues we speak, Scat-tered are the lands,
   Yet our hearts are one in God And his love's de-mands.
   E'en in dark-ness hope ap-pears, Call-ing age and youth:
   Je-sus, teach-er, dwell with us, For you are the Truth.

3. Na-ture's se-crets o-pen wide, Chang-es nev-er cease;
   Where, O where, can wea-ry men Find the source of peace?
   Un-to all those sore dis-tressed, Torn by end-less strife:
   Je-sus, heal-er, bring your balm, For you are the Life.

4. Grant, O God, an age re-newed, Filled with death-less love,
   Help us as we work and pray, Send us from a-bove
   Truth and cour-age, faith and power Need-ed in our strife:
   Je-sus, Mas-ter, be our way, Be our truth, our life.

Words used by permission of Tokuo Yamaguchi and Everett M. Stowe. Music used by permission of the copyright owners, The Japanese Society of Rights of Authors and Composers, License, 462534.

418 Here, O Our Lord, We See You Face to Face
ERFYNIAD 10.10.10.10.

Horatius Bonar, 1855; alt., 1972
Welsh hymn melody
Harm. by David Evans, 1920

1. Here, O our Lord, we see you face to face;
   Here would we touch and handle things unseen,
   Here grasp with firmer hand eternal grace,
   And all our weariness upon you lean.

2. We have no help but yours, nor do we need
   Another arm save yours to lean upon;
   It is enough, O Lord, enough indeed;
   Our strength is in your might, your might alone.

3. This is the hour of banquet and of song;
   This is the heavenly table for us spread;
   Here let us feast, and, feasting, still prolong
   The fellowship of living wine and bread.

4. Too soon we rise; the symbols disappear.
   The feast, though not the love, is past and gone;
   The bread and wine remove, but you are here,
   Nearer than ever, still our shield and sun. A-men.

Music used by permission of the Executors of the late Professor Evans.

Holy Ghost, Dispel Our Sadness

419

HYFRYDOL 8.7.8.7.D.

Paul Gerhardt, 1648
Trans. by J. C. Jacobi, ca. 1725
Alt. by Augustus M. Toplady, 1776, and others

Rowland H. Prichard, 1855

1. Ho-ly Ghost, dis-pel our sad-ness; Pierce the clouds of na-ture's night;
2. Au-thor of the new cre-a-tion, Come with bless-ing and with power.

Come, great source of joy and glad-ness, Breathe your life, and spread your light.
Make our hearts your hab-i-ta-tion; On our souls your grac-es shower.

From the height which knows no mea-sure, As a gra-cious shower de-scend,
Hear, O hear our sup-pli-ca-tion, Bless-ed Spir-it, God of peace!

Bring-ing down the rich-est trea-sure Man can wish, or God can send.
Rest up-on this con-gre-ga-tion, With the full-ness of your grace. A-men.

420 Holy God, We Praise Your Name
GROSSER GOTT, WIR LOBEN DICH 7.8.7.8.7.7.

Allgemeines Katholisches Gesangbuch, ca. 1774
Trans. by Clarence A. Walworth, 1853; alt., 1972

Allgemeines Katholisches Gesangbuch, ca. 1774
Alt. in Schicht's *Choral-Buch*, 1819

1. Holy God, we praise your name; Lord of all, we bow before you; All on earth your scepter claim, All in heaven above adore you. Infinite your vast domain, Everlasting is your reign.
2. Hark, the glad celestial hymn Angel choirs above are raising; Cherubim and seraphim In unceasing chorus praising, Fill the heavens with sweet accord: Holy, holy, holy Lord.
3. All apostles join the strain As your sacred name they hallow; Prophets swell the glad refrain, And the blessed martyrs follow, And from morn to set of sun, Through the church the song goes on.
4. Holy Father, Holy Son, Holy Spirit: Three we name you While in essence only One; Undivided God we claim you, And adoring bend the knee While we own the mystery. A-men.

Holy, Holy, Holy! Lord God Almighty! 421
NICAEA 11.12.12.10.

Reginald Heber, 1826
John B. Dykes, 1861

1. Ho - ly, ho - ly, ho - ly! Lord God Al - might - y!
2. Ho - ly, ho - ly, ho - ly! all the saints a - dore thee,
3. Ho - ly, ho - ly, ho - ly! though the dark - ness hide thee,
4. Ho - ly, ho - ly, ho - ly! Lord God Al - might - y!

Ear - ly in the morn - ing our song shall rise to thee;
Cast - ing down their gold - en crowns a - round the glass - y sea;
Though the eye of sin - ful man thy glo - ry may not see,
All thy works shall praise thy name, in earth and sky and sea;

Ho - ly, ho - ly, ho - ly! Mer - ci - ful and might - y!
Cher - u - bim and ser - a - phim fall - ing down be - fore thee,
On - ly thou art ho - ly; there is none be - side thee
Ho - ly, ho - ly, ho - ly! Mer - ci - ful and might - y!

God in three Per - sons, bless - ed Trin - i - ty!
Who wert, and art, and ev - er - more shalt be.
Per - fect in power, in love, and pu - ri - ty.
God in three Per - sons, bless - ed Trin - i - ty! A - men.

422 Holy Spirit, Truth Divine
SONG 13 7.7.7.7.

Samuel Longfellow, 1864; alt., 1972 — Orlando Gibbons, 1623

1. Holy Spirit, truth divine, Dawn upon this soul of mine; Word of God, and inward light, Wake my spirit, clear my sight.
2. Holy Spirit, love divine, Glow within this heart of mine; Kindle every high desire; Perish self in your pure fire.
3. Holy Spirit, power divine, Fill and nerve this will of mine; By you may I strongly live, Bravely bear, and nobly strive.
4. Holy Spirit, peace divine, Still this restless heart of mine; Speak to calm this tossing sea, Stayed in your tranquility.
5. Holy Spirit, right divine, King within my conscience reign; Be my law, and I shall be Firmly bound, forever free. A-men.

Hope of the World

423

DONNE SECOURS 11.10.11.10.

Georgia Harkness, 1953; alt., 1972

Comp. or adapted by Louis Bourgeois, 1551

1. Hope of the world, O Christ of great com-pas-sion,
Speak to our fear-ful hearts by con-flict rent.
Save us, your peo-ple, from con-sum-ing pas-sion,
Who by our own false hopes and aims are spent.

2. Hope of the world, God's gift from high-est heav-en,
Bring-ing to hun-gry souls the bread of life,
Still let your Spir-it un-to us be giv-en
To heal earth's wounds and end her bit-ter strife.

3. Hope of the world, a-foot on dust-y high-ways,
Show-ing to wan-dering souls the path of light,
Walk close be-side us, lest the tempt-ing by-ways
Lure us from you and in-to end-less night.

4. Hope of the world, who by your cross did save us
From death and dark de-spair, from guilt and sin,
We ren-der back the love your mer-cy gave us;
O bless our lives that we may oth-ers win!

*5. Hope of the world, O Christ, o'er death vic-to-rious,
Who by this sign did con-quer grief and pain,
We would be faith-ful to your gos-pel glo-rious.
Our sov-ereign Lord, now and for-ev-er reign! A-men.

Words copyright 1954 by The Hymn Society of America; altered from *Eleven Ecumenical Hymns*; used by permission.

424 Hosanna, Loud Hosanna

ELLACOMBE 7.6.7.6.D.

Jennette Threlfall, 1873

Gesangbuch der herzogl. Wirtembergischen Katholischen Hofkapelle, 1784

1. Ho-san-na, loud ho-san-na, The lit-tle chil-dren sang;
Through pil-lared court and tem-ple The love-ly an-them rang;
To Je-sus, who had blessed them Close fold-ed to his breast,
The chil-dren sang their prais-es, The sim-plest and the best.

2. From Ol-i-vet they fol-lowed Mid an ex-ult-ant crowd,
The vic-tor palm branch wav-ing, And chant-ing clear and loud;
The Lord of men and an-gels Rode on in low-ly state,
Nor scorned that lit-tle chil-dren Should on his bid-ding wait.

3. "Ho-san-na in the high-est!" That an-cient song we sing,
For Christ is our Re-deem-er, The Lord of heaven our King.
O may we ev-er praise him With heart and life and voice,
And in his bliss-ful pres-ence E-ter-nal-ly re-joice. A-men.

How Firm a Foundation 425

FOUNDATION 11.11.11.11.

"K"
Rippon's *A Selection of Hymns*, 1787; alt.

American folk hymn

1. How firm a foundation, O saints of the Lord,
Is laid for your faith in his excellent Word!
What more can he say than to you he has said,
To you who for refuge to Jesus have fled?

2. "Fear not, I am with you, O be not dismayed,
For I am your God, and will still give you aid;
I'll strengthen you, help you, and cause you to stand,
Upheld by my righteous, omnipotent hand.

3. "When through the deep waters I call you to go,
The rivers of sorrow shall not overflow;
For I will be near you, your troubles to bless,
And sanctify to you your deepest distress.

4. "The soul that on Jesus has leaned for repose,
I will not, I will not desert to his foes;
That soul, though all hell should endeavor to shake,
I'll never, no, never, no, never forsake." A-men.

426 I Danced in the Morning
(Lord of the Dance)

Sydney Carter, 1963
Based on a Shaker tune
Arr. and adapted by Sydney Carter, 1963

1. I danced in the morn-ing when the world was be-gun, And I danced in the moon and the stars and the sun And I came down from heav-en and I danced on the earth— At Beth-le-hem I had my birth.
2. I danced for the scribe and the Phar-i-see, But they would not dance and they would-n't fol-low me; I danced for the fish-er-men, for James and John— They came with me and the dance went on.
3. I danced on the Sab-bath and I cured the lame; The ho-ly peo-ple said it was a shame; They whipped and they stripped and they hung me high, And they left me there on a cross to die.
4. I danced on a Fri-day and the sky turned black. It's hard to dance with the dev-il on your back; They bur-ied my bod-y and they thought I'd gone. But I am the dance and I still go on.

Words and music © copyright 1963 by Galliard, Ltd. All rights reserved. Reprinted by permission of Galaxy Music Corp., N.Y., sole U.S. agent.

I Danced in the Morning (cont.) 427

Refrain

Dance, then, wher-ev-er you may be, I am the Lord of the Dance, said he, And I'll lead you all, wher-ev-er you may be, And I'll lead you all in the dance, said he.

Melody for stanza 5

5. They cut me down and I leap up high— I am the life that-'ll nev-er, nev-er die; I'll live in you if you'll live in me— I am the Lord of the Dance, said he.

(Refrain)

428 I Sing as I Arise Today
ST. PATRICK and DEIRDRE P.M.

Attr. to St. Patrick (ca. 389-ca. 461)
Para. by Joseph W. Clokey, 1964

Ancient Irish melodies
Harm. by Donald D. Kettring, 1972

1. I sing as I arise today; I call upon the Trinity; I now invoke the Father, Son, And Holy Spirit, One in Three, In whom creation now is joined, The vaulted sky, the sun so bright, The shining
2. I sing as I arise today; I call upon the Father's might; The will of God to be my guide, The eye of God to be my sight, The word of God to be my speech, The hand of God to be my stay, The shield of

Words copyright 1964 by Concordia Publishing House; from "I Sing as I Arise"; used by permission. Music copyright 1972 by The Westminster Press.

I Sing as I Arise Today (cont.) 429

stars, the sea so deep, The rush-ing wind, the snow so white.
God to be my strength, The path of God to be my way.

Christ with-in me, Christ be-side me, Christ be-fore me, Christ to guide me, Christ in ris-ing, Christ in sleep-ing, Christ in work-ing, Christ in speak-ing.
Christ in heart of all who love me, Christ in mouth of neigh-bors near me, Christ in eye of all who see me, Christ in ear of all who hear me. A-men.

430 I to the Hills Will Lift My Eyes
DUNDEE (FRENCH) C.M.

From Psalm 121
The Psalter, 1912; alt., 1972

Scottish Psalter, 1615

1. I to the hills will lift my eyes; From whence shall come our aid? Our help is from the Lord alone, Who heaven and earth has made.
2. He will not let your foot be moved, Your guardian never sleeps; With watchful and unslumbering care His own he safely keeps.
3. Your faithful keeper is the Lord, Your Shelter and your Shade; 'Neath sun or moon, by day or night, You shall not be afraid.
4. From evil he will keep you safe, For you he will provide; Your going out, your coming in, Forever he will guide. A-men.

If You Will Only Let God Guide You

431

NEUMARK 9.8.9.8.8.8.

Georg Neumark, 1657
Trans. by Catherine Winkworth, 1855, 1863; alt., 1972

Georg Neumark, 1657

1. If you will only let God guide you, And hope in him through all your ways, What-ev-er comes, he'll stand be-side you, To bear you through the e - vil days; Who trusts in God's un-chang-ing love Builds on the rock that can-not move.

2. On - ly be still, and wait his lei - sure In cheer-ful hope, with heart con - tent To take what-e'er the Fa-ther's plea-sure And all dis-cern-ing love have sent; Nor doubt our in-most wants are known To him who chose us for his own.

3. Sing, pray, and swerve not from his ways, But do your part in con-science true; Trust his rich prom - is - es of grace, So shall they be ful - filled in you; God hears the call of those in need, The souls that trust in him in - deed. A - men.

432. I'm So Glad Troubles Don't Last Always

Negro spiritual
Negro spiritual
Harm. by Joan M. Salmon, 1972

1. I'm so glad troubles don't last always. (always.)
2. Make more room, Lord, in my heart for you. (for you.)

I'm so glad troubles don't last always.
Make more room, Lord, in my heart for you.

I'm so glad troubles don't last always.
Make more room, Lord, in my heart for you.

Oh, my Lord, oh, my Lord, what shall I do? (I do?)

Music copyright 1972 by The Westminster Press.

NOTE: Additional stanzas may be improvised.

Immortal, Invisible, God Only Wise

ST. DENIO 11.11.11.11.

Walter Chalmers Smith, 1867, 1884; alt.

Welsh folk song
Adapted as hymn tune, 1839

1. Immortal, invisible, God only wise,
In light inaccessible hid from our eyes,
Most blessed, most glorious, the Ancient of Days,
Almighty, victorious, thy great name we praise.

2. Unresting, unhasting, and silent as light,
Nor wanting, nor wasting, thou rulest in might;
Thy justice like mountains high soaring above
Thy clouds which are fountains of goodness and love.

3. To all, life thou givest— to both great and small;
In all life thou livest, the true life of all;
We blossom and flourish as leaves on the tree,
And wither and perish— but naught changeth thee.

4. Great Father of glory, pure Father of light,
Thine angels adore thee, all veiling their sight;
All praise we would render; O help us to see
'Tis only the splendor of light hideth thee! Amen.

434 Immortal Love, Forever Full
SERENITY C.M.

John Greenleaf Whittier, 1866
William V. Wallace, 1856
Arr. by Uzziah C. Burnap, 1869

1. Immortal Love, forever full, Forever flowing free, Forever shared, forever whole, A never-ebbing sea!
2. We may not climb the heavenly steeps To bring the Lord Christ down; In vain we search the lowest deeps, For him no depths can drown.
3. But warm, sweet, tender, even yet A present help is he; And faith has still its Olivet, And love its Galilee.
4. The healing of his seamless dress Is by our beds of pain; We touch him in life's throng and press, And we are whole again.
5. O Lord and Master of us all, Whate'er our name or sign, We own thy sway, we hear thy call, We test our lives by thine. A-men.

In Christ There Is No East or West

435

ST. PETER C.M.
(First Tune)

John Oxenham, 1908

Alexander R. Reinagle, ca. 1836

1. In Christ there is no East or West, In him no South or North; But one great fellowship of love Throughout the whole wide earth.
2. In him shall true hearts everywhere Their high communion find; His service is the golden cord Close-binding all mankind.
3. Join hands, then, brothers of the faith, Whate'er your race may be! Who serves my Father as a son Is surely kin to me.
4. In Christ now meet both East and West, In him meet South and North; All Christly souls are one in him Throughout the whole wide earth. A-men.

Words from *Bees in Amber*, by John Oxenham; used by permission.

436 In Christ There Is No East or West

MCKEE C.M.
(Second Tune)

John Oxenham, 1908

Negro spiritual
Adapted by Harry T. Burleigh, 1939

1. In Christ there is no East or West, In him no South or North; But one great fellowship of love Throughout the whole wide earth.
2. In him shall true hearts ev-ery-where Their high communion find; His service is the golden cord Close-binding all mankind.
3. Join hands, then, brothers of the faith, What-e'er your race may be! Who serves my Father as a son Is surely kin to me.
4. In Christ now meet both East and West, In him meet South and North; All Christ-ly souls are one in him Throughout the whole wide earth. A-men.

Words from *Bees in Amber*, by John Oxenham; used by permission.

In the Cross of Christ I Glory

RATHBUN 8.7.8.7.

John Bowring, 1825

Ithamar Conkey, 1851

1. In the cross of Christ I glory, Tow-ering o'er the wrecks of time; All the light of sacred story Gathers round its head sublime.
2. When the woes of life o'er-take me, Hopes deceive, and fears annoy, Never shall the cross forsake me: Lo! it glows with peace and joy.
3. When the sun of bliss is beaming Light and love upon my way, From the cross the radiance streaming Adds more luster to the day.
4. Bane and blessing, pain and pleasure, By the cross are sanctified; Peace is there that knows no measure, Joys that through all time abide.
5. In the cross of Christ I glory, Towering o'er the wrecks of time; All the light of sacred story Gathers round its head sublime. A-men.

438 It Came Upon the Midnight Clear
CAROL C.M.D.

Edmund H. Sears, 1849; alt. Richard Storrs Willis, 1850

1. It came upon the midnight clear, That glorious song of old,
From angels bending near the earth, To touch their harps of gold:
"Peace on the earth, good will to men, From heaven's all-gracious King":
The world in solemn stillness lay, To hear the angels sing.

2. Still through the cloven skies they come, With peaceful wings unfurled,
And still their heavenly music floats O'er all the weary world:
Above its sad and lowly plains They bend on hovering wing,
And ever o'er its Babel sounds The blessed angels sing.

3. And ye, beneath life's crushing load, Whose forms are bending low,
Who toil along the climbing way With painful steps and slow,
Look now! for glad and golden hours Come swiftly on the wing:
O rest beside the weary road, And hear the angels sing.

4. For lo, the days are hastening on, By prophet bards foretold,
When with the ever-circling years Comes round the age of gold;
When peace shall over all the earth Its ancient splendors fling,
And the whole world give back the song Which now the angels sing. A-men.

Jesus Calls Us

439

GALILEE 8.7.8.7.

Cecil Frances Alexander, 1852; alt., 1972

William H. Jude, 1887

1. Jesus calls us: o'er the tumult Of our life's wild, restless sea, Day by day his voice is sounding, Saying, "Christian, follow me."
2. As of old, Saint Andrew heard it By the Galilean lake, Turned from home and toil and kindred, Leaving all for his dear sake.
3. Jesus calls us from the worship Of the vain world's golden store, From each idol that would keep us, Saying, "Christian, love me more."
4. In our joys and in our sorrows, Days of toil and hours of ease, Still he calls, in cares and pleasures, "Christian, love me more than these."
5. Jesus calls us; by your mercies, Savior, may we hear your call, Give our hearts to your obedience, Serve and love you best of all. A-men.

440 Jesus Christ Is Risen Today

EASTER HYMN 7.7.7.7. with Alleluias

St. 1, Latin carol, 14th century
Para. in *Lyra Davidica*, 1708; alt.
Sts. 2, 3, *The Compleat Psalmodist*, ca. 1750; alt.
St. 4, Charles Wesley, 1740; alt., 1972

Lyra Davidica, 1708
Alt. in *The Compleat Psalmodist*, ca. 1750

1. Jesus Christ is risen today, Alleluia!
   Our triumphant holy day,
   Who did once, upon the cross, Alleluia!
   Suffer to redeem our loss.

2. Hymns of praise then let us sing, Alleluia!
   Unto Christ, our heavenly King,
   Who endured the cross and grave, Alleluia!
   Sinners to redeem and save.

3. But the pains which he endured, Alleluia!
   Our salvation have procured;
   Now above the sky he's King, Alleluia!
   Where the angels ever sing.

4. Sing we to our God above,
   Praise eternal as his love;
   Praise him, all you heavenly host,
   Father, Son, and Holy Ghost. Amen.

Alternative Tune: LLANFAIR

Jesus, Lead the Way 441
SEELENBRÄUTIGAM 5.5.8.8.5.5.

Nicolaus L. von Zinzendorf, 1721
Recast by Christian Gregor, 1778
Trans. by Arthur W. Farlander, 1939; alt., 1972

Adam Drese, 1698

1. Jesus, lead the way Through our life's long day, And with faithful footstep steady, We will follow, always ready. Guide us by your hand To the heavenly land.
2. Should our lot be hard, Keep us on our guard; Even through severest trial Make us brave in self-denial: Transient pain may come But your will be done.
3. When we need relief From an inner grief, Or when evils come alluring, Make us patient and enduring: Let us follow still Your most holy will.
4. Order then our ways, Savior, all our days. If you lead us through rough places, Grant us your sustaining graces. When our course is o'er, Open heaven's door. A-men.

Words used by permission of The Church Pension Fund.

442 Jesus, Priceless Treasure
JESU, MEINE FREUDE P.M.

Johann Franck, 1653
Trans. by Catherine Winkworth, 1863; alt.

Crüger's *Praxis Pietatis Melica*, 1653
Harm. by J. S. Bach, 1723

1. Jesus, priceless treasure, Source of purest pleasure, Truest friend to me; Long my heart hath panted, Till it well-nigh fainted, Thirsting after thee. Thine I am, O spotless Lamb, I will suffer naught to hide thee, Ask for naught beside thee.

2. In thine arm I rest me; Foes who would molest me Cannot reach me here. Though the earth be shaking, Every heart be quaking, God dispels our fear; Sin and hell in conflict fell With their heaviest storms assail us: Jesus will not fail us.

3. Hence, all thoughts of sadness! For the Lord of gladness, Jesus, enters in: Those who love the Father, Though the storms may gather, Still have peace within; Yea, what-e'er we here must bear, Still in thee lies purest pleasure, Jesus, priceless treasure! A-men.

Jesus Shall Reign
DUKE STREET L.M.

443

Based on Psalm 72
Isaac Watts, 1719

John Hatton, 1793

1. Jesus shall reign where'er the sun Does his successive journeys run, His kingdom stretch from shore to shore, Till moons shall wax and wane no more.
2. For him shall endless prayer be made, And praises throng to crown his head; His name, like sweet perfume, shall rise With every morning sacrifice.
3. People and realms of every tongue Dwell on his love with sweetest song, And infant voices shall proclaim Their early blessings on his name.
4. Blessings abound where'er he reigns, The prisoner leaps to lose his chains, The weary find eternal rest, And all the sons of want are blest.
5. Let every creature rise and bring Peculiar honors to our King; Angels descend with songs again, And earth repeat the loud Amen! Amen.

444 Joy to the World!
ANTIOCH C.M.

Based on Psalm 98: 5-9
Isaac Watts, 1719

Attr. to George Frederick Handel, 1742
Mason's *The Modern Psalmist*, 1839
Arr. by Robert Carwithen, 1972

1. Joy to the world! the Lord is come: Let earth receive her King; Let ev-ery heart pre-pare him room, And heaven and na-ture sing, And heaven and na-ture sing, And heaven and na-ture sing,
2. Joy to the earth! the Sav-ior reigns: Let men their songs em-ploy; While fields and floods, rocks, hills, and plains Re-peat the sound-ing joy, Re-peat the sound-ing joy, Re-peat the sound-ing joy,
3. No more let sins and sor-rows grow, Nor thorns in-fest the ground; He comes to make his bless-ings flow Far as the curse is found, Far as the curse is found, Far as the curse is found,
4. He rules the world with truth and grace, And makes the na-tions prove The glo-ries of his righ-teous-ness, And won-ders of his love, And won-ders of his love, And won-ders of his love,

Joy to the World! (cont.) 445

sing, And heaven, and heaven and na-ture sing.
joy, Re - peat, re - peat the sound-ing joy.
found, Far as, far as the curse is found.
love, And won - ders, won - ders of his love. A - men.

heaven and na-ture sing, And
peat the sound-ing joy, Re -
as the curse is found, Far
won-ders of his love, And

446 Joyful, Joyful, We Adore Thee

HYMN TO JOY 8.7.8.7.D.

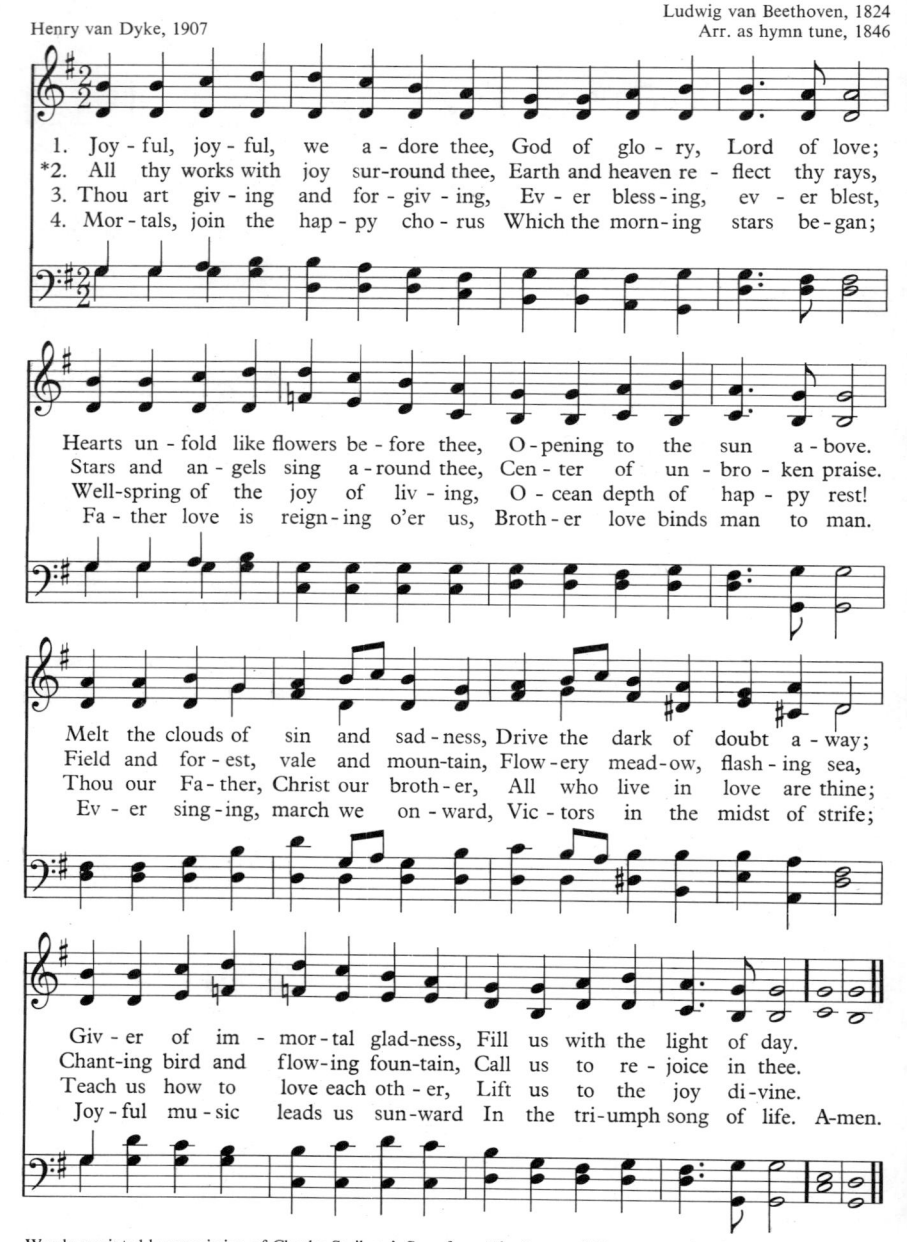

Henry van Dyke, 1907
Ludwig van Beethoven, 1824
Arr. as hymn tune, 1846

1. Joy - ful, joy - ful, we a - dore thee, God of glo - ry, Lord of love;
*2. All thy works with joy sur-round thee, Earth and heaven re - flect thy rays,
3. Thou art giv - ing and for - giv - ing, Ev - er bless-ing, ev - er blest,
4. Mor - tals, join the hap - py cho - rus Which the morn-ing stars be - gan;

Hearts un - fold like flowers be - fore thee, O - pening to the sun a - bove.
Stars and an - gels sing a - round thee, Cen - ter of un - bro - ken praise.
Well-spring of the joy of liv - ing, O - cean depth of hap - py rest!
Fa - ther love is reign-ing o'er us, Broth - er love binds man to man.

Melt the clouds of sin and sad - ness, Drive the dark of doubt a - way;
Field and for - est, vale and moun-tain, Flow-ery mead - ow, flash - ing sea,
Thou our Fa - ther, Christ our broth - er, All who live in love are thine;
Ev - er sing-ing, march we on - ward, Vic - tors in the midst of strife;

Giv - er of im - mor - tal glad-ness, Fill us with the light of day.
Chant-ing bird and flow-ing foun-tain, Call us to re - joice in thee.
Teach us how to love each oth - er, Lift us to the joy di - vine.
Joy - ful mu - sic leads us sun-ward In the tri-umph song of life. A-men.

Words reprinted by permission of Charles Scribner's Sons from *The Poems of Henry van Dyke*. Copyright 1911 Charles Scribner's Sons; renewal copyright 1939 Tertius van Dyke.

Judge Eternal, Throned in Splendor 447
RHUDDLAN 8.7.8.7.8.7.

Henry Scott Holland, 1902; alt.
Traditional Welsh melody
Adapted in *The English Hymnal*, 1906

1. Judge e-ter-nal, throned in splen-dor, Lord of lords and King of kings, With the liv-ing fire of judg-ment Purge this realm of bit-ter things: Sol-ace all its wide do-min-ion With the heal-ing of your wings.
2. Still the wea-ry folk are pin-ing For the hour that brings re-lease; And the cit-y's crowd-ed clang-or Cries a-loud for sin to cease; And the home-steads and the wood-lands Plead in si-lence for their peace.
3. Crown, O God, your own en-deav-or: Cleave our dark-ness with your sword; Feed the faint and hun-gry peo-ples With the rich-ness of your Word; Cleanse the bod-y of this na-tion Through the glo-ry of the Lord. A-men.

448 Lead On, O King Eternal
LLANGLOFFAN 7.6.7.6.D.

Ernest W. Shurtleff, 1888; alt., 1972

Welsh hymn melody
Evans' *Hymnau a Thonau*, 1865

1. Lead on, O King eternal, The day of march has come;
2. Lead on, O King eternal, Till sin's fierce war shall cease,
3. Lead on, O King eternal: We follow, not with fears;

Henceforth in fields of conquest Your tents shall be our home:
And Holiness shall whisper The sweet Amen of peace;
For gladness breaks like morning Where'er your face appears;

Through days of preparation Your grace has made us strong,
For not with swords' loud clashing, Nor roll of stirring drums,
Your cross is lifted o'er us; We journey in its light:

And now, O King eternal, We lift our battle song.
But deeds of love and mercy, The heavenly kingdom comes.
The crown awaits the conquest; Lead on, O God of might. Amen.

Alternative Tune: LANCASHIRE

Let All Mortal Flesh Keep Silence

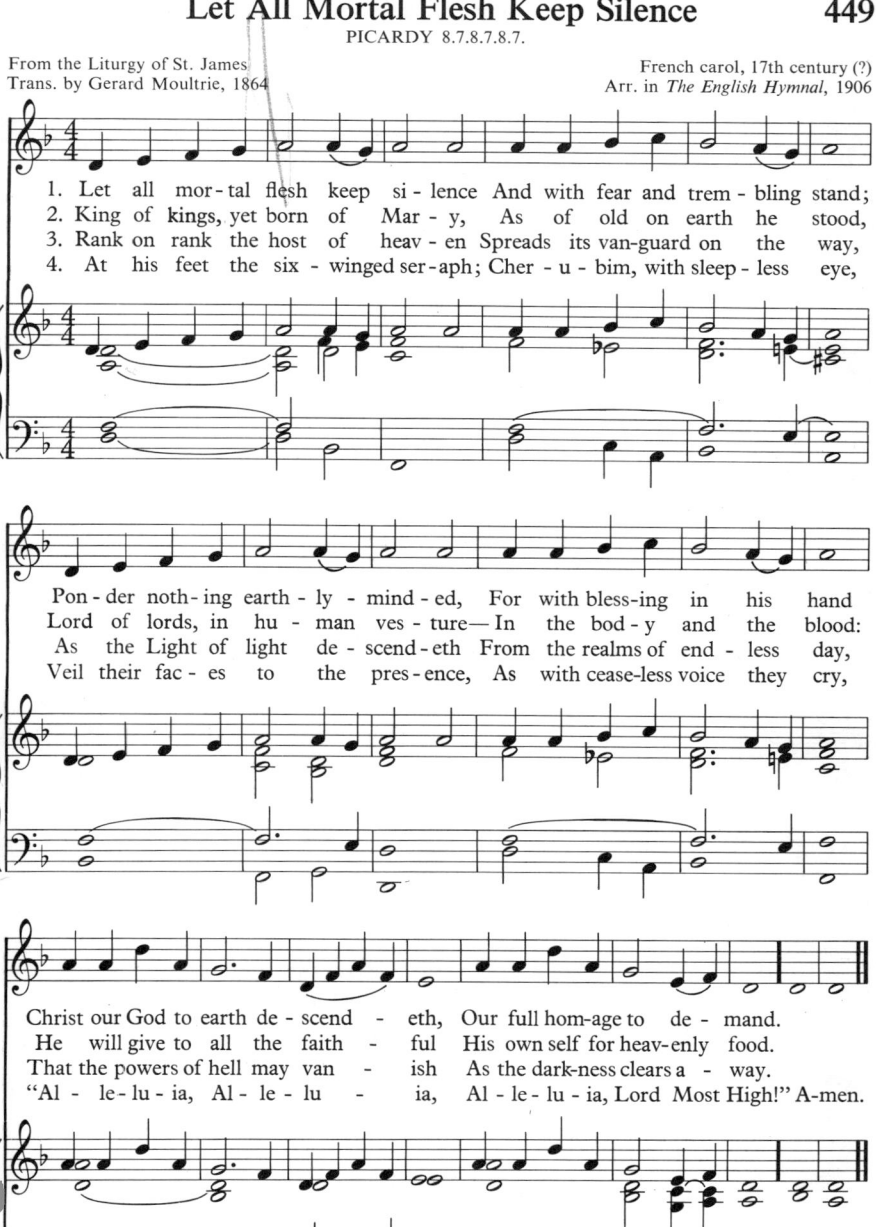

PICARDY 8.7.8.7.8.7.

From the Liturgy of St. James
Trans. by Gerard Moultrie, 1864

French carol, 17th century (?)
Arr. in *The English Hymnal*, 1906

1. Let all mortal flesh keep silence And with fear and trembling stand;
2. King of kings, yet born of Mar-y, As of old on earth he stood,
3. Rank on rank the host of heav-en Spreads its van-guard on the way,
4. At his feet the six-winged ser-aph; Cher-u-bim, with sleep-less eye,

Pon-der noth-ing earth-ly-mind-ed, For with bless-ing in his hand
Lord of lords, in hu-man ves-ture— In the bod-y and the blood:
As the Light of light de-scend-eth From the realms of end-less day,
Veil their fac-es to the pres-ence, As with cease-less voice they cry,

Christ our God to earth de-scend-eth, Our full hom-age to de-mand.
He will give to all the faith-ful His own self for heav-en-ly food.
That the powers of hell may van-ish As the dark-ness clears a-way.
"Al-le-lu-ia, Al-le-lu-ia, Al-le-lu-ia, Lord Most High!" A-men.

450 Let All Together Praise Our God
LOBT GOTT, IHR CHRISTEN C.M.

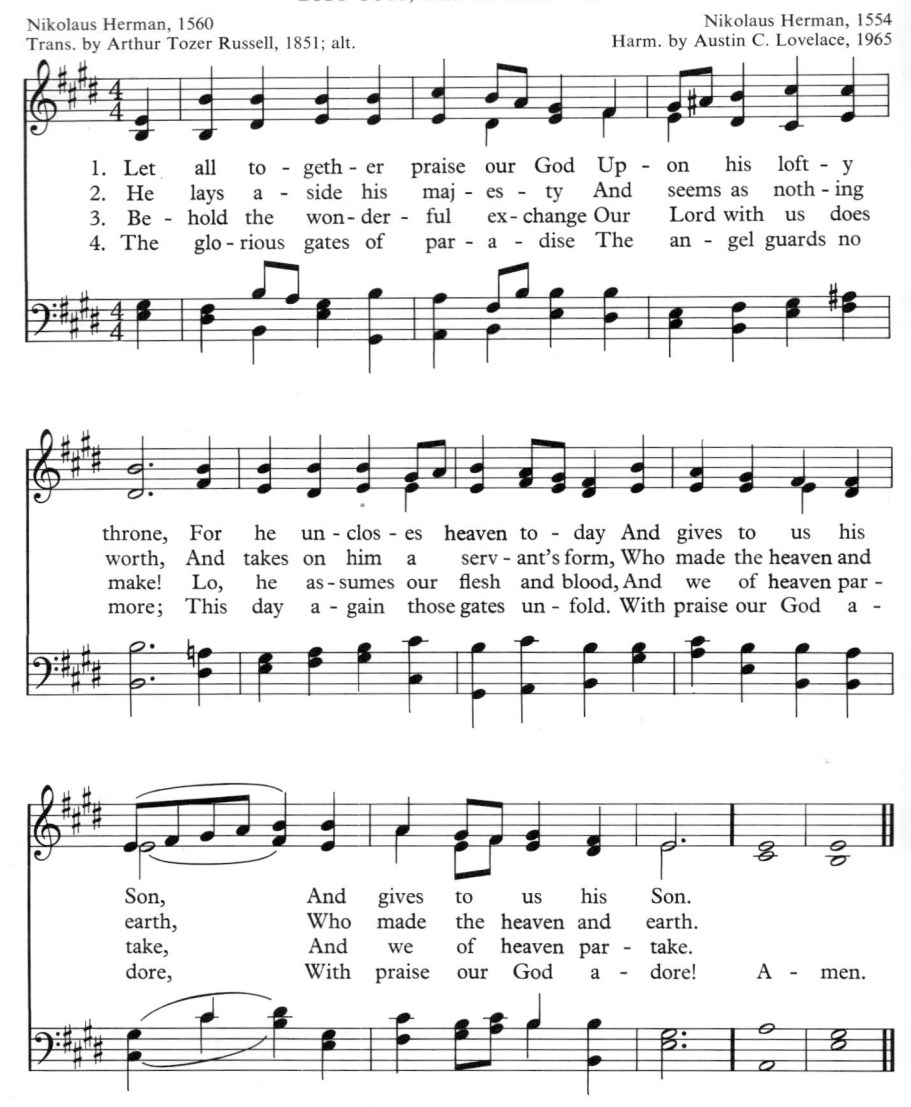

Nikolaus Herman, 1560
Trans. by Arthur Tozer Russell, 1851; alt.

Nikolaus Herman, 1554
Harm. by Austin C. Lovelace, 1965

1. Let all to-geth-er praise our God Up-on his loft-y throne, For he un-clos-es heaven to-day And gives to us his Son, And gives to us his Son.
2. He lays a-side his maj-es-ty And seems as noth-ing worth, And takes on him a serv-ant's form, Who made the heaven and earth, Who made the heaven and earth.
3. Be-hold the won-der-ful ex-change Our Lord with us does make! Lo, he as-sumes our flesh and blood, And we of heaven par-take, And we of heaven par-take.
4. The glo-rious gates of par-a-dise The an-gel guards no more; This day a-gain those gates un-fold. With praise our God a-dore, With praise our God a-dore! A-men.

Harmonization copyright © 1965 by Abingdon Press; from *The Methodist Hymnal*; used by permission.

Let There Be Light, Lord God of Hosts 451
SONG 34 L.M.

William Merrell Vories, 1908; alt., 1972

Orlando Gibbons, 1623
As in *Hymnal for Colleges and Schools*, 1956

1. Let there be light, Lord God of hosts, Let there be wisdom on the earth! Let broad humanity have birth! Let there be deeds instead of boasts!
2. Within our passioned hearts instill The calm that ends all strain and strife; Make us your ministers of life; Purge us from lusts that curse and kill!
3. Give us the peace of vision clear To see our brothers' good our own, To joy and suffer not alone — The love that casts away all fear!
4. Let woe and waste of warfare cease, That useful labor yet may build Its homes with love and laughter filled! God, give your wayward children peace! Amen.

452 Let Us Break Bread Together

Negro spiritual
Arr. for *The Hymnbook*, 1955

Negro spiritual

1. Let us break bread to-geth-er on our knees;
2. Let us drink wine to-geth-er on our knees; (on our knees;)
3. Let us praise God to-geth-er on our knees;

Let us break bread to-geth-er on our knees.
Let us drink wine to-geth-er on our knees. (on our knees.)
Let us praise God to-geth-er on our knees.

When I fall on my knees, with my face to the ris-ing sun, O Lord, have mer-cy on me. A-men.

Let Us with a Gladsome Mind
453
MONKLAND 7.7.7.7.

Psalm 136:1, 2, 7, 25
Para. by John Milton, ca. 1624; alt.

John Antes (1740-1811)
Arr. by John B. Wilkes, 1861

1. Let us with a gladsome mind Praise the Lord, for he is kind:
2. Let us sound his name abroad, For of gods he is the God:
3. He, with all-commanding might, Filled the new-made world with light: For his mercies shall endure,
4. All things living he does feed; His full hand supplies their need:
5. Let us then with gladsome mind Praise the Lord, for he is kind:

Ever faithful, ever sure. A-men.

454 Lift Up Your Heads, O Mighty Gates
TRURO L.M.

Georg Weissel, 1642
Trans. by Catherine Winkworth, 1855; alt.

Psalmodia Evangelica, 1789

1. Lift up your heads, O mighty gates; Behold, the King of glory waits; The King of kings is drawing near; The Savior of the world is here!
2. O blest the land, the city blest, Where Christ the ruler is confessed! O happy hearts and happy homes To whom this King in triumph comes!
3. Fling wide the portals of your heart; Make it a temple set apart From selfish use for his employ, Adorned with prayer, and love, and joy.
4. Redeemer, come! We open wide Our hearts to you; here, Lord, abide. Let us your inner presence feel; Your grace and love in us reveal. A-men.

Lo, How a Rose E'er Blooming   455
ES IST EIN' ROS' 7.6.7.6.6.7.6.

Attr. to Brother Conrad of Mainz, 1588
Trans. by Theodore Baker, 1894; alt., 1972

Rhineland folk melody
Harm. by Michael Praetorius, 1609

1. Lo, how a Rose e'er bloom-ing From ten-der stem has sprung!
Of Jes-se's lin-eage com-ing As men of old have sung.
It came, a flow-eret bright, A-mid the cold of win-ter, When half spent was the night.

2. I-sa-iah 'twas fore-told it, The Rose I have in mind,
With Mar-y we be-hold it, The Vir-gin Moth-er kind.
To show God's love a-right, She bore to men a Sav-ior, When half spent was the night. A-men.

456 Lord, Bless and Pity Us
ST. MICHAEL S.M.

From Psalm 67
The Psalter, 1912; alt., 1972

Comp. or adapted by Louis Bourgeois, 1551
Adapted by William Crotch, 1836
As in *Pilgrim Hymnal*, 1958

1. Lord, bless and pity us, Shine on us with your face, That all the earth your way may know And men may see your grace.
2. Your praise, O gracious God, Let all the nations sing; Let all men worship you with joy And songs of gladness bring.
3. The nations you will judge And lead them in your ways; Let all men praise your name, O God, Let all the people praise.
4. The earth her fruit shall yield, For God, our God, will bless; We shall be blest, and all the world His glory shall confess. A-men.

Lord, by Whose Breath All Souls and Seeds 457
ZU MEINEM HERRN 11.10.11.10.

Andrew Young, 1960; alt., 1972
Johann Gottfried Schicht, 1819

1. Lord, by whose breath all souls and seeds are living
With life that is and life that is to be,
First-fruits of earth, we offer with thanksgiving
For fields in flood with summer's golden sea.

2. Lord of the earth, accept these gifts in token;
You in your works are to be all adored,
From whom the light as daily bread is broken,
Sunset and dawn as wine and milk are poured.

3. Poor is our praise, but these shall be our psalter;
Lo, like yourself they rose up from the dead;
Lord, give them back when at your holy altar
We feed on you, who are the living bread. A-men.

Words from *The Collected Poems of Andrew Young*; used by permission of the publisher, Rupert Hart-Davis Ltd.

458 Lord, Dismiss Us with Your Blessing
SICILIAN MARINERS 8.7.8.7.8.7.

Attr. to John Fawcett, 1773; alt.
St. 3 alt. by Godfrey Thring (1823-1903)

Sicilian folk song (?)

1. Lord, dismiss us with your blessing; Fill our hearts with joy and peace; Let us each, your love possessing, Triumph in redeeming grace. O refresh us, O refresh us, Traveling through this wilderness.

2. Thanks we give and adoration For your gospel's joyful sound; May the fruits of your salvation In our hearts and lives abound. Ever faithful, Ever faithful To the truth may we be found;

3. So that when your love shall call us, Savior, from the world away, Let no fear of death appall us, Glad your summons to obey. May we ever, May we ever Reign with you in endless day. A-men.

Lord, from the Depths to You I Cry 459
SONG 67 C.M.

Psalm 130
Para. in the Scottish Psalter, 1650; alt.

Prys's Welsh Psalter, 1621

1. Lord, from the depths to you I cry; My call, Lord, you will hear: Unto my supplication's voice Give an attentive ear.
2. Lord, who shall stand, if you, O Lord, Should mark iniquity? But yet with you forgiveness is, That feared you still may be.
3. I wait for God, my soul does wait; My hope is in his word. More than they who for morning watch, My soul waits for the Lord;
4. I say, more than all they who watch The morning light to see. Let Israel hope ever found with him: And from all his iniquities He Israel shall redeem. A-men.
5. Redemption also plenteous Is in the Lord, For with him mercies be.

460 Lord God of Hosts, Whose Purpose

WELWYN 11.10.11.10.

Shepherd Knapp, 1907; alt., 1972

Alfred Scott-Gatty, 1900
As in *The English Hymnal*, 1906

1. Lord God of hosts, whose purpose, never swerving,
Leads toward the day of Jesus Christ your Son,
Grant us to march among your faithful legions,
Armed with your courage, till the world is won.

2. Strong Son of God, whose work was his that sent you,
One with the Father, thought and deed and word,
One make us all, true comrades in your service,
And make us one in you with God the Lord.

3. O Prince of Peace, the bringer of good tidings,
Teach us to speak your word of hope and cheer—
Rest for the soul, and strength for all man's striving,
Light for the path of life, and God brought near.

4. Lord God, whose grace has called us to your service,
How good your thoughts toward us, how great their sum!
We work with you, we go where you will lead us,
Until in all the earth your kingdom come. A-men.

Lord Jesus Christ, Our Lord Most Dear

461

VOM HIMMEL HOCH L.M.

Heinrich von Laufenberg, 1429(?)
Trans. by Catherine Winkworth, 1869; alt.

Geystliche Lieder, Leipzig, 1539

Lord Jesus Christ, our Lord most dear,
As you were once an infant here,
So give this child of yours, we pray,
Your grace and blessing day by day. A-men.

462 Lord, Look Upon Our Working Days
AUDREY L.M.

Ian M. Fraser, 1964; alt., 1972
Donald D. Kettring, 1972

1. Lord, look up-on our work-ing days, Bus-ied in fac-tory, of-fice, store; May word-less work your name a-dore, The com-mon round spell out your praise?
2. Bent to the lot our crafts as-sign, Swayed by deep tides of need and fear, In loy-al-ties torn, the truth un-clear, How may we build to your de-sign?
3. You are the work-man, Lord, not we: All worlds were made at your com-mand. Christ, their sus-tain-er, bared his hand, Res-cued them from fu-til-i-ty.
4. Our part to do what he'll com-mit, Who strides the world, and calls men all Part-ners in pain and car-ni-val, To grasp the hope he won for it.
5. Cov-er our faults with par-don full, Shield those who suf-fer when we shirk; Take what is wor-thy in our work, Give it due por-tion in your rule. A-men.

Words © copyright 1969 by Galliard, Ltd. All rights reserved. Used by permission of Galaxy Music Corp., N.Y., sole U.S. agent. Music copyright 1972 by The Westminster Press.

Lord of All Being, Throned Afar 463
LOUVAN L.M.

Oliver Wendell Holmes, 1859; alt., 1972
Virgil C. Taylor, 1846; alt., 1931, 1958

1. Lord of all be-ing, throned a-far, Your glo-ry flames from sun and star; Cen-ter and soul of ev-ery sphere, Yet to each lov-ing heart how near!
2. Sun of our life, your quick-ening ray Sheds on our path the glow of day; Star of our hope, your soft-ened light Cheers the long watch-es of the night.
3. Lord of all life, be-low, a-bove, Whose light is truth, whose warmth is love, Be-fore your ev-er-blaz-ing throne We ask no lus-ter of our own.
4. Grant us your truth for which we yearn, And kin-dling hearts that for you burn, Till all your liv-ing al-tars claim One ho-ly light, one heav-enly flame. A-men.

464. Lord of All Majesty and Might

VATER UNSER 8.8.8.8.8.8.

George Wallace Briggs, 1931
Geystliche Lieder, Leipzig, 1539
Harm. by J. S. Bach (1685-1750)

1. Lord of all majesty and might, Whose presence fills th'unfathomed deep, Wherein uncounted worlds of light Through countless ages vigil keep; Eternal God, can such as we, Frail mortal men, know aught of thee?

2. Beyond all knowledge thou art wise, With wisdom that transcends all thought: Yet still we seek with straining eyes, Yea, seek thee as our fathers sought; Nor will we from the quest depart Till we shall know thee as thou art.

*3. Frail though our form, and brief our day, Our mind has bridged the gulf of years, Our puny balances can weigh The magnitude of starry spheres: Within us is eternity; Whence comes it, Father, but from thee?

4. For, when thy wondrous works we scan, And mind gives answer back to mind, Thine image stands revealed in man; And, seeking, he shall surely find. Thy sons, our heritage we claim: Shall not thy children know thy name?

5. We know in part: enough we know To walk with thee, and walk aright; And thou shalt guide us as we go, And lead us into fuller light, Till, when we stand before thy throne, We know at last as we are known. A-men.

Words from *Songs of Praise*, Enlarged Edition; used by permission of Oxford University Press.

Lord of All Nations, Grant Me Grace 465
BEATUS VIR L.M.

Olive Wise Spannaus, 1960; alt., 1972

Slovak melody, 16th century
Arr. by Richard Hillert, 1967

1. Lord of all nations, grant me grace To love all men of every race, And in each fellow-man to view My brother, loved, redeemed by you.
2. Break down the wall that would divide Your children, Lord, on every side. Let me seek first my neighbor's good, In bonds of Christian brotherhood.
3. Forgive me, Lord, where I have erred By loveless act and thoughtless word. Make me to see the wrong I do Will crucify my Lord anew.
4. Give me your courage, Lord, to speak Whenever strong oppress the weak. Should I myself the victim be, Help me forgive, from anger free.
5. With your own love may I be filled And by your Holy Spirit willed, That all I touch whate'er I do May be divinely touched by you. A-men.

Words and music copyright 1967 by Concordia Publishing House; from *A New Song* (words slightly altered); used by permission.

466 Lord of the Strong, When Earth You Trod
CHARLOTTE 8.8.8.8.8.6.

Donald Hankey (1884-1916) — Richard M. Peek, 1972

1. Lord of the strong, when earth you trod, You calm-ly faced the an-gry sea, The fierce un-masked hy-poc-ri-sy, The trai-tor's kiss, the rab-ble's hiss, The aw-ful death up-on the tree,
2. Lord of the weak, when earth you trod, Op-pres-sors writhed be-neath your scorn; The weak, de-spised, de-praved, for-lorn, You taught to hope and know the scope Of love di-vine for all who mourn:
3. Lord of the rich, when earth you trod, To Mam-mon's power you nev-er bowed, But taught how men with wealth en-dowed In meek-ness' school might learn to rule The de-mon that en-slaves the proud: All glo-ry be to God.
4. Lord of the poor, when earth you trod, The lot you chose was hard and poor; You taught us hard-ness to en-dure, And so to gain through hurt and pain The wealth that lasts for-ev-er-more:
*5. Lord of us all, when earth you trod, The life you led was per-fect, free, De-fi-ant of all tyr-an-ny: Now give us grace that we may face Our foes with like te-mer-i-ty,

A-men.

Music copyright 1972 by The Westminster Press.

Lord Our God, with Praise We Come

467

GUD ER GUD P.M.

Petter Dass (1647-1707)
Trans. by Peter A. Sveeggen, 1951; alt., 1972

Leland B. Sateren, 1951, 1970

1. Lord our God, with praise we come before you! Let all nations humbly now implore you! All endeavor to praise you ever! And ceasing never, may we forever adore you!
2. God is God, though lands were all forsaken. God is God, though death had all men taken. Though all races had left no traces— In starry spaces God's love embraces creation.
3. Vales and hills shall move from their foundations; Heaven and earth shall crash in consternation; Mounts transcending will have their ending. Then morn ascending shall bring unending salvation. A-men.

Words and music reprinted from "God Is God," 1970 based on ACL No. 1380, 1951; used by permission of Augsburg Publishing House, Minneapolis, Minnesota, copyright owner.

468 Lord, We Thank You for Our Brothers
BLAENHAFREN 8.7.8.7.D.

Roger K. Powell, 1948; alt., 1965

Traditional Welsh melody
As in *Hymns of the Kingdom of God*, 1923

1. Lord, we thank you for our brothers Keeping faith with us and you, Joining heart to heart with others, Thus our oneness to renew. With the
2. God be praised for congregations Joining now in charity; Many tongues of many nations, Sing the greater unity. Welcome
3. May your name be praised forever! Heal our differences of old; Bless your church's new endeavor; For your kingdom make us bold. One our

Words used by permission of Roger K. Powell.

Lord, We Think You for Our Brothers (cont.) 469

cross our on-ly stan-dard Let us sing with
sound of psalm and car-ol When our song is
Christ and one our gos-pel, Make us one, we

one great voice, Glo-ry, glo-ry, yours the
raised as one. Glo-ry, glo-ry, yours the
now im-plore. Glo-ry, glo-ry, yours the

king-dom; Church-es in your church re-joice.
pow-er, As in heaven your will be done.
glo-ry Through the ag-es ev-er-more. A-men.

470 Lord, Who Throughout These Forty Days
ST. FLAVIAN C.M.

Claudia F. Hernaman, 1873; alt., 1972

Day's Psalter, 1562
Adapted in *Church Hymn Tunes*, 1853

1. Lord, who through-out these for-ty days For us did fast and pray, Teach us with you to mourn our sins, And close by you to stay.
2. As you with Sa-tan did con-tend, And did the vic-tory win, O give us strength in you to fight, In you to con-quer sin.
3. And through these days of pen-i-tence, And through your Pas-sion-tide, Yes, ev-er-more, in life and death, O Lord, with us a-bide.
4. A-bide with us, so when this course Of life on earth is past, An Eas-ter of un-end-ing joy We may at-tain at last! A-men.

Love Divine, All Loves Excelling

HYFRYDOL 8.7.8.7.D.

Charles Wesley, 1747; alt.

Rowland Hugh Prichard, 1855
Harm. by Ralph Vaughan Williams, 1906

471

1. Love divine, all loves excelling, Joy of heaven, to earth come down, Fix in us thy humble dwelling, All thy faithful mercies crown! Jesus,
2. Breathe, O breathe thy loving Spirit Into every troubled breast! Let us all in thee inherit, Let us find the promised rest; Take away
3. Come, Almighty to deliver, Let us all thy life receive; Suddenly return, and never, Nevermore thy temples leave. Thee we
4. Finish, then, thy new creation; Pure and spotless let us be; Let us see thy great salvation Perfectly restored in thee; Changed from

Music from *The English Hymnal*; used by permission of Oxford University Press.

See following page.

472 Love Divine, All Loves Excelling (cont.)

thou art all com-pas-sion, Pure, un-bound-ed love thou art; Vis-it us with thy sal-va-tion, En-ter ev-ery trem-bling heart.

way the love of sin-ning; Al-pha and O-meg-a be; End of faith, as its Be-gin-ning, Set our hearts at lib-er-ty.

would be al-ways bless-ing, Serve thee as thy hosts a-bove, Pray, and praise thee with-out ceas-ing, Glo-ry in thy per-fect love.

glo-ry in-to glo-ry, Till in heaven we take our place, Till we cast our crowns be-fore thee, Lost in won-der, love, and praise. A-men.

Lovely Child, Holy Child   473
BETHLEHEM 6.6.6.7. with Alleluias

David N. Johnson, 1968

Folk carol
Adapted by David N. Johnson, 1968

1. Lovely Child, holy Child, Gentle, mild, undefiled;
   Infant King, fairest King, Gifts we'll bring and anthems sing:
   Alleluia, alleluia,
   Alleluia, alleluia! Amen.

2. Child of light, born tonight, Our delight, promise bright;
   Child so fair: see him there; Now declare him everywhere:
   Alleluia, alleluia,
   Alleluia, alleluia! Amen.

3. Rest thy head, sweetest head; Gifts we'll spread at thy bed.
   Jesus Lord, be adored, May this word now be outpoured:
   Alleluia, alleluia,
   Alleluia, alleluia! Amen.

4. To this Boy, our great joy, We employ hymns of joy;
   Child so fair: see him there; Now declare him everywhere:
   Alleluia, alleluia,
   Alleluia, alleluia! Amen.

Words and music reprinted from *Twelve Folksongs and Spirituals*, compiled and arranged by David N. Johnson, 1968; used by permission of Augsburg Publishing House, Minneapolis, Minnesota, copyright owner.

474 Mine Eyes Have Seen the Glory
BATTLE HYMN OF THE REPUBLIC P.M.

Julia Ward Howe, 1861 — Arr. from camp meeting song

1. Mine eyes have seen the glo-ry of the com-ing of the Lord;
2. I have seen him in the watch-fires of a hun-dred cir-cling camps;
3. He has sound-ed forth the trum-pet that shall nev-er call re-treat;
4. In the beau-ty of the lil-ies Christ was born a-cross the sea,

He is tram-pling out the vin-tage where the grapes of wrath are stored;
They have build-ed him an al-tar in the eve-ning dews and damps;
He is sift-ing out the hearts of men be-fore his judg-ment seat;
With a glo-ry in his bos-om that trans-fig-ures you and me;

He hath loosed the fate-ful light-ning of his ter-ri-ble swift sword;
I can read his righ-teous sen-tence by the dim and flar-ing lamps;
O be swift, my soul, to an-swer him; be ju-bi-lant, my feet!
As he died to make men ho-ly, let us die to make men free!

Mine Eyes Have Seen the Glory (cont.) 475

His truth is march-ing on.
His day is march-ing on.
Our God is march-ing on.
While God is march-ing on. Glo-ry! glo-ry! Hal-le-lu-jah! Glo-ry! glo-ry! Hal-le-lu-jah! Glo-ry! glo-ry! Hal-le-lu-jah! His truth is march-ing on. A-men.

476 My Country, 'Tis of Thee

AMERICA 6.6.4.6.6.6.4.

Samuel F. Smith, 1831
Source unknown

1. My country, 'tis of thee, Sweet land of liberty, Of thee I sing; Land where my fathers died, Land of the pilgrims' pride, From every mountainside Let freedom ring.

2. My native country, thee, Land of the noble free, Thy name I love; I love thy rocks and rills, Thy woods and templed hills; My heart with rapture thrills Like that above.

3. Let music swell the breeze, And ring from all the trees Sweet freedom's song: Let mortal tongues awake; Let all that breathe partake; Let rocks their silence break, The sound prolong.

4. Our fathers' God, to thee, Author of liberty, To thee we sing: Long may our land be bright With freedom's holy light; Protect us by thy might, Great God, our King. A-men.

My Shepherd Will Supply My Need

RESIGNATION C.M.D.

477

Psalm 23
Para. by Isaac Watts, 1719; alt., 1972

Southern Harmony, 1835
Harm. in *Hymnal for Colleges and Schools*, 1956

1. My Shepherd will supply my need; Jehovah is his name: In pastures fresh he makes me feed, Beside the living stream. He brings my wandering spirit
2. When I walk through the shades of death Your presence is my stay; One word of your supporting breath Drives all my fears away. Your hand, in sight of all my
3. The sure provisions of my God Attend me all my days; O may your house be my abode, And all my work be praise. There would I find a settled

Music from *Hymnal for Colleges and Schools*, edited by E. Harold Geer;
used by permission of Yale University Press.

See following page.

478. My Shepherd Will Supply My Need (cont.)

back, When I forsake his ways; And leads me, for his mercy's sake, In paths of truth and grace.
foes, Does still my table spread; My cup with blessings overflows, Your oil anoints my head.
rest, While others go and come; No more a stranger, or a guest, But like a child at home. A-men.

Not Alone for Mighty Empire

479

GENEVA 8.7.8.7.D.

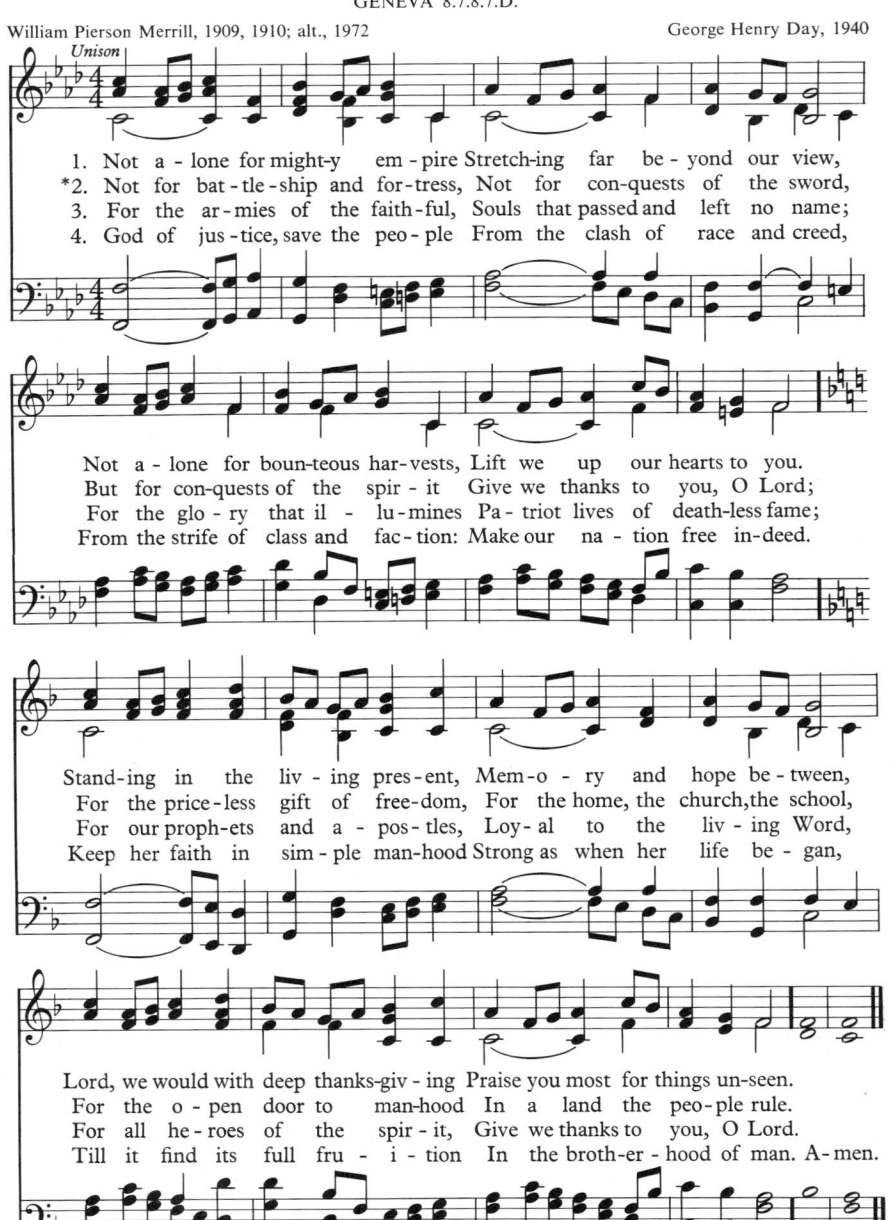

William Pierson Merrill, 1909, 1910; alt., 1972   George Henry Day, 1940

1. Not alone for mighty empire Stretching far beyond our view,
*2. Not for battleship and fortress, Not for conquests of the sword,
3. For the armies of the faithful, Souls that passed and left no name;
4. God of justice, save the people From the clash of race and creed,

Not alone for bounteous harvests, Lift we up our hearts to you.
But for conquests of the spirit Give we thanks to you, O Lord;
For the glory that illumines Patriot lives of deathless fame;
From the strife of class and faction: Make our nation free indeed.

Standing in the living present, Memory and hope between,
For the priceless gift of freedom, For the home, the church, the school,
For our prophets and apostles, Loyal to the living Word,
Keep her faith in simple manhood Strong as when her life began,

Lord, we would with deep thanksgiving Praise you most for things unseen.
For the open door to manhood In a land the people rule.
For all heroes of the spirit, Give we thanks to you, O Lord.
Till it find its full fruition In the brotherhood of man. Amen.

Music used by permission of The Church Pension Fund.   *Alternative Tune:* HYFRYDOL

480 Now, on Land and Sea Descending
VESPER HYMN 8.7.8.7.8.6.8.7.

Samuel Longfellow, 1859
Refrain added

Russian melody (?)
Arr. by John A. Stevenson, 1818

1. Now, on land and sea de-scend-ing, Brings the night its peace pro-found;
2. Soon as dies the sun-set glo-ry, Stars of heaven shine out a-bove,
3. Now, our wants and bur-dens leav-ing To his care who cares for all,
4. As the dark-ness deep-ens o'er us, Lo! e-ter-nal stars a-rise;

Let our ves-per hymn be blend-ing With the ho-ly calm a-round.
Tell-ing still the an-cient sto-ry—Their Cre-a-tor's change-less love.
Cease we fear-ing, cease we griev-ing: At his touch our bur-dens fall.
Hope and faith and love rise glo-rious, Shin-ing in the spir-it's skies.

Ju-bi-la-te! Ju-bi-la-te! Ju-bi-la-te! A-men!

Let our ves-per hymn be blend-ing With the ho-ly calm a-round.
Tell-ing still the an-cient sto-ry—Their Cre-a-tor's change-less love.
Cease we fear-ing, cease we griev-ing: At his touch our bur-dens fall.
Hope and faith and love rise glo-rious, Shin-ing in the spir-it's skies. A-men.

Now Thank We All Our God
NUN DANKET 6.7.6.7.6.6.6.6.

Martin Rinkart, 1636
Trans. by Catherine Winkworth, 1858; alt., 1972

Johann Crüger, 1647
As alt. by Felix Mendelssohn, 1840

481

1. Now thank we all our God With heart and hands and voices,
Who wondrous things has done, In whom his world rejoices;
Who, from our mothers' arms Has blessed us on our way
With countless gifts of love, And still is ours today.

2. O may this bounteous God Through all our life be near us,
With ever-joyful hearts And blessed peace to cheer us;
And keep us in his grace, And guide us when perplexed,
And free us from all ills In this world and the next.

3. All praise and thanks to God The Father now be given,
The Son, and him who reigns With them in highest heaven,
The one eternal God, Whom earth and heaven adore;
For thus it was, is now, And shall be evermore. A-men.

482 O Be Joyful in the Lord!

ROCK OF AGES (MOOZ TSUR) 7.7.7.7.5.7.6.7.

Based on Psalm 100
Curtis Beach, 1958; alt., 1972

Traditional Hebrew melody
As in *Pilgrim Hymnal*, 1958

1. O be joy-ful in the Lord! Sing be-fore him, all the earth!
Praise him with a glad ac-cord And with lives of no-blest worth.
Sons of ev-ery land, Hum-bly now be-fore him stand!
Raise your voice and re-joice In the boun-ty of his hand.

2. Know then that the Lord is King! All his works his wis-dom prove!
By his might the heav-ens ring; In his love we live and move.
By him we are made, So we trust him un-a-fraid.
Stand-ing fast to the last, By his hand our lives are stayed.

3. En-ter now his ho-ly gate; Let our bur-dened hearts be still;
In the sa-cred si-lence wait, As we seek to know his will.
Let our lives ex-press Our a-bun-dant thank-ful-ness;
All our days, all our ways, Shall our Fa-ther's love con-fess.

4. For the Lord our God is kind, And his love shall con-stant be;
In his will our peace we find; In his serv-ice, lib-er-ty.
Yea, his law is sure; In his light we walk se-cure;
Ev-er-more, as of yore, Shall his change-less truth en-dure. A-men.

Words copyright 1958 by The Pilgrim Press; used by permission of the author and the United Church Press.

O Beautiful for Spacious Skies

MATERNA C.M.D.

483

Katharine Lee Bates, 1893, 1904

Samuel A. Ward, 1882

1. O beautiful for spacious skies, For amber waves of grain,
For purple mountain majesties Above the fruited plain!
America! America! God shed his grace on thee
And crown thy good with brotherhood From sea to shining sea!

2. O beautiful for pilgrim feet, Whose stern, impassioned stress
A thoroughfare for freedom beat Across the wilderness!
America! America! God mend thine every flaw,
Confirm thy soul in self-control, Thy liberty in law!

3. O beautiful for heroes proved In liberating strife,
Who more than self their country loved, And mercy more than life!
America! America! May God thy gold refine
Till all success be nobleness And every gain divine!

4. O beautiful for patriot dream That sees beyond the years
Thine alabaster cities gleam, Undimmed by human tears!
America! America! God shed his grace on thee
And crown thy good with brotherhood From sea to shining sea! A-men!

484. O Brother Man, Fold to Your Heart
WELWYN 11.10.11.10.

John Greenleaf Whittier, 1848; alt., 1972

Alfred Scott-Gatty, 1900
As in *The English Hymnal*, 1906

1. O brother man, fold to your heart your brother;
   Where pity dwells, the peace of God is there;
   To worship rightly is to love each other,
   Each smile a hymn, each kindly deed a prayer.

2. For he whom Jesus loved has truly spoken:
   The holier worship which he deigns to bless
   Restores the lost, and binds the spirit broken,
   And feeds the widow and the fatherless.

3. Follow with reverent steps the great example
   Of him whose holy work was doing good;
   So shall the wide earth seem our Father's temple,
   Each loving life a psalm of gratitude.

4. Then shall all shackles fall; the stormy clangor
   Of wild war music o'er the earth shall cease;
   Love shall tread out the baleful fire of anger,
   And in its ashes plant the tree of peace. A-men.

O Christ, Whose Love Has Sought Us Out   485
DAS NEUGEBORNE KINDELEIN L.M.

John Edgar Park, 1953; alt., 1972

Melchior Vulpius, 1609
Harm. by J. S. Bach, 1724

1. O Christ, whose love has sought us out
   Alone and lost in desert ways;
   We gather round your cross again
   In wonder and united praise.

2. Your life is still the miracle,
   Our way of living far above,
   Beyond the reaches of our minds:
   We cannot understand; we love.

3. Ancestral gifts within our hands,
   The cherished treasures from the past,
   We lay before your feet, O Lord:
   Cleanse, use them, make them yours at last.

4. So may we all be one in you,
   Whose revelations never cease,
   Whose love and truth are ever new,
   And in whose service is our peace. Amen.

Words altered from *Eleven Ecumenical Hymns;* copyright 1954 by The Hymn Society of America; used by permission.

486 O Come, All Ye Faithful
ADESTE FIDELES Irregular

Attr. to John Francis Wade, ca. 1743
Trans. by Frederick Oakeley, 1841; alt.

Attr. to John Francis Wade, ca. 1743

1. O come, all ye faithful, Joyful and triumphant, O come ye, O come ye to Bethlehem! Come and behold him, Born the King of angels!
2. The Brightness of glory, Light of light eternal, Our lowly nature he hath not abhorred: Son of the Father, Word of God incarnate,
3. O sing, choirs of angels, Sing in exultation! O sing, all ye citizens of heaven above! Glory to God, all glory in the highest!
4. Amen, Lord, we greet thee, Born this happy morning, O Jesus, to thee be all glory given; Word of the Father, Now in flesh appearing!

O Come, All Ye Faithful (cont.) 487

O come, let us adore him, O come, let us adore him, O come, let us adore him, Christ the Lord! A-men.

488 O Come and Sing Unto the Lord
IRISH C.M.

From Psalm 95:1-6
The Psalter, 1912; alt., 1955

A Collection of Hymns and Sacred Poems, 1749

1. O come and sing unto the Lord, To him our voices raise; Let us in our most joyful songs The Lord, our Savior, praise.
2. Before his presence let us come With praise and thankful voice; Let us sing psalms to him with grace, With grateful hearts rejoice.
3. The Lord our God is King of kings, Above all gods his throne; The depths of earth are in his hand, The mountains are his own.
4. To him the spacious sea belongs, He made its waves and tides; And by his hand the rising land Was formed, and still abides.
5. O come, and bowing down to him Our worship let us bring; Yea, let us kneel before the Lord, Our Maker and our King. A-men.

O Come, O Come, Emmanuel

VENI EMMANUEL 8.8.8.8.8.8.

Psalteriolum Cantionum Catholicarum, 1710
Sts. 1, 2 trans. by John Mason Neale, 1851, 1854; alt.
Sts. 3, 4 trans. by Henry Sloane Coffin, 1916

French Processional, 15th century
Adapted by Thomas Helmore, 1854
As in *Hymnal for Colleges and Schools*, 1956

May be sung in unison

1. O come, O come, Emmanuel, And ransom captive Israel, That mourns in lonely exile here, Until the Son of God appear.
2. O come, thou Day-spring, come and cheer Our spirits by thine advent here; Disperse the gloomy clouds of night, And death's dark shadows put to flight.
3. O come, thou Wisdom from on high, And order all things, far and nigh; To us the path of knowledge show, And cause us in her ways to go.
4. O come, Desire of nations, bind All peoples in one heart and mind; Bid envy, strife, and quarrels cease; Fill the whole world with heaven's peace.

Rejoice! Rejoice! Emmanuel Shall come to thee, O Israel! A-men.

Music from *Hymnal for Colleges and Schools*, edited by E. Harold Geer; used by permission of Yale University Press.

490 O Come, O Come, Emmanuel

Psalteriolum Cantionum Catholicarum, 1710
Trans. by T. A. Lacey, 1906
James Minchin, 1964

(Solo instrument ad lib.)

1. O come, O come, Emmanuel! Redeem thy captive Israel, That into exile drear has gone Far from the face of God's dear Son.
2. O come, O come, thou Dayspring bright! Pour on our souls thy healing light; Dispel the long night's lingering gloom, And pierce the shadows of the tomb.
3. O come, thou Lord of David's Key! The royal door fling wide and free; Safeguard for us the heav'nward road, And bar the way to death's abode. Re-

Words from *The English Hymnal*; used by permission of Oxford University Press. Music from *Jazz in the Church*; © 1964 by James Minchin; used by permission.

O Come, O Come, Emmanuel (cont.)   491

492 O Day of God, Draw Nigh
ST. MICHAEL S.M.

R. B. Y. Scott, 1937, 1939; alt., 1972

Comp. or adapted by Louis Bourgeois, 1551
Adapted by William Crotch, 1836
As in *Pilgrim Hymnal*, 1958

1. O Day of God, draw nigh In beauty and in power, Come with your timeless judgment now To match our present hour.
2. Bring to our troubled minds, Uncertain and afraid, The quiet of a steadfast faith, Calm of a call obeyed.
3. Bring justice to our land, That all may dwell secure, And finely build for days to come Foundations that endure.
4. Bring to our world of strife Your sovereign word of peace, That war may haunt the earth no more And desolation cease.
5. O Day of God, draw nigh As at creation's birth; Let there be light again, and set Your judgments in the earth. A-men.

Words used by permission of R. B. Y. Scott.

O for a Thousand Tongues to Sing

AZMON C.M.

Charles Wesley, 1739; alt., 1972

Carl G. Gläser, 1828
Arr. by Lowell Mason, 1839

493

1. O for a thousand tongues to sing Our dear Redeemer's praise, The glories of our God and King, The triumphs of his grace!
2. Jesus, the name that charms our fears, That bids our sorrows cease— Its music in the sinner's ears Brings life, and health, and peace.
3. Our gracious Master and our God, Assist us to proclaim, To spread through all the earth abroad, The honors of your name.
4. Glory to God and praise and love Be ever, ever given By saints below and saints above, The church in earth and heaven. A-men.

494 O Gladsome Light, O Grace
NUNC DIMITTIS 6.6.7.D.

Greek hymn, 3d century or earlier
Trans. by Robert Bridges, 1899

Comp. or adapted by Louis Bourgeois, 1549

1. O glad-some Light, O Grace Of God the Fa-ther's face, Th'e-ter-nal splen-dor wear-ing; Ce-les-tial, ho-ly, blest, Our Sav-ior Je-sus Christ, Joy-ful in thine ap-pear-ing!
2. Now, ere day fad-eth quite, We see the eve-ning light, Our wont-ed hymn out-pour-ing; Fa-ther of might un-known, Thee, his in-car-nate Son, And Ho-ly Spirit a-dor-ing.
3. To thee of right be-longs All praise of ho-ly songs, O Son of God, Life-giv-er; Thee, there-fore, O Most High, The world doth glo-ri-fy And shall ex-alt for-ev-er. A-men.

Words from *The Yattendon Hymnal*; used by permission of Oxford University Press.

O God, Beneath Your Guiding Hand   495
DUKE STREET L.M.

Leonard Bacon, 1833, 1845; alt., 1972 — John Hatton, 1793

1. O God, beneath your guiding hand Our exiled fathers crossed the sea; And echoed o'er the wintry strand Their psalms and prayers in worship free.
2. You heard, well-pleased, the song, the prayer; Your blessing came, and still its power Shall onward through all ages bear The memory of that holy hour.
3. Laws, freedom, truth, and faith in God Came with those exiles o'er the waves, And where their pilgrim feet have trod, The God they trusted guards their graves.
4. And here your name, O God of love, Their children's children shall adore, Till these eternal hills remove, And spring adorns the earth no more. A-men.

496. O God of Bethel, by Whose Hand

DUNDEE (FRENCH) C.M.

Philip Doddridge, 1736, and others
As in Scottish Paraphrases, 1781; alt., 1972

Scottish Psalter, 1615

1. O God of Beth-el, by whose hand Your people still are fed, Who through this weary pil-grim-age Have all our fa-thers led,

2. Our vows, our prayers, we now pre-sent Be-fore your throne of grace; God of our fa-thers, be the God Of their suc-ceed-ing race.

3. Through each per-plex-ing path of life Our wan-dering foot-steps guide; Give us each day our dai-ly bread, And rai-ment fit pro-vide.

4. O spread your cov-ering wings a-round Till all our wan-derings cease, And at our Fa-ther's loved a-bode Our souls ar-rive in peace.

5. Such bless-ings from your gra-cious hand Our hum-ble prayers im-plore; And you shall be our cho-sen God And por-tion ev-er-more. A-men.

O God of Earth and Altar

497

LLANGLOFFAN 7.6.7.6.D.

Gilbert K. Chesterton, 1906

Welsh hymn melody
Evans' *Hymnau a Thonau*, 1865

1. O God of earth and altar, Bow down and hear our cry; Our earthly rulers falter; Our people drift and die; The walls of gold entomb us; The swords of scorn divide; Take not thy thunder from us, But take away our pride.

2. From all that terror teaches, From lies of tongue and pen, From all the easy speeches That comfort cruel men, From sale and profanation Of honor and the sword, From sleep and from damnation, Deliver us, good Lord!

3. Tie in a living tether The priest and prince and thrall; Bind all our lives together; Smite us and save us all; In ire and exultation, Aflame with faith, and free, Lift up a living nation, A single sword to thee. A-men.

Words from *The English Hymnal*; used by permission of Oxford University Press.

498 O God of Every Nation

LLANGLOFFAN 7.6.7.6.D.

William W. Reid, Jr., 1958; alt., 1972

Welsh hymn melody
Evans' *Hymnau a Thonau*, 1865

1. O God of every nation, Of every race and land,
Redeem the whole creation With your almighty hand;
Where hate and fear divide us And bitter threats are hurled,
In love and mercy guide us And heal our strife-torn world.

2. From search for wealth and power And scorn of truth and right,
From trust in bombs that shower Destruction through the night,
From pride of race and station And blindness to your way,
Deliver every nation, Eternal God, we pray.

3. Lord, strengthen all who labor That men may find release
From fear of rattling saber, From dread of war's increase;
When hope and courage falter, Your still small voice be heard;
With faith that none can alter, Your servants undergird.

4. Keep bright in us the vision Of days when war shall cease,
When hatred and division Give way to love and peace,
Till dawns the morning glorious When brotherhood shall reign
And Christ shall rule victorious O'er all the world's domain. A-men.

Words copyright 1958 by The Hymn Society of America; altered from *Twelve New World Order Hymns*; used by permission.

O God of Light, Your Word, a Lamp Unfailing 499
CHARTERHOUSE 11.10.11.10.

Sarah E. Taylor, 1952; alt., 1972
David Evans, 1927

1. O God of light, your Word, a lamp unfailing, Shines through the darkness of our earthly way, O'er fear and doubt, o'er black despair prevailing, Guiding our steps to your eternal day.

2. From days of old, through swiftly rolling ages, You have revealed your will to mortal men, Speaking to saints, to prophets, kings, and sages, Who wrote the message with immortal pen.

3. Undimmed by time, the Word is still revealing To sinful men your justice and your grace; And questing hearts that long for peace and healing See your compassion in the Savior's face.

4. To all the world the message you are sending, To every land, to every race and clan; And myriad tongues, in one great anthem blending, Acclaim with joy your wondrous gift to man. A-men.

Words altered from *Ten New Hymns on the Bible*; copyright 1952 by The Hymn Society of America; used by permission.
Music from *The Church Hymnary*, Revised Edition, 1927; used by permission of Oxford University Press.

500 O God, Our Faithful God
O GOTT, DU FROMMER GOTT 6.7.6.7.6 6 6 6.

Johann Heermann, 1630
Trans. by Catherine Winkworth, 1858; alt., 1956, 1972

Attr. to Ahasuerus Fritsch, 1679
Harm. by J. S. Bach, 1726

1. O God, our faithful God, O fountain ever flowing, Without whom nothing is, All perfect gifts bestowing, Grant us a faithful life, And give us, Lord, within, Commitment free from strife, A soul unhurt by sin.

2. And grant us, Lord, to do, With ready heart and willing, Whatever you command, Our calling here fulfilling; And do it when we ought, With zeal and joyfulness; And bless the work we've wrought, For you must give success.

3. If dangers gather round, Still keep us calm and fearless; Help us to bear the cross When life is dark and cheerless, To overcome our foes With words and actions kind; O God, your will disclose, Your counsel let us find. Amen.

Words altered from *Hymnal for Colleges and Schools*, edited by E. Harold Geer; used by permission of Yale University Press.

O God, This Child from You Did Come   501
SHEPHERDS' PIPES C.M.D.

Frank A. Brooks, Jr., 1972　　　　　　　　　　　　　　Annabeth McClelland Gay, 1952

1. O God, this child from you did come, To you it shall return;
   But to our trust and love you chose To send it for some years.
   Because we thank you for this life That to our lives has come,
   Together we do pledge ourselves To help this child serve you. Amen.

2. Real acts of love and words of truth We hope to teach this child,
   And constant may our guidance be In likeness of your Son.

3. Of flesh and blood this child is made, In image of yourself.
   To men we come; on earth we live—Our purpose clear to serve.

Words copyright 1972 by The Westminster Press. Music copyright by The Pilgrim Press; used by permission of the United Church Press.

502 O God, Who by a Star Did Guide
ST. BERNARD C.M.

John Mason Neale, 1842; alt., 1972

Tochter Sion, Cologne, 1741
Arr. attr. to John Richardson, 1851

1. O God, who by a star did guide The Wise Men on their way, Until it came and stood beside The place where Jesus lay:
2. Although by stars you do not lead Your servants now below, Your Holy Spirit, when they need, Will show them how to go.
3. As yet we know you but in part, But still we trust your word, That blessed are the pure in heart, For they shall see the Lord.
4. O Savior, give us then your grace, For pure in heart we'd be, That we may see you, face to face, Through all eternity. Amen.

O God, Whose Will Is Life and Peace 503
THIRD MODE MELODY C.M.D.

Rolland W. Schloerb, 1948; alt., 1972

Thomas Tallis, ca. 1567
Rhythm alt.

1. O God, whose will is life and peace For all the sons of men,
Let not our hu-man hates re-lease The sword's dread power a-gain.
For-give our nar-row-ness of mind; De-stroy false pride, we plead;
De-liv-er us and all man-kind From self-ish-ness and greed.

2. O God, whose ways shall lead to peace, En-light-en us, we pray;
Dis-pel our dark-ness and in-crease The light a-long our way.
Il-lu-mine those who lead the lands, That they may make at length
The laws of right to guide the hands That wield the na-tions' strength.

3. O God, who calls all men to peace, We join with ev-ery-one
Who does his part that wars may cease And jus-tice may be done.
En-a-ble us to take the way The Prince of Peace has trod;
Cre-ate the will to build each day The fam-i-ly of God. A-men.

Words used by permission of Mrs. Rolland W. Schloerb.

504 O God, You Are the Father

GOSTERWOOD 7.6.7.6.D.

St. Columba (521-597)
Trans. by Duncan Macgregor, 1897; alt., 1972

Traditional English melody, collected and harm. by Ralph Vaughan Williams, 1906

1. O God, you are the Father Of all that have believed,
From whom all hosts of people Have life and power received.
O God, you are the Maker Of all created things,
The righteous Judge of judges, Th' almighty King of kings.

2. High in the heavenly Zion You reign, our God adored,
And in the coming glory You shall be sovereign Lord;
Beyond our knowledge shining, The everlasting light:
Ineffable in loving, Unthinkable in might.

3. You to the meek and lowly Your secrets do unfold;
O God, who can do all things, All things good, new and old.
We walk secure and blessed In every clime or coast,
In name of God the Father, And Son, and Holy Ghost. A-men.

Music from *The English Hymnal*; used by permission of Oxford University Press.

O Holy City, Seen of John 505
MORNING SONG 8.6.8.6.8.6.

Walter Russell Bowie, 1909; alt., 1972
Kentucky Harmony, ca.1815
Harm. by C. Winfred Douglas, 1940

May be sung in unison

1. O holy city, seen of John, Where Christ, the Lamb, does reign, Within whose four-square walls shall come No night, nor need, nor pain, And where the tears are wiped from eyes That shall not weep again!

2. O shame to us who rest content While lust and greed for gain In street and shop and tenement Wring gold from human pain, And bitter lips in blind despair Cry, "Christ has died in vain"!

3. Give us, O God, the strength to build The city that has stood Too long a dream, whose laws are love, Whose ways are brotherhood, And where the sun that shines becomes God's grace for human good.

4. Already in the mind of God That city rises fair: Lo, how its splendor challenges The souls that greatly dare, And bids us seize the whole of life And build its glory there. A-men.

Music used by permission of The Church Pension Fund.

506 O How Shall We Receive You

ST. THEODULPH 7.6.7.6.D.

Paul Gerhardt, 1653
Trans. by Arthur Tozer Russell, 1851, and others
As in *Hymnal for Colleges and Schools*, 1956; alt., 1972

Melchior Teschner, 1615

1. O how shall we re-ceive you, How meet you on your way,
Blest hope of ev-ery na-tion, Our soul's de-light and stay?
O Je-sus, Je-sus, give us Now by your own pure light
To know what-e'er is pleas-ing And wel-come in your sight.

2. Your Zi-on palms is spread-ing, And branch-es fresh and fair;
Our souls, to praise a-wak-ing, An an-them shall pre-pare.
Un-end-ing thanks and prais-es From our glad hearts shall spring;
And to your name the serv-ice Of all our powers we bring.

3. Love caused your in-car-na-tion; Love blessed hu-man-i-ty.
Your thirst for our sal-va-tion Pro-cured our lib-er-ty.
O love be-yond all tell-ing, That led you to em-brace.
In love all loves ex-cel-ling, Our lost and trou-bled race.

4. You came, O Lord, with glad-ness, In mer-cy and good-will,
To bring an end to sad-ness And bid our fears be still.
We wel-come you, our Sav-ior; Come, gath-er us to you,
That in your light e-ter-nal Our joy-ous home we'll view. A-men.

Words altered from *Hymnal for Colleges and Schools*, edited by E. Harold Geer; used by permission of Yale University Press.

O I Know the Lord

507

Negro spiritual

Negro spiritual

O I know the Lord, I know the Lord, I know the Lord's laid his hands on me. O I know the Lord, I know the Lord, I know the Lord's laid his hands on me.

Fine

1. Did ev-er you see the like be-fore—
2. O was-n't that a hap-py day
3. Some seek the Lord and don't seek him right,
4. My Lord's done just what he said,

I know the Lord's laid his

Music from *American Negro Songs and Spirituals*, by John W. Work III, copyright 1940 by John W. Work III; used by permission.

See following page.

508   O I Know the Lord (cont.)

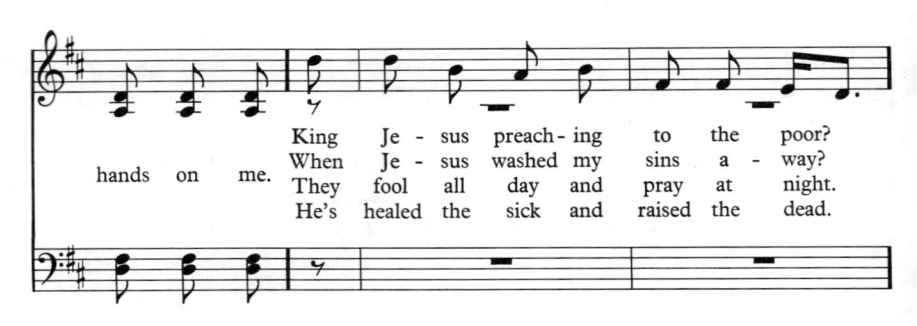

hands on me.
King Jesus preaching to the poor?
When Jesus washed my sins away?
They fool all day and pray at night.
He's healed the sick and raised the dead.

I know the Lord's laid his hands on me.

D.C.

O Jesus Christ, to You May Hymns Be Rising 509
CITY OF GOD 11.10.11.10.

Bradford G. Webster, 1954, 1969 — Daniel Moe, 1957

1. O Jesus Christ, to you may hymns be rising,
In every city for your love and care;
Inspire our worship, grant the glad surprising
That your blest Spirit brings men everywhere.

2. Show us your Spirit, brooding o'er each city,
As you once wept above Jerusalem,
Seeking to gather all in love and pity,
And healing those who touch your garment's hem.

3. Grant us new courage, sacrificial, humble,
Strong in your strength to venture and to dare;
To lift the fallen, guide the feet that stumble,
Seek out the lonely and God's mercy share. Amen.

Words copyright 1954 by The Hymn Society of America; revised from *Five New Hymns on the City*; used by permission. Music reprinted from *Hymns and Songs for Church Schools*, edited by Ruth Olson, 1962; used by permission of Augsburg Publishing House, Minneapolis, Minnesota, copyright owner.

510 O Jesus, Joy of Loving Hearts
FEDERAL STREET L.M.

Latin, 12th century
Trans. by Ray Palmer, 1858; alt., 1972

Henry K. Oliver, 1832

1. O Jesus, joy of loving hearts, O fount of life, O light of men, From the best bliss that earth imparts, We turn unfilled to you again.
2. Your truth unchanged has ever stood; You save those who upon you call; To those who seek you, you are good, To them who find you all in all.
3. We taste you, Lord, our living Bread, And long to feast upon you still; We drink of you, the fountain head, And thirst our souls from you to fill.
4. For you our restless spirits yearn, Wher-e'er our changeful lot is cast, Glad when to you our gaze we turn, Blest when our faith can hold you fast.
5. O Jesus, ever with us stay, Make all our moments calm and bright; Chase the dark night of sin away, Shed o'er the world your holy light. A-men.

Words copyright 1972 by The Westminster Press.

O Little Town of Bethlehem 511
ST. LOUIS 8.6.8.6.7.6.8.6.

Phillips Brooks, 1868
Lewis H. Redner, 1868

1. O little town of Bethlehem, How still we see thee lie;
2. For Christ is born of Mary; And gathered all above,
3. How silently, how silently The wondrous gift is given!
4. O holy Child of Bethlehem, Descend to us, we pray;

Above thy deep and dreamless sleep The silent stars go by.
While mortals sleep, the angels keep Their watch of wondering love.
So God imparts to human hearts The blessings of his heaven.
Cast out our sin, and enter in, Be born in us today.

Yet in thy dark streets shineth The everlasting Light;
O morning stars, together Proclaim the holy birth;
No ear may hear his coming, But in this world of sin,
We hear the Christmas angels The great glad tidings tell;

The hopes and fears of all the years Are met in thee tonight.
And praises sing to God the King, And peace to men on earth.
Where meek souls will receive him, still The dear Christ enters in.
O come to us, abide with us, Our Lord Emmanuel. A-men.

Alternative Tune: FOREST GREEN

512 O Lord of Every Shining Constellation
LOMBARD STREET 11.10.11.10.

Albert F. Bayly, 1950; alt., 1968   Frederick George Russell, 1925

1. O Lord of every shining constellation
That wheels in splendor through the midnight sky;
Grant us your Spirit's true illumination
To read the secrets of your work on high.

2. You, Lord, have made the atom's hidden forces,
Your laws its mighty energies fulfill;
Teach us, to whom you give such rich resources,
In all we use, to serve your holy will.

3. You, Lord, have stamped your image on your creatures,
And, though they mar that image, love them still;
Lift up our eyes to Christ, that in his features
We may discern the beauty of your will.

4. Great Lord of nature, shaping and renewing,
You made us more than nature's sons to be;
You help us tread, with grace our souls enduing,
The road to life and immortality. A-men.

Words used by permission of Albert F. Bayly. Music used by permission of Industrial Christian Fellowship, London.

O Lord of Life, Where'er They Be 513

GELOBT SEI GOTT 8.8.8. with Alleluias

Frederick Lucian Hosmer, 1888; alt., 1972

Attr. to Melchior Vulpius, 1609
As in *Pilgrim Hymnal*, 1958

1. O Lord of life, wher-e'er they be, Safe in your own e-ternity, Now live your chil-dren glo-rious-ly:
2. All souls you call, both here and there Do rest with-in your shel-tering care; One prov-i-dence a-like they share;
3. Your word is true, your ways are just; A-bove the chant-ed "Dust to dust" Shall rise our song of grate-ful trust:
4. Hap-py are they in God who rest, No more by fear and doubt op-pressed, Liv-ing or dy-ing, they are blest:

Al-le-lu-ia! Al-le-lu-ia! Al-le-lu-ia! A-men.

514   *O Lord, Our God, Most Earnestly*
STRACATHRO C.M.

From Psalm 63:1-8   Charles Hutcheson, 1832
The Psalter, 1912; alt., 1972   Harm. by Geoffrey Shaw, 1925

1. O Lord, our God, most earnestly Our hearts would seek your face, Within your holy house once more To see your glorious grace.
2. Apart from you we long and thirst, And none can satisfy; We wander in a desert land Where all the streams run dry.
3. The lovingkindness of our God Is life's security; So we will bless you while we live And pray unceasingly.
4. In you our souls are satisfied, Our darkness turns to light, And joyful meditations fill The watches of the night.
5. O Savior, 'neath your sheltering wings Our souls delight to dwell; Still closer to your side we press, For near you all is well. A-men.

Music from *Songs of Praise*, Enlarged Edition; used by permission of Oxford University Press.

O Lord, Our Lord, in All the Earth 515
DUNFERMLINE C.M.

From Psalm 8
The Psalter, 1912; alt., 1972

Scottish Psalter, 1615

1. O Lord, our Lord, in all the earth How ex-cel-lent your name! Your glo-ry you have spread a-far In all the star-ry frame.
2. When I re-gard the won-drous heavens, Your hand-i-work on high, The moon and stars you have or-dained, Oh, what is man! I cry.
3. Oh, what is man, in your re-gard To hold so large a place! And what the Son of man, that you Do vis-it him in grace!
4. On man your wis-dom has be-stowed A power none else has known; With hon-or you have crowned his head With glo-ry like your own.
5. Your might-y works and won-drous grace Your glo-ry, Lord, pro-claim. O Lord, our Lord, in all the earth How ex-cel-lent your name! A-men.

516 O Lord, Whose Gracious Presence Shone

PUER NOBIS (Praetorius) L.M.

Sts. 1, 2, 4, Marion Franklin Ham, 1912; alt., 1972
St. 3, Dalton E. McDonald, 1972

Trier MS., 15th century
Adapted by Michael Praetorius, 1609
Harm. by George R. Woodward, 1902

1. O Lord, whose gracious presence shone A light to bless your fellowmen, To you we fondly turn again, As to a friend that we have known.
2. Your grace and truth, your life that shed Undying radiance through all time, Your tender love, your faith sublime— Remembering these, we break the bread.
3. We taste the wine, and so recall Your sacrifice upon the cross— A life divine become as loss, That love should live again in all.
4. And lo, again we seem to hear Your blessing on the loaf and cup—The presence that was lifted up Again to loving hearts brought near. A-men.

Stanza 3 copyright 1972 by The Westminster Press. Music altered from *The Cowley Carol Book*, No. 21; used by permission of A. R. Mowbray & Co. Limited.

O Lord, You Are Our God and King 517
DUKE STREET L.M.

From Psalm 145:1-7
The Psalter, 1912; alt., 1972

John Hatton, 1793

1. O Lord, you are our God and King, And we will ev - er bless your name; We will ex - tol you ev - ery day, And ev - er - more your praise pro - claim.
2. The Lord is great - ly to be praised; His great - ness is be - yond our thought; From age to age the sons of men Shall tell the won - ders God has wrought.
3. Up - on your glo - rious maj - es - ty And won - drous works our minds shall dwell; Your deeds shall fill the world with awe, And of your great - ness we will tell.
4. Your match - less good - ness and your grace Your peo - ple shall com - mem - o - rate, And all your truth and righ - teous - ness Our joy - ful songs shall cel - e - brate. A - men.

518 O Love, How Deep, How Broad, How High!
DEO GRACIAS L.M.

Latin, 15th century
Trans. by Benjamin Webb, 1851; alt.

"The Agincourt Song," England, ca. 1415
Arr. for *The Hymnal*, 1933

1. O love, how deep, how broad, how high!
Beyond man's gift to prophesy,
That God, the Son of God, should take
Our mortal form for mortals' sake!

2. For us baptized, for us he bore
His holy fast, and hungered sore;
For us temptations sharp he knew;
For us the tempter overthrew.

3. For us to wicked men betrayed,
Scourged, mocked, in purple robe arrayed,
He bore the shameful cross and death,
For us gave up his dying breath.

4. For us he rose from death again,
For us he went on high to reign;
For us he sent his Spirit here
To guide, to strengthen, and to cheer. A-men.

Music copyright 1933 by Presbyterian Board of Christian Education, renewed 1961.

O Love That Wilt Not Let Me Go 519

ST. MARGARET 8.8.8.8.8.6.

George Matheson, 1882
Albert L. Peace, 1884

1. O Love that wilt not let me go, I rest my weary soul in thee; I give thee back the life I owe, That in thine o-cean depths its flow May rich-er, full-er be.
2. O Light that fol-lowest all my way, I yield my flick-ering torch to thee; My heart re-stores its bor-rowed ray, That in thy sun-shine's blaze its day May bright-er, fair-er be.
3. O Joy that seek-est me through pain, I can-not close my heart to thee; I trace the rain-bow through the rain, And feel the prom-ise is not vain That morn shall tear-less be.
4. O Cross that lift-est up my head, I dare not ask to fly from thee; I lay in dust life's glo-ry dead, And from the ground there blos-soms red Life that shall end-less be. A-men.

520 O Master, Let Me Walk with Thee
MARYTON L.M.

Washington Gladden, 1879 — Henry Percy Smith, 1874

1. O Master, let me walk with thee In lowly paths of service free; Tell me thy secret; help me bear The strain of toil, the fret of care.
2. Help me the slow of heart to move By some clear, winning word of love; Teach me the wayward feet to stay, And guide them in the homeward way.
3. Teach me thy patience; still with thee In closer, dearer company, In work that keeps faith sweet and strong, In trust that triumphs over wrong;
4. In hope that sends a shining ray Far down the future's broadening way; In peace that only thou canst give, With thee, O Master, let me live. Amen.

O Morning Star, How Fair and Bright   521
FRANKFORT P.M.

Philipp Nicolai, 1599
Trans. by Catherine Winkworth, 1863; alt.

Attr. to Philipp Nicolai, 1599
Harm. by J. S. Bach, 1740

1. O Morning Star, how fair and bright Your beams shine forth in truth and light! O Sovereign meek and lowly! O Root of Jesse, David's Son, Our Lord and Master,
*2. Come, heavenly Brightness! Light divine! O deep within our hearts now shine, And make you there an altar! Fill us with joy and strength to be Your members joined with
3. Rejoice, O heavens; and earth reply! With praise, you sinners, fill the sky, For this his incarnation. Incarnate God, put forth your power; Ride on, ride on, great

See following page.

522 O Morning Star, How Fair and Bright (cont.)

you have won Our hearts to serve you sole-ly! You are ho-ly,
u-ni-ty In love that can-not fal-ter! Toward you long-ing
Con-quer-or, Till all know your sal-va-tion. A-men, A-men!

Fair and glo-rious, all-vic-to-rious, Rich in bless-ing,
Does pos-sess us; turn and bless us; Here in sad-ness
Al-le-lu-ia! Al-le-lu-ia! Praise be giv-en

Rule and might o'er all pos-sess-ing.
Eye and heart long for your glad-ness!
Ev-er-more by earth and heav-en. A-men.

O My Soul, Bless God, the Father 523
STUTTGART 8.7.8.7.

From Psalm 103
Para. in *The Book of Psalms*, 1871; alt.

Psalmodia Sacra, 1715
Adapted in *Hymns Ancient & Modern*, 1861

1. O my soul, bless God, the Father; All within me bless his name; Bless the Father, and forget not All his mercies to proclaim;
2. He forgives all your transgressions, Each disease he gently heals; He redeems you from destruction, And with you so kindly deals.
3. Far as east from west is distant, He has put away our sin; Like the pity of a father Has the Lord's compassion been.
4. As it was without beginning, So it lasts without an end; To their children's children ever Shall his righteousness extend:
5. Unto such as keep his covenant And are steadfast in his way; Unto those who still remember His commandments and obey.
6. Bless the Father, all his creatures, Ever under his control, All throughout his vast dominion; Bless the Father, O my soul. A-men.

524 O Sacred Head, Now Wounded
PASSION CHORALE 7.6.7.6.D.

Based on medieval Latin poem
Paul Gerhardt, 1656
Trans. by James W. Alexander, 1830

Hans Leo Hassler, 1601
Harm. by J. S. Bach, 1729

1. O sa-cred Head, now wound-ed, With grief and shame weighed down, Now scorn-ful-ly sur-round-ed With thorns, thine on-ly crown; O sa-cred Head, what glo-ry, What bliss, till now was thine! Yet, though de-spised and gor-y, I joy to call thee mine.

2. What thou, my Lord, hast suf-fered Was all for sin-ners' gain; Mine, mine was the trans-gres-sion, But thine the dead-ly pain. Lo, here I fall, my Sav-ior! 'Tis I de-serve thy place; Look on me with thy fa-vor, Vouch-safe to me thy grace.

3. What lan-guage shall I bor-row To thank thee, dear-est Friend, For this thy dy-ing sor-row, Thy pit-y with-out end? O make me thine for-ev-er; And should I faint-ing be, Lord, let me nev-er, nev-er Out-live my love to thee. A-men.

O Sing a New Song to the Lord

525

SONG 67 C.M.

From Psalm 96
Para. in the Scottish Psalter, 1650; alt.

Prys's Welsh Psalter, 1621

1. O sing a new song to the Lord; Sing all the earth to God, To God sing, bless his name, show still His saving health abroad.
2. Great honor is before his face, And majesty divine; Strength is within his holy place, And there does beauty shine.
*3. O give unto the living Lord, You men of every tribe, All glory give unto the Lord, And mighty power ascribe.
4. O give the glory to the Lord That to his name is due; Come all into his courts, and bring An offering with you.
5. In beauty of his holiness, O all the earth throughout Fear him whom we implore. A-men.

526 O Sing a Song of Bethlehem
KINGSFOLD C.M.D.

Louis F. Benson, 1899

Traditional English melody collected by Lucy Broadwood (1858-1929)
Arr. and harm. by Ralph Vaughan Williams, 1906

1. O sing a song of Bethlehem, Of shepherds watching there,
And of the news that came to them From angels in the air:
The light that shone on Bethlehem Fills all the world today;
Of Jesus' birth and peace on earth The angels sing alway.

2. O sing a song of Nazareth, Of sunny days of joy;
O sing of fragrant flow'rs' breath, And of the sinless boy:
For now the flowers of Nazareth In ev'ery heart may grow;
Now spreads the fame of his dear name On all the winds that blow.

3. O sing a song of Galilee, Of lake and woods and hill,
Of him who walked upon the sea And bade its waves be still:
For though, like waves on Galilee, Dark seas of trouble roll,
When faith has heard the Master's word, Falls peace upon the soul.

4. O sing a song of Calvary, Its glory and dismay;
Of him who hung upon the tree, And took our sins away:
For he who died on Calvary Is risen from the grave,
And Christ, our Lord, by heaven adored, Is mighty now to save. A-men.

Music from *The English Hymnal*; used by permission of Oxford University Press.

O Sons and Daughters, Let Us Sing! 527

O FILII ET FILIAE 8.8.8. with Alleluias

Jean Tisserand (d. 1494) and others
Trans. by John Mason Neale, 1851; alt.

Probably French, ca. 15th century
As in *Pilgrim Hymnal*, 1958

Alleluia! Alleluia! Alleluia!

1. O sons and daughters, let us sing! The King of heaven, the glorious King, O'er death today rose triumphing.
2. That Easter morn at break of day, The faithful women went their way To seek the tomb where Jesus lay.
3. An angel clad in white they see, Who sat, and spoke unto the three, "Your Lord has gone to Galilee." Alleluia!
4. How blest are they who have not seen, And yet whose faith has constant been; For they eternal life shall win.
5. On this most holy day of days, Our hearts and voices, Lord, we raise To you, in jubilee and praise. A-men.

528 O Spirit of the Living God
WINCHESTER NEW L.M.

James Montgomery, 1823; alt., 1972
Musikalisches Handbuch, Hamburg, 1690
Arr. in *Old Church Psalmody*, 1864

1. O Spirit of the living God, In all the fullness of your grace, Where'er the foot of man has trod, Descend on our rebellious race.

2. Give tongues of fire and hearts of love To preach the reconciling word; Give power and blessing from above, When'er the joyful sound is heard.

3. Be darkness, at your coming, light; Confusion, order in your path; Souls without strength inspire with might; Bid mercy triumph over wrath.

4. O Spirit of the Lord, prepare All the round earth her God to meet; And breathe abroad like morning air, Till hearts of stone begin to beat.

5. Baptize the nations; far and nigh The triumphs of the cross record; The name of Jesus glorify, Till every kindred call him Lord. A-men.

O Splendor of God's Glory Bright 529
WAREHAM L.M.

Ambrose of Milan (ca. 340-397)
Translation composite
As in *The Methodist Hymnal*, 1935; alt., 1972

William Knapp, 1738

1. O splendor of God's glory bright, From light eternal bringing light; O Light of life, light's living spring, True day, all days illumining.
2. Confirm our will to do the right, And keep our hearts from envy's blight; Let faith her eager fires renew, And hate the false, and love the true.
3. O joyful be the passing day With thoughts as clear as morning's ray, With faith like noontide shining bright, Our souls unshadowed by the night.
4. Dawn's glory gilds the earth and skies; Let Him, our perfect morn, arise; The Father's help his children claim, And sing the Father's glorious name. A-men.

Alternative Tune: PUER NOBIS

530   O Where Are Kings and Empires Now
ST. ANNE C.M.

Arthur Cleveland Coxe, 1839; alt.   Attr. to William Croft, 1708

1. O where are kings and empires now Of old that went and came? But, Lord, your church is praying yet, A thousand years the same.
2. We mark her goodly battlements And her foundations strong; We hear within the solemn voice Of her unending song.
3. For not like kingdoms of the world Your holy church, O God, Though earthquake shocks are threatening her And tempests are abroad,
4. Unshaken as eternal hills, Immovable she stands, A mountain that shall fill the earth, A house not made by hands. Amen.

O Wondrous Type, O Vision Fair 531
DEO GRACIAS L.M.

Latin hymn, 15th century
Trans. by John Mason Neale, 1854; alt.

"The Agincourt Song," England, ca. 1415
Arr. for *The Hymnal*, 1933

1. O wondrous type, O vision fair
Of glory that the church shall share,
Which Christ upon the mountain shows
Where brighter than the sun he glows.

2. With shining face and bright array,
Christ deigns to manifest today
What glory shall be theirs above
Who joy in God with perfect love.

3. And faithful souls in vision see
The heights of God's own mystery;
For which in joyful strains we raise
The voice of prayer, the hymn of praise.

4. O Father, with th' eternal Son,
And Holy Spirit, ever One,
Be pleased to bring us by your grace
To see your glory face to face. A-men.

Music copyright 1933 by Presbyterian Board of Christian Education, renewed 1961.

532 O Word of God Incarnate
MUNICH 7.6.7.6.D.

William Walsham How, 1867; alt., 1972

Neuvermehrtes...Meiningisches Gesangbuch, 1693
Adapted by Felix Mendelssohn, 1847

1. O Word of God incarnate, O Wisdom from on high,
   O Truth unchanged, unchanging, O Light of our dark sky,
   We praise you for the radiance That from the hallowed page,
   A lantern to our footsteps, Shines on from age to age.

2. The church from her dear Master Received the gift divine,
   And still that light is lifted O'er all the earth to shine.
   It is the chest so precious Where gems of truth are stored;
   It is the heaven-drawn picture Of Christ, the living Word.

3. It floats e'er like a banner Before God's host unfurled;
   It shines out like a beacon Above the darkening world.
   It is the chart and compass That o'er life's surging waves,
   'Mid mists and rocks and quicksands, Still guides to Christ who saves.

4. O make your church, dear Savior, A lamp of purest gold,
   To bear before the nations Your true light, as of old.
   O teach your wandering pilgrims By this their path to trace,
   Till, clouds and darkness ended, They see you face to face. A-men.

O Worship the King All-glorious Above 533
LYONS 10.10.11.11.

Based on Psalm 104
Robert Grant, 1833; alt.

Attr. to J. Michael Haydn (1737-1806)
Gardiner's *Sacred Melodies*, 1815

1. O worship the King all-glorious above,
O gratefully sing his power and his love;
Our Shield and Defender, the Ancient of Days,
Pavilioned in splendor and girded with praise.

2. O tell of his might, O sing of his grace,
Whose robe is the light, whose canopy space.
His chariots of wrath the deep thunder-clouds form,
And dark is his path on the wings of the storm.

3. The earth with its store of wonders untold,
Almighty, your power has founded of old,
Established it fast by a changeless decree,
And round it has cast, like a mantle, the sea.

4. Your bountiful care, what tongue can recite?
It breathes in the air, it shines in the light;
It streams from the hills; it descends to the plain,
And sweetly distills in the dew and the rain.

5. We children of dust are feeble and frail;
In you we do trust, nor find you to fail;
Your mercies how tender, how firm to the end,
Our Maker, Defender, Redeemer, and Friend! A-men.

For lower key, see "You Servants of God, Your Master Proclaim."

534 Of the Father's Love Begotten
DIVINUM MYSTERIUM 8.7.8.7.8.7.7.

Aurelius Clemens Prudentius (348-ca. 410)
Trans. by John Mason Neale, 1851,
and Henry W. Baker, 1859; alt., 1972

Plainsong, Mode V, 12th century (?)
Harm. by C. Winfred Douglas, 1940

1. Of the Father's love be-got-ten, Ere the worlds be-gan to be,
   He is Al-pha and O-meg-a, He the Source, the End-ing he,
   Of the things that are, that have been, And that fu-ture years shall see,
   Ev-er-more and ev-er-more!

2. O you heights of heaven, a-dore him; An-gel hosts, his prais-es sing;
   Powers, do-min-ions, bow be-fore him, And ex-tol our God and King;
   Let no tongue on earth be si-lent, Ev-ery voice in con-cert ring,
   Ev-er-more and ev-er-more!

3. Christ, to you, with God the Fa-ther, And the Spir-it, one in three,
   Hymn and chant and high thanks-giv-ing And un-wea-ried prais-es be:
   Hon-or, glo-ry, and do-min-ion, And e-ter-nal vic-to-ry,
   Ev-er-more and ev-er-more! A-men.

Music used by permission of The Church Pension Fund.

Oh, Freedom!

535

Negro spiritual
Harm. by Joan M. Salmon, 1972

Negro spiritual

1. Oh, free-dom! oh, free-dom! oh, free-dom for me!
2. Dy-ing sin-ner! dy-ing sin-ner! dy-ing sin-ner all my days!
3. Trust-ing Je-sus! trust-ing Je-sus! trust-ing Je-sus all my days!

And be-fore I'd be a slave, I'd be bur-ied in my grave,

And go home to my Lord and be free. (and be free.)

Music copyright 1972 by The Westminster Press.

536 On a Bethlehem Hill

Peter Scholtes, 1967

White spiritual
Harm. by Richard D. Wetzel, 1972

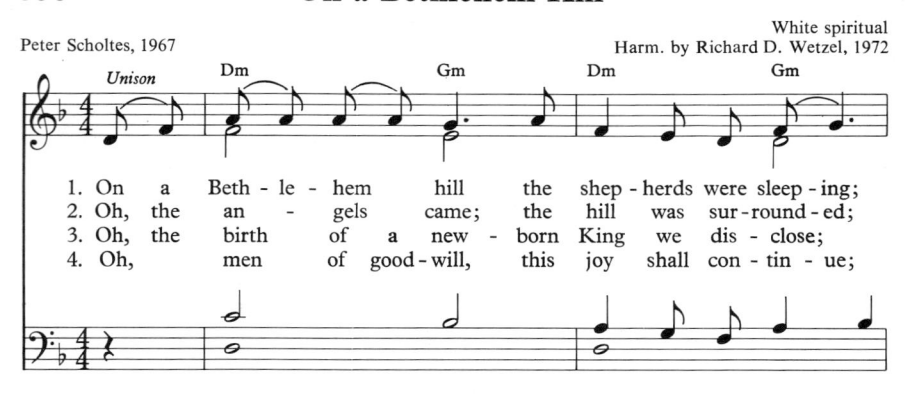

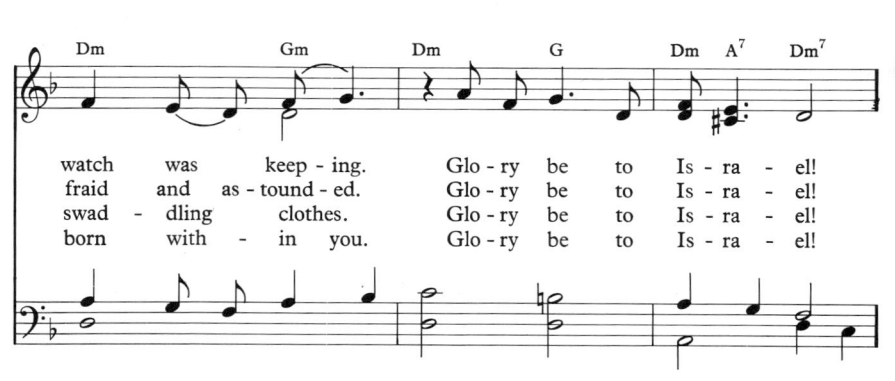

1. On a Beth-le-hem hill the shep-herds were sleep-ing;
2. Oh, the an - gels came; the hill was sur-round-ed;
3. Oh, the birth of a new-born King we dis-close;
4. Oh, men of good-will, this joy shall con-tin-ue;

Glo-ry be to Is-ra-el! One young boy the watch was keep-ing.
Glo-ry be to Is-ra-el! The shep-herd boy was a-fraid and as-tound-ed.
Glo-ry be to Is-ra-el! You will find him in a cave wrapped in swad-dling clothes.
Glo-ry be to Is-ra-el! For the King of Peace has been born with-in you.

Glo-ry be to Is-ra-el!
Glo-ry be to Is-ra-el!
Glo-ry be to Is-ra-el!
Glo-ry be to Is-ra-el!

Words copyright © 1967 by F.E.L. Church Publications, Ltd.; from *Hymnal for Young Christians*; used by permission.
Music copyright 1972 by The Westminster Press.

On a Bethlehem Hill (cont.) 537

Glo-ry, glo-ry, glo-ry, glo-ry, Glo-ry be to Is-ra-el!

Glo-ry, glo-ry, glo-ry, glo-ry, Glo-ry be to Is-ra-el!

538 On This Day Earth Shall Ring

PERSONENT HODIE 6.6.6.6.6. with Refrain

Piae Cantiones, 1582
Trans. by Jane M. Joseph, 1924

Piae Cantiones, 1582
As in *Hymnal for Colleges and Schools*, 1956

1. On this day earth shall ring With the song chil-dren sing
To the Lord, Christ our King, Born on earth to save us;
Him the Fa-ther gave us.

2. His the doom, ours the mirth; When he came down to earth
Beth-le-hem saw his birth; Ox and ass be-side him
From the cold would hide him.

3. God's bright star, o'er his head, Wise Men three to him led;
Kneel they low by his bed, Lay their gifts be-fore him,
Praise him and a-dore him.

4. On this day an-gels sing; With their song earth shall ring,
Prais-ing Christ, heav-en's King, Born on earth to save us;
Peace and love he gave us.

Refrain:
Id-e-o-o-o, Id-e-o-o-o,
O, Id-e-o, Id-e-o, Id-e-o-o,
O, Id-e-o-o-o,

Unison
Id-e-o glo-ri-a in ex-cel-sis De-o!*

Words copyright by J. Curwen & Sons, Ltd.; used by permission of G. Schirmer, Inc. Music from *Hymnal for Colleges and Schools*, edited by E. Harold Geer; used by permission of Yale University Press.

*"Therefore let us give glory to God in the highest."

Once in Royal David's City   539
IRBY 8.7.8.7.8.7.

Cecil Frances Alexander, 1848; alt.   Henry J. Gauntlett, 1849

1. Once in royal David's city Stood a lowly cattle shed, Where a mother laid her baby In a manger for his bed: Mary was that mother mild, Jesus Christ, her little child.
2. He came down to earth from heaven Who is God and Lord of all, And his shelter was a stable, And his cradle was a stall: With the poor, and mean, and lowly, Lived on earth our Savior holy.
3. Jesus is our childhood's pattern, Day by day like us he grew; He was little, weak, and helpless, Tears and smiles like us he knew: And he comforts us in sadness, And he shares in all our gladness.
4. And our eyes at last shall see him, Through his own redeeming love; For that child so dear and gentle Is our Lord in heaven above, And he leads his children on To the place where he is gone. A-men.

540 Once to Every Man and Nation

EBENEZER (TON-Y-BOTEL) 8.7.8.7.D.

James Russell Lowell, 1845; alt.
Thomas John Williams, 1890

1. Once to ev-ery man and na-tion Comes the mo-ment to de-cide,
   In the strife of truth with false-hood, For the good or e-vil side;
   Some great cause, God's new Mes-si-ah, Of-fering each the bloom or blight,
   And the choice goes by for-ev-er 'Twixt that dark-ness and that light.

2. Then to side with truth is no-ble, When we share her wretch-ed crust,
   Ere her cause bring fame and prof-it, And 'tis pros-perous to be just;
   Then it is the brave man choos-es While the cow-ard stands a-side,
   Till the mul-ti-tude make vir-tue Of the faith they had de-nied.

3. By the light of burn-ing mar-tyrs, Christ, your bleed-ing feet we track,
   Toil-ing up new Cal-varies ev-er With the cross that turns not back;
   New oc-ca-sions teach new du-ties, Time makes an-cient good un-couth;
   They must up-ward still and on-ward, Who would keep a-breast of truth.

4. Though the cause of e-vil pros-per, Yet 'tis truth a-lone is strong;
   Though her por-tion be the scaf-fold, And up-on the throne be wrong,
   Yet that scaf-fold sways the fu-ture, And, be-hind the dim un-known,
   Stands our God with-in the shad-ow Keep-ing watch a-bove his own. A-men.

Music copyright by Gwenlyn Evans, Ltd.; used by permission.

One Table Spread

541

MANNITTO 10.4.10.4.12.10.

Dalton E. McDonald, 1972

Donald D. Kettring, 1972

1. One ta-ble spread through-out the whole wide earth—The King's own feast! / From ev-ery na-tion men shall come to share, From west and east. / All now is read-y, and our Host in-vites us in: / "Both bad and good are guests. Let us be-gin."

2. See bread and wine, the to-kens of God's grace—This is our meal. / Here we re-call our Lord up-on the cross—His love is real! / Take it not light-ly; this is God's own sac-ri-fice / For all our need, and his love will suf-fice.

3. Give thanks to God that peace may here be found With-in his plan; / Our part to hear and heed his new com-mand: "Love God and man!" / Now is re-vealed the glo-ry of the Fa-ther, Son, / And God the Ho-ly Spir-it, three in one. A-men.

Words and music copyright 1972 by The Westminster Press.

542 Onward, Christian Soldiers

ST. GERTRUDE 6.5.6.5.D. with Refrain

Sabine Baring-Gould, 1864; alt.
Arthur S. Sullivan, 1871

1. On-ward, Chris-tian sol - diers, March-ing as to war,
2. Like a might-y ar - my Moves the church of God;
3. Crowns and thrones may per - ish, King-doms rise and wane,
4. On-ward, then, you peo - ple, Join our hap-py throng,

With the cross of Je - sus Go-ing on be - fore:
Broth-ers, we are tread - ing Where the saints have trod;
But the church of Je - sus Con-stant will re - main;
Blend with ours your voic - es In the tri - umph song;

Christ the roy - al mas - ter Leads a-gainst the foe;
We are not di - vid - ed, All one bod - y we,
Gates of hell can nev - er 'Gainst that church pre - vail;
Glo - ry, laud, and hon - or Un - to Christ the King;

Words used by permission of Gordon A. Hitchcock and the Executors of the estate of the late Sabine Baring-Gould.

Onward, Christian Soldiers (cont.) 543

For-ward in-to bat - tle, See, his ban-ners go.
One in hope and doc - trine, One in char - i - ty.
We have Christ's own prom - ise, And that can - not fail.
This through count-less ag - es Men and an - gels sing.

On-ward, Chris-tian sol - diers, March-ing as to war,
With the cross of Je - sus Go-ing on be - fore. A - men.

544. Open Now the Gates of Beauty

NEANDER (UNSER HERRSCHER) 8.7.8.7.7.7.

Benjamin Schmolck, 1732
Trans. by Catherine Winkworth, 1863; alt., 1972
Joachim Neander, 1680

1. O-pen now the gates of beau-ty, Zi-on, let us en-ter there, Where we may in joy-ful du-ty Wait for him who an-swers prayer. O how bless-ed is this place, Filled with sol-ace, light, and grace!

2. Here, O God, we come be-fore you; To this com-pa-ny come down; Where we find you and a-dore you, There with joy our lives you crown; In our hearts to you we bow, Let them be your tem-ple now.

3. Here our faith in-crease and quick-en, Let us keep your gift di-vine; And when-e'er temp-ta-tions thick-en May your word still o'er us shine, As our guid-ing star through life, As our com-fort in all strife.

4. Speak, O Lord, and we will hear you; Let your will be done in-deed. May we un-dis-turbed draw near you While your peo-ple you do feed; Here of life the foun-tain flows, Here is balm for all our woes. A-men.

Our Faith Is in the Christ Who Walks with Men 545
WAREHAM L.M.

Thomas Curtis Clark (1877-1953) William Knapp, 1738

1. Our faith is in the Christ who walks With men to-day, in street and mart; The constant friend who thinks and talks With those who seek him with the heart.

2. His gospel calls for living men, With singing minds alert; Strong men, who fall to rise again, Who strive and bleed, with courage girt.

3. We serve no God whose work is done, Who rests within his firmament; Our God, his labors but begun, Toils evermore, with power unspent.

4. God was and is and e'er shall be; Christ lived and loved—and loves us still; And man goes forward, proud and free, God's present purpose to fulfill. A-men.

546 Our Father, by Whose Name

RHOSYMEDRE 6.6.6.6.8.8.8.8.

F. Bland Tucker, 1941, 1972
John D. Edwards, ca. 1840

1. Our Father, by whose name All fatherhood is known, Who in your love proclaim Each family your own, Bless now all parents, guarding well, With constant love as sentinel, The homes in which your people dwell.

*2. O Christ, yourself a child Within an earthly home, With heart still undefiled, You did to manhood come; Our children bless, in every place, That they may all behold your face, And, knowing you, may grow in grace.

3. O Spirit, who can bind Our hearts in unity, And teach us so to find The love from self set free, In all our hearts such love increase, That every home, by this release, May be the dwelling place of peace. A-men.

Words used by permission of The Church Pension Fund.

Our Father, Which Art in Heaven 547

West Indian folk tune
Melody set down by Olive Pattison, 1945
Harm. by Richard D. Wetzel, 1972

Our Father, which art in heav-en, Hal-low-ed-a-be thy name.
Thy king-dom come, thy will be done, Hal-low-ed-a-be thy name.
On the earth as it is in heav-en. Give us this day our dai-ly bread;
And for-give us all our tres-pass-es, As we for-give those who
tres-pass a-gainst us; And leave us not to the dev-il to be tempt-ed,

Words and melody from *Edric Connor Collection of West Indian Spirituals and Folk Tunes*; copyright 1945 by Boosey and Company, Ltd.; reprinted by permission of Boosey and Hawkes, Inc.

*Repeat Refrain A or B as indicated after alternate lines.

See following page.

548 Our Father, Which Art in Heaven (cont.)

But deliver us from all that is evil.

For thine is the kingdom, The power and the glory,

For-ever, for-ever, for-ever and ever.

Amen, Amen, Amen, Amen, Amen, Amen,

Amen, Amen. Hallowed-a-be thy name.

Our God, Our Help in Ages Past
ST. ANNE C.M.

549

Based on Psalm 90:1-5
Isaac Watts, 1719; alt.

Attr. to William Croft, 1708

1. Our God, our help in ages past, Our hope for years to come, Our shelter from the stormy blast, And our eternal home:
2. Before the hills in order stood, Or earth received her frame, From everlasting you are God, To endless years the same.
3. A thousand ages in your sight Are like an evening gone; Short as the watch that ends the night Before the rising sun.
4. Time, like an ever-rolling stream, Bears all its sons away; They fly forgotten, as a dream Dies at the opening day.
5. Our God, our help in ages past, Our hope for years to come, O be our guard while life shall last, And our eternal home. A-men.

550 Pardoned Through Redeeming Grace
AUS DER TIEFE 7.7.7.7.

Edward Osler, 1836; alt., 1972
Attr. to Martin Herbst, 1676

1. Pardoned through redeeming grace, In your blessed Son revealed, Worshiping before your face, Lord, to you ourselves we yield.
2. This our sacrifice receive, Humbly offered through your Son; Quicken us in him to live; Lord, in us your will be done.
3. By the hallowed outward sign, By the cleansing grace within, Seal us with your own design; Wash and keep us pure from sin.
4. Called to bear the Christian name, May our vows and life accord, And our every deed proclaim "Holiness unto the Lord!" A-men.

Praise, My Soul, the King of Heaven 551
LAUDA ANIMA (PRAISE, MY SOUL) 8.7.8.7.8.7.

Based on Psalm 103
Henry Francis Lyte, 1834; alt.
John Goss, 1869

1. Praise, my soul, the King of heaven; To his feet your tribute bring; Ransomed, healed, restored, forgiven, Evermore his praises sing: Alleluia! Alleluia! Praise the everlasting King.

2. Praise him for his grace and favor To our fathers in distress; Praise him still the same as ever, Slow to chide, and swift to bless: Alleluia! Alleluia! Glorious in his faithfulness.

3. Father-like he tends and spares us; Well our feeble frame he knows; In his hands he gently bears us, Rescues us from all our foes. Alleluia! Alleluia! Widely yet his mercy flows.

4. Come, then, help us to adore him, Till we see him face to face; Gladly worship we before him, Dwellers now in time and space. Alleluia! Alleluia! Praise with us the God of grace. A-men.

552 Praise the Lord, His Glories Show

LLANFAIR 7.7.7.7. with Alleluias

Based on Psalm 150
Henry Francis Lyte, 1834; alt., 1972

Robert Williams, 1817
Harm. by David Evans, 1927

1. Praise the Lord, his glories show,
Saints within his courts below,
Angels round his throne above,
All that see and share his love.
Alleluia!

2. Earth to heaven, and heaven to earth,
Tell his wonders, sing his worth,
Age to age and shore to shore,
Praise him, praise him evermore!
Alleluia!

3. Praise the Lord, his mercies trace,
Praise his providence and grace,
All that he for man has done,
All he sends us through his Son.
Alleluia! A-men.

Music from *The Church Hymnary*, Revised Edition, 1927; used by permission of Oxford University Press.

Praise the Lord, Who Reigns Above

553

AMSTERDAM 7.6.7.6.7.7.7.6.

Based on Psalm 150
Charles Wesley, 1743

Foundery Collection, 1742

1. Praise the Lord, who reigns above And keeps his court below;
   Praise the holy God of love, And all his greatness show;
   Praise him for his noble deeds, Praise him for his matchless power;
   Him from whom all good proceeds Let earth and heaven adore.

2. Celebrate th' eternal God With harp and psaltery;
   Timbrels soft and cymbals loud In his high praise agree;
   Praise him, every tuneful string; All the reach of heavenly art,
   All the powers of music bring, The music of the heart.

3. Him, in whom they move and live, Let every creature sing,
   Glory to their Maker give, And homage to their King.
   Hallowed be his name beneath, As in heaven on earth adored;
   Praise the Lord in every breath; Let all things praise the Lord. A-men.

554 Praise the Lord! You Heavens, Adore Him
AN DIE FREUDE 8.7.8.7.D.

Based on Psalm 148
Sts. 1, 2, anon., ca. 1801; alt., 1972
St. 3, Edward Osler, 1836; alt., 1972

Anon. setting of Schiller's
"Hymn to Joy," Berlin, 1799

1. Praise the Lord! you heavens, adore him; Praise him, angels in the height; Sun and moon, rejoice before him, Praise him, all you stars of light. Praise the Lord, for he has
2. Praise the Lord! for he is glorious; Never shall his promise fail. God has made his saints victorious; Sin and death shall not prevail. Praise the God of our sal-
3. Worship, honor, glory, blessing, Lord, we offer as our gift. Young and old, your praise expressing, Our glad songs to you we lift. All the saints in heaven a-

Alternative Tune: AUSTRIAN HYMN

Praise the Lord! You Heavens, Adore Him (cont.) 555

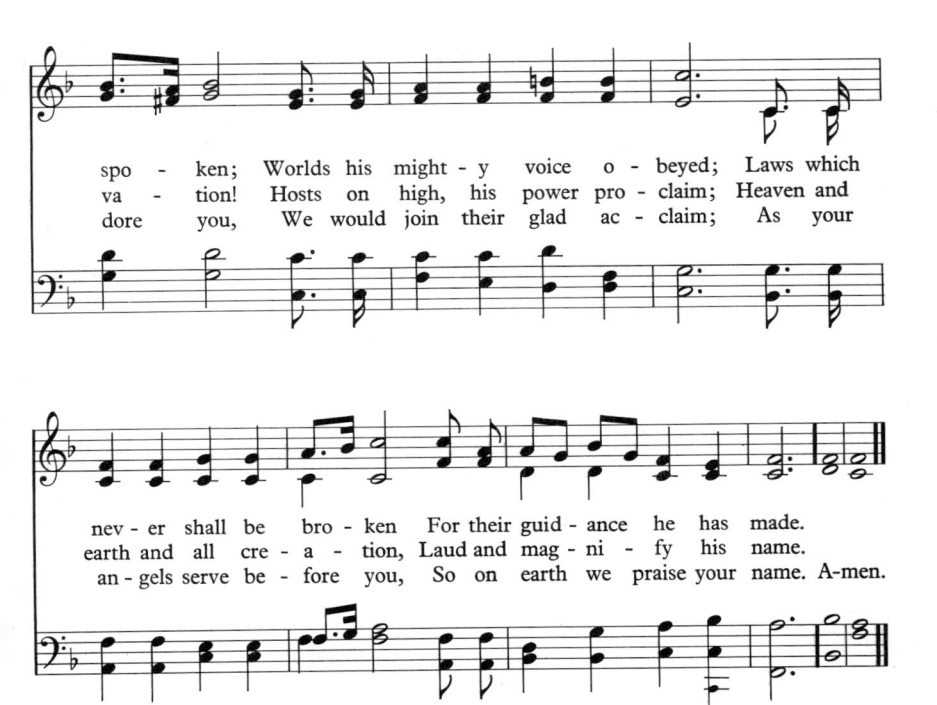

spo - ken; Worlds his might-y voice o-beyed; Laws which nev-er shall be bro-ken For their guid-ance he has made.
va - tion! Hosts on high, his power pro-claim; Heaven and earth and all cre-a-tion, Laud and mag-ni-fy his name.
dore you, We would join their glad ac-claim; As your an-gels serve be-fore you, So on earth we praise your name. A-men.

556 Praise to God, Immortal Praise

ORIENTIS PARTIBUS 7.7.7.7.

Anna L. Barbauld, 1772; alt.

Medieval French melody
Harm. by Ralph Vaughan Williams, 1906

1. Praise to God, immortal praise, For the love that crowns our days; Bounteous source of every joy, Let your praise our tongues employ.
2. Flocks that whiten all the plain, Yellow sheaves of ripened grain, Clouds that drop their fattening dews, Suns that temperate warmth diffuse;
3. All that spring with bounteous hand Scatters o'er the smiling land! All that liberal autumn pours From her rich o'erflowing stores—
4. These to you, our God, we owe, Source whence all our blessings flow, And for these our souls shall raise Grateful vows and solemn praise. A-men.

Music altered from *The English Hymnal*; used by permission of Oxford University Press.

Praise to the Lord, the Almighty 557
LOBE DEN HERREN P.M.

Joachim Neander, 1680
Trans. by Catherine Winkworth, 1863; alt.

Adapted from Stralsund Gesangbuch, 1665
As in *The Chorale Book for England*, 1863

1. Praise to the Lord, the Al-might-y, the King of cre-a-tion!
2. Praise to the Lord, who o'er all things is won-drous-ly reign-ing,
3. Praise to the Lord, who does pros-per your way and de-fend you;
4. Praise to the Lord! O let all that is in me a-dore him!

O my soul, praise him, for he is your health and sal-va-tion!
Shel-tering you un-der his wings and so gen-tly sus-tain-ing.
Sure-ly his good-ness and mer-cy shall ev-er at-tend you!
All that have life and breath, come now with prais-es be-fore him!

All you that hear, Now to his tem-ple draw near;
Have you not seen? All that is need-ful has been
Pon-der a-new What the Al-might-y can do,
Let the A-men Sound from his peo-ple a-gain:

Join-ing in glad ad-o-ra-tion.
Grant-ed in all his or-dain-ing.
Who with his love does be-friend you.
Glad-ly al-ways we a-dore him. A-men.

558 Praise We Our Maker While We've Breath
OLD 113TH 8.8.8.D.

From Psalm 146
Para. by Isaac Watts, 1719; alt., 1737, 1972

Attr. to Matthäus Greiter, 1525
Alt. and abr. in English use
Harm. by V. Earle Copes, 1964

1. Praise we our Maker while we've breath; And when our voice is lost in death, Praise shall employ our nobler powers. Our days of praise shall ne'er be past, While life, and thought, and being last, Or immortality endures.

2. The Lord gives vision to the blind; The Lord supports the fainting mind; He sends the laboring conscience peace. He helps the stranger in distress, The widow and the fatherless, And grants the prisoner sweet release.

3. Blest is the man whose hopes rely On Israel's God; he made the sky And earth and seas, with all their train. His truth forever stands secure; He saves th'op-pressed, he feeds the poor, And none shall find his promise vain. A-men.

Harmonization copyright © 1964 by Abingdon Press; from *The Methodist Hymnal*; used by permission.

Put Forth, O God, Your Spirit's Might 559
DUNDEE (FRENCH) C.M.

Howard Chandler Robbins, 1937; alt., 1972 — Scottish Psalter, 1615

1. Put forth, O God, your Spirit's might And bid your church increase, In breadth and length, in depth and height, Her unity and peace.
2. Let works of darkness disappear Before your conquering light. Let hatred and tormenting fear Pass with the passing night.
3. Let the apostles' constancy Be ours from age to age; Their steadfast faith our heritage. Their peace our heritage.
4. O Judge divine of human strife! O Vanquisher of pain! To know you is eternal life, To serve you is to reign. A-men.

Words altered from *The New Church Hymnal*; used by permission of Fleming H. Revell Company, publisher.

560 Rejoice and Be Merry
GALLERY CAROL 11.11.11.11.

Old church gallery book

Old church gallery book
Arr. by Martin Shaw, 1928

1. Rejoice and be merry in songs and in mirth!
   O praise our Redeemer, all mortals on earth!
   For this is the birthday of Jesus our King,
   Who brought us salvation—his praises we'll sing!

2. A heavenly vision appeared in the sky;
   Vast numbers of angels the shepherds did spy,
   Proclaiming the birthday of Jesus our King,
   Who brought us salvation—his praises we'll sing!

3. Likewise a bright star in the sky did appear,
   Which led the Wise Men from the east to draw near;
   They found the Messiah, sweet Jesus our King,
   Who brought us salvation—his praises we'll sing!

4. And when they were come, they their treasures unfold,
   And unto him offered myrrh, incense, and gold.
   So blessed for ever be Jesus our King,
   Who brought us salvation—his praises we'll sing!

Music from *The Oxford Book of Carols*; used by permission of Oxford University Press.

Rejoice, O Pure in Heart

561

MARION S.M. with Refrain

Edward H. Plumptre, 1865; alt.
Refrain added, 1883

Arthur H. Messiter, 1883

1. Rejoice, O pure in heart; Rejoice, give thanks and sing; Your glorious banner wave on high, The cross of Christ your King.
2. Bright youth and snow-crowned age, Strong men and maidens fair, Raise high your free, exulting song, God's wondrous praise declare.
3. With voice as full and strong As ocean's surging praise, Send forth the hymns our fathers loved, The psalms of ancient days.
4. Yes on, through life's long path, Still chanting as you go, From youth to age, by night and day, In gladness and in woe.
5. Still lift your standard high, Still march in firm array, As warriors through the darkness toil Till dawns the golden day.

Rejoice, rejoice, Rejoice, give thanks and sing! A-men.

562 Rejoice, the Lord Is King
DARWALL'S 148TH 6.6.6.6.8.8.

Charles Wesley, 1746; alt.   John Darwall, 1770; alt., ca. 1778

1. Rejoice, the Lord is King: Your Lord and King adore!
   Rejoice, give thanks, and sing, And triumph evermore:
   Lift up your heart, lift up your voice!
   Rejoice, again I say, rejoice!

2. His Kingdom cannot fail, He rules o'er earth and heaven;
   The keys of death and hell Are to our Jesus given:
   Lift up your heart, lift up your voice!
   Rejoice, again I say, rejoice!

3. He all his foes shall quell, Shall all our sins destroy,
   The church his work shall tell With everlasting joy:
   Lift up your heart, lift up your voice!
   Rejoice, again I say, rejoice! Amen.

Ride On! Ride On in Majesty! 563
ST. DROSTANE L.M.

Henry H. Milman, 1827; alt., 1972
John B. Dykes, 1862

1. Ride on! Ride on in majesty! Hark! all the tribes hosanna cry; Your humble beast pursues his way Where crowds the palms and garments lay.
2. Ride on! Ride on in majesty! In lowly pomp ride on to die: O Christ, your triumphs now begin O'er captive death and conquered sin.
3. Ride on! Ride on in majesty! The winged squadrons of the sky Look down with sad and wondering eyes To see th' approaching sacrifice.
4. Ride on! Ride on in majesty! Your last and fiercest strife is nigh; The Father on his sapphire throne Expects his own anointed Son.
5. Ride on! Ride on in majesty! In lowly pomp ride on to die; Bow your meek head to mortal pain, Then take, O God, your power, and reign. A-men.

564. Rise Up, O Men of God!
FESTAL SONG S.M.

William Pierson Merrill, 1911; alt., 1972
William H. Walter, 1894

1. Rise up, O men of God! Have done with lesser things; Give heart and soul and mind and strength To serve the King of kings.
2. Rise up, O men of God! His kingdom tarries long; Bring in the day of brotherhood And end the night of wrong.
3. Rise up, O men of God! How long the church must wait, Her strength unequal to her task. Rise up, and make her great!
4. Lift high the cross of Christ! Tread where his feet have trod; As brothers of the Son of Man, Rise up, O men of God. A-men.

Savior of the Nations, Come 565
NUN KOMM, DER HEIDEN HEILAND 7.7.7.7.

Attr. to Ambrose of Milan (ca. 340-397)
Para. by Martin Luther, 1524
Trans. by William M. Reynolds, 1850; alt.

Based on plainsong melody
Eyn Enchiridion..., Erfurt, 1524
As in *Songs of Syon*, 1910

1. Savior of the nations, come, Virgin's Son, make here your home. Marvel now, O heaven and earth, That the Lord chose such a birth.
2. From the Father forth he came, And returns unto the same, Captive leading death and hell. High the song of triumph swell!
3. You, the Father's only Son, Have o'er sin the victory won. Boundless shall your kingdom be; When shall we its glories see?
4. Brightly does your manger shine; Glorious is its light divine. Let not sin o'ercloud this light; Ever be our faith thus bright. A - men.

Music used by permission of Mrs. J. Meredith Tatton.

566 Send Down Your Truth, O God

AYLESBURY S.M.

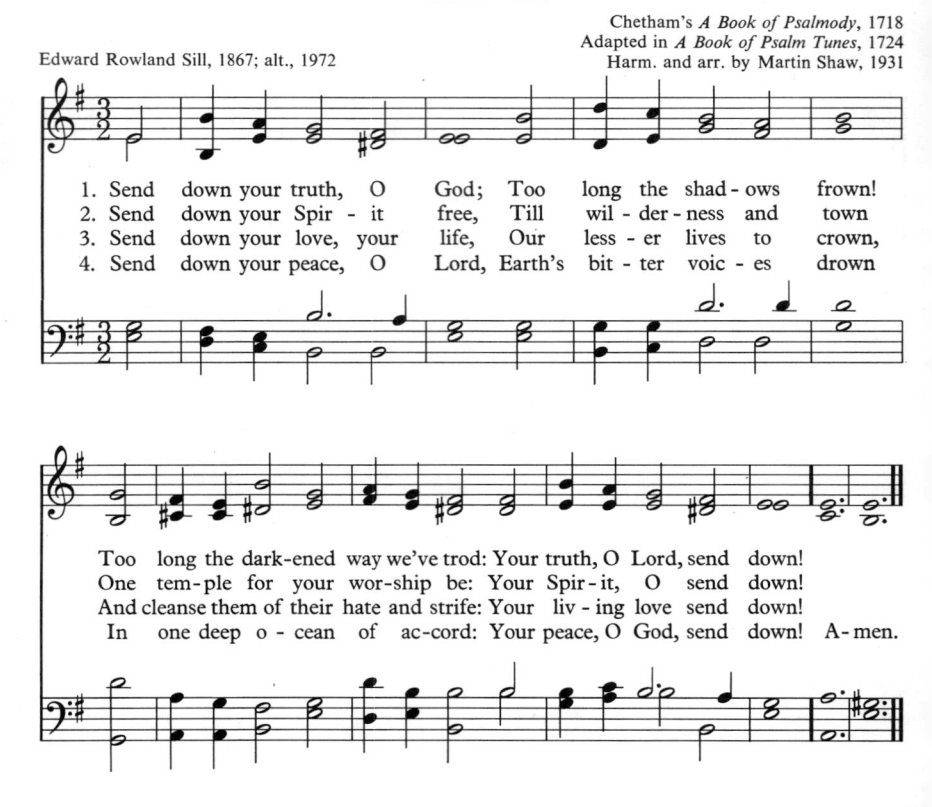

Edward Rowland Sill, 1867; alt., 1972

Chetham's *A Book of Psalmody*, 1718
Adapted in *A Book of Psalm Tunes*, 1724
Harm. and arr. by Martin Shaw, 1931

1. Send down your truth, O God; Too long the shadows frown!
Too long the darkened way we've trod: Your truth, O Lord, send down!

2. Send down your Spirit free, Till wilderness and town
One temple for your worship be: Your Spirit, O send down!

3. Send down your love, your life, Our lesser lives to crown,
And cleanse them of their hate and strife: Your living love send down!

4. Send down your peace, O Lord, Earth's bitter voices drown
In one deep ocean of accord: Your peace, O God, send down! A-men.

Music from *Songs of Praise*, Enlarged Edition; used by permission of Oxford University Press.

Silent Night, Holy Night

567

STILLE NACHT Irregular

Joseph Mohr, 1818
Trans. by John Freeman Young, ca. 1863

Franz Grüber, 1818

1. Si - lent night, ho - ly night! All is calm, all is bright
2. Si - lent night, ho - ly night! Shep - herds quake at the sight;
3. Si - lent night, ho - ly night! Son of God, love's pure light

Round yon vir - gin moth - er and Child. Ho - ly In - fant so ten - der and mild,
Glo - ries stream from heav - en a - far, Heav - enly hosts sing al - le - lu - ia:
Ra - diant beams from thy ho - ly face, With the dawn of re - deem - ing grace,

Sleep in heav - en - ly peace, Sleep in heav - en - ly peace.
Christ, the Sav - ior, is born! Christ, the Sav - ior, is born!
Je - sus, Lord, at thy birth, Je - sus, Lord, at thy birth. A - men.

---

1. *Stille Nacht, heilige Nacht!*
   Alles schläft, einsam wacht
   Nur das traute, hochheilige Paar.
   Holder Knabe im lockigen Haar,
   Schlaf' in himmlischer Ruh',
   Schlaf' in himmlischer Ruh'!

2. *Stille Nacht, heilige Nacht!*
   Hirten erst kundgemacht
   Durch der Engel Alleluja,
   Tönt es laut von fern und nah:
   Christ der Retter ist da,
   Christ der Retter ist da!

3. *Stille Nacht, heilige Nacht!*
   Gottes Sohn, o wie lacht
   Lieb' aus deinem göttlichen Mund,
   Da uns schlägt die rettende Stund':
   Christ, in deiner Geburt,
   Christ, in deiner Geburt!

568   Sing Praise to God, Who Reigns Above
MIT FREUDEN ZART 8.7.8.7.8.8.7.

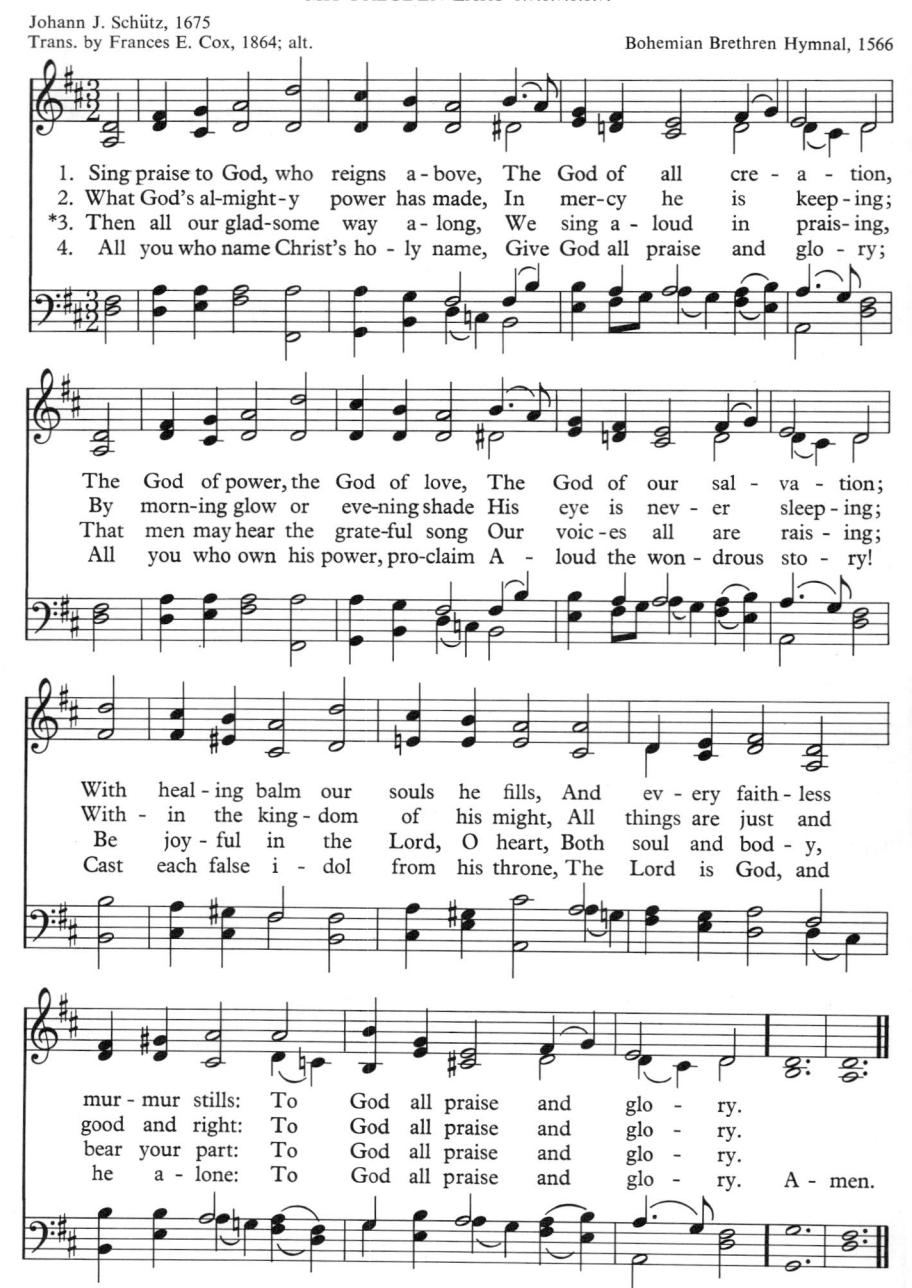

Johann J. Schütz, 1675
Trans. by Frances E. Cox, 1864; alt.

Bohemian Brethren Hymnal, 1566

1. Sing praise to God, who reigns a-bove, The God of all cre-a-tion,
2. What God's al-might-y power has made, In mer-cy he is keep-ing;
*3. Then all our glad-some way a-long, We sing a-loud in prais-ing,
4. All you who name Christ's ho-ly name, Give God all praise and glo-ry;

The God of power, the God of love, The God of our sal-va-tion;
By morn-ing glow or eve-ning shade His eye is nev-er sleep-ing;
That men may hear the grate-ful song Our voic-es all are rais-ing;
All you who own his power, pro-claim A-loud the won-drous sto-ry!

With heal-ing balm our souls he fills, And ev-ery faith-less
With-in the king-dom of his might, All things are just and
Be joy-ful in the Lord, O heart, Both soul and bod-y,
Cast each false i-dol from his throne, The Lord is God, and

mur-mur stills: To God all praise and glo-ry.
good and right: To God all praise and glo-ry.
bear your part: To God all praise and glo-ry.
he a-lone: To God all praise and glo-ry. A-men.

Sing to the Lord of Harvest

569

WIE LIEBLICH IST DER MAIEN 7.6.7.6.D.

John S. B. Monsell, 1866; alt.

Johann Steurlein, 1581
Arr. as hymn tune by Jan Bender, 1967

1. Sing to the Lord of har-vest, Sing songs of love and praise:
With joy-ful hearts and voic-es Your al-le-lu-ias raise.
By him the roll-ing sea-sons In fruit-ful or-der move;
Sing to the Lord of har-vest A joy-ous song of love.

2. By him the clouds drop fat-ness, The des-erts bloom and spring,
The hills leap up in glad-ness, The val-leys laugh and sing.
He bless-es from his full-ness All things with large in-crease,
He crowns the year with good-ness, With plen-ty and with peace.

3. Bring to his sa-cred al-tar The gifts his good-ness gave,
The gold-en sheaves of har-vest, The souls he died to save.
Your hearts lay down be-fore him When at his feet you fall,
And with your lives a-dore him, Who gave his life for all. A-men.

Music copyright 1967 by Concordia Publishing House; slightly altered from *A New Song*; used by permission.

570 Sinner, Please Don't Let This Harvest Pass

Negro spiritual

Negro spiritual
Harm. by Robert E. Grooters, 1972

Sin-ner, please don't let this har-vest pass. (har-vest pass.)

Sin-ner, please don't let this har-vest pass.

Sin-ner, please don't let this har-vest pass,

And die and lose your soul at last. (at last.)

Music copyright 1972 by The Westminster Press.

So Lowly Does the Savior Ride

EPWORTH CHURCH C.M.

Almer M. Pennewell, 1946; alt., 1972

V. Earle Copes, 1964

1. So lowly does the Savior ride A paltry borrowed beast, Nor pomp, nor show, nor lofty pride, Nor boast above the least.
2. His scepter is his kindliness, His grandeur is his grace, His royalty is holiness, And love is in his face.
3. 'Tis thus the great Messiah came To break the tyrants' will, To heal the people of their shame, And nobleness instill.
4. Ride on, O King, ride on your way, While men of low degree Exalt and usher in the day Of peace we long to see. A-men.

Words used by permission of Myra S. Pennewell. Music copyright © 1964 by Abingdon Press; from *The Methodist Hymnal*; used by permission.

572 Somebody's Knocking at Your Door

Negro spiritual
Negro spiritual

Somebody's knocking at your door, Somebody's knocking at your door. O sinner, why don't you answer? Somebody's knocking at your door.

1. Knocks like Jesus,
2. Can't you hear him? Somebody's knocking at your door.
3. Answer Jesus.

Knocks like Jesus,
Can't you hear him? Somebody's knocking at your door.
Answer Jesus.

O sinner, why don't you answer? Somebody's knocking at your door.

Son of God, Eternal Savior

573

IN BABILONE 8.7.8.7.D.

Somerset Corry Lowry, 1893; alt., 1972

Traditional Dutch melody
Harm. by Julius Röntgen, ca. 1906

1. Son of God, e-ter-nal Sav-ior, Source of life and truth and grace,
Son of Man, whose birth in-car-nate Hal-lows all our hu-man race;
You, our Head, who, throned in glo-ry, For your own do ev-er plead,
Fill us with your love and pit-y, Heal our wrongs, and help our need.

2. Lord, as you have lived for oth-ers, So may we for oth-ers live;
Free-ly have your gifts been grant-ed, Free-ly may your serv-ants give.
Yours the gold and yours the sil-ver, Yours the wealth of land and sea,
We, the stew-ards of your boun-ty, Faith-ful to our trust should be.

*3. Come, O Christ, and reign a-mong us, King of love and Prince of Peace;
Hush the storm of strife and pas-sion, Bid its cru-el dis-cords cease.
By your pa-tient years of toil-ing, By your si-lent hours of pain,
Quench our fe-vered thirst of plea-sure, Shame our self-ish greed of gain.

4. See the Christ-like host ad-vanc-ing, High and low-ly, great and small,
Linked in bonds of com-mon serv-ice For the com-mon Lord of all.
As you prayed and as you la-bored That your peo-ple should be one,
Grant, O grant our hope's fru-i-tion: Here on earth your will be done. A-men.

Words altered from *The English Hymnal*; used by permission of Oxford University Press. Music used by permission of F. E. Röntgen.

574. Spirit Divine, Attend Our Prayers
NUN DANKET ALL' (GRÄFENBERG) C.M.

Andrew Reed, 1829
Crüger's *Praxis Pietatis Melica*, 1653

1. Spirit divine, attend our prayers, And make this house your home; Descend with all your gracious powers; O come, great Spirit, come!
2. Come as the light: to us reveal Our emptiness and woe; And lead us in those paths of life Where all the righteous go.
3. Come as the fire: and purge our hearts Like sacrificial flame; Let our whole soul an offering be To our redeemer's name.
4. Come as the dove: and spread your wings, The wings of peaceful love; And let the church on earth become Blest as the church above.
5. Spirit divine, attend our prayers; Make a lost world your home; Descend with all your gracious powers; O come, great Spirit, come! A-men.

Spirit of God, Descend Upon My Heart

MORECAMBE 10.10.10.10.

Attr. to George Croly, 1867
Frederick C. Atkinson, 1870

575

1. Spirit of God, descend upon my heart;
   Wean it from earth; through all its pulses move;
   Stoop to my weakness, mighty as thou art,
   And make me love thee as I ought to love.

2. I ask no dream, no prophet ecstasies,
   No sudden rending of the veil of clay,
   No angel visitant, no opening skies;
   But take the dimness of my soul away.

3. Hast thou not bid us love thee, God and King?
   All, all thine own, soul, heart, and strength, and mind;
   I see thy cross— there teach my heart to cling:
   O let me seek thee, and O let me find!

4. Teach me to feel that thou art always nigh;
   Teach me the struggles of the soul to bear,
   To check the rising doubt, the rebel sigh;
   Teach me the patience of unanswered prayer.

5. Teach me to love thee as thine angels love,
   One holy passion filling all my frame;
   The baptism of the heaven-descended Dove,
   My heart an altar, and thy love the flame. A-men.

576 Spirit of God, Man's Hope in All the Ages
L'OMNIPOTENT 11.10.11.10.

Frank von Christierson, 1967

Comp. or adapted by Louis Bourgeois, 1551
As in *Pilgrim Hymnal*, 1958

1. Spirit of God, man's hope in all the ages,
Bringer of light in darkness, love in strife;
Wisdom of all the wise, and truth of sages,
Show us the meaning and the goal of life.

2. Spirit of love, grant us the holy wisdom
To love you first, and then our brother man;
To give ourselves in love to all who need us;
To work with all according to your plan.

3. Spirit of justice, lead us in the battle
For human rights against all human sin.
Help us be bold when man exploits his brother
To stand with Christ, and in his spirit win.

4. Spirit of Christ, the brother of the fallen;
Friend of the friendless, champion of the poor,
Lead forth your church in joyous consecration,
Serving the Kingdom goals forevermore. A-men.

Words copyright 1972 by The Westminster Press.

Spread, O Spread the Mighty Word

GOTT SEI DANK 7.7.7.7.

Jonathan Friedrich Bahnmaier, 1827
Trans. by Catherine Winkworth, 1858; alt.; and
Arthur W. Farlander and C. Winfred Douglas, 1938

Freylinghausen's *Geistreiches Gesangbuch*, 1704; alt.

1. Spread, O spread the mighty word, Spread the kingdom of the Lord, That to earth's remotest bound Men may heed the joyful sound.
2. Word of how the Father's will Made the world, and keeps it, still; How his only Son he gave, Man from sin and death to save.
3. Word of how the Savior's love Earth's sore burden does remove; How for ever, in its need, Through his death the world is freed.
4. Mighty word God's Spirit gave, Man for heavenly life to save; Word through whose all-holy might Man can will and do the right.
5. Word of life, most pure and strong, Word for which the nations long, Spread abroad, until from night All the world awakes to light. A-men.

Words used by permission of The Church Pension Fund.

578 Strong Son of God, Immortal Love
ROCKINGHAM OLD L.M.

Alfred Tennyson, 1850
Psalmody in Miniature, 1783
Adapted by Edward Miller, 1790

1. Strong Son of God, immortal Love, Whom we, that have not seen thy face, By faith, and faith alone, embrace, Believing where we cannot prove,

2. Thou seemest human and divine, The highest, holiest manhood, thou. Our wills are ours, we know not how; Our wills are ours to make them thine.

3. Our little systems have their day; They have their day and cease to be; They are but broken lights of thee, And thou, O Lord, art more than they.

4. Let knowledge grow from more to more, But more of reverence in us dwell, That mind and soul, according well, May make one music as before. A-men.

Take Thou Our Minds, Dear Lord 579

HALL 10.10.10.10.

William H. Foulkes; sts. 1-3, 1918;
st. 4, ca. 1920

Calvin W. Laufer, 1918

1. Take thou our minds, dear Lord, we humbly pray;
   Give us the mind of Christ each passing day;
   Teach us to know the truth that sets us free;
   Grant us in all our thoughts to honor thee.

2. Take thou our hearts, O Christ, they are thine own;
   Come thou within our souls and claim thy throne;
   Help us to shed abroad thy deathless love;
   Use us to make the earth like heaven above.

3. Take thou our wills, Most High! Hold thou full sway;
   Have in our inmost souls thy perfect way;
   Guard thou each sacred hour from selfish ease;
   Guide thou our ordered lives as thou dost please.

4. Take thou ourselves, O Lord, heart, mind, and will;
   Through our surrendered souls thy plans fulfill.
   We yield ourselves to thee—time, talents, all;
   We hear, and henceforth heed, thy sovereign call. A-men.

580 Thanks to God, Whose Word Was Spoken

LAUDA ANIMA (PRAISE, MY SOUL) 8.7.8.7.8.7.

R. T. Brooks, 1954

John Goss, 1869

1. Thanks to God, whose Word was spo-ken In the deed that made the earth. His the voice that called a na-tion, His the fires that tried her worth. God has spo-ken; God has spo-ken; Praise him for his o-pen Word.

2. Thanks to God, whose Word in-car-nate Glo-ri-fied the flesh of man. Deeds and words and death and ris-ing Tell the grace in heav-en's plan. God has spo-ken; God has spo-ken; Praise him for his o-pen Word.

3. Thanks to God, whose Word is an-swered By the Spir-it's voice with-in. Here we drink of joy un-mea-sured, Life re-deemed from death and sin. God is speak-ing; God is speak-ing; Praise him for his o-pen Word. A-men.

Words copyright; used by permission of R. T. Brooks.

That Easter Day with Joy Was Bright 581
PUER NOBIS (Praetorius) L.M.

Latin hymn, before 8th century
Trans. by John Mason Neale, 1851; alt.

Trier MS., 15th century
Adapted by Michael Praetorius, 1609
Harm. by George R. Woodward, 1902

1. That Easter Day with joy was bright, The sun shone out with fairer light, When, to their longing eyes restored, Th' apostles saw their risen Lord.
2. O Jesus, King of gentleness, Do all our inmost hearts possess, And we to you will ever raise The tribute of our grateful praise.
3. O Lord of all, with us abide In this our joyful Eastertide; From every weapon death can wield, Your own redeemed forever shield.
4. All praise, O risen Lord, we give To you, who, dead, again do live; To God the Father equal praise, And God the Holy Ghost, we raise. A-men.

Music altered from *The Cowley Carol Book*, No. 21; used by permission of A. R. Mowbray & Co. Limited.

582 The Church's One Foundation
AURELIA 7.6.7.6.D.

Samuel J. Stone, 1866, 1868; alt., 1972
Samuel S. Wesley, 1864

1. The church's one foundation Is Jesus Christ her Lord;
   She is his new creation By water and the word:
   From heaven he came and sought her To be his holy bride;
   With his own blood he bought her, And for her life he died.

2. Elect from every nation, Yet one o'er all the earth,
   Her charter of salvation One Lord, one faith, one birth;
   One holy name she blesses, Partakes one holy food,
   And to one hope she presses, With every grace endued.

3. Mid toil and tribulation, And tumult of her war,
   She waits the consummation Of peace forevermore;
   Till with the vision glorious Her longing eyes are blest,
   And the great church victorious Shall be the church at rest.

4. Yet she on earth has union With God the Three in One,
   And mystic sweet communion With those whose rest is won:
   O happy ones and holy! Lord, give us grace that we,
   Like them, the meek and lowly, May live eternally. A-men.

The Day of Pentecost Arrived 583
LAND OF REST C.M.

Frank A. Brooks, Jr., 1972
Folk song, adapted as American folk hymn
Arr. by Annabel Morris Buchanan, 1938

1. The day of Pentecost arrived, To one place many came. Tongues as of fire appeared to them. They spoke in different ways.
2. Unharnessed joy was there released. Strong power they received. No explanations were required. They celebrated faith.
3. Not only laws and ancient creeds We sometimes fail to grasp, But acts of love and brotherhood, O God, we would affirm.
4. Our inhibitions make us die, To you and to all men, Do make us free, O God our friend, And hear our new-found praise.
5. In narrow ways of life and faith We all do surely walk. But Pentecost is never far, And grace to all is free. A-men.

Words copyright 1972 by The Westminster Press. Music from *Folk Songs of America*, by Annabel Morris Buchanan; copyright 1938 by J. Fischer & Bro., renewed 1966; assigned to Belwin Mills Publishing Corp.; used by permission.

584 The Day of Resurrection!

LANCASHIRE 7.6.7.6.D.

John of Damascus (675?-749?)
Trans. by John Mason Neale, 1862; alt.

Henry Smart, 1836

1. The day of res-ur-rec-tion! Earth, tell it out a-broad! The Pass-o-ver of glad-ness, The Pass-o-ver of God! From death to life e-ter-nal, From this world to the sky, Our Christ has brought us o-ver With hymns of vic-to-ry.

2. Our hearts be pure from e-vil, That we may see a-right The Lord in rays e-ter-nal Of res-ur-rec-tion light, And, lis-tening to his ac-cents, May hear, so calm and plain, His own "All hail!" and, hear-ing, May raise the vic-tor strain.

3. Now let the heavens be joy-ful, Let earth her song be-gin; Let the round world keep tri-umph, And all that is there-in; Let all things seen and un-seen Their notes of glad-ness blend, For Christ the Lord has ris-en, Our Joy that has no end. A-men.

The First Nowell the Angel Did Say 585
THE FIRST NOWELL Irregular

Traditional English carol

Traditional English carol
Harm. by John Stainer, 1871

1. The first Now-ell the an-gel did say Was to cer-tain poor shep-herds, in fields as they lay, In fields where they lay keep-ing their sheep, On a cold win-ter's night that was so deep.
2. They look-ed up and saw a star Shin-ing in the east be-yond them far, And to the earth it gave great light, And so it con-tin-ued both day and night.
3. And by the light of that same star, Three Wise Men came from coun-try far; To seek for a king was their in-tent, And to fol-low the star wher-ev-er it went.
4. This star drew nigh to the north-west, O'er Beth-le-hem it took its rest, And there it did both stop and stay, Right o-ver the place where Je-sus lay.
5. Then en-tered in those Wise Men three, Fell rev-erent-ly up-on their knee, And of-fered there in his pres-ence Their gold, and myrrh, and fran-kin-cense.

Now-ell, Now-ell, Now-ell, Now-ell, Born is the King of Is-ra-el! A-men.

586. The Friends of Christ Together

ES FLOG EIN KLEINS WALDVÖGELEIN 7.6.7.6.D.

David W. Romig, 1965
Memmingen MS., 17th century
Harm. by George R. Woodward, 1904

1. The friends of Christ together, In patience born of love
For God and for each other, Sought wisdom from above.
They heard the Master saying, His last words in that hour,
"Stay in the city praying Till you are clothed with power."

2. Our faith grows tired of waiting; The church is torn apart,
Our selfishness and hating, A spear thrust to his heart!
The hungry cry for feeding, Injustice rules again,
And Christ's hands are still bleeding Because of cruel men.

3. The thunder of the Spirit Will burst on us anew,
If we, like them, can hear it And find God's work to do.
Come, Holy Spirit, burn us, Enflame us with your power,
And by your might return us To Jesus in this hour! A-men.

Words copyright 1972 by The Westminster Press. Music slightly altered from *Songs of Syon;* used by permission of Mrs. J. Meredith Tatton.

The God of Abraham Praise 587
LEONI (YIGDAL) 6.6.8.4.D.

Daniel ben Judah Dayyan, ca. 1400
Trans. by Newton Mann, 1885;
and William Channing Gannett, 1910; alt.

Traditional Hebrew melody
Transcribed by Meyer Lyon, ca. 1770

1. The God of Abraham praise, All praised be his name,
   Who was, and is, and is to be, And still the same!
   The one eternal God, Ere aught that now appears;
   The first, the last: beyond all thought His timeless years!

2. His spirit still flows free, High surging where it will;
   In prophet's word he spoke of old And he speaks still.
   Established is his law, And changeless it shall stand,
   Deep writ upon the human heart, On sea, or land.

3. He has eternal life Implanted in the soul;
   His love shall be our strength and stay, While ages roll.
   Praise to the living God! All praised be his name
   Who was, and is, and is to be, And still the same! A-men.

588. The Great Creator of the Worlds

TALLIS' ORDINAL C.M.

From Epistle to Diognetus, 2d or 3d century
Para. by F. Bland Tucker, 1939, 1972

Thomas Tallis, ca. 1567

1. The great Creator of the worlds, The sovereign God of heaven, His holy and immortal truth To men on earth has given.
2. He sent no angel of his host To bear this mighty word, But him through whom the worlds were made, The everlasting Lord.
3. He sent him not in wrath and power, But grace and peace to bring, In kindness, as a king might send His son, himself a king.
4. He sent him down as sending God; As man he came to men; As one with us he dwelt with us, And died and lives again. A-men.

Words used by permission of The Church Pension Fund.

The Head That Once Was Crowned with Thorns 589
ST. MAGNUS C.M.

Thomas Kelly, 1820
Attr. to Jeremiah Clark, 1707

1. The head that once was crowned with thorns Is crowned with glory now; A royal diadem adorns The mighty victor's brow.
2. The highest place that heaven affords Is his, is his by right; The King of kings, and Lord of lords, And heaven's eternal light.
3. The joy of all who dwell above, The joy of all below, To whom he manifests his love And grants his name to know.
4. To them the cross, with all its shame, With all its grace, is given; Their name an everlasting name, Their joy the joy of heaven. A-men.

590 The King of Love My Shepherd Is
ST. COLUMBA 8.7.8.7.

Psalm 23
Para. by Henry W. Baker, 1868; alt., 1972

Ancient Irish melody
Arr. by Robert Carwithen, 1972

1. The King of love my shepherd is, Whose goodness fails me never; I nothing lack if I am his, And he is mine forever.
2. Where streams of living water flow My ransomed soul he's leading, And where the verdant pastures grow With food celestial feeding.
*3. Perverse and foolish oft I strayed, But yet in love he sought me, And on his shoulder gently laid, And home, rejoicing, brought me.
*4. In death's dark vale I fear no ill With you, dear Lord, beside me; Your rod and staff my comfort still, Your cross before to guide me.
5. You spread a table in my sight; Your grace so rich bestowing; And O what transport of delight From your pure cup is flowing!
6. And so through all the length of days Your goodness fails me never; Good Shepherd, may I sing your praise Within your house forever. A-men.

The Lone, Wild Bird   591
PROSPECT L.M.

Henry Richard McFadyen, 1925; alt., 1968

Southern folk hymn
Harm. by David N. Johnson, 1968

1. The lone, wild bird in lof-ty flight Is still with thee, nor leaves thy sight. And I am thine! I rest in thee. Great Spir-it, come, and rest in me. A-men.

2. The ends of earth are in thy hand, The sea's dark deep and far-off land.

Words copyright 1927 by *The Homiletic Review*, used by permission. Music reprinted from *Twelve Folksongs and Spirituals*, compiled and arranged by David N. Johnson, 1968; used by permission of Augsburg Publishing House, Minneapolis, Minnesota, copyright owner.

592 The Lord's My Shepherd

CRIMOND C.M.
(First Tune)

Psalm 23
Para. in the Scottish Psalter, 1650

Jessie Seymour Irvine, 1872
Harm. by T. C. L. Pritchard, 1929; alt., 1955

1. The Lord's my shepherd, I'll not want; He makes me down to lie In pastures green; He leadeth me The quiet waters by.
2. My soul he doth restore again; And me to walk doth make Within the paths of righteousness, E'en for his own name's sake.
3. Yea, though I walk in death's dark vale, Yet will I fear none ill; For thou art with me; and thy rod And staff me comfort still.
4. My table thou hast furnished In presence of my foes; My head thou dost with oil anoint, And my cup overflows.
5. Goodness and mercy all my life Shall surely follow me; And in God's house forevermore My dwelling place shall be. A-men.

Music slightly altered from *The Scottish Psalter*, 1929; used by permission of Oxford University Press.

The Lord's My Shepherd

593

EVAN C.M.
(Second Tune)

Psalm 23
Para. in the Scottish Psalter, 1650

William H. Havergal, 1846

1. The Lord's my shepherd, I'll not want; He makes me down to lie In pastures green; He leadeth me The quiet waters by.
2. My soul he doth restore again; And me to walk doth make With-in the paths of righteousness, E'en for his own name's sake.
3. Yea, though I walk in death's dark vale, Yet will I fear none ill; For thou art with me; And thy rod And staff me comfort still.
4. My table thou hast furnished In presence of my foes; My head thou dost with oil anoint, And my cup overflows.
5. Goodness and mercy all my life Shall surely follow me; And in God's house forevermore My dwelling place shall be. A-men.

594 The Man Who Once Has Found Abode

TALLIS' CANON L.M.

From Psalm 91
Para. in *The Book of Psalms*, 1871; alt., 1972

Thomas Tallis, ca. 1657

1. The man who once has found abode With-in the secret place of God Shall with almighty God abide And in his shadow safely hide.
2. I of the Lord my God will say, "He is my refuge and my stay; To him for safety I will flee; My God, in him my trust shall be."
3. His outspread pinions shall you hide; Beneath his wings shall you abide; His faithfulness assured and true Shall be a shield protecting you.
4. No nightly terrors shall alarm; No deadly shaft by day shall harm, Nor pestilence that walks by night, Nor plagues that waste in noonday light.
5. Because your trust is God alone, Your dwelling place the Highest One, No evil shall upon you come, Nor plague approach your guarded home. A-men.

*May be sung as a canon.

The Spacious Firmament on High 595
CREATION L.M.D.

Joseph Addison, 1712
Franz Joseph Haydn, 1798

1. The spacious firmament on high, With all the blue ethereal sky, And spangled heavens, a shining frame, Their great Original proclaim: Th'unwearied sun, from
2. Soon as the evening shades prevail, The moon takes up the wondrous tale, And nightly to the listening earth Repeats the story of her birth; While all the stars that
3. What though in solemn silence all Move round this dark terrestrial ball? What though no real voice nor sound Amid the radiant orbs be found? In reason's ear they

See following page.

596   The Spacious Firmament on High (cont.)

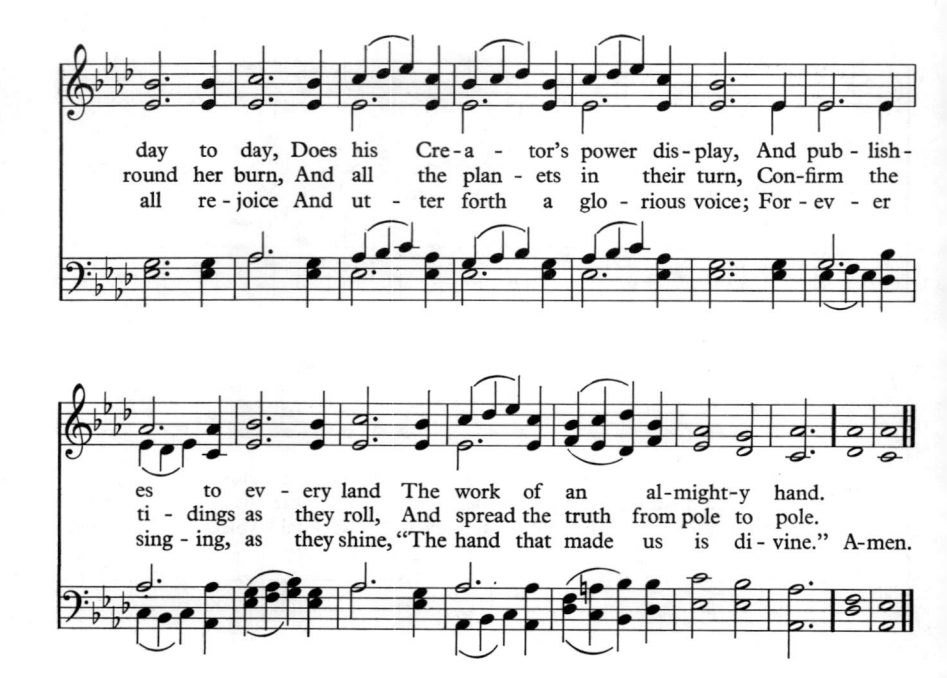

day to day, Does his Cre-a - tor's power dis-play, And pub-lish-
round her burn, And all the plan - ets in their turn, Con-firm the
all re - joice And ut - ter forth a glo - rious voice; For - ev - er

es to ev - ery land The work of an al-might-y hand.
ti - dings as they roll, And spread the truth from pole to pole.
sing - ing, as they shine, "The hand that made us is di - vine." A-men.

The Strife Is O'er, the Battle Done   597
VICTORY (PALESTRINA) 8.8.8. with Alleluias

Symphonia Sirenum Selectarum, 1695
Trans. by Francis Pott, 1861; alt.

Giovanni P. da Palestrina, 1591
Adapted by William Henry Monk, 1861

Alleluia! Alleluia! Alleluia!

1. The strife is o'er, the battle done;
The victory of life is won;
The song of triumph has begun.

2. The powers of death have done their worst,
But Christ their legions has dispersed:
Let shouts of holy joy outburst.

3. The three sad days have quickly sped;
He rises glorious from the dead:
All glory to our risen Head!

4. He closed the yawning gates of hell;
The bars from heaven's high portals fell:
Let hymns of praise his triumphs tell.

5. Lord, by your wounds on Calvary
From death's dread sting your servants free,
That we may live eternally.

Alleluia!

A-men.

598. The True Light That Enlightens Man

Based on John 1:9-17
John Ylvisaker, 1964

Spiritual (?)
Arr. by John Ylvisaker, 1964
Harm. by Paul Abels, 1966

1. The true light that en-light-ens man,
Came to earth from God's right hand,
Glo-ry be to thee, O Lord, Al-le-lu-ia!
Praise to thee, O Son of God, Al-le-lu-ia!

2. And to all who be-lieve in him,
Gave he free-dom from the bonds of sin, Al-le-lu-ia!
Glo-ry be to thee, O Lord, Al-le-lu-ia!
Praise to thee, O Son of God, Al-le-lu-ia!

3. Word made flesh has dwelt with man,
We shall live with him a-gain, Al-le-lu-ia!
Glo-ry be to thee, O Lord, Al-le-lu-ia!
Praise to thee, O Son of God, Al-le-lu-ia!

4. For the law through Mo-ses came,
Grace and truth in Je-sus' name, Al-le-lu-ia!
Glo-ry be to thee, O Lord, Al-le-lu-ia!
Praise to thee, O Son of God, Al-le-lu-ia!

Words and arrangement of music copyright 1964 by The Youth Department of The American Lutheran Church; from *Songs for Today*; used by permission. Harmonization from *Risk*, Vol. II, No. 3, 1966, published by World Council of Churches; used by permission.

Thee We Adore, O Hidden Savior, Thee 599
ADORO TE DEVOTE 10.10.10.10.

Attr. to Thomas Aquinas (ca. 1225-1274)
Trans. by James Russell Woodford, 1850; alt.

Plainsong, Solesmes form
Arr. by J. H. Arnold, 1933

1. Thee we a-dore, O hid-den Sav-ior, thee,
   Who at this bless-ed feast art pleased to be;
   Both flesh and spir-it in thy pres-ence fail,
   Yet here thy pres-ence we de-vout-ly hail.

2. O blest me-mo-rial of our dy-ing Lord,
   Who liv-ing Bread to men doth here af-ford!
   O may our souls for-ev-er feed on thee,
   And thou, O Christ, for-ev-er pre-cious be!

3. Foun-tain of good-ness, Je-sus, Lord and God,
   Cleanse us, un-clean, with thy most cleans-ing blood;
   In-crease our faith and love, that we may know
   The hope and peace which from thy pres-ence flow.

4. O Christ, whom now be-neath a veil we see,
   May what we thirst for soon our por-tion be,
   To gaze on thee un-veiled, and see thy face,
   The vi-sion of thy glo-ry and thy grace. A-men.

Music from *The English Hymnal*; used by permission of Oxford University Press.

600 There Is a Balm in Gilead

Negro spiritual
Arr. by Harold Moyer, 1956

There is a balm in Gil-e-ad To make the wound-ed whole,

There is a balm in Gil-e-ad To heal the sin-sick soul.

1. Some-times I feel dis-cour-aged, And think my work's in vain, But then the Ho-ly Spir-it Re-vives my soul a-gain.
2. Don't ev-er feel dis-cour-aged, For Je-sus is your friend, And if you lack for knowl-edge, He'll not re-fuse to lend.
3. If you can-not preach like Pe-ter, If you can-not pray like Paul, You can tell the love of Je-sus And say, "He died for all."

Arrangement of music from *The Youth Hymnary*; used by permission of Faith and Life Press.

There's a Wideness in God's Mercy   601
IN BABILONE 8.7.8.7.D.

Frederick W. Faber, 1854

Traditional Dutch melody
Harm. by Julius Röntgen, ca. 1906

1. There's a wide-ness in God's mer-cy, Like the wide-ness of the sea;
2. For the love of God is broad-er Than the mea-sure of man's mind;

There's a kind-ness in his jus-tice, Which is more than lib-er-ty.
And the heart of the E-ter-nal Is most won-der-ful-ly kind.

There is no place where earth's sor-rows Are more felt than up in heaven;
If our love were but more sim-ple, We should take him at his word;

There is no place where earth's fail-ings Have such kind-ly judg-ment given.
And our lives would be all sun-shine In the sweet-ness of our Lord. A-men.

Music used by permission of F. E. Röntgen.

602 This Is My Father's World
TERRA BEATA S.M.D.

Maltbie D. Babcock, 1901

Traditional English melody
Adapted by Franklin L. Sheppard, 1915; alt.
Harm. for *The Hymnbook*, 1955

1. This is my Father's world, And to my lis-tening ears All na-ture sings, and round me rings The mu-sic of the spheres. This is my Father's world: I rest me in the thought Of rocks and trees, of skies and seas; His hand the won-ders wrought.

2. This is my Father's world: The birds their car-ols raise, The morn-ing light, the lil-y white, De-clare their mak-er's praise. This is my Father's world: He shines in all that's fair; In the rus-tling grass I hear him pass, He speaks to me ev-ery-where.

3. This is my Father's world: Oh, let me ne'er for-get That though the wrong seems oft so strong, God is the rul-er yet. This is my Father's world: The bat-tle is not done; Je-sus who died shall be sat-is-fied, And earth and heaven be one. A-men.

Thou Whose Purpose Is to Kindle

603

LADUE CHAPEL 8.7.8.7.D.

Elton Trueblood, 1966

Ronald Arnatt, 1968

1. Thou whose pur-pose is to kin-dle Now ig-nite us with thy fire; While the earth a-waits thy burn-ing, With thy pas-sion us in-spire. O-ver-come our sin-ful calm-ness,
2. Thou who, in thy ho-ly gos-pel, Wills that man should tru-ly live, Make us sense our share of fail-ure, Our tran-quil-li-ty for-give. Teach us cour-age as we strug-gle
3. Lord, who still a sword de-liv-ers Rath-er than a plac-id peace, With thy sharp-ened word dis-turb us, From com-pla-cen-cy re-lease! Save us now from sat-is-fac-tion,

Words from *The Incendiary Fellowship*, by Elton Trueblood; copyright © 1967 by David Elton Trueblood; used by permission of Harper & Row, Publishers. Music used by permission of Ronald Arnatt.

See following page.

Alternative Tune: AUSTRIAN HYMN

604 Thou Whose Purpose Is to Kindle (cont.)

Rouse us with re-demp-tive shame; Bap-tize with thy fier-y spir-it, Crown our lives with tongues of flame.
In all lib-er-a-ting strife; Lift the small-ness of our vi-sion By thine own a-bun-dant life.
When we pri-vate-ly are free, Yet are un-dis-turbed in spir-it By our broth-er's mis-er-y. A-men.

Throned Upon the Awful Tree

ARFON 7.7.7.7.7.7.

John Ellerton, 1875; alt., 1972

Traditional melody, France and Wales
Adapted by Hugh Davies, ca. 1906

1. Throned upon the awful tree, Lamb of God, your grief we see. Darkness veils your anguished face; None its lines of woe can trace. None can tell what pangs unknown Hold you silent and alone—
2. Silent through those three dread hours, Wrestling with the evil powers, Left alone with human sin, Gloom around you and within, Till th'appointed time is nigh, Till the Lamb of God may die.
3. Hark, that cry that peals aloud Upward through the whelming cloud! You, the Father's only Son, You, his own anointed one, You are asking— can it be?—"Why have you forsaken me?"
4. Lord, should fear and anguish roll Darkly o'er our sinful soul, You, who once were thus bereft That your own might ne'er be left, Teach us by that bitter cry In the gloom to know you nigh. A-men.

606 'Tis the Gift to Be Simple
(Simple Gifts)

Shaker song
Harm. by Richard D. Wetzel, 1972

Shaker song

Unison

'Tis the gift to be sim-ple, 'tis the gift to be free, 'Tis the gift to come down where we ought to be, And when we find our-selves in the place just right, 'Twill be in the val-ley of love and de-light.

Music copyright 1972 by The Westminster Press.

'Tis the Gift to Be Simple (cont.)   607

When true sim-plic-i-ty is gained, To bow and to bend we shan't be a-shamed, To turn, turn will be our delight Till by turn-ing, turn-ing we come round right.

608   To Abraham the Promise Came
THE BABE OF BETHLEHEM 8.7.8.7.D.

Traditional carol
Southern Harmony, 1835

American folk tune
Southern Harmony, 1835
Harm. by John Powell, 1934

1. To Abraham the promise came, And to his seed forever, A light to shine in Isaac's line, By Scripture we discover; Hail, promised morn! the Savior's
2. His parents poor in earthly store, To entertain the stranger They found no bed to lay his head, But in the ox's manger: No royal things, as used by
3. On that same night a glorious light To shepherds there appeared, Bright angels came in shining flame, They saw and greatly feared. The angels said, "Be not a-
4. "The city's name is Bethlehem, In which God hath appointed, This glorious morn a Savior's born, For him hath God anointed; By this you'll know, if you will
5. When this was said, straightway was made A glorious sound from heaven: Each flaming tongue an anthem sung, "To men a Savior's given, In Jesus' name, the glorious

Music from *Twelve Folk Hymns*, by John Powell; copyright 1934 by J. Fischer & Bro., renewed 1962; assigned to Belwin Mills Publishing Corp.; used by permission.

To Abraham the Promise Came (cont.) 609

born, The glorious Mediator— God's blessed Word made flesh and blood, Assumed the human nature.
kings, Were seen by those that found him, But in the hay the stranger lay, With swaddling bands around him.
fraid, Although we much alarm you, We do appear good news to bear, As now we will inform you.
go To see this little stranger, His lovely charms in Mary's arms, Both lying in a manger."
theme, We elevate our voices, At Jesus' birth be peace on earth, Meanwhile all heaven rejoices."

610 To Thee with Joy I Sing

Appalachian carol
Arr. by David N. Johnson, 1968

Appalachian carol
Adapted by David N. Johnson, 1968

1. To thee with joy I sing, Sweet Child that heaven did bring, Now Ju-dah's land shall ring With thy prais-es. Gen-tle Stran-ger, In that man-ger, In Ju-dah's land we find thee, In-fant Sav-ior.
2. I greet thee, Prince of Peace: From sin give thy re-lease! Nor shall my tongue e'er cease From thy prais-es. Gen-tle Stran-ger, In that man-ger, In Ju-dah's land we find thee, In-fant Sav-ior.
3. Thy crib can scarce con-tain Thy love, our pre-cious gain; May hymns new heights at-tain With thy prais-es. Gen-tle Stran-ger, In that man-ger, In Ju-dah's land we find thee, In-fant Sav-ior.
4. Now twi-light soft-ly comes: The Babe to sleep suc-cumbs; Play soft-ly, flute and drums, To his prais-es. Gen-tle Stran-ger, In that man-ger, In Ju-dah's land we find thee, Bless-ed Sav-ior. A-men.

Words and adaptation of music reprinted from *Twelve Folksongs and Spirituals* (words alt.), compiled and arranged by David N. Johnson, 1968; used by permission of Augsburg Publishing House, Minneapolis, Minnesota, copyright owner. Melody used by permission of Berea College.

Upon Your Great Church Universal 611
RENDEZ À DIEU 9.8.9.8.D

J. M. de Carbon-Ferrière, 1823
Trans. by Margaret House, 1949; alt., 1972
Comp. or adapted by Louis Bourgeois, 1543, 1551

1. Upon your great church universal, The constant object of your love, May your abundant grace paternal Be poured out freely from above. Your children trusting in your
2. O God, be mindful of your promise Made to your people through your Word; The Holy Spirit give us comfort, And teach us how to call you Lord. Open our eyes to see your
3. Spread the good news to all your people From rising unto setting sun; And let us hear the myriad voices In theme and music raised as one! And on the farthest distant

Words altered from *Cantate Domino*; used by permission of the World Student Christian Federation.

See following page.

612 Upon Your Great Church Universal (cont.)

mer - cy In ev - ery place ex - pect - ant pray; Grant that their hopes be not con-found - ed; O Lord, be in our midst to - day.

glo - ry, In trans-formed hearts al - le - giance win, And may your church in in - stant prayer Through you tri - um-phant con-quer sin.

beach - es The na - tions all their trib - ute bring, And there be - neath the cross as - sem - bled Praise Je - sus Christ their Lord and King. A-men.

Veiled in Darkness Judah Lay

613

PITTSBURGH 7.7.7.7.7.7.

Douglas LeTell Rights, 1915; alt., 1972

Roland Leich, 1969

1. Veiled in darkness Judah lay, Waiting for the promised day, While across the shadowy night Streamed a flood of glorious light, Heavenly voices chanting then, "Peace on earth, peace on earth, goodwill, goodwill to men." Amen.

2. Still the earth in darkness lies. Up from death's dark vale arise Voices of a world in grief. Prayers of men who seek relief: Now our darkness pierce again, "Peace on earth, peace on earth, goodwill, goodwill to men." Amen.

3. Light of light, we humbly pray, Shine upon your world today; Break the gloom of our dark night, Fill our souls with love and light, Send your blessed word again, "Peace on earth, peace on earth, goodwill, goodwill to men." Amen.

Words used by permission of Burton J. Rights. Music copyright 1972 by The Westminster Press.

614 Wake, Awake, for Night Is Flying
WACHET AUF P.M.

Philipp Nicolai, 1599
Trans. by Catherine Winkworth, 1858, 1863; alt., 1972

Attr. to Philipp Nicolai, 1599
Harm. by J. S. Bach, 1731

1. Wake, a-wake, for night is fly-ing, The watch-men on the heights are cry-ing: A-wake, Je-ru-sa-lem, at last! Mid-night hears the wel-come voic-es, And at the thrill-ing
2. Zi-on hears the watch-men sing-ing, And all her heart with joy is spring-ing; She wakes, she ris-es from her gloom; For her Lord comes down all-glo-rious, The strong in grace, in

Wake, Awake, for Night Is Flying (cont.) 615

cry re-joices; Come forth, you virgins, night is past! The Bridegroom comes; awake, Your lamps with gladness take; Alleluia! And for his marriage feast prepare, For you must go to meet him there.

truth victorious, Her Star is risen, her Light is come! Ah, come now, blessed Lord, O Jesus, Son of God! Alleluia! We follow till the halls we view Where you have bid us sup with you. Amen.

616 Walk Tall, Christian
WOOSTER 4.6.8.6.

Miriam Drury, 1969 — Richard T. Gore, 1969

1. Walk tall, Christian, Walk tall and have no fear; The Christ of God, whose child you are, He holds you in his care.
2. Walk true, Christian, Keep faith come weal or woe; To upright, pure, forgiving souls, His bounties overflow.
3. Walk free, Christian, Lay hold on deep, deep joy That age, nor loss, nor rude rebuff, Nor failure, can destroy.
4. Walk proud, Christian, As Christ's ambassador; His gospel and his church are judged By what his people are. A-men.

Words and music copyright 1972 by The Westminster Press.

Watchman, Tell Us of the Night

ABERYSTWYTH 7.7.7.7.D.

John Bowring, 1825; alt., 1972

Joseph Parry, 1879

1. Watch-man, tell us of the night, What its signs of prom-ise are.
   Trav - eler, o'er yon moun-tain's height, See that glo - ry - beam-ing star.
   Watch-man, does its beau - teous ray Aught of joy or hope fore - tell?
   Trav - eler, yes; it brings the day, Prom - ised day of Is - ra - el.

2. Watch-man, tell us of the night, High-er yet that star as-cends.
   Trav - eler, bless-ed - ness and light, Peace and truth its course por-tends.
   Watch-man, will its beams a - lone Gild the spot that gave them birth?
   Trav - eler, ag - es are its own; See, it bursts o'er all the earth.

3. Watch-man, tell us of the night, For the morn-ing seems to dawn.
   Trav - eler, dark-ness takes its flight, Doubt and ter - ror are with-drawn.
   Watch-man, let your wan-derings cease; Has - ten to your qui - et home.
   Trav - eler, lo, the Prince of Peace, Lo, the Son of God is come! A-men.

618 We Are Living, We Are Dwelling

BLAENHAFREN 8.7.8.7.D.

Arthur Cleveland Coxe, 1840; alt.

Traditional Welsh melody
as in *Hymns of the Kingdom of God*, 1923

1. We are living, we are dwelling In a grand and awful time.
In an age on ages telling; To be living is sublime.
Hark! the waking up of nations, Hosts advancing to the fray;
Hark! what sounds is all creation's Groaning for the latter day.

2. Will you play, then? will you dally Far behind the battle line?
Up! it is Jehovah's rally; Your full strength with God's combine.
Worlds are charging, heaven beholding; You have but an hour to fight;
Now, the blazoned cross unfolding, On, right onward for the right!

3. Sworn to yield, to waver, never; Consecrated, born again;
Sworn to be Christ's soldiers ever, O for Christ at least be men!
O let all the soul within you For the truth's sake go abroad!
Strike! let every nerve and sinew Tell on ages, tell for God. Amen.

We Are One in the Spirit
(They'll Know We Are Christians by Our Love)

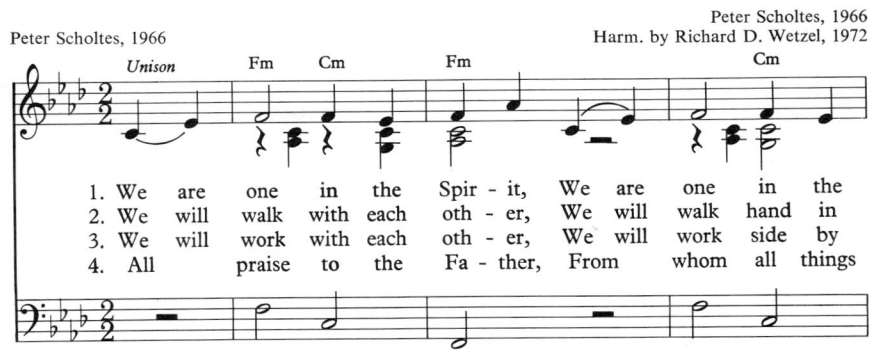

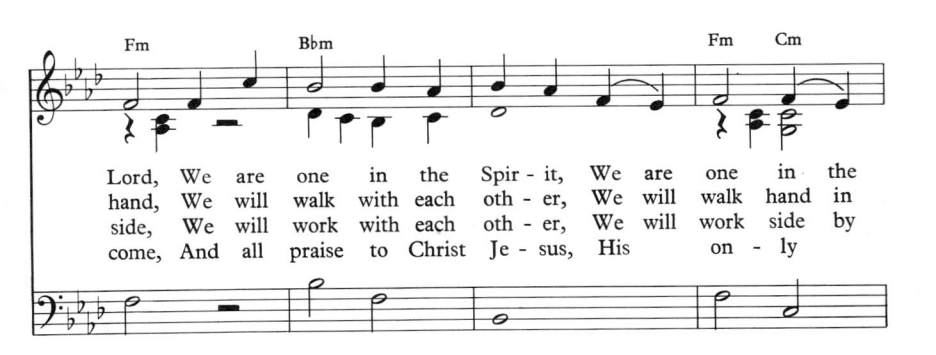

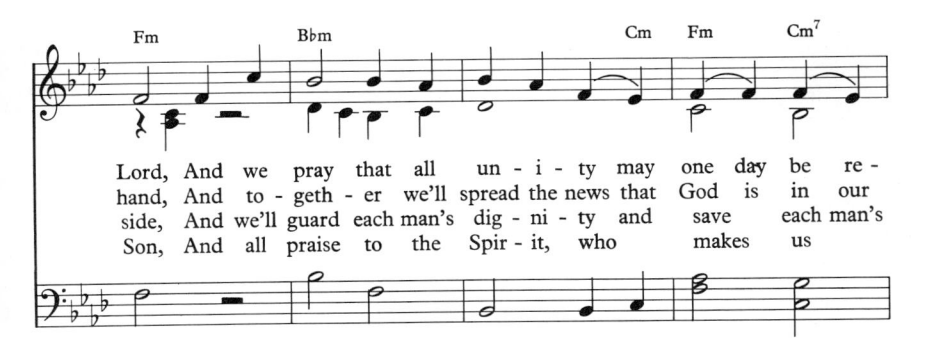

Peter Scholtes, 1966
Harm. by Richard D. Wetzel, 1972

1. We are one in the Spir-it, We are one in the Lord, We are one in the Spir-it, We are one in the Lord, And we pray that all un-i-ty may one day be re-
2. We will walk with each oth-er, We will walk hand in hand, We will walk with each oth-er, We will walk hand in hand, And to-geth-er we'll spread the news that God is in our
3. We will work with each oth-er, We will work side by side, We will work with each oth-er, We will work side by side, And we'll guard each man's dig-ni-ty and save each man's
4. All praise to the Fa-ther, From whom all things come, And all praise to Christ Je-sus, His on-ly Son, And all praise to the Spir-it, who makes us

Words and melody copyright © 1966 by F.E.L. Church Publications, Ltd.;
from *They'll Know We Are Christians* and *Missa Bossa Nova*; used by permission.
Harmonization copyright 1972 by The Westminster Press.

See following page.

620 We Are One in the Spirit (cont.)

stored.
land.
pride. And they'll know we are Christians by our love, by our
one.

love, Yes, they'll know we are Christians by our love.

We Bear the Strain of Earthly Care 621
AZMON C.M.

Ozora S. Davis, 1909

Carl G. Gläser, 1828
Arr. by Lowell Mason, 1839

1. We bear the strain of earthly care, But bear it not alone; Beside us walks our brother Christ And makes our task his own.
2. Through din of market, whirl of wheels, And thrust of driving trade, We follow where the Master leads, Serene and unafraid.
3. The common hopes that make us men Were his in Galilee; The tasks he gives are those he gave Beside the restless sea.
4. Our brotherhood still rests in him, The brother of us all, And o'er the centuries still we hear The Master's winsome call. A-men.

622 We Believe in One True God

RATISBON 7.7.7.7.7.7.

Tobias Clausnitzer, 1668
Trans. by Catherine Winkworth, 1863; alt.

German melody, adapted in
J. G. Werner's *Choralbuch*, 1815

1. We believe in one true God, Father, Son, and Holy Ghost,
Ever-present help in need, Praised by all the heavenly host;
By whose mighty power alone All is made and wrought and done.

2. We believe in Jesus Christ, Son of God and Mary's Son,
Who descended from his throne And for us salvation won;
By whose cross and death are we Rescued from sin's misery.

3. We confess the Holy Ghost, Who from both for e'er proceeds;
Who upholds and comforts us In all trials, fears, and needs.
Blest and Holy Trinity, Praise we all eternally. A-men.

We Come Unto Our Fathers' God

NUN FREUT EUCH 8.7.8.7.8.8.7.

Thomas H. Gill, 1868; alt., 1972 *Geistliche Lieder*, Wittenberg, 1535

623

1. We come unto our fathers' God; Their Rock is our salvation;
The eternal arms, their dear abode, We make our habitation.
We bring you, Lord, the praise they brought, We seek you as your saints have sought In every generation.

2. Their joy unto their Lord we bring; Their song to us descending;
The Spirit who in them did sing To us is music lending:
His song in them, in us, is one; We raise it high, we send it on. The song is never ending.

3. You saints to come, take up the strain, The same sweet theme endeavor;
Unbroken be the golden chain! Keep on the song forever!
Safe in the same dear dwelling place, Rich with the same eternal grace, Bless the same boundless Giver. A-men.

624 We Gather Together to Ask the Lord's Blessing
KREMSER 12.11.12.11.

Netherlands folk song
Trans. by Theodore Baker, 1919; alt., 1972

Netherlands folk song
Arr. by Eduard Kremser, 1877

1. We gather together to ask the Lord's blessing;
   He chastens and hastens his will to make known;
   The wicked oppressing now cease from distressing.
   Sing praises to his name; he forgets not his own.

2. Beside us to guide us, our God with us joining,
   Ordaining, maintaining his kingdom always;
   So from the beginning the fight we were winning;
   You, Lord, were at our side, to you be all praise.

3. We all do extol you, O leader triumphant,
   And pray that you still our defender will be.
   Let your congregation escape tribulation.
   Your name be ever praised! O Lord, make us free! A-men.

We Greet You, Sure Redeemer from All Strife 625
TOULON 10.10.10.10.

Attr. to John Calvin, 1545
Trans. by Elizabeth L. Smith, 1868; alt.

Comp. or adapted by Louis Bourgeois, 1551
Abr. in English Psalters

1. We greet you, sure Redeemer from all strife,
   Our only Trust and Savior of our life,
   Who pain did undergo for our poor sake;
   We pray you from our hearts all cares to take.

2. You are the King of mercy and of grace,
   Reigning omnipotent in every place:
   So come, O King, and our whole being sway;
   Shine on us with the light of your pure day.

3. You are the life, in which we do believe,
   From you all substance and our strength receive;
   Sustain us by your faith and by your power,
   And give us strength in every trying hour.

*4. You have the true and perfect gentleness,
   You have no harshness and no bitterness:
   O grant to us the grace in you we see,
   That we may dwell in perfect unity.

5. Our hope is in no other save in you;
   Our faith is built upon your promise true;
   Lord, give us peace, and make us calm and sure,
   That in your strength we evermore endure. A-men.

626 We Love Your Kingdom, Lord
ST. THOMAS S.M.

Timothy Dwight, 1800; alt., 1972
Williams' *The Universal Psalmodist*, 1763
Abr. in *The New Universal Psalmodist*, 1770

1. We love your kingdom, Lord, The house of your abode, The church our blest Redeemer saved With his own precious blood.
2. We love your church, O God, Her walls reflect your plan, A symbol of love's covenant Uniting God and man.
3. For her our tears shall fall, For her our prayers ascend; To her our cares and toils be given, Till toils and cares shall end.
4. Beyond our highest joy We prize her heavenly ways, Her sweet communion, solemn vows, Her hymns of love and praise. A-men.

We Praise You, O God, Our Redeemer, Creator 627
KREMSER 12.11.12.11.

Julia Cady Cory, 1902, 1956; alt., 1972

Netherlands folk song
Arr. by Eduard Kremser, 1877

1. We praise you, O God, our Re-deem-er, Cre-a-tor,
   In grate-ful de-vo-tion our trib-ute we bring.
   We lay it be-fore you, we kneel and a-dore you,
   We bless your ho-ly name, glad prais-es we sing.

2. We wor-ship you, God of our fa-thers, we bless you;
   Through life's storm and tem-pest our guide you have been.
   When per-ils o'er-take us, you will not for-sake us,
   And with your help, O Lord, life's bat-tles we win.

3. With voic-es u-nit-ed our prais-es we of-fer,
   And glad-ly our songs of true wor-ship we raise.
   Our sins now con-fess-ing, we pray for your bless-ing;
   To you, our great Re-deem-er, for-ev-er be praise! A-men.

628. We Sing the Mighty Power of God

ELLACOMBE C.M.D.

Isaac Watts, 1715; alt.
Gesangbuch der herzogl. Wirtembergischen Katholischen Hofkapelle, 1784

1. We sing the might-y power of God, That made the moun-tains rise;
That spread the flow-ing seas a-broad, And built the loft-y skies.
We sing the Wis-dom that or-dained The sun to rule the day;
The moon shines full at his com-mand, And all the stars o-bey.

2. We sing the good-ness of the Lord, That filled the earth with food;
He formed the crea-tures with his word, And then pro-nounced them good.
Lord, how your won-ders are dis-played, Wher-e'er we turn our eyes:
If we sur-vey the ground we tread, Or gaze up-on the skies!

3. There's not a plant or flower be-low But makes your glo-ries known;
And clouds a-rise, and tem-pests blow, By or-der from your throne;
All crea-tures, man-y as they be, Are ev-er in your care,
And ev-ery-where that man can be, We see your pres-ence there. A-men.

We Thank You, Lord, for Strength of Arm 629
O JESU 8.4.8.4.8.8.

Robert Davis, 1908; alt., 1972
Attr. to Johann Balthasar Reimann, 1747

1. We thank you, Lord, for strength of arm
To win our bread, And that, be-yond our need, is meat
For friends un-fed: We thank you much for bread to live; We thank you more for bread to give.

2. We thank you, Lord, for shel-tered home
In cold and storm, And that, be-yond our need, is room
For friends for-lorn: We thank you much for place to rest, But more for shel-ter for our guest.

3. We thank you, Lord, for lav-ish love
On us be-stowed, E-nough to share with love-less folk
To ease their load: Your love to us we ill could spare, Yet dear-er is your love we share. A-men.

630 What Child Is This

GREENSLEEVES 8.7.8.7.6.8.6.7.

William Chatterton Dix, 1861 — Traditional English melody

1. What child is this, who, laid to rest, On Mary's lap is sleeping?
Whom angels greet with anthems sweet, While shepherds watch are keeping?
This, this is Christ the King, Whom shepherds guard and angels sing!
Haste, haste to bring him laud, The Babe, the Son of Mary!

2. Why lies he in such mean estate, Where ox and ass are feeding?
Good Christian, fear, for sinners here The silent Word is pleading.
Nails, spear, shall pierce him through, The cross be borne for me, for you.
Hail, hail, the Word made flesh, The Babe, the Son of Mary!

3. So bring him incense, gold, and myrrh; Come, peasant, king, to own him.
The King of kings salvation brings; Let loving hearts enthrone him.
Raise, raise the song on high! The virgin sings her lullaby.
Joy, joy, for Christ is born, The Babe, the Son of Mary!

What Makes a City Great and Strong? 631

LEICESTER 8.8.8.8.8.8.

Sts. 1-3, author unknown; alt., 1964
St. 4, Donald D. Kettring, 1972

John Bishop, ca. 1711
As in *Hymns for the Celebration of Life*, 1964

1. What makes a cit-y great and strong? Not ar-chi-tec-ture's graceful strength, Not fac-to-ries' ex-tend-ed length, But men who see the civ-ic wrong, And give their lives to make it right, And turn its dark-ness in-to light.
2. What makes a cit-y man can love? Not things that charm the out-ward sense, Not gross dis-play of op-u-lence, But right that wrong can-not re-move, And truth that fac-es civ-ic shame To ban-ish it in hon-or's name.
3. This is a cit-y that shall stand, A light up-on a na-tion's hill, A voice that e-vil can-not still, A source of bless-ing to the land; Its strength not brick, nor stone, nor wood, But jus-tice, love, and broth-er-hood.
4. A cit-y warm with man's in-tent To serve the Christ who came in love, As bea-cons light-ed from a-bove, With ra-diance of the One God sent; And quick-ened by the Spir-it's power We serve God in this place and hour. A-men.

Stanza 4 copyright 1972 by The Westminster Press.

632 What Star Is This, with Beams So Bright

PUER NOBIS (Praetorius) L.M.

Charles Coffin, 1736
Trans. by John Chandler, 1837; alt.

Trier MS., 15th century
Adapted by Michael Praetorius, 1609
Harm. by George R. Woodward, 1902

1. What star is this, with beams so bright, More lovely than the noon-day light? 'Tis sent to announce a new-born King, Glad tidings of our God to bring.
2. 'Tis now fulfilled what God decreed, "From Jacob shall a star proceed"; And lo! the Eastern sages stand, To read in heaven the Lord's command.
3. O Jesus, while the star of grace Impels us on to seek your face, Let not our slothful hearts refuse The guidance of your light to use.
4. To God the Father, heavenly Light, To Christ, revealed in earthly night, To God the Holy Ghost we raise An endless song of thankful praise! A-men.

Music altered from *The Cowley Carol Book*, No. 21; used by permission of A. R. Mowbray & Co. Limited.

Whate'er Our God Ordains Is Right 633
WAS GOTT TUT 8.7.8.7.4.4.8.8.

Samuel Rodigast, ca. 1674
Trans. by Catherine Winkworth, 1858, 1863; alt., 1972

Attr. to Severus Gastorius, 1681
Harm. in *Common Service Book*, 1917

1. What-e'er our God or-dains is right, His ho-ly will a-bid-ing;
   We will be still, what-e'er he does, And fol-low where he's guid-ing.
   He is our God; Though dark our road, He holds us that we
   shall not fall; Where-fore to him we leave it all.

2. What-e'er our God or-dains is right; He nev-er will de-ceive us.
   He leads us by the prop-er path; We know he will not leave us,
   And take, con-tent, What he has sent; His hand can turn our
   griefs a-way, And pa-tient-ly we wait his day.

3. What-e'er our God or-dains is right; Here shall our stand be tak-en.
   Though sor-row, need, or death be ours, Yet we are not for-sak-en.
   Our Fa-ther's care Is round us there; He holds us that we
   shall not fall, And so to him we leave it all. A-men.

Music slightly altered from *Common Service Book* of the United Lutheran Church; used by permission.

634 When Christ Comes to Die on Calvary

Henry L. Lettermann, 1966
Richard Hillert, 1966

1. When Christ comes to die on Calvary, Created things all hold their breath, They hide their face in the darkened sky, And nothing moves on that hillside except A white lily blows, A white lily blows in the dark heart of spring!

2. When Mary in doubt that Easter dawn Believes her Lord among the dead, She weeps her shuddering grief against The stubborn stone in the garden and there A white lily blows, A white lily blows in the dark heart of spring!

3. When death with its terror comes by night Disquieting my solitude, My Christ who rose from the dead proclaims The empty grave in the garden, and then A white lily blows, A white lily blows in the dark heart of spring!

Words and music from "A White Lily Blows" ("When Christ Comes to Die on Calvary"), copyright 1966 by Concordia Publishing House; used by permission.

When I Survey the Wondrous Cross 635
HAMBURG L.M.

Isaac Watts, 1707, 1709
Comp. or arr. by Lowell Mason, 1825

1. When I survey the wondrous cross On which the Prince of glory died, My richest gain I count but loss, And pour contempt on all my pride.
2. Forbid it, Lord, that I should boast, Save in the death of Christ my God. All the vain things that charm me most, I sacrifice them to his blood.
3. See, from his head, his hands, his feet, Sorrow and love flow mingled down. Did e'er such love and sorrow meet, Or thorns compose so rich a crown?
4. Were the whole realm of nature mine, That were a present far too small; Love so amazing, so divine, Demands my soul, my life, my all. A-men.

Alternative Tune: ROCKINGHAM OLD

636 When Jesus Wept

St. 1, William Billings, 1770
Sts. 2-4, Frank A. Brooks, Jr., 1972

William Billings, 1770
Harm. by Richard D. Wetzel, 1972

1. When Jesus wept, the falling tear
   In mercy flowed beyond all bound;
   When Jesus groaned, a trembling fear
   Seized all the guilty world around.

2. When Jesus saw Jerusalem
   Amid the palms and rowdy cheer,
   He stopped to look. His eyes grew dim.
   For misled men, he shed the tear.

3. When Jesus looks upon our towns;
   Our churches rich; our brothers poor;
   "Hosannas" seem but empty sounds
   To him who is our Savior sure.

4. Then let us haste to serve his cause
   Forgetting race and station,
   Lest once again our chance is lost,
   And gone his visitation.

Stanzas 2-4 and music copyright 1972 by The Westminster Press.

*May be sung as a four-part canon unaccompanied.

When Morning Gilds the Skies   637
LAUDES DOMINI 6.6.6.D.

German hymn, 18th(?) century
Trans. by Edward Caswall, 1854, 1858; alt.

Joseph Barnby, 1868

1. When morning gilds the skies, My heart awaking cries: May Jesus Christ be praised! Alike at work and prayer To Jesus I repair: May Jesus Christ be praised!
2. Does sadness fill my mind? A solace here I find: May Jesus Christ be praised! Or fades my earthly bliss? My comfort still is this: May Jesus Christ be praised!
3. Let earth's wide circle round In joyful notes resound: May Jesus Christ be praised! Let air and sea and sky, From depth to height, reply: May Jesus Christ be praised!
4. Be this, while life is mine, My canticle divine: May Jesus Christ be praised! Be this th'eternal song, Through all the ages long: May Jesus Christ be praised! A-men.

638 When Stephen, Full of Power and Grace
SALVATION C.M.D.

Based on Acts, chs. 6, 7
Jan Struther, 1931; alt., 1972

Kentucky Harmony, ca. 1815
Harm. by Kenneth Munson, 1964

1. When Stephen, full of power and grace, Went forth throughout the land, He bore no shield before his face, No weapon in his hand; But only in his heart a flame
2. When Stephen preached against the laws And by those laws was tried, He had no friend to plead his cause, No spokesman at his side; But only in his heart a flame
3. When Stephen, young and doomed to die, Fell crushed beneath the stones, He had no curse nor vengeful cry For those who broke his bones; But only in his heart a flame
4. Let me, O Lord, your cause defend, A knight without a sword; No shield I ask, no faithful friend, No vengeance, no reward; But only in my heart a flame

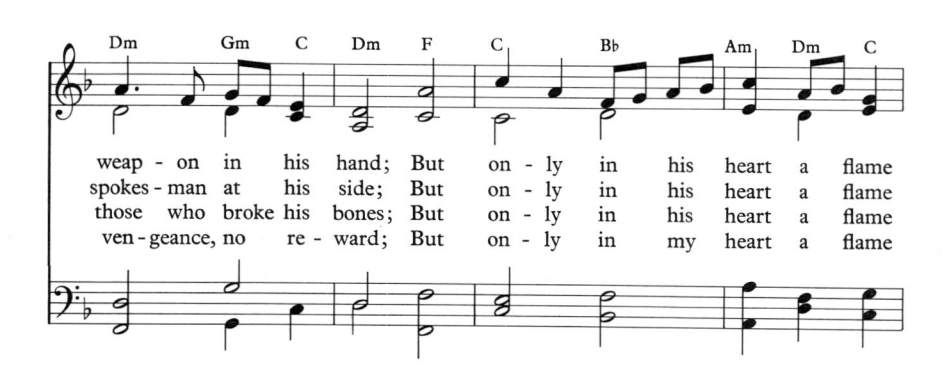

Words altered from *Songs of Praise*, Enlarged Edition; used by permission of Oxford University Press. Music copyright © 1964 by Unitarian Universalist Association; reprinted by permission of Beacon Press.

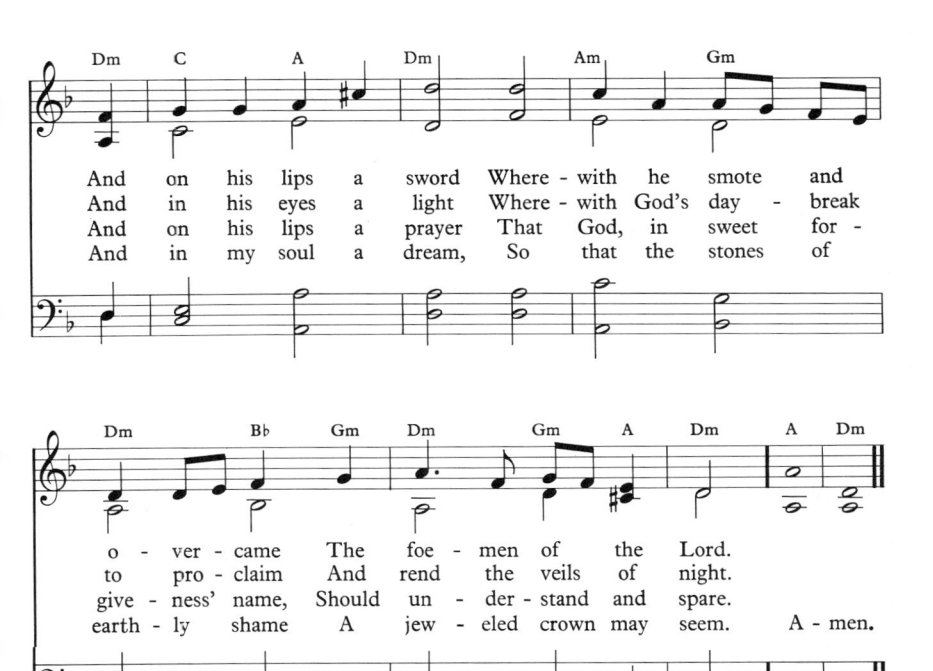

When Stephen, Full of Power and Grace (cont.) 639

And on his lips a sword Where-with he smote and
And in his eyes a light Where-with God's day-break
And on his lips a prayer That God, in sweet for-
And in my soul a dream, So that the stones of

o-ver-came The foe-men of the Lord.
to pro-claim And rend the veils of night.
give-ness' name, Should un-der-stand and spare.
earth-ly shame A jew-eled crown may seem. A-men.

640 When We Are Tempted to Deny Your Son

PSALM 22 (abr.) 10.10.10.6.

David W. Romig, 1965

Comp. or adapted by Louis Bourgeois, 1542

1. When we are tempt-ed to de-ny your Son,
Because we fear the an-ger of the world,
And we are few who bear the in-sults hurled,
Your will, O God, be done. A-men.

2. When we are tempt-ed to be-tray your Son,
Because he leads us in a hard-er way,
And makes de-mands we do not want to pay,
Your will, O God, be done. A-men.

3. When we for-get the cross that held your Son,
And would a-void the bur-den of this life,
The cry for jus-tice and an end to strife,
Your will, O God, be done. A-men.

4. When doubt ob-scures the vic-tory of your Son,
And faith is weak and all re-solve has fled,
Help us to know him ris-en from the dead,
Your will, O God, be done. A-men.

Words copyright 1972 by The Westminster Press.

Where Charity and Love Prevail

CHRISTIAN LOVE C.M. — 641

Latin hymn, ca. 9th century
Para. by J. Clifford Evers, 1960
Paul Benoit (b. 1893)

1. Where charity and love prevail, There God is ever found; Brought here together by Christ's love, By love are we thus bound.
2. With grateful joy and holy fear His charity we learn; Let us with heart and mind and soul Now love him in return.
3. Forgive we now each other's faults As we our faults confess; And let us love each other well In Christian holiness.
4. Let strife among us be unknown, Let all contention cease; Be his the glory that we seek, Be ours his holy peace.
5. Let us recall that in our midst Dwells God's begotten Son; As members of his body joined, We are in him made one.
6. No race nor creed can love exclude If honored be God's name; Our brotherhood embraces all Whose Father is the same. A-men.

Words and music used by permission of World Library Publications, Inc., Cincinnati, Ohio.

642 Where Cross the Crowded Ways of Life

GERMANY L.M.

Frank Mason North, 1903; alt., 1972

Attr. to Ludwig van Beethoven (1770-1827)
Gardiner's *Sacred Melodies*, 1815

1. Where cross the crowd-ed ways of life, Where sound the cries of race and clan, A-bove the noise of self-ish strife, We hear your voice, O Son of Man.
2. In haunts of wretch-ed - ness and need, On shad-owed thresh-olds dark with fears, From paths where hide the lures of greed, We catch the vi-sion of your tears.
*3. From ten-der child-hood's help - less - ness, From wom-an's grief, man's bur-dened toil, From fam-ished souls, from sor-row's stress, Your heart has nev-er known re-coil.
*4. The cup of wa-ter given for you Still holds the fresh-ness of your grace; Yet long these mul-ti-tudes to view The sweet com-pas-sion of your face.
5. O Mas-ter, from the moun-tain-side Make haste to heal these hearts of pain; A-mong these rest-less throngs a-bide, O tread the cit-y's street a-gain;
6. Till sons of men shall learn your love, And fol-low where your feet have trod; Till glo-rious from your heaven a-bove Shall come the cit-y of our God. A-men.

While Shepherds Watched Their Flocks by Night 643
CHRISTMAS C.M.

Nahum Tate, 1702; alt., 1972
George Frederick Handel, 1728

1. While shepherds watched their flocks by night, All seated on the ground, The angel of the Lord came down, And glory shone around, And glory shone around.
2. "Fear not," said he — for mighty dread Had seized their troubled mind — "Glad tidings of great joy I bring To you and all mankind, To you and all mankind.
3. "To you, in David's town this day, Is born of David's line, The Savior, who is Christ, the Lord, And this shall be the sign: And this shall be the sign:
4. "The heavenly Babe you there shall find To human view displayed, All meanly wrapped in swathing bands, And in a manger laid, And in a manger laid."
5. Thus spoke the seraph, and forthwith Appeared a shining throng Of angels praising God, who thus Addressed their joyful song: Addressed their joyful song:
6. "All glory be to God on high, And to the earth be peace: Goodwill henceforth, from heaven to men, Begin and never cease! Begin and never cease!" A-men.

644 You, Holy Father, We Adore

LASST UNS ERFREUEN L.M. with Alleluias

Calvin W. Laufer, 1931; alt., 1972

Geistliche Kirchengesäng, Cologne, 1623
Arr. and harm. by Ralph Vaughan Williams, 1906

1. You, ho-ly Fa-ther, we a-dore; We sing your prais-es o'er and o'er; Al-le-lu-ia, Al-le-lu-ia! With ser-aph throngs join heart and voice, Ac-claim your glo-ry and re-joice; Al-le-lu-ia, Al-le-lu-ia, Al-le-lu-ia, Al-le-lu-ia! A-men.

2. You fill the heaven and earth and sea With sov-ereign power and maj-es-ty; Al-le-lu-ia, Al-le-lu-ia! Yet where the poor in spir-it meet, There is your bless-ed mer-cy seat:

3. Our souls on wings of rap-ture rise To swell the choirs of Par-a-dise: Al-le-lu-ia, Al-le-lu-ia! En-thralled and thrilled, we you a-dore, Our Lord and God for-ev-er-more.

Words copyright 1933 by C. W. Laufer, renewed 1961 by E. B. Laufer; used by permission. Music from *The English Hymnal*; used by permission of Oxford University Press.

You Servants of God, Your Master Proclaim 645
LYONS 10.10.11.11.

Charles Wesley, 1744; alt.
Attr. to J. Michael Haydn (1737-1806)
Gardiner's *Sacred Melodies*, 1815

1. You servants of God, your Master proclaim,
And publish abroad his wonderful name;
The name, all-victorious, of Jesus extol;
His kingdom is glorious, and rules over all.

2. Our God rules on high, almighty to save;
And still he is nigh, his presence we have.
The great congregation his triumph shall sing,
Ascribing salvation to Jesus, our King.

3. Salvation to God who sits on the throne!
Let all cry aloud and honor the Son.
The praises of Jesus the angels proclaim,
Fall down on their faces and worship the Lamb.

4. Then let us adore, and give him his right,
All glory and power, and wisdom and might,
All honor and blessing, with angels above,
And thanks never ceasing, and infinite love. A-men.

646 Your Love, O God, Has All Mankind Created
L'OMNIPOTENT 11.10.11.10.

Albert F. Bayly, 1947; alt., 1972

Comp. or adapted by Louis Bourgeois, 1551
As in *Pilgrim Hymnal*, 1958

1. Your love, O God, has all mankind created,
And led your people to this present hour.
In Christ we see love's glory consummated,
Your spirit manifests his living power.

2. We bring you, Lord, in fervent intercession
The children of your world-wide family;
With contrite hearts we offer our confession,
For we have sinned against your charity.

3. In pity look upon your children's striving
For life and freedom, peace and brotherhood;
Till, at the fullness of your truth arriving,
We find in Christ the crown of every good.

4. Inspire the church, mid earth's discordant voices,
To preach the gospel of her Lord above;
Until the day this warring world rejoices
To hear the mighty harmonies of love.

5. Until the tidings men have long awaited,
From north to south, from east to west shall ring;
And all mankind, by Jesus liberated,
Proclaims in jubilation Christ is King! A-men.

Words used by permission of Albert F. Bayly.

Indexes

Index of Scripture and Scriptural Allusions

Scriptural quotations and allusions to be found in this book are listed below. Translations used in the services and prayers are the Revised Standard Version, the Phillips translation, the Jerusalem Bible, and the New English Bible. The page numbers printed in boldface type refer to hymns.

	Page		Page		Page
Genesis 1	42	Psalm 37:3	61	Psalm 103:8	296
Genesis 1:3–4	56	Psalm 43:3	180	Psalm 103:17	179, 601
Genesis 1:4–6, 25–26	35	Psalm 45:2	360	Psalm 104	409, **533**
Genesis 1:26	180	Psalm 46		Psalm 104:28–29	128
Genesis 1:26–27	362		274, 276, 283, 396	Psalm 105	409
Genesis 1:31	99, 180	Psalm 46:1	72, 179	Psalm 106	409
Genesis 2:21–25	184	Psalm 47:7–8	15	Psalm 106:1	**481**
Genesis 9:9	191	Psalm 51:1	392	Psalm 107:1	27
Genesis 11:9	190	Psalm 54:4	357	Psalm 113:1, 3	
Genesis 28:20–22	**496**	Psalm 55:22	323, 431		16, 25, 56, 67, 71
Exodus 3:16	201	Psalm 59:16	464	Psalm 113:3	292
Exodus 6:6–7	145	Psalm 63	514	Psalm 116:5–7	**633**
Exodus 15:2	**530**	Psalm 63:3	59	Psalm 117	**373**
Exodus 20:1–17	17, 35	Psalm 66:1	**446**	Psalm 118:5	182
Exodus 33:12	181	Psalm 66:1–2	378	Psalm 118:24	56
Numbers 6:24	**624**	Psalm 67	**456**	Psalm 119:105	193, **499**
Numbers 6:24–26	**458**	Psalm 67:4	**467**	Psalm 121	77, **430**
Deuteronomy 6:4–7	100	Psalm 68:5–6	186	Psalm 121:8	356
Deuteronomy 7:6	194, 197	Psalm 72	**443**	Psalm 124:8	25, 71
Deuteronomy 31:24–26	199	Psalm 78:3–4	100	Psalm 130	75, **459**
Deuteronomy 33:27	**513**	Psalm 82:8	**447**	Psalm 136	376, **453**
Joshua 24:14–15	**540**	Psalm 89	**628**	Psalm 136:1	34, 39
I Samuel 7:12	341	Psalm 90	72–73, 549	Psalm 136:1–3	62
I Kings 19:11–12	179	Psalm 90:4	138	Psalm 137	321, **626**
I Chronicles 16:34	114, 115	Psalm 90:17	**462**	Psalm 139	74–75, **460**
Job 37:14	192	Psalm 91	322, **594**	Psalm 139:9–10	183
Psalm 1	**569**	Psalm 92:2	59	Psalm 139:11–12	59
Psalm 8	372, **466, 495, 515**	Psalm 93	403	Psalm 139:23–24	59
Psalm 8:6	99	Psalm 95	**488**	Psalm 145	**517**
Psalm 9	**568**	Psalm 95:1–2	114	Psalm 146	**558**
Psalm 17:15	337	Psalm 95:6	**644**	Psalm 148	**554**
Psalm 19		Psalm 96	**525**	Psalm 149	354
	281, 415, **512**, **595**	Psalm 96:10	187	Psalm 150	
Psalm 20:6	**394**	Psalm 98:1	**597**		354, **552, 553, 557**
Psalm 22:28	139, 187, 189	Psalm 100	288, 306, **482**	Isaiah 2:4	164
Psalm 23		Psalm 102:26–27	278	Isaiah 2:12–17	**492**
	77–78, **477, 590, 592, 593**	Psalm 103		Isaiah 6:1	151
Psalm 23:5	16		76–77, **523, 551, 557, 629**	Isaiah 6:3	35
Psalm 24	454, **602**	Psalm 103:1–2	37	Isaiah 9:6	
Psalm 27:1–3	**388**	Psalm 103:3	**432**		179, **438, 489, 490**

648

SCRIPTURE AND SCRIPTURAL ALLUSIONS

	Page		Page		Page
Isaiah 11:10	455	Matthew 5:5	199	Matthew 17:16–20	183
Isaiah 21:11	617	Matthew 5:5–7	106	Matthew 18:19–20	155
Isaiah 35:4	342	Matthew 5:6	53, 106, 143	Matthew 18:32–35	155
Isaiah 40:1–8	347	Matthew 5:7–9	107	Matthew 19:6	68, 70, 186
Isaiah 40:3–5	416	Matthew 5:9	188	Matthew 19:13–14	310
Isaiah 40:10–11	358	Matthew 5:10–12	108, 140	Matthew 19:19	179
Isaiah 42:1–7	26	Matthew 5:14, 16	108	Matthew 20:10–12	155
Isaiah 43:1–7	425	Matthew 5:14–15	140, 195	Matthew 21:1–9	563, 571
Isaiah 44:9–20	116	Matthew 5:17	201	Matthew 21:1–11	41
Isaiah 46:13	379	Matthew 5:27–37	141	Matthew 21:4–5	121
Isaiah 53:3	182	Matthew 5:43–48	141	Matthew 21:8–9	144
Isaiah 55:8	151	Matthew 5:44	112, 202	Matthew 21:9	
Isaiah 61:1–2	410	Matthew 6:7	202		35, 187, **284, 424**
Isaiah 61:3	366	Matthew 6:9	**547**	Matthew 21:11	121
Jeremiah 5:14	189	Matthew 6:9–13	36, 39	Matthew 21:28–32	156
Jeremiah 8:22	600	Matthew 6:13	126	Matthew 21:34	156
Jeremiah 31:3	556	Matthew 6:34	141	Matthew 22:1–5	156
Jeremiah 36:4	199	Matthew 7:3–4	182	Matthew 22:36–39	156
Lamentations 1:12	294	Matthew 7:14	200	Matthew 22:37	**579**
Lamentations 3:41		Matthew 7:22	179	Matthew 22:37–40	17
16, 34, 35, 38, 39, 54, 67		Matthew 7:24	153	Matthew 22:39	53
Daniel 2:22	391	Matthew 8:16	181, 183	Matthew 23:34–40	191
Amos 5:21	202	Matthew 8:20	190	Matthew 24:35	202
Micah 4:1–4	498	Matthew 9:6	43, 153	Matthew 24:42, 44	135
Micah 4:3	503	Matthew 9:9	153	Matthew 25:1–13	157, **614**
Micah 6:8	631	Matthew 9:10–13	15	Matthew 25:14–30	157
Zechariah 14:7	59	Matthew 9:11	197	Matthew 25:23	99
Malachi 3:10	301	Matthew 9:20–21	**434**	Matthew 25:31–40	157
		Matthew 9:35	193	Matthew 25:36	182
		Matthew 10:5–7	197	Matthew 26:29	149
Matthew 1	608	Matthew 10:7–8	153, 179	Matthew 26:30–41	146
Matthew 1:1–3	136	Matthew 10:32	48	Matthew 26:69–75	**640**
Matthew 1:20–22	137	Matthew 10:32–33	108, 153	Matthew 29:1–10	
Matthew 1:23	384	Matthew 10:38	108, 154		291, 327, 527
Matthew 2:1–2		Matthew 11:5	181	Matthew 28:18–20	43, **621**
136, 139, 302		Matthew 11:5, 19	35	Matthew 28:19	
Matthew 2:1, 11	312	Matthew 11:25	154		25, 42, 45, 119, 139
Matthew 2:2	632	Matthew 11:28	59, 71	Matthew 28:19–20	44, 100
Matthew 2:2, 9–10	40	Matthew 12:49–50	138, 182	Mark 1:1–4	136
Matthew 2:5–6	116, 137	Matthew 13:3–9	154	Mark 1:8	45
Matthew 2:7–11	630	Matthew 13:44–46	154	Mark 1:9	140
Matthew 2:9–10	502	Matthew 13:45–46	**442**	Mark 1:9–11	47
Matthew 2:10–11		Matthew 14:17	**377**	Mark 1:16–20	140
136, 138, 289		Matthew 14:19	154	Mark 1:23–26	140
Matthew 3:3	116	Matthew 14:26–27	154	Mark 2:9–11	153
Matthew 3:11	45	Matthew 15:27	155	Mark 3:25	153
Matthew 3:13	140	Matthew 16:2–3	618	Mark 4:26–32	154
Matthew 3:16	**591**	Matthew 16:16	30	Mark 4:37–40	154
Matthew 4:2	**470**	Matthew 16:16–28	155	Mark 6:34	154
Matthew 4:1–11	143	Matthew 16:18	116	Mark 6:38–44	62
Matthew 4:18–19		Matthew 16:24		Mark 8:34	143, **414**
140, 197, 201		143, 147, 155		Mark 9:2–8, 14–29	143
Matthew 4:18–22	350	Matthew 17:1–2	**642**	Mark 10:35–45	143, 156
Matthew 4:23–25	190	Matthew 17:1–8	143	Mark 10:43–45	89
Matthew 5:3–4	105	Matthew 17:2	**531**	Mark 11:1–10	41

SCRIPTURE AND SCRIPTURAL ALLUSIONS

	Page		Page		Page
Mark 11:8–10	144	Luke 12:15	154	John 7:40–44	539
Mark 13:37	135	Luke 13:29	34, 541	John 8:1–11	189
Mark 14:22	197	Luke 14:10–11	155	John 8:12	
Mark 14:57–63	200	Luke 15:3–7	155		40, 55, 59, 139, 316, 529
Mark 14:65	182	Luke 15:11–24, 32	142, 143	John 10:3	181
Mark 15:13	182	Luke 15:18–19	53	John 10:11	154
Mark 15:34	605	Luke 17:7–10	156	John 10:14, 16	149
Mark 16:6	86, 330	Luke 18:6	501	John 11:17–27	79
Mark 16:7	201	Luke 19:1–10	188	John 11:25–26	71, 87
Luke 1:1–4	199	Luke 19:10	140, 142	John 12:32	
Luke 1:30–33	201	Luke 19:28–38	41, 144		41, 139, 150, 198
Luke 1:78–79	332	Luke 19:41	636	John 12:47	145
Luke 2:1–18	279	Luke 19:45–46	144	John 13:3–16	41
Luke 2:1–20	585	Luke 21:38	637	John 13:5–10	146
Luke 2:4	511	Luke 22:15–20	146	John 13:34	100
Luke 2:6–7		Luke 22:28–30	36, 145	John 14:1	149
	380, 401, 406, 538	Luke 23:5, 10, 43	41	John 14:1–6	79
Luke 2:7	375	Luke 23:20–24	280	John 14:2	85, 149
Luke 2:8	567	Luke 23:32–43	78	John 14:3	113
Luke 2:8–11	374	Luke 23:33	182, 188	John 14:6	
Luke 2:8–14	299, 643	Luke 23:34	147		54, 121, 136, 193, 198, 413
Luke 2:8–15	136	Luke 24:29	278	John 14:16–18	412
Luke 2:8–20	289	Luke 24:30	340	John 14:19	87
Luke 2:10	444	Luke 24:30–31	34, 41, 54	John 14:26	422
Luke 2:10–11	287	Luke 24:34	31, 581	John 14:27	86
Luke 2:13–14		John 1:1–4	84	John 15:5	37, 55, 161
	124, 128, 137, 138, 189,	John 1:1–8	598	John 15:9–12	70
	298, 411	John 1:3	191	John 15:13–15	147, 182
Luke 2:13–15	438	John 1:5	314, 480	John 15:16	48
Luke 2:14		John 1:5, 9, 12		John 15:19	507
	215, 237, 255, 420		40, 136, 137, 139, 195	John 15:20	202
Luke 2:15	486	John 1:9	494	John 16:13	41, 419
Luke 2:20	137, 138, 140	John 1:12	506	John 16:33	143, 149
Luke 2:21	201	John 1:14	449, 565	John 17:9	113
Luke 2:22–35	318	John 1:17	191	John 17:9, 17–18	149
Luke 2:39–52	116, 201	John 1:29	307	John 17:11	201
Luke 3:1–6	136	John 1:41	189	John 17:21–23	160, 161
Luke 3:16	45	John 2:1–2	65	John 19:2–5	524
Luke 4:1–13	143	John 2:1–11	140	John 19:7	182
Luke 4:16–24, 33–35	140	John 3:14	150	John 20:1–14	344
Luke 4:18	187	John 3:16	450	John 20:21–23	152, 196
Luke 4:43	195	John 3:16–17		John 20:28	30
Luke 5:30	15		25, 41, 88, 142, 143	Acts 1:1–14	586
Luke 6:12–16	140	John 3:16–18	588	Acts 1:5	461
Luke 6:20	199	John 3:19	139	Acts 1:8	334
Luke 6:28	57	John 4:11–15	143	Acts 1:9–11	41
Luke 6:35–36	141	John 4:23–24	15, 145	Acts 1:11	283
Luke 7:50	58, 61, 64	John 4:35	570	Acts 2:1–4	611
Luke 8:48	58, 61, 64	John 6:32–34	313	Acts 2:1–5	152, 153
Luke 9:28–36	143	John 6:35		Acts 2:1–21	583
Luke 9:49–50	200		37, 53, 55, 146, 154, 161,	Acts 2:3	528
Luke 9:61–62	154		317	Acts 2:3–4	353
Luke 10:25–37	147, 156	John 6:41, 48	41	Acts 2:17	199
Luke 11:9–10	154	John 6:58	155	Acts 2:17–18	393
Luke 11:28	309	John 6:68–69	72, 155	Acts 2:24	185

SCRIPTURE AND SCRIPTURAL ALLUSIONS

	Page
Acts 2:28	516
Acts 2:39	501
Acts 3:13	201, 623
Acts 3:22–25	195
Acts 3:25	398
Acts 4:10	201
Acts 4:10–12	36, 116, 428
Acts 4:12	189
Acts 6:8	638
Acts 7:32	361
Acts 7:48–49	198
Acts 8:18–24	183
Acts 10:43	382
Acts 13:32–33	407
Acts 14:15	404
Acts 15:6–28	199
Acts 17:24–25	457
Acts 17:26	465
Acts 17:28	184
Acts 20:28	599
Acts 26:22	408
Romans 1:2	40
Romans 4:16	201
Romans 4:20–21	466
Romans 5:2, 5	85, 148
Romans 5:8	26
Romans 5:9–10	107
Romans 6:3–11	43, 85, 148
Romans 6:4	584
Romans 6:13	36, 39, 45
Romans 6:23	148
Romans 8:1	85
Romans 8:2–3	182
Romans 8:6	566
Romans 8:9–11	336
Romans 8:15	200
Romans 8:17, 23	43
Romans 8:20	113
Romans 8:26	33, 576
Romans 8:26–27	111, 188, 338
Romans 8:26–30	15
Romans 8:28	85, 111, 368
Romans 8:31	183
Romans 8:31–39	81–82
Romans 8:32	371
Romans 8:34	27, 71
Romans 8:35–39	519
Romans 8:37–39	485
Romans 8:38–39	33, 148
Romans 8:39	65
Romans 10:15	577
Romans 10:17	188, 190
Romans 11:1–2, 28–32	201
Romans 12:1	162

	Page
Romans 12:1–2	301
Romans 12:6–9, 11, 17	38, 40, 58, 96
Romans 13:8–10	195
Romans 13:10–11	463
Romans 13:11–12	365
Romans 13:12	613
Romans 14:11	509
Romans 15:13	423
Romans 16:27	56
I Corinthians 1:9	48
I Corinthians 1:18	635
I Corinthians 2:7	580
I Corinthians 3:9	183
I Corinthians 3:11	122, 192
I Corinthians 3:16–17	122, 123
I Corinthians 10:4	122
I Corinthians 10:26	127
I Corinthians 11:17–22	161
I Corinthians 11:20, 33	149
I Corinthians 11:23–26	36, 37, 55, 146, 418
I Corinthians 11:27–28	452
I Corinthians 12:4–7	89, 96
I Corinthians 12:5–11	195
I Corinthians 12:12–30	15, 122, 123, 160
I Corinthians 12:13	200, 201
I Corinthians 12:27	89
I Corinthians 12:28	196
I Corinthians 13	641
I Corinthians 13:4–8	67
I Corinthians 13:12	139
I Corinthians 13:13	15
I Corinthians 15:1–6	30
I Corinthians 15:3–8, 12–20, 35–38, 42–44, 50	79–80
I Corinthians 15:20–22	183
I Corinthians 15:23–25	36
I Corinthians 15:26	191
I Corinthians 15:47–49	72
I Corinthians 15:57	87, 597
I Corinthians 16:23	61, 99
II Corinthians 1:22	43
II Corinthians 2:14	448
II Corinthians 4:6	35, 56, 139, 364, 451
II Corinthians 4:11	72
II Corinthians 4:11 to 5:9	81–82
II Corinthians 4:13	622
II Corinthians 4:14	72
II Corinthians 4:17	606

	Page
II Corinthians 5:17	27, 180, 646
II Corinthians 5:18–20	25, 43, 94, 97, 107, 189, 199
II Corinthians 8:9	105
II Corinthians 9:10–12	346
II Corinthians 11:23–26	305
II Corinthians 13:14	38, 40, 46, 50, 52, 68, 70, 86
Galatians 2:20	116
Galatians 3:6–8	587
Galatians 3:11	504
Galatians 3:28	138, 435, 436
Galatians 4:7	106
Galatians 5:1	535
Galatians 5:22	381
Galatians 5:22–23	575
Galatians 5:25	574
Galatians 6:2	484
Galatians 6:14	308, 437
Ephesians 1:3–10	136
Ephesians 1:7	550
Ephesians 1:9–11	389
Ephesians 1:22–23	48
Ephesians 2:7–8	341
Ephesians 2:8	296
Ephesians 2:13–19	417
Ephesians 2:14–15	107
Ephesians 2:17–19	187
Ephesians 2:19	45, 198
Ephesians 2:19–21	325
Ephesians 2:19–22	46, 152, 320
Ephesians 2:20	582
Ephesians 3:12	26
Ephesians 3:14–21	83–84, 88, 183, 200
Ephesians 3:14–15	546
Ephesians 3:18–19	518
Ephesians 4:1	520
Ephesians 4:3–6	149, 153
Ephesians 4:3, 13	15, 31
Ephesians 4:4–6	51, 619
Ephesians 4:15–16	123, 160, 195
Ephesians 4:22–24	627
Ephesians 5:8–9	56, 99
Ephesians 5:21	66, 69
Ephesians 5:23	198, 199
Ephesians 5:24–26	65, 69
Ephesians 6:10–20	616

	Page		Page		Page
Ephesians 6:11–13	149	I Timothy 1:17	28	I John 1:8–9	26, 142
Ephesians 6:18	185	I Timothy 3:15	121, 122	I John 2:25	183
Philippians 1:3	468	I Timothy 6:12	542	I John 3:1	45
Philippians 1:27 to 2:4	200	I Timothy 6:15	40	I John 3:14	36, 39, 45
Philippians 2:5–6	46, 50, 52, 93, 120	I Timothy 6:15–16	328	I John 3:23	27
Philippians 2:5–7	359	II Timothy 1:8–10	433	I John 3:23–24	63
Philippians 2:5–11	290	II Timothy 2:8	54	I John 4:7	33, 63
Philippians 2:6–7	138, 193	Titus 2:13, 14	573	I John 4:7–8	386
Philippians 2:8	35–36, 147	Hebrews 1:3–4	181	I John 4:9	471
Philippians 2:9	54	Hebrews 2:7–8	349	I John 4:9–11	33, 161
Philippians 2:9–10	285, 286, 303	Hebrews 2:10	589	I John 4:11–12	63
Philippians 2:10–11	25, 90, 120, 348	Hebrews 4:12	405	I John 4:16	72
		Hebrews 4:14–15	35, 54, 109, 147	I John 4:17–18	41
				I John 4:19–21	32
Philippians 3:14	304, 399	Hebrews 4:15–16	545	I John 5:13–14	625
Philippians 3:20	122, 123	Hebrews 5:5	121, 147	Jude 24–25	68
Philippians 4:4	562	Hebrews 10:19–22	441	Revelation 1:5	150
Philippians 4:4–7	561	Hebrews 11:17–27	116	Revelation 1:8	534
Philippians 4:19	363	Hebrews 12:1	369	Revelation 1:17–18	87
Colossians 1:13	43	Hebrews 12:2	199, 324	Revelation 1:18	181, 440
Colossians 1:13–14	493	Hebrews 13:4	65	Revelation 3:19	53
Colossians 1:15–17	192	Hebrews 13:7	198	Revelation 3:20	572
Colossians 2:15	105	Hebrews 13:21	559	Revelation 4:8	54, 421
Colossians 3:1	564	James 1:22–27	479	Revelation 5:13	311
Colossians 3:13–14	27, 67, 202	James 4:1–10	32	Revelation 7:9–12	645
		James 5:16	185	Revelation 7:12	28
Colossians 3:15	123	I Peter 1:3	25, 87	Revelation 11:15	25, 343
Colossians 3:15–17	46, 49	I Peter 1:3–9	83, 85, 148	Revelation 14:2–4	185
Colossians 3:16	333	I Peter 1:6–7	345	Revelation 15:3	35, 54
Colossians 3:17	94, 97	I Peter 1:8	510	Revelation 15:4	109
I Thessalonians 4:13–14	79	I Peter 1:23–25	532	Revelation 17:14	136, 137, 138
I Thessalonians 4:13–15	397	I Peter 1:25	202	Revelation 19:6–7	37
		I Peter 2:9	46, 50, 52, 86, 94, 97, 121, 123	Revelation 21	544
I Thessalonians 5:13–19	38, 40	I Peter 2:16	38, 40	Revelation 21:1–4, 22–25; 22:3–5	82–83
I Thessalonians 5:28	37, 55, 58, 64	I Peter 2:24	27	Revelation 21:2	505
II Thessalonians 3:3	500	I Peter 3:14	202	Revelation 21:2–3	128, 186
II Thessalonians 3:16	125	I Peter 4:10	194	Revelation 21:4	33, 191
I Timothy 1:1	137	II Peter 1:19	499, 521	Revelation 21:23	186–187
I Timothy 1:15	26	II Peter 3:8	395	Revelation 22:13	30, 180
		I John 1:5	56, 59	Revelation 22:20	339
		I John 1:7	326		

Guide for the Use of Prayers

The Guide for the Use of Prayers will help those who lead worship to locate particular prayers in this book. Prayers are indexed according to topics and the seasons of the Christian Year.

References in the Guide indicate the page on which a prayer may be found, and the location of the prayer on the page. Thus, 154:5 refers to the fifth prayer printed on page 154; and 31:2 to the second prayer on page 31.

In addition to the prayers listed in the Guide, leaders of worship will discover that there are prayers within the litanies (see pp. 105–131). There are also petitions in the litanies that may be converted into brief and useful prayers with the addition of an address to God and a conclusion.

Addicts, 182:4
Advent, 40:1; 135:1; 135:2; 135:3; 136:1; 136:2; 136:3; 136:4; 136:5; 157:1; 157:2
Agape, prayers for an, 62:1; 63:1
Anxiety, deliverance from, 141:3; 156:3; 181:4; 184:2. *See also* Fear
Armed Forces, 187:3
Ascension Day, 41:6; 150:1; 150:2; 150:3
Ash Wednesday, 142:3

Baptism:
   prayers for, 45:1; 46:1; 46:2; 47:1; 47:2; 139:1; 139:2; 140:2
   thanks for, 42:1; 45:1; 139:2; 140:2
Breaking bread, 31:3; 62:1; 149:5. *See also* Lord's Supper
Brotherhood, 32:2; 179:2; 180:3

Candidates for church vocations, 196:2
Changing times, 180:1
Chaplains. *See* Church
Charitable agencies, 194:1
Childbirth, 183:3
Children, 183:4; 205:1

Christ:
   coming of, 40:1; 135:1; 135:3; 136:1; 136:3; 138:2; 144:2; 157:1; 157:2
   following him, 57:1; 140:4; 143:2; 143:6; 144:3; 146:3; 147:2; 149:3; 153:4; 154:1; 154:4; 161:2
   good shepherd, 149:3; 154:4
   light of the world, 59:1; 139:1
   lordship of, 40:2; 41:2; 41:6; 150:1; 150:2; 157:3
   mind of, 46:1; 50:1; 52:1
   presence of, 136:5; 148:2
   rule of, 40:2; 136:3; 150:2
   Savior, 40:3; 41:2
   thanks for, 39:2; 40:2; 40:3; 41:2; 41:4; 41:6; 45:2; 61:1; 86:1; 137:2; 137:3; 139:2; 142:2; 144:2; 147:2; 150:2; 156:3; 158:2; 159:2; 160:2; 162:2
   union with, 16:3; 45:1; 138:3; 139:3; 143:3; 150:3
   victory of, 135:1; 148:1; 148:4; 157:1
Christian unity, 159:1; 159:2; 159:3; 201:2
Christmas, 40:2; 136:4; 136:5; 137:1; 137:2; 137:3; 138:1; 138:2; 139:3; 140:1

Church:
  building, 198:4
  candidates for church vocations, 196:2
  chaplains, 195:4
  colleges, 197:1
  courage by, 200:5
  courts of, 196:5; 197:3
  decision by, 199:2
  division in, 200:4
  enemies of, 202:2
  evangelists, 195:1
  families in, 202:1
  founders of, 198:2
  fraternal workers, 195:1
  gifts, acknowledgment of, 198:3
  inclusiveness of, 200:2
  meetings of, 196:5; 197:3
  minister, leaving or retiring, 196:4
  ministers of the word, 93:1; 195:3; 196:4
  ministries, 195:1; 195:2; 195:3; 195:4; 196:3
  mission of, 94:2; 97:1; 143:2; 194:4; 194:5
  moderator, 196:1
  money, right use of, 199:1
  new members, 46:1; 50:1; 52:1; 198:1
  other churches, 201:2
  peace in, 200:3; 200:4
  presbytery, meeting of, 196:5; 197:3
  property, 198:4; 199:1
  schools, 197:1
  Scripture in, 199:3
  seminaries, 197:2
  servant purpose of, 26:1; 46:1; 50:1; 52:1; 156:2
  supper, 197:4
  synod, meeting of, 196:5; 197:3
  teachers, 101:1; 195:2
  trustees, 99:1
  unity of, 15:1; 31:3; 63:1; 149:5; 152:1; 152:2; 153:4; 159:1; 159:2; 159:3; 160:1; 160:2; 160:3; 200:3; 200:4; 201:2
City people, 186:5
Comfort, 33:1; 85:4; 87:2; 88:1; 88:2; 181:1; 182:1
Communion. See Lord's Supper
Communion of saints, 33:3
Compassion, 143:2; 154:3; 163:1; 181:3
Conduct. See Righteousness
Confession, prayer of, 26:1; 26:2; 53:1; 60:2; 65:1; 71:1; 135:1; 137:1; 139:1; 142:1; 143:4; 144:1; 146:1; 147:1; 148:1; 150:1; 152:1; 158:1; 159:1; 160:1; 161:1; 162:1; 163:1
Confidence, 184:2; 186:2
Conscientious objectors, 187:4
Conservation. See Natural resources
Courage, 85:4; 94:2; 97:1; 143:6; 154:1; 154:7; 157:2; 161:3; 180:1; 200:5; 201:4
Courtesy, 156:4
Creation:
  enjoyment of, 31:2; 162:3; 180:5
  thanks for, 35:1; 42:3; 61:1; 63:1; 162:2; 163:1
Criminals, 188:4
Crisis, times of, 179:1; 180:2

Darkness, deliverance from, 56:1; 59:1; 72:1; 136:5
Death:
  deliverance from, 145:2
  faith in the face of, 84:2; 85:1; 85:4; 87:1; 87:2; 87:3; 88:1; 148:1; 149:1
  thanks for those who have died, 85:3
Dedication, prayer of, 39:2; 45:2; 57:2; 86:1; 136:4; 136:5; 153:6
Disaster, natural, 179:4
Divorced or separated persons, 186:2
Doubt, deliverance from, 57:1; 193:5
Dying, for the, 185:3

Easter, 41:5; 148:1; 148:2; 148:3; 148:4
Election time, 180:4
Enemies, that we may love, 140:5; 141:2; 202:2
Engaged to marry, 184:3
Epiphany, 40:3; 139:1; 139:2; 139:3; 140:1; 140:2; 140:6
Eternal life, 143:3; 145:2; 148:2; 148:3; 150:3; 155:2; 185:3
Eucharistic prayer, 34:1; 35:1; 54:1
Evangelists. See Church
Evening prayers, 59:1; 59:2; 60:1; 205:5; 205:6

Faith, 60:1; 72:1; 85:4; 87:2; 88:1; 135:3; 138:2; 140:3; 143:1; 149:1; 153:2

GUIDE FOR THE USE OF PRAYERS

Families, for our, 33:2; 202:1; 205:2
Families with one parent, 186:3
Family prayers, 205:1; 205:2; 205:3; 205:4; 205:5; 205:6; 206:3; 206:5
Fear, deliverance from, 57:1; 141:3; 143:6; 148:1; 149:4; 154:7; 158:3; 185:3
Feast, heavenly, 149:2; 156:3
Food, workers who provide, 189:5
Forgive, that we may, 155:5
Forgiveness, thanks for, 41:1; 142:2; 147:2
Fraternal workers. *See* Church
Freedom, 31:2
Friends, 33:2; 206:3

General Assembly, meeting of, 196:5; 197:3
Gifts, acknowledgment of. *See* Church
God:
  glory to, 16:3; 31:3; 137:2; 137:3; 150:2; 158:2; 162:2
  guidance of, 32:5; 99:1; 138:4; 140:1; 158:3; 180:3
  help of, 15:4; 31:2; 32:6
  judge, 157:3; 158:2
  love toward, 152:3; 156:5
  mystery of, 149:2; 153:2
  power of, 148:1; 148:4; 179:4; 181:4
  protection by, 183:2; 186:3
  rule of, 15:2; 32:3; 135:2; 136:2; 143:5; 151:1; 179:1
  salvation by, 136:2; 156:6
  thanks to, 41:7; 42:3; 158:2
Good Friday, 41:4; 147:1; 147:2; 147:3; 147:4
Government, for those in, 189:2; 193:2
Grace at table, 197:4; 206:1; 206:2; 206:3; 206:4
Graduates, 184:2

Handicapped, 181:3
Hardness of heart, deliverance from, 147:3
Healing, for, 32:6; 183:3; 191:2
Hearing God's word, 28:1; 28:2; 136:1; 138:2; 143:2; 153:3; 154:2; 155:4
Holy Spirit:
  guidance of, 16:4; 32:5; 87:3
  power of, 45:1; 136:3; 139:1; 152:1; 152:2; 152:3; 153:1; 161:1; 205:4
  presence of, 15:2; 15:5; 16:3; 155:4; 199:4
  thanks for, 160:2; 161:2
  unity in, 46:1; 50:1; 52:1; 149:5; 152:1; 152:2; 161:3; 199:4
Home, prayer for use at, 205:1; 205:2; 205:3; 205:4; 205:5; 205:6; 206:1; 206:2; 206:3; 206:4
Hope, 72:1; 84:2; 85:1; 85:4; 135:2; 140:6; 145:2; 148:2; 148:3
Humility, 143:5; 155:3; 156:4
Hungry, for the, 62:1; 189:5

Illumination, prayer for, 16:4; 28:1; 28:2; 72:1; 72:2; 84:1; 153:3; 154:2; 154:3; 155:4; 156:6
Installation service, prayers for, 93:1; 94:1; 94:2; 97:1
Intercession, general prayers, 31:2; 57:3; 60:3
International crisis, 179:1

Jesus. *See* Christ
Jewish friends, 201:1
Joy, 138:1; 140:5; 148:1; 148:3; 148:4; 154:5; 155:5; 157:3
Judging, against, 155:6; 182:2; 182:4; 188:4
Judgment, 135:1; 142:1

Kingdom, 135:2; 153:5; 156:3; 156:4

Labor and management, agreement between, 187:2
Law, 41:1; 141:1; 156:6; 182:2; 191:5
Lawmakers, 32:3; 193:2
Leaders in government, 32:3; 32:4; 180:2
Lent, 41:1; 142:1; 142:2; 142:3; 143:1; 143:4; 143:6; 144:4
Life eternal. *See* Eternal life
Life, newness of, 71:1; 140:3; 180:1
Light, for, 56:1; 57:1; 72:1; 136:5; 157:1; 180:2; 185:3
Lonely, for the, 182:1; 186:3
Lord's Supper:
  preparation for, 15:3; 16:5; 146:1
  thanks for, 37:1; 40:1; 41:3; 41:5; 42:2; 55:1; 146:2
Lord's table, 15:3; 16:5; 146:1; 146:2; 160:1; 160:2

Love, for, 136:4; 140:2; 156:4; 158:1; 182:1; 183:5; 185:4; 186:1; 205:2

Management and labor, agreement between, 187:2
Marital difficulty, for those in, 186:1
Marriage service, prayers for, 67:1; 70:1
Married, newly, 67:1; 70:1; 184:4
Maundy Thursday, 41:3; 146:1; 146:2; 146:3
Men in the church, 201:4
Mental distress, for those in, 181:4
Middle years, for those in, 185:1
Military service, for those in, 187:3
Military service, for those who refuse, 187:4
Ministers of the word. See Church
Misfits, 182:3
Money, right use of, 199:1
Morning prayers, 56:1; 57:1; 57:2; 60:1; 205:3; 205:4

Nation, for the, 180:2
National crisis, in times of, 180:2
National significance, days of, 163:1; 163:2; 163:3
Natural resources, for right use of, 180:5
Neighbors, love of, 156:1; 156:5; 157:3; 179:2; 179:3; 182:3; 184:3; 205:2
New Year's Day, 138:4; 158:1; 158:2; 158:3
Night. See Evening prayers

Obedience, for, 28:1; 28:2; 47:2; 94:2; 97:1; 135:2; 140:3; 140:4; 141:1; 144:3; 149:2; 150:1; 152:1; 153:3; 154:1; 154:4; 156:1; 156:2; 161:3; 163:3
Oppression, victims of, 181:2
Ordination, prayers for, 93:1; 94:1; 94:2; 97:1
Orphans, 186:4
Overcome, that we may, 143:1; 149:1

Palm Sunday, 41:2; 144:1; 144:2; 144:3
Parents, 47:1; 183:4; 205:1
Patience, for, 140:5
Patriotism, for a right, 163:1

Peace:
between races, 179:3
inner, 72:1; 87:1; 141:3; 181:4
in the world, 32:1; 32:4; 136:2; 179:1; 179:2; 189:2
Pentecost, 41:7; 152:1; 152:2; 152:3; 153:1
Play, for a spirit of, 188:1
Power, a right use of, 180:3
Praise, that we may, 15:3; 15:5; 16:1; 135:3; 137:3; 138:2; 140:1; 150:1; 154:2; 155:1; 163:2
Prayer:
answer to, 33:4
for those we may forget in, 188:3
guidance in, 31:1; 188:3
Prayer after the Lord's Supper, 37:1; 55:1; 146:2; 160:2
Prayer for the Communion of Saints. See Communion of Saints
Prayer of confession. See Confession
Prayer of dedication. See Dedication
Prayer, eucharistic. See The Thanksgiving
Prayer for illumination. See Illumination
Prayer of intercession. See Intercession
Prayer of thanksgiving. See Thanksgiving
Prayer for use at home. See Home
Preach the good news, that we may, 140:5; 53:5; 188:2
Prejudice, 32:2; 179:3
Presbytery, meeting of. See Church
President, 32:3
Pride, 147:1; 155:3; 157:3
Prisoners, 182:2
Property, right use of, 199:1
Prophets, modern-day, 189:3
Prostitutes, 189:1

Racial peace. See Peace
Racketeers, 188:4
Reconciliation between men, 32:2; 200:4
Reformation Sunday, 161:1; 161:2; 161:3
Renewal, for, 136:3; 137:1; 147:1; 151:1; 160:1; 161:1; 161:3
Repentance, for, 26:2; 136:1; 142:2; 142:3; 143:4; 144:4; 147:3; 147:4; 161:1; 180:2

Resolve, 59:2; 138:4; 143:1
Rest, for, 59:1; 59:2; 87:1
Resurrection:
  faith in, 88:1; 148:1; 148:3; 148:4; 149:2
  thanks for, 41:5; 84:2
Retired people, 185:2
Righteousness, for, 32:3; 57:1; 136:5; 153:3
Rural areas, those living in, 187:1

Sacraments, thanks for, 45:1; 152:2
Schools, for, 197:1
Scripture in the church, 199:3
Seek, that we may, 154:5
Seminaries. *See* Church
Serve, that we may, 32:5; 41:3; 47:2; 55:1; 57:2; 59:1; 59:2; 65:1; 71:1; 138:3; 143:2; 143:5; 146:2; 147:2; 154:5; 154:7; 155:2; 155:3; 156:1; 158:1; 162:3; 163:2; 205:3
Sexual confusion, those in, 185:4
Share, that we may, 62:1; 154:6
Sick, for the, 32:6; 183:3
Sin, deliverance from, 26:1; 140:3; 145:2; 146:3; 147:1; 150:1; 158:1
Sorrow, for those in, 33:1; 85:4; 88:2; 181:1
Strength, for, 72:2; 87:1; 88:2; 143:1
Students, for, 184:2; 193:5; 197:2
Synod, meeting of. *See* Church

Table of the Lord. *See* Lord's table
Temptation, strength in, 143:1
Thanks for food. *See* Grace at table
Thanksgiving Day, 162:1; 162:2; 162:3
Thanksgiving, for a spirit of, 62:1; 147:2; 154:6
Thanksgiving, prayer of, 38:1; 39:1; 61:1; 135:2; 137:2; 139:2; 142:2; 144:2; 146:2; 147:2; 148:2; 150:2; 152:2; 158:2; 159:2; 160:2; 161:2; 162:2; 163:2
The thanksgiving, 34:1; 35:1; 54:1
Tragedy, in times of, 181:1
Travelers, 183:2; 190:3
Trinity, 42:1; 153:2
Trust, for, 72:2; 85:1; 85:4; 87:2; 140:5; 144:1; 144:3; 148:4; 149:4; 153:6; 179:4

Trustees. *See* Church
Truth, for, 180:2; 181:4

Unbelievers, for, 188:2
Unemployed, for the, 183:1
United Nations, 32:4

Vocations:
  architects, 192:2
  Armed Forces, those in, 187:3
  artists, 192:4
  builders, 192:2
  business, those in, 191:1
  clerical workers, 192:1
  commerce, those in, 191:1
  communications workers, 190:2
  counselors, 193:1
  dangerous occupations, 194:3
  decorators, 192:2
  domestic workers, 193:3
  education, those in, 193:4
  entertainers, 192:3
  farmers, 189:5
  food preparers and distributors, 189:5
  government, those in, 193:2
  industrial workers, 190:4
  international government, those in, 189:2
  janitors, 191:4
  journalists, 191:3
  legal workers, 191:5
  maintenance men, 191:4
  manufacturers, 190:4
  mechanics, 194:2
  medical services, 191:2
  migrant workers, 190:1
  military service, those in, 187:3
  musicians, 192:3; 192:4
  printers, 191:3
  prostitutes, 189:1
  publishers, 191:3
  racketeers and criminals, 188:4
  refuse collectors, 191:4
  repairmen, 194:2
  salesmen, 190:4
  scientists, 189:4
  secretaries, 192:1
  social service workers, 194:1
  students, 193:5

teachers, 193:4
trades, skilled, 194:2
transportation workers, 190:3
waiters, 193:3

Waiting, patience in, 137:1; 157:1
War, deliverance from, 32:1; 179:2
Watchfulness, for, 135:3; 137:1; 157:1
Witness of the church, 94:2; 97:1; 139:1; 140:6; 144:1; 145:1; 152:3; 153:1; 155:2; 156:1; 194:4; 195:1
Women in the church, 201:3
Wonder, for, 136:4; 147:4; 200:1
Word of God, faithful to hear, 28:1; 28:2; 138:2; 143:2; 153:3; 155:4
Work, 157:2

World:
  good management of, 32:5; 99:1; 180:5
  peace. *See* Peace
World Communion, 42:2; 160:1; 160:2; 160:3
Worship:
  for leaders of, 16:3; 16:5
  for a right, 15:2; 15:4; 15:5; 144:4; 200:1
  preparation for, 15:1; 15:2; 15:4; 15:5; 16:1; 16:2; 16:5; 138:1; 200:1
Writers of prayers, 202:3

Youth, 184:1; 184:2; 193:5

Guide for the Use of Hymns

The Guide for the Use of Hymns will enable the worship leader to find hymns appropriate to a part of the Service for the Lord's Day, a sacrament or act of the church, a season of the Christian or civil year, or one of several other observances.

The Guide includes thirty-five categories arranged under six major headings.

SERVICE FOR THE LORD'S DAY
- Opening of Worship
- After Confession and Pardon
- After Old Testament Lesson
- After Creed
- After Offering
- Conclusion of Worship

SACRAMENTS
- Baptism
- Lord's Supper

ACTS OF THE CHURCH
- Confirmation
- The Marriage Service
- Witness to the Resurrection
   —Funeral
- Ordination
- Installation

CHRISTIAN YEAR
- Advent
- Christmas
- Epiphany
- Lent
- Palm Sunday
- Good Friday
- Easter Day
- Ascension
- Pentecost
- Trinity Sunday

CIVIL YEAR
- New Year
- Memorial Day
- Independence Day
- Labor Day
- Thanksgiving Day

OTHER OBSERVANCES
- Christian Education
- Ecumenism
- Mission
- Reformation Day
- Stewardship
- World Communion
- World Peace

Service for the Lord's Day

OPENING OF WORSHIP

	Page
A hymn of glory let us sing	273
A mighty fortress	274, 276
All beautiful the march of days	281
All creatures of our God and King	282
All glory be to God on high	283
All glory, laud, and honor	284
All hail the power of Jesus' name	285, 286
All people that on earth do dwell	288
All praise be yours; for you, O King divine	290
All praise to God in highest heaven	291
All praise to thee, our God, this night	292
Ancient of Days, who sit enthroned in glory	297
At the name of Jesus	303
Be thou my vision	304
Before the Lord Jehovah's throne	306
Blessed Jesus, at your word	309
Blessing and honor and glory and power	311
Built on the rock the church does stand	320
Christ, above all glory seated	324
Christ is made the sure foundation	325
Christ is the world's true light	326
Christ, whose glory fills the skies	332
Come, Christians, join to sing	333
Come, Holy Spirit, God	336
Come, my soul, you must be waking	337
Come, thou fount of every blessing	341
Come to us, mighty King	343
Come, you people, rise and sing	345
Creator of the stars of night	348
Crown him with many crowns	349
Earth and all stars	354
Father, we praise you, now the night is over	365
For the beauty of the earth	372
From all that dwell below the skies	373
Give to our God immortal praise	376
God himself is with us	384
God of our fathers, whose almighty hand	394
God of our life, through all the circling years	395
God, the Lord, a King remaineth	403
Heaven and earth, and sea	415
Heralds of Christ, who bear	416
Here, O Lord, your servants gather	417
Holy God, we praise your name	420
Holy, holy, holy! Lord God Almighty!	421
Hosanna, loud hosanna	424
How firm a foundation	425
I sing as I arise today	428
Immortal, invisible, God only wise	433
Jesus, priceless treasure	442
Jesus shall reign where'er the sun	443
Joyful, joyful, we adore thee	446
Let us with a gladsome mind	453
Lord of all being, throned afar	463
Lord of all majesty and might	464
Lord our God, with praise we come	467
Lord, we thank you for our brothers	468
Love divine, all loves excelling	471
Now, on land and sea descending	480
Now thank we all our God	481
O come and sing unto the Lord	488
O for a thousand tongues	493
O gladsome Light, O Grace	494
O God, our faithful God	500
O God, you are the Father	504
O Lord, our Lord, in all	515
O Lord, you are our God	517
O my soul, bless God	523
O sing a new song to the Lord	525
O splendor of God's glory bright	529
O wondrous type, O vision fair	531
O worship the King	533
Of the Father's love begotten	534
Open now the gates of beauty	544
Our God, our help in ages past	549
Praise, my soul, the King of heaven	551
Praise the Lord, his glories show	552
Praise the Lord, who reigns above	553
Praise the Lord! you heavens, adore him	554
Praise to God, immortal praise	556
Praise to the Lord, the Almighty	557
Praise we our Maker	558
Rejoice, O pure in heart	561
Rejoice, the Lord is King	562
Rise up, O men of God	564
Sing praise to God, who reigns above	568
Son of God, eternal Savior	573
Thanks to God, whose Word was spoken	580
The church's one foundation	582
The God of Abraham praise	587
The head that once was crowned with thorns	589
The Lord's my shepherd	592, 593
The spacious firmament on high	595
This is my Father's world	602
To thee with joy I sing	610

SERVICE FOR THE LORD'S DAY

	Page
Wake, awake, for night is flying	614
We come unto our fathers' God	623
We gather together to ask the Lord's blessing	624
We greet you, sure Redeemer from all strife	625
We praise you, O God, our Redeemer, Creator	627
We sing the mighty power of God	628
When morning gilds the skies	637
You, holy Father, we adore	644
You servants of God, your Master proclaim	645

AFTER CONFESSION AND PARDON

	Page
Blessing and honor and glory and power	311
Cast your burden on the Lord	323
Christ is made the sure foundation	325
Christ, whose glory fills the skies	332
Come, Holy Ghost, our souls inspire	335
Come, you thankful people, come	346
For the beauty of the earth	372
God, the Lord, a King remaineth	403
I to the hills will lift my eyes	430
Lord, from the depths to you I cry	459
Love divine, all loves excelling	471
O be joyful in the Lord!	482
O God of Bethel, by whose hand	496
O Lord, our God, most earnestly	514
Our Father, which art in heaven	547
Pardoned through redeeming grace	550
Praise the Lord, his glories show	552
Praise the Lord! you heavens, adore him	554
Praise to God, immortal praise	556
Praise to the Lord, the Almighty	557
Sing to the Lord of harvest	569
There's a wideness in God's mercy	601
We love your kingdom, Lord	626
We praise you, O God, our Redeemer, Creator	627

AFTER OLD TESTAMENT LESSON

	Page
Abide with me	278
All beautiful the march of days	281
All creatures of our God and King	282
All praise to thee, our God, this night	292
Before the Lord Jehovah's throne	306

	Page
Break thou the bread of life	317
Christ is made the sure foundation	325
Christ was the Word who spake it	331
Earth and all stars	354
Eternal Father, strong to save	356
Give to the winds your fears	377
God is our strong salvation	388
God's word is like a flaming sword	405
Great God, we sing that mighty hand	408
Guide me, O thou great Jehovah	409
Heaven and earth, and sea	415
Holy Spirit, truth divine	422
I to the hills will lift my eyes	430
Jesus calls us	439
Lord, bless and pity us	456
Lord of all being, throned afar	463
My Shepherd will supply my need	477
O come and sing unto the Lord	488
O Lord, our Lord, in all the earth	515
O sing a new song to the Lord	525
O Word of God incarnate	532
O worship the King	533
Praise, my soul, the King of heaven	551
Praise the Lord, his glories show	552
Praise the Lord, who reigns above	553
Praise the Lord! you heavens, adore him	554
Praise to God, immortal praise	556
Praise to the Lord, the Almighty	557
Put forth, O God	559
Rejoice, the Lord is King	562
Sing praise to God, who reigns above	568
Spirit divine, attend our prayers	574
The God of Abraham praise	587
The King of love my shepherd is	590
The Lord's my shepherd	592, 593
The man who once has found abode	594
The spacious firmament on high	595
This is my Father's world	602
We sing the mighty power of God	628
Whate'er our God ordains is right	633

AFTER CREED

	Page
Abide with me	278
Ah, dearest Jesus, holy child	279
Ah, holy Jesus, how have you offended	280
All glory, laud, and honor	284
All who love and serve your city	293
At the name of Jesus	303
Be thou my vision	304
Before the Lord Jehovah's throne	306
Break forth, O living light of God	316

GUIDE FOR THE USE OF HYMNS

	Page
Built on the rock the church does stand	320
By the Babylonian rivers we sat down and wept	321
Cast your burden on the Lord	323
Christ, whose glory fills the skies	332
Come, my soul, you must be waking	337
Come, O thou God of grace	339
Come, thou long-expected Jesus	342
Crown him with many crowns	349
Dear Lord and Father of mankind	350
Descend, O Spirit, purging flame	353
Eternal God, whose power upholds	357
Every star shall sing a carol	359
Faith of our fathers	361
Father eternal, ruler of creation	362
Father, we praise you, now the night is over	365
For all the saints	369
Glorious is your name, Most Holy	378
Glorious things of you are spoken	379
God himself is with us	384
God is working his purpose out	389
God of compassion, in mercy befriend us	392
Heaven and earth, and sea	415
Holy, holy, holy! Lord God Almighty	421
Hope of the world, O Christ	423
How firm a foundation	425
If you will only let God guide you	431
Immortal Love, forever full	434
Jesus, priceless treasure	442
Joyful, joyful, we adore thee	446
Lord God of hosts, whose purpose never swerving	460
Lord, we thank you for our brothers	468
Now, on land and sea descending	480
O God, beneath your guiding hand	495
O God of Bethel, by whose hand	496
O God of light, your Word a lamp unfailing	499
O God, you are the Father	504
O Holy City, seen of John	505
O Lord, you are our God	517
O splendor of God's glory bright	529
O where are kings and empires now	530
Of the Father's love begotten	534
Once to every man and nation	540
Onward, Christian soldiers	542
Our faith is in the Christ	545
Send down your truth, O God	566
Sing praise to God, who reigns above	568
Spirit of God, man's hope	576

	Page
The church's one foundation	582
To thee with joy I sing	610
Upon your great church universal	611
We are one in the Spirit	619
We bear the strain of earthly care	621
We believe in one true God	622
We greet you, sure Redeemer from all strife	625
We love your kingdom, Lord	626
Whate'er our God ordains is right	633
When morning gilds the skies	637
Where charity and love prevail	641
Where cross the crowded ways	642
You servants of God, your Master proclaim	645
Your love, O God, has all mankind created	646

AFTER OFFERING

Ah, holy Jesus, how have you offended	280
As men of old their firstfruits brought	301
As with gladness men of old	302
Behold the Lamb of God	307
Cast your burden on the Lord	323
Come, Christians, join to sing	333
Come, you thankful people, come	346
Father, we thank you that you planted	366
God of compassion, in mercy befriend us	392
Jesus calls us	439
Lord, by whose breath all souls and seeds	457
Now thank we all our God	481
O Morning Star, how fair and bright	521
O worship the King	533
When I survey the wondrous cross	635

CONCLUSION OF WORSHIP

All creatures of our God and King	282
All glory, laud, and honor	284
All hail the power of Jesus' name	285, 286
All people that on earth do dwell	288
All praise be yours; for you, O King divine	290
All praise to thee, our God, this night	292
Ancient of Days, who sit enthroned in glory	297

SERVICE FOR THE LORD'S DAY

	Page		Page
Be thou my vision	304	O God, whose will is life and peace	503
Blessing and honor and glory and power	311	O Lord of every shining constellation	512
Call Jehovah your salvation	322	O Lord, our Lord, in all the earth	515
Christ, above all glory seated	324	O Lord, you are our God	517
Christ is made the sure foundation	325	O Love that wilt not let me go	519
Christ is the world's true light	326	O my soul, bless God	523
Christ the Lord is risen again	328	O Spirit of the living God	528
Come, Christians, join to sing	333	O Word of God incarnate	532
Come to us, mighty King	343	Of the Father's love begotten	534
Crown him with many crowns	349	Oh, freedom!	535
Dear Lord and Father of mankind	350	Once to every man and nation	540
Eternal Father, strong to save	356	Onward, Christian soldiers	542
For all the saints	369	Our Father, which art in heaven	547
From all that dwell below the skies	373	Our God, our help in ages past	549
Give to our God immortal praise	376	Praise, my soul, the King of heaven	551
God gives his people strength	381	Praise the Lord, his glories show	552
God is love: let heaven adore him	386	Praise the Lord, who reigns above	553
God is our strong salvation	388	Praise the Lord! you heavens, adore him	554
God moves in a mysterious way	391	Rejoice, O pure in heart	561
God of compassion, in mercy befriend us	392	Rejoice, the Lord is King	562
God of our fathers, whose almighty hand	394	Rise up, O men of God	564
God of the ages, by whose hand	396	Sing praise to God, who reigns above	568
God of the prophets! bless the prophets' sons	398	Sinner, please don't let this harvest pass	570
Guide me, O thou great Jehovah	409	Somebody's knocking at your door	572
He who would valiant be	414	Son of God, eternal Savior	573
Hope of the world, O Christ	423	Spread, O spread the mighty word	577
How firm a foundation	425	Take thou our minds, dear Lord	579
If you will only let God guide you	431	Thanks to God, whose Word was spoken	580
Immortal, invisible, God only wise	433	The church's one foundation	582
Immortal Love, forever full	434	The God of Abraham praise	587
Jesus, lead the way	441	The King of love my shepherd is	590
Jesus shall reign where'er the sun	443	The Lord's my shepherd	592, 593
Joy to the world	444	The man who once has found abode	594
Lead on, O King eternal	448	The true light that enlightens man	598
Let us with a gladsome mind	453	This is my Father's world	602
Lord, dismiss us with your blessing	458	Veiled in darkness Judah lay	613
Lord God of hosts, whose purpose never swerving	460	Wake, awake, for night is flying	614
Lord of all majesty and might	464	Walk tall, Christian	616
Mine eyes have seen the glory	474	We bear the strain of earthly care	621
My Shepherd will supply my need	477	We praise you, O God, our Redeemer, Creator	627
Now, on land and sea descending	480	Whate'er our God ordains is right	633
O brother man	484	When morning gilds the skies	637
O Christ, whose love has sought us out	485	When we are tempted to deny your Son	640
O Day of God, draw nigh	492	Where charity and love prevail	641
O for a thousand tongues	493	Where cross the crowded ways	642
O gladsome Light, O Grace	494	You, holy Father, we adore	644
O God of earth and altar	497	You servants of God, your Master proclaim	645
O God, our faithful God	500		

GUIDE FOR THE USE OF HYMNS

Sacraments

BAPTISM

	Page
All people that on earth do dwell	288
Blessed Jesus, we are here	310
Built on the rock the church does stand	320
Come down, O Love divine	334
Come, Holy Spirit, God	336
Come, O come, great quickening Spirit	338
Creator of the stars of night	348
Descend, O Spirit, purging flame	353
Father, in your mysterious presence	363
Father, we thank you that you planted	366
Glorious things of you are spoken	379
God himself is with us	384
God of our life, through all the circling years	395
He is the Way	413
Holy Spirit, truth divine	422
Lord Jesus Christ, our Lord most dear	461
O God, this child from you did come	501
O my soul, bless God	523
O splendor of God's glory bright	529
Once in royal David's city	539
Our Father, by whose name	546
Our Father, which art in heaven	547
Pardoned through redeeming grace	550
The lone, wild bird	591
The Lord's my shepherd	592, 593
We are one in the Spirit	619
We love your kingdom, Lord	626
Your love, O God, has all mankind created	646

LORD'S SUPPER

	Page
A hymn of glory let us sing	273
Ah, holy Jesus, how have you offended	280
All hail the power of Jesus' name	285, 286
All people that on earth do dwell	288
Alone you journey forth, O Lord	294
At the name of Jesus	303
Become to us the living bread	305
Behold the Lamb of God	307
Beneath the cross of Jesus	308
Bread of heaven, on thee we feed	313
Built on the rock the church does stand	320
Christ was the Word who spake it	331

	Page
Come, risen Lord, and deign to be our guest	340
Deck yourself, my soul, with gladness	351
Eternal Ruler of the ceaseless round	358
Fairest Lord Jesus	360
Father, we greet you	364
Father, we thank you that you planted	366
For perfect love so freely spent	371
Here, O our Lord, we see you face to face	418
I'm so glad troubles don't last always	432
In the cross of Christ I glory	437
Jesus, priceless treasure	442
Joy to the world	444
Let all mortal flesh keep silence	449
Let us break bread together	452
O God of Bethel, by whose hand	496
O Jesus, joy of loving hearts	510
O Lord, whose gracious presence shone	516
O sacred Head, now wounded	524
One table spread	541
Open now the gates of beauty	544
Our Father, which art in heaven	547
Pardoned through redeeming grace	550
Thanks to God, whose Word was spoken	580
The church's one foundation	582
The great Creator of the worlds	588
The Lord's my shepherd	592, 593
Thee we adore, O hidden Savior, thee	599
There is a balm in Gilead	600
There's a wideness in God's mercy	601
Throned upon the awful tree	605
Wake, awake, for night is flying	614
We are one in the Spirit	619
We come unto our fathers' God	623
We greet you, sure Redeemer from all strife	625
When I survey the wondrous cross	635
When Jesus wept	636
Where charity and love prevail	641

Acts of the Church

CONFIRMATION

	Page
All praise be yours; for you, O King divine	290
Amazing grace! How sweet	296
At the name of Jesus	303

ACTS OF THE CHURCH

	Page		Page
Be thou my vision	304	Father, in your mysterious presence	363
Blessed Jesus, at your word	309	Father, we greet you	364
Blessing and honor and glory and power	311	For the beauty of the earth	372
Break forth, O living light of God	316	God of our life, through all the circling years	395
Call Jehovah your salvation	322	God of the ages, by whose hand	396
Come down, O Love divine	334	Great God, we sing that mighty hand	408
Father eternal, ruler of creation	362	Jesus, lead the way	441
God gives his people strength	381	Lord of all being, throned afar	463
God is our strong salvation	388	Love divine, all loves excelling	471
God of compassion, in mercy befriend us	392	O be joyful in the Lord!	482
God of our life, through all the circling years	395	O Jesus, joy of loving hearts	510
God of the ages, by whose hand	396	O my soul, bless God	523
God our Father, you our Maker	399	Our Father, by whose name	546
Guide me, O thou great Jehovah	409	Praise, my soul, the King of heaven	551
I sing as I arise today	428	Praise to the Lord, the Almighty	557
If you will only let God guide you	431	Spirit divine, attend our prayers	574
My Shepherd will supply my need	477	There's a wideness in God's mercy	601
O Christ, whose love has sought us out	485	We greet you, sure Redeemer from all strife	625
O God, our faithful God	500	Where charity and love prevail	641
O I know the Lord	507		
O Master, let me walk with thee	520	**WITNESS TO THE RESURRECTION—FUNERAL**	
Open now the gates of beauty	544		
Somebody's knocking at your door	572	A mighty fortress	274, 276
Spirit of God, descend upon my heart	575	Abide with me	278
Take thou our minds, dear Lord	579	All glory be to God on high	283
The day of Pentecost arrived	583	All people that on earth do dwell	288
The Lord's my shepherd	592, 593	Cast your burden on the Lord	323
'Tis the gift to be simple	606	Christ the Lord is risen again	328
Upon your great church universal	611	Come, Christians, join to sing	333
Walk tall, Christian	616	Father, we praise you, now the night is over	365
We bear the strain of earthly care	621	For all the saints	369
We believe in one true God	622	Give to the winds your fears	377
We gather together to ask the Lord's blessing	624	Glorious things of you are spoken	379
We greet you, sure Redeemer from all strife	625	God is our strong salvation	388
When I survey the wondrous cross	635	God moves in a mysterious way	391
You servants of God, your Master proclaim	645	God of compassion, in mercy befriend us	392
		God of our life, through all the circling years	395
THE MARRIAGE SERVICE		God of the ages, by whose hand	396
		God of the living, in whose eyes	397
All creatures of our God and King	282	God, who made the earth and heaven	404
All people that on earth do dwell	288	Holy Ghost, dispel our sadness	419
Be thou my vision	304	How firm a foundation	425
Blessed Jesus, at your word	309	I to the hills will lift my eyes	430
Christ is made the sure foundation	325	Jesus, priceless treasure	442
Come, O come, great quickening Spirit	338	My Shepherd will supply my need	477
Eternal Ruler of the ceaseless round	358	O God, you are the Father	504
		O Lord of life, where'er they be	513
		O Lord, you are our God	517
		O Love that wilt not let me go	519

GUIDE FOR THE USE OF HYMNS

	Page		Page
Of the Father's love begotten	534	God our Father, you our Maker	399
Oh, freedom!	535	I sing as I arise today	428
Our God, our help in ages past	549	My Shepherd will supply my need	477
Praise, my soul, the King of heaven	551	O God, our faithful God	500
Praise we our Maker	558	O I know the Lord	507
The God of Abraham praise	587	O Master, let me walk with thee	520
The King of love my shepherd is	590	Veiled in darkness Judah lay	613
The Lord's my shepherd	592, 593	Walk tall, Christian	616
The man who once has found abode	594	We greet you, sure Redeemer from all strife	625
The strife is o'er	597	When Stephen, full of power	638
We come unto our fathers' God	623		
Whate'er our God ordains is right	633		

ORDINATION

Christian Year

ADVENT

A mighty fortress	274, 276	All beautiful the march of days	281
All glory be to God on high	283	All poor men and humble	289
All hail the power of Jesus' name	285, 286	Angels, from the realms	298
All people that on earth do dwell	288	Be thou my vision	304
At the name of Jesus	303	Break forth, O living light of God	316
Be thou my vision	304	Bring a torch, Jeannette	319
Blessing and honor and glory and power	311	By the Babylonian rivers we sat down and wept	321
Call Jehovah your salvation	322	Christ, whose glory fills the skies	332
Christ is made the sure foundation	325	Come, O thou God of grace	339
Come down, O Love divine	334	Come, thou long-expected Jesus	342
Come, O thou God of grace	339	Come to us, mighty King	343
God has spoken—by his prophets	382	Comfort, comfort you, my people	347
God of the prophets! bless the prophets' sons	398	Father eternal, ruler of creation	362
Guide me, O thou great Jehovah	409	God's word is like a flaming sword	405
I sing as I arise today	428	Guide me, O thou great Jehovah	409
My Shepherd will supply my need	477	Hark! the glad sound; the Savior comes	410
O God, our faithful God	500	I danced in the morning, when the world was begun	426
O I know the Lord	507	It came upon the midnight clear	438
O Master, let me walk with thee	520	Let all mortal flesh keep silence	449
Take thou our minds, dear Lord	579	Lift up your heads, O mighty gates	454
The Lord's my shepherd	592, 593	Lord our God, with praise we come	467
Veiled in darkness Judah lay	613	Love divine, all loves excelling	471
		O be joyful in the Lord!	482

INSTALLATION

A mighty fortress	274, 276	O come, O come, Emmanuel	489, 490
All glory be to God on high	283	O Day of God, draw nigh	492
All hail the power of Jesus' name	285, 286	O God of every nation	498
At the name of Jesus	303	O how shall we receive you	506
Be thou my vision	304	O splendor of God's glory bright	529
Blessing and honor and glory and power	311	O Word of God incarnate	532
Christ is made the sure foundation	325	Praise we our Maker	558
Come down, O Love divine	334	Rejoice and be merry	560
Come, O thou God of grace	339	Savior of the nations, come	565
God has spoken—by his prophets	382	The great Creator of the worlds	588
God of the prophets! bless the prophets' sons	398	Veiled in darkness Judah lay	613
		Wake, awake, for night is flying	614
		Watchman, tell us of the night	617

CHRISTIAN YEAR

CHRISTMAS

	Page
Ah, dearest Jesus, holy child	279
All my heart today rejoices	287
All poor men and humble	289
Angels, from the realms	298
Angels we have heard on high	299
Born in the night	312
Break forth, O beauteous heavenly light	314
Bring a torch, Jeannette	319
Every star shall sing a carol	359
From shepherding of stars	374
Gentle Mary laid her child	375
Go, tell it on the mountain	380
God rest you merry, gentlemen	401
Good Christian men, rejoice	406
Hark! the herald angels sing	411
I danced in the morning, when the world was begun	426
It came upon the midnight clear	438
Joy to the world	444
Let all together praise our God	450
Lo, how a Rose e'er blooming	455
Lovely Child, holy Child	473
O come, all ye faithful	486
O gladsome Light, O Grace	494
O little town of Bethlehem	511
O sing a song of Bethlehem	526
Of the Father's love begotten	534
On a Bethlehem hill	536
On this day earth shall ring	538
Once in royal David's city	539
Rejoice and be merry	560
Savior of the nations, come	565
Silent night, holy night	567
The first Nowell	585
The true light that enlightens man	598
To Abraham the promise came	608
To thee with joy I sing	610
Veiled in darkness Judah lay	613
What child is this	630
What star is this	632
While shepherds watched their flocks by night	643

EPIPHANY

	Page
Ah, dearest Jesus, holy child	279
All my heart today rejoices	287
Angels, from the realms	298
As with gladness men of old	302
Brightest and best of the sons of the morning	318
Christ is the world's true light	326
Christ, whose glory fills the skies	332
Creator of the stars of night	348
Fairest Lord Jesus	360
Gentle Mary laid her child	375
Go, tell it on the mountain	380
God himself is with us	384
Hark! the herald angels sing	411
Let there be light, Lord God of hosts	451
O God of light, your Word a lamp unfailing	499
O God, who by a star did guide	502
O Lord, whose gracious presence shone	516
O Morning Star, how fair and bright	521
O sing a song of Bethlehem	526
Once in royal David's city	539
Rejoice and be merry	560
The true light that enlightens man	598
To Abraham the promise came	608
Veiled in darkness Judah lay	613
What star is this	632

LENT

	Page
Ah, holy Jesus, how have you offended	280
All praise be yours; for you, O King divine	290
Alone you journey forth, O Lord	294
"Am I my brother's keeper?"	295
Amazing grace! How sweet	296
At the name of Jesus	303
Behold the Lamb of God	307
Beneath the cross of Jesus	308
Bread of heaven, on thee we feed	313
Christ is made the sure foundation	325
Dear Lord and Father of mankind	350
Eternal Ruler of the ceaseless round	358
Every star shall sing a carol	359
Fairest Lord Jesus	360
Father eternal, ruler of creation	362
Father, we greet you	364
God of grace and God of glory	393
He did not want to be far	412
He who would valiant be	414
Here, O Lord, your servants gather	417
Hope of the world, O Christ	423
I danced in the morning, when the world was begun	426
I'm so glad troubles don't last always	432
In the cross of Christ I glory	437
Lord, who throughout these forty days	470
O Christ, whose love has sought us out	485
O Jesus, joy of loving hearts	510
O love, how deep, how broad	518

GUIDE FOR THE USE OF HYMNS

	Page
O Love that wilt not let me go	519
O sacred Head, now wounded	524
O sing a song of Bethlehem	526
O wondrous type, O vision fair	531
Strong Son of God, immortal Love	578
The Lord's my shepherd	592, 593
There is a balm in Gilead	600
There's a wideness in God's mercy	601
Throned upon the awful tree	605
When I survey the wondrous cross	635
When Jesus wept	636
When we are tempted to deny your Son	640

PALM SUNDAY

All glory, laud, and honor	284
Hosanna, loud hosanna	424
Lift up your heads, O mighty gates	454
O how shall we receive you	506
O Jesus Christ, to you may hymns be rising	509
Ride on! Ride on in majesty!	563
So lowly does the Savior ride	571
When Jesus wept	636

GOOD FRIDAY

Ah, holy Jesus, how have you offended	280
Alone you journey forth, O Lord	294
"Am I my brother's keeper?"	295
Behold the Lamb of God	307
Beneath the cross of Jesus	308
Bread of heaven, on thee we feed	313
By the Babylonian rivers we sat down and wept	321
I danced in the morning, when the world was begun	426
I'm so glad troubles don't last always	432
In the cross of Christ I glory	437
O sacred Head, now wounded	524
Once to every man and nation	540
Throned upon the awful tree	605
When Christ comes to die	634
When I survey the wondrous cross	635
When Jesus wept	636
When we are tempted to deny your Son	640

EASTER DAY

All praise to God in highest heaven	291
Christ Jesus lay in death's strong bands	327

	Page
Christ the Lord is risen again	328
"Christ the Lord is risen today"	330
Come, you faithful, raise the strain	344
Fairest Lord Jesus	360
Good Christian men, rejoice	406
Good Christian men, rejoice and sing	407
I danced in the morning, when the world was begun	426
Jesus Christ is risen today	440
O love, how deep, how broad	518
O sons and daughters	527
Of the Father's love begotten	534
That Easter Day with joy	581
The day of resurrection!	584
The strife is o'er	597
When Christ comes to die	634
When we are tempted to deny your Son	640

ASCENSION

A hymn of glory let us sing	273
All hail the power of Jesus' name	285, 286
All praise be yours; for you, O King divine	290
At the name of Jesus	303
Christ, above all glory seated	324
Christ the Lord is risen again	328
Crown him with many crowns	349
Give to our God immortal praise	376
Holy Ghost, dispel our sadness	419
In Christ there is no East or West	435, 436
Jesus shall reign where'er the sun	443
Lord of all nations, grant me grace	465
O for a thousand tongues	493
The day of resurrection!	584
The head that once was crowned with thorns	589

PENTECOST

Blessing and honor and glory and power	311
Christ is made the sure foundation	325
Come down, O Love divine	334
Come, Holy Ghost, our souls inspire	335
Come, Holy Spirit, God	336
Come, O come, great quickening Spirit	338
Come, you people, rise and sing	345
Descend, O Spirit, purging flame	353
Eternal Ruler of the ceaseless round	358
Father, in your mysterious presence	363
God has spoken—by his prophets	382
God of grace and God of glory	393

Civil Year

	Page
God of the prophets! bless the prophets' sons	398
God our Father, you our Maker	399
Here, O Lord, your servants gather	417
Holy Ghost, dispel our sadness	419
Holy Spirit, truth divine	422
How firm a foundation	425
Lord, by whose breath all souls and seeds	457
Love divine, all loves excelling	471
O Lord of every shining constellation	512
O love, how deep, how broad	518
O Spirit of the living God	528
O splendor of God's glory bright	529
Put forth, O God, your Spirit's might	559
Send down your truth, O God	566
Spirit divine, attend our prayers	574
Spirit of God, descend upon my heart	575
Spirit of God, man's hope	576
The day of Pentecost arrived	583
The friends of Christ together	586
The lone, wild bird	591
Thou whose purpose is to kindle	603
Upon your great church universal	611
We are one in the Spirit	619
We believe in one true God	622
Your love, O God, has all mankind created	646

TRINITY SUNDAY

All creatures of our God and King	282
All glory be to God on high	283
Ancient of Days, who sit enthroned in glory	297
Christ is made the sure foundation	325
Come, Holy Ghost, our souls inspire	335
Come, O thou God of grace	339
Come to us, mighty King	343
Come, you people, rise and sing	345
Come, you thankful people, come	346
Creator of the stars of night	348
Eternal Father, strong to save	356
Eternal God, whose power upholds	357
Father, we praise you, now the night is over	365
God has spoken—by his prophets	382
God our Father, you our Maker	399
Holy God, we praise your name	420
Holy, holy, holy! Lord God Almighty!	421
How firm a foundation	425
I sing as I arise today	428
O wondrous type, O vision fair	531
Of the Father's love begotten	534
Our Father, by whose name	546
We believe in one true God	622

NEW YEAR

	Page
Ah, dearest Jesus, holy child	279
All beautiful the march of days	281
All creatures of our God and King	282
All people that on earth do dwell	288
As with gladness men of old	302
Christ is the world's true light	326
Eternal God, whose power upholds	357
God is working his purpose out	389
God of grace and God of glory	393
God of our life, through all the circling years	395
God of the ages, by whose hand	396
God, the Lord, a King remaineth	403
How firm a foundation	425
If you will only let God guide you	431
Immortal, invisible, God only wise	433
Jesus, lead the way	441
Joyful, joyful, we adore thee	446
Lead on, O King eternal	448
O sing a song of Bethlehem	526
On this day earth shall ring	538
Onward, Christian soldiers	542
Open now the gates of beauty	544
Praise to God, immortal praise	556
Sinner, please don't let this harvest pass	570
Somebody's knocking at your door	572
Wake, awake, for night is flying	614
Watchman, tell us of the night	617
We are living, we are dwelling	618

MEMORIAL DAY

A mighty fortress	274, 276
Abide with me	278
All people that on earth do dwell	288
Call Jehovah your salvation	322
Cast your burden on the Lord	323
Christ the Lord is risen again	328
Eternal Ruler of the ceaseless round	358
Faith of our fathers	361
For all the saints	369
Give to the winds your fears	377
God of our fathers, whose almighty hand	394
God of our life, through all the circling years	395
God of the living, in whose eyes	397
How firm a foundation	425
Mine eyes have seen the glory	474
My country, 'tis of thee	476
Not alone for mighty empire	479
O Day of God, draw nigh	492

GUIDE FOR THE USE OF HYMNS

	Page
O God, beneath your guiding hand	495
O God of earth and altar	497
O God of every nation	498
O God, you are the Father	504
O Lord of life, where'er they be	513
O Love that wilt not let me go	519
Open now the gates of beauty	544
The head that once was crowned with thorns	589
The Lord's my shepherd	592, 593
The man who once has found abode	594
The strife is o'er	597
We come unto our fathers' God	623

INDEPENDENCE DAY

A mighty fortress	274, 276
Cast your burden on the Lord	323
Eternal God, whose power upholds	357
God of grace and God of glory	393
God of our fathers, whose almighty hand	394
If you will only let God guide you	431
Judge eternal, throned in splendor	447
Lord, bless and pity us	456
Mine eyes have seen the glory	474
My country, 'tis of thee	476
Not alone for mighty empire	479
O beautiful for spacious skies	483
O Day of God, draw nigh	492
O God, beneath your guiding hand	495
O God of earth and altar	497
O God of every nation	498
Our faith is in the Christ	545
Thanks to God, whose Word was spoken	580
What makes a city great and strong?	631

LABOR DAY

All who love and serve your city	293
Earth and all stars	354
God gives his people strength	381
God of grace and God of glory	393
God, who made the earth and heaven	404
Judge eternal, throned in splendor	447
Let there be light, Lord God of hosts	451
Lord, bless and pity us	456
Lord, look upon our working days	462
O God of earth and altar	497
O God of every nation	498
Our faith is in the Christ	545
We thank you, Lord, for strength of arm	629
What makes a city great and strong?	631

THANKSGIVING DAY

	Page
All creatures of our God and King	282
All people that on earth do dwell	288
As men of old their firstfruits brought	301
Blessing and honor and glory and power	311
Call Jehovah your salvation	322
Come, you thankful people, come	346
Fairest Lord Jesus	360
For the beauty of the earth	372
From all that dwell below the skies	373
God of our fathers, whose almighty hand	394
Heaven and earth, and sea	415
Lord, by whose breath all souls and seeds	457
My country, 'tis of thee	476
Not alone for mighty empire	479
Now thank we all our God	481
O be joyful in the Lord!	482
O beautiful for spacious skies	483
O God, beneath your guiding hand	495
Praise to God, immortal praise	556
Praise to the Lord, the Almighty	557
Sing to the Lord of harvest	569
Sinner, please don't let this harvest pass	570
This is my Father's world	602
We gather together to ask the Lord's blessing	624
We praise you, O God, our Redeemer, Creator	627

Other Observances

CHRISTIAN EDUCATION

"Am I my brother's keeper?"	295
As with gladness men of old	302
Be thou my vision	304
Blessed Jesus, at your word	309
Blessing and honor and glory and power	311
Break forth, O living light of God	316
Break thou the bread of life	317
Brightest and best of the sons of the morning	318
Built on the rock the church does stand	320
Christ, whose glory fills the skies	332
Come, Holy Spirit, God	336
Come, my soul, you must be waking	337
Come, O come, great quickening Spirit	338

OTHER OBSERVANCES

	Page		Page
Dear Lord and Father of mankind	350	O Lord, whose gracious presence shone	516
Every star shall sing a carol	359	Of the Father's love begotten	534
God's word is like a flaming sword	405	One table spread	541
He did not want to be far	412	Put forth, O God, your Spirit's might	559
He who would valiant be	414	Send down your truth, O God	566
Holy Spirit, truth divine	422	Son of God, eternal Savior	573
Lord of the strong, when earth you trod	466	Take thou our minds, dear Lord	579
O Lord of every shining constellation	512	The friends of Christ together	586
O Master, let me walk with thee	520	There is a balm in Gilead	600
O Morning Star, how fair and bright	521	To Abraham the promise came	608
O sing a song of Bethlehem	526	Upon your great church universal	611
Oh, freedom!	535	We are one in the Spirit	619
Once in royal David's city	539	We greet you, sure Redeemer from all strife	625
Sinner, please don't let this harvest pass	570	Where charity and love prevail	641
Somebody's knocking at your door	572		
Spread, O spread the mighty word	577	**MISSION**	
Strong Son of God, immortal Love	578		
Take thou our minds, dear Lord	579	All praise be yours; for you, O King divine	290
'Tis the gift to be simple	606	All who love and serve your city	293
We believe in one true God	622	"Am I my brother's keeper?"	295
What star is this	632	As men of old their firstfruits brought	301
When Stephen, full of power	638	At the name of Jesus	303
		Break forth, O living light of God	316
ECUMENISM		Christ is made the sure foundation	325
All creatures of our God and King	282	Christ is the world's true light	326
All hail the power of Jesus' name	285, 286	Come, O thou God of grace	339
All praise be yours; for you, O King divine	290	Come, thou long-expected Jesus	342
As men of old their firstfruits brought	301	Come, you people, rise and sing	345
At the name of Jesus	303	Comfort, comfort you, my people	347
Break forth, O living light of God	316	Descend, O Spirit, purging flame	353
Built on the rock the church does stand	320	Eternal God, whose power upholds	357
Christ is the world's true light	326	Eternal Ruler of the ceaseless round	358
Come, Holy Spirit, God	336	Fairest Lord Jesus	360
Come, risen Lord, and deign to be our guest	340	Father, we greet you	364
God is love: let heaven adore him	386	Father, whose will is life and good	368
God is working his purpose out	389	From all that dwell below the skies	373
God of grace and God of glory	393	Glorious is your name, Most Holy	378
God our Father, you our Maker	399	Glorious things of you are spoken	379
He is the Way	413	Go, tell it on the mountain	380
Holy God, we praise your name	420	God gives his people strength	381
Hope of the world, O Christ	423	God is love: let heaven adore him	386
Let us break bread together	452	God is working his purpose out	389
Lord God of hosts, whose purpose never swerving	460	God of grace and God of glory	393
Lord, we thank you for our brothers	468	God of our life, through all the circling years	395
O brother man	484	God of the prophets! bless the prophets' sons	398
O Christ, whose love has sought us out	485	Great God, we sing that mighty hand	408
O God, whose will is life and peace	503	Guide me, O thou great Jehovah	409
		Hark! the glad sound; the Savior comes	410
		He is the Way	413

GUIDE FOR THE USE OF HYMNS

	Page
Heralds of Christ, who bear	416
Here, O Lord, your servants gather	417
Hope of the world, O Christ	423
In Christ there is no East or West	435, 436
Jesus shall reign where'er the sun	443
Joyful, joyful, we adore thee	446
Lead on, O King eternal	448
Let there be light, Lord God of hosts	451
Lord, bless and pity us	456
Lord God of hosts, whose purpose never swerving	460
Lord of all nations, grant me grace	465
Lord of the strong, when earth you trod	466
Lord our God, with praise we come	467
Lord, we thank you for our brothers	468
O brother man	484
O God of light, your Word a lamp unfailing	499
O Jesus Christ, to you may hymns be rising	509
O Master, let me walk with thee	520
O Spirit of the living God	528
O where are kings and empires now	530
Onward, Christian soldiers	542
Our faith is in the Christ	545
Praise we our Maker	558
Put forth, O God, your Spirit's might	559
Send down your truth, O God	566
Sinner, please don't let this harvest pass	570
Somebody's knocking at your door	572
Spirit of God, man's hope	576
Spread, O spread the mighty word	577
The day of Pentecost arrived	583
There is a balm in Gilead	600
To Abraham the promise came	608
Upon your great church universal	611
We are living, we are dwelling	618
We bear the strain of earthly care	621
We love your kingdom, Lord	626
We thank you, Lord, for strength of arm	629
What makes a city great and strong?	631
When morning gilds the skies	637
When Stephen, full of power	638
Where cross the crowded ways	642
You servants of God, your Master proclaim	645
Your love, O God, has all mankind created	646

REFORMATION DAY

A mighty fortress	274, 276
All glory be to God on high	283

	Page
All people that on earth do dwell	288
Call Jehovah your salvation	322
Come, thou long-expected Jesus	342
Come to us, mighty King	343
Faith of our fathers	361
For all the saints	369
Glorious things of you are spoken	379
God is love: let heaven adore him	386
God's word is like a flaming sword	405
Immortal, invisible, God only wise	433
O where are kings and empires now	530
O Word of God incarnate	532
Of the Father's love begotten	534
Once to every man and nation	540
Our God, our help in ages past	549
Praise, my soul, the King of heaven	551
Spread, O spread the mighty word	577
The church's one foundation	582
The head that once was crowned with thorns	589
We are living, we are dwelling	618
We come unto our fathers' God	623
We greet you, sure Redeemer from all strife	625
We love your kingdom, Lord	626
Whate'er our God ordains is right	633
When Stephen, full of power	638

STEWARDSHIP

All people that on earth do dwell	288
All who love and serve your city	293
As men of old their firstfruits brought	301
At the name of Jesus	303
Be thou my vision	304
Earth and all stars	354
Eternal Father, strong to save	356
Fairest Lord Jesus	360
Father, we greet you	364
Glorious is your name, Most Holy	378
God gives his people strength	381
God of grace and God of glory	393
He is the Way	413
He who would valiant be	414
Hope of the world, O Christ	423
In Christ there is no East or West	435, 436
Jesus calls us	439
Let there be light, Lord God of hosts	451
Lord, by whose breath all souls and seeds	457
Lord God of hosts, whose purpose never swerving	460
Lord, look upon our working days	462
O beautiful for spacious skies	483
O brother man	484
O God, beneath your guiding hand	495

OTHER OBSERVANCES

	Page		Page
O God of earth and altar	497	O Holy City, seen of John	505
O Holy City, seen of John	505	O Lord, whose gracious presence shone	516
O Lord of every shining constellation	512	O sacred Head, now wounded	524
O Master, let me walk with thee	520	One table spread	541
O sing a new song	525	Our Father, which art in heaven	547
Once to every man and nation	540	Spirit divine, attend our prayers	574
Praise, my soul, the King of heaven	551	Spirit of God, man's hope	576
Rise up, O men of God	564	Thee we adore, O hidden Savior, thee	599
Sinner, please don't let this harvest pass	570	Upon your great church universal	611
Son of God, eternal Savior	573	We are one in the Spirit	619
Spirit of God, man's hope	576	We bear the strain of earthly care	621
The great Creator of the worlds	588	We greet you, sure Redeemer from all strife	625
To Abraham the promise came	608	We love your kingdom, Lord	626
Walk tall, Christian	616	Where charity and love prevail	641
We are living, we are dwelling	618	Your love, O God, has all mankind created	646
We praise you, O God, our Redeemer, Creator	627		
We sing the mighty power of God	628		
We thank you, Lord, for strength of arm	629	**WORLD PEACE**	
What makes a city great and strong?	631	A mighty fortress	274, 276
When I survey the wondrous cross	635	All glory be to God on high	283
When Stephen, full of power	638	All people that on earth do dwell	288
Where cross the crowded ways	642	All praise be yours; for you, O King divine	290
		"Am I my brother's keeper?"	295
WORLD COMMUNION		As men of old their firstfruits brought	301
A hymn of glory let us sing	273	At the name of Jesus	303
Ah, holy Jesus, how have you offended	280	Before the Lord Jehovah's throne	306
All hail the power of Jesus' name	285, 286	By the Babylonian rivers we sat down and wept	321
All people that on earth do dwell	288	Christ is the world's true light	326
Alone you journey forth, O Lord	294	Come, you people, rise and sing	345
At the name of Jesus	303	Comfort, comfort you, my people	347
Become to us the living bread	305	Crown him with many crowns	349
Behold the Lamb of God	307	Eternal Father, strong to save	356
Beneath the cross of Jesus	308	Eternal God, whose power upholds	357
Bread of heaven, on thee we feed	313	Eternal Ruler of the ceaseless round	358
Built on the rock the church does stand	320	Every star shall sing a carol	359
Christ, above all glory seated	324	Fairest Lord Jesus	360
Christ is the world's true light	326	Father eternal, ruler of creation	362
Come, risen Lord, and deign to be our guest	340	Father, we greet you	364
Deck yourself, my soul, with gladness	351	Father, we thank you that you planted	366
Eternal Father, strong to save	356	Father, whose will is life and good	368
Eternal Ruler of the ceaseless round	358	From all that dwell below the skies	373
Fairest Lord Jesus	360	God gives his people strength	381
Father, we greet you	364	God is love: let heaven adore him	386
Father, we thank you that you planted	366	God is working his purpose out	389
For perfect love so freely spent	371	God of compassion, in mercy befriend us	392
Holy, holy, holy! Lord God Almighty	421	God of grace and God of glory	393
I'm so glad troubles don't last always	432	God of our fathers, whose almighty hand	394
In Christ there is no East or West	435, 436		
Let us break bread together	452		
Lord of all nations, grant me grace	465		

	Page		*Page*
God of the ages, by whose hand	396	Not alone for mighty empire	479
Guide me, O thou great Jehovah	409	O brother man	484
Hark! the glad sound; the Savior comes	410	O Day of God, draw nigh	492
		O God of every nation	498
He is the Way	413	O God, whose will is life and peace	503
Heralds of Christ, who bear	416	O Holy City, seen of John	505
Here, O Lord, your servants gather	417	Rise up, O men of God	564
Jesus calls us	439	Send down your truth, O God	566
Judge eternal, throned in splendor	447	So lowly does the Savior ride	571
Lead on, O King eternal	448	The Lord's my shepherd	592, 593
Let there be light, Lord God of hosts	451	There is a balm in Gilead	600
		To Abraham the promise came	608
Lord of all nations, grant me grace	465	Upon your great church universal	611
Lord of the strong, when earth you trod	466	Watchmen, tell us of the night	617
		Where cross the crowded ways	642
Lord our God, with praise we come	467	Your love, O God, has all mankind created	646
Mine eyes have seen the glory	474		

Index of Familiar Hymns with Unfamiliar First Lines

The hymns in this book are arranged in alphabetical order. However, the user of *The Worshipbook—Services and Hymns* is advised when searching to remember that the wording of many hymns has been modernized. In such cases *thee, thou,* and *ye* become *you; thy* becomes *your; hast* becomes *have.* "Cast thy burden" now reads, "Cast your burden." Similarly, "God hath spoken" now reads, "God has spoken." The user can generally locate such hymns without assistance.

The index below includes commonly used titles that differ from first lines. It includes familiar first lines that have been extensively altered for use in this book.

A white lily blows
 see When Christ comes to die on Calvary, 634

All praise to thee, for thou, O King divine
 see All praise be yours; for you, O King divine, 290

Almighty Father, strong to save
 see Eternal Father, strong to save, 356

Baptism by fire
 see Thou whose purpose is to kindle, 603

Before Jehovah's awful throne
 see Before the Lord Jehovah's throne, 306

Come, thou almighty King
 see Come to us, mighty King, 343

Glory be to Israel!
 see On a Bethlehem Hill, 536

God, that madest earth and heaven
 see God, who made the earth and heaven, 404

Hymn for those in captivity
 see By the Babylonian rivers, 321

I greet thee, who my sure Redeemer art
 see We greet you, sure Redeemer from all strife, 625

I know the Lord
 see O I know the Lord, 507

I love thy kingdom, Lord
 see We love your kingdom, Lord, 626

UNFAMILIAR FIRST LINES

I sing the mighty power of God
  see We sing the mighty power of God, 628

I thank thee, Lord, for strength of arm
  see We thank you, Lord, for strength of arm, 629

I'll praise my Maker while I've breath
  see Praise we our Maker while we've breath, 558

Jesus, thou joy of loving hearts
  see O Jesus, joy of loving hearts, 510

Lord of the dance
  see I danced in the morning, 426

Mary's Child
  see Born in the night, Mary's Child, 312

O God, our help in ages past
  see Our God, our help in ages past, 549

O God, thou faithful God
  see O God, our faithful God, 500

O Lord, my God, most earnestly
  see O Lord, our God, most earnestly, 514

O thou, who by a star didst guide
  see O God, who by a star did guide, 502

O thou, whose gracious presence shone
  see O Lord, whose gracious presence shone, 516

Rejoice, ye pure in heart
  see Rejoice, O pure in heart, 561

Simple gifts
  see 'Tis the gift to be simple, 606

The Babe of Bethlehem
  see To Abraham the promise came, 608

Thee, holy Father, we adore
  see You, holy Father, we adore, 644

They'll know we are Christians by our love
  see We are one in the Spirit, 619

Thy love, O God, has all mankind created
  see Your love, O God, has all mankind created, 646

Thy word is like a flaming sword
  see God's word is like a flaming sword, 405

Unto the hills around do I lift up
  see I to the hills will lift my eyes, 430

Ye servants of God, your Master proclaim
  see You servants of God, your Master proclaim, 645

Index of Authors, Translators, and Sources

Abelard, Peter (1079–1142), 294
Adderley, James G. (1861–1942), 364
Addison, Joseph (1672–1719), 595
Ainger, Arthur Campbell (1841–1919), 389
Ainger, Geoffrey (b. 1925), 312
Alexander, Cecil Frances (1823–1895), 439, 539
Alexander, James W. (1804–1859), 524
Alford, Henry (1810–1871), 346
Alington, Cyril A. (1872–1955), 345, 407
Allgemeines Katholisches Gesangbuch (ca. 1774), 420
Ambrose of Milan (ca. 340–397), 529, 565
Anonymous, 406
  Dutch, 624
  English, 343, 380, 401, 432, 452, 507, 535, 554, 560, 570, 572, 585, 600, 606, 608, 610, 631
  French, 299, 319
  German, 360, 637
  Greek, 366, 494
  Irish, 304
  Latin, 324, 325, 335, 336, 348, 440, 510, 518, 524, 531, 581, 641
  Welsh, 289
Aquinas, Thomas (ca. 1225–1274), 599
Arnold, Thomas (1795–1842), 337
Auden, W. H. (b. 1907), 413

Babcock, Maltbie D. (1858–1901), 602
Bacon, Leonard (1802–1881), 495
Bahnmaier, Jonathan Friedrich (1774–1841), 577
Baker, Henry W. (1821–1877), 534, 590
Baker, Theodore (1851–1934), 455, 624
Barbauld, Anna L. (1743–1825), 556
Barclay, Margaret (b. 1923), 291
Baring-Gould, Sabine (1834–1924), 542
Bash, Ewald (b. 1924), 321
Bateman, Christian Henry (1813–1889), 333
Bates, Katharine Lee (1859–1929), 483
Bayly, Albert F. (b. 1901), 512, 646
Beach, Curtis (b. 1914), 482
Bede, The Venerable (ca. 672–735), 273
Benson, Louis F. (1855–1930), 526
Bianco da Siena (d. 1434), 334
Billings, William (1746–1800), 636
Bonar, Horatius (1808–1889), 311, 418

Book of Psalms, The (1871), 523, 594
Bowie, Walter Russell (1882–1969), 505
Bowring, John (1792–1872), 437, 617
Brenner, Scott Francis (b. 1903), 353
Bridges, Matthew (1800–1894), 307, 349
Bridges, Robert (1844–1930), 280, 494
Briggs, George Wallace (1875–1959), 326, 340, 382, 464
Brokering, Herbert (b. 1926), 354
Brooks, Frank A. (b. 1935), 501, 583, 636
Brooks, Phillips (1835–1893), 511
Brooks, R. T. (b. 1918), 580
Buckoll, Henry J. (1803–1871), 337
Bunyan, John (1628–1688), 414
Burrowes, Elisabeth (b. 1885), 396
Byrne, Mary (1880–1931), 304

Calvin, John (1509–1564), 625
Canitz, Friedrich R. L. von (1654–1699), 337
Carbon-Ferrière, J. M. de (ca. 1823), 611
Carter, Sydney (b. 1915), 359, 426
Caswall, Edward (1814–1878), 637
Chadwick, John W. (1840–1904), 358
Chandler, John (1806–1876), 632
Charles, Elizabeth Rundle (1828–1896), 273
Chesterton, Gilbert K. (1874–1936), 497
Christierson, Frank von (b. 1900), 301, 316, 576
Church Book (1868), 415
Church Chorals and Choir Studies (1850), 360
Clark, Thomas Curtis (1877–1953), 545
Clausnitzer, Tobias (1619–1684), 309, 622
Clephane, Elizabeth C. (1830–1869), 308
Clokey, Joseph W. (1890–1961), 428
Coffin, Charles (1676–1749), 632
Coffin, Henry Sloane (1877–1954), 489
Compleat Psalmodist, The (ca. 1750), 440
Conder, Josiah (1789–1855), 313
Conrad of Mainz (ca. 1588), 455
Cook, Joseph Simpson (1859–1933), 375
Copenhaver, Laura S. (1868–1940), 416
Cory, Julia Cady (1882–1963), 627
Cosin, John (1594–1672), 335
Cowper, William (1731–1800), 391
Cox, Frances E. (1812–1897), 568
Coxe, Arthur Cleveland (1818–1896), 530, 618

AUTHORS, TRANSLATORS, AND SOURCES

Croly, George (1780–1860), 575
Crown of Jesus (1862), 299

Dass, Petter (1647–1707), 467
Davis, Ozora S. (1866–1931), 621
Davis, Robert (1881–1950), 629
Dayyan, Daniel ben Judah (14th century), 587
Dearmer, Percy (1867–1936), 365, 414
Decius, Nikolaus (ca. 1485–ca. 1541), 283
De Vries, C. Michael (b. 1923), 412
Dix, William Chatterton (1837–1898), 302, 630
Doane, William C. (1832–1913), 297
Doddridge, Philip (1702–1751), 408, 410, 496
Douglas, C. Winfred (1867–1944), 310, 577
Döving, Carl (1867–1937), 320
Draper, William H. (1855–1933), 282
Drury, Miriam (b. 1900), 305, 616
Dwight, Timothy (1752–1817), 626

Elizabeth I (1533–1603), 331
Ellerton, John (1826–1893), 397, 605
Elliot, Ruth, 378
Epistle to Diognetus (2d or 3d century), 588
Evans, William E. (1851–1915), 339
Evers, J. Clifford (b. 1916), 276, 641

Faber, Frederick W. (1814–1863), 361, 601
Farlander, Arthur W. (1898–1952), 441, 577
Fawcett, John (1740–1817), 458
Fécamp, Jean de (d. 1078), 280
Ferguson, Ian (b. 1921), 295
Fosdick, Harry Emerson (1878–1969), 393
Foulkes, William H. (1877–1961), 579
Francis of Assisi (1182–1226), 282
Franck, Johann (1618–1677), 351, 442
Fraser, Ian M. (b. 1917), 462

Gannett, William Channing (1840–1923), 587
Garve, Carl Bernhard (1763–1841), 405
Gerhardt, Paul (1607–1676), 287, 377, 419, 506, 524
Gill, Thomas H. (1819–1906), 623
Gladden, Washington (1836–1918), 520
Gloria in excelsis, 283
Grant, Robert (1779–1838), 533
Gregor, Christian (1723–1801), 441
Gregory I (540–604), 365
Grundtvig, Nicolai F. S. (1783–1872), 320

Ham, Marion Franklin (1867–1956), 516
Hankey, Donald (1884–1916), 466
Harkness, Georgia (b. 1891), 423
Heber, Reginald (1783–1826), 318, 404, 421

Hedge, Frederick H. (1805–1890), 274, 276
Heermann, Johann (1595–1647), 280, 500
Held, Heinrich (d. ca. 1659), 338
Herman, Nikolaus (ca. 1490–1561), 450
Hernaman, Claudia F. (1838–1898), 470
Hill, Rowland, *Psalms and Hymns* (1783), 323
Holland, Henry Scott (1847–1918), 447
Holmes, Oliver Wendell (1809–1894), 463
Horn, Edward Traill III (b. 1909), 338
Hosmer, Frederick Lucian (1840–1929), 404, 513
House, Margaret (b. 1908), 611
Housman, Laurence (1865–1959), 362
How, William Walsham (1823–1897), 369, 532
Howe, Julia Ward (1819–1910), 474
Hull, Eleanor (1860–1935), 304
Hymnal, The (1941), 384
Hymnal for Colleges and Schools (1956), 506
Hymnal 1940, The, 348

John of Damascus (675?–749?), 344, 584
Johnson, David N. (b. 1922), 473, 610
Johnson, Samuel (1822–1882), 363
Jacobi, J. C. (1670–1750), 419
Janzow, F. Samuel (b. 1913), 374
Joseph, Jane M. (ca. 1894–1929), 538

"K", Rippon's *A Selection of Hymns* (1787), 425
Keble, John (1792–1866), 403
Kelly, Thomas (1769–1855), 589
Ken, Thomas (1637–1711), 224, 266, 272, 292
Kerr, Hugh T. (1871–1950), 395
Kethe, William (d. 1593), 288
Kettring, Donald D. (b. 1907), 308, 631
Knapp, Shepherd (1873–1946), 460

Lacey, T. A. (1853–1931), 490
Lathbury, Mary Ann (1841–1913), 317
Laufenberg, Heinrich von (ca. 1385–ca. 1460), 461
Laufer, Calvin W. (1874–1938), 644
Lettermann, Henry L. (b. 1932), 634
Littledale, Richard F. (1833–1890), 334
Liturgy of St. James, 449
Longfellow, Samuel (1819–1892), 422, 480
Lowell, James Russell (1819–1891), 540
Lowry, Somerset Corry (1855–1932), 573
Luther, Martin (1483–1546), 274, 276, 279, 327, 336, 565
Lyra Davidica (1708), 440
Lyte, Henry Francis (1793–1847), 278, 551, 552

AUTHORS, TRANSLATORS, AND SOURCES

McClellan, Robert W. (b. 1921), 399
McDonald, Dalton E. (b. 1910), 291, 308, 314, 516, 541
McDowell, Louise Marshall, 371
McFadyen, Henry Richard (1877–1964), 591
Macgregor, Duncan (1854–1923), 504
Mann, Newton (1836–1926), 587
Marlatt, Earl (b. 1892), 299
Massie, Richard (1800–1887), 327
Matheson, George (1842–1906), 519
Mattes, John Caspar (1876–1948), 351
Merrill, William Pierson (1867–1954), 479, 564
Methodist Hymnal, The (1935), 529
Milman, Henry H. (1791–1868), 563
Milton, John (1608–1674), 453
Mohr, Joseph (1792–1848), 567
Moment, John J. (1875–1959), 392
Monsell, John S. B. (1811–1875), 569
Montgomery, James (1771–1854), 298, 322, 388, 528
Moultrie, Gerard (1829–1885), 449
Münster MS. (1662), 360

Neale, John Mason (1818–1866), 284, 325, 344, 348, 406, 489, 502, 527, 531, 534, 581, 584
Neander, Joachim (1650–1680), 415, 557
Negro spirituals, 380, 432, 452, 507, 535, 570, 572, 600
Neumark, Georg (1621–1681), 431
Newton, John (1725–1807), 296, 379
Nicolai, Philipp (1566–1608), 521, 614
Noel, Caroline Maria (1817–1877), 303
North, Frank Mason (1850–1935), 642
Nunn, E. Cuthbert (1868–1914), 319

Oakeley, Frederick (1802–1880), 486
Olearius (1611–1684), 347
Oosterhuis, Huub, 412
Osler, Edward (1798–1863), 550, 554
Oxenham, John (1852–1941), 435

Palmer, Ray (1808–1887), 510
Park, John Edgar (1879–1956), 485
Pennewell, Almer M. (1876–1969), 571
Perronet, Edward (1726–1792), 285, 286
Piae Cantiones (1582), 538
Pierpoint, Folliott S. (1835–1917), 372
Plumptre, Edward H. (1821–1891), 561
Pott, Francis (1832–1909), 597
Powell, Roger K. (b. 1914), 468
Prudentius, Aurelius Clemens (ca. 348–413), 534

Psalms and Hymns, Rowland Hill's (1783), 323
Psalter, The (1912), 430, 456, 488, 514, 515, 517
Psalteriolum Cantionum Catholicarum (1710), 489, 490

Rawnsley, Hardwicke D. (1851–1920), 368
Reed, Andrew (1787–1862), 574
Rees, Timothy (1874–1939), 386
Reid, William W., Jr. (b. 1923), 498
Reynolds, William M. (1812–1876), 565
Rights, Douglas LeTell (1891–1956), 613
Rinkart, Martin (1586–1649), 481
Rippon, John (1751–1836), 285, 286
Rippon's *A Selection of Hymns* (1787), 425
Rist, Johann von (1607–1667), 314
Robbins, Howard Chandler (1876–1952), 559
Roberts, Daniel C. (1841–1907), 394
Roberts, Katherine E. (1877–1962), 289
Robinson, Robert (1735–1790), 341
Rodigast, Samuel (1649–1708), 633
Romig, David W. (b. 1926), 586, 640
Routley, Erik (b. 1917), 293
Russell, Arthur Tozer (1806–1874), 450, 506

St. Columba (521–597), 504
St. Patrick (ca. 389–ca. 461), 428
Schloerb, Rolland W. (1893–1958), 503
Schmolck, Benjamin (1672–1737), 310, 544
Scholtes, Peter (b. 1938), 536, 619
Schütz, Johann J. (1640–1690), 568
Scott, R. B. Y. (b. 1899), 492
Scottish Paraphrases (1781), 496
Scottish Psalter (1650), 459, 525, 592, 593
Sears, Edmund H. (1810–1876), 438
Seiss, Joseph A. (1823–1904), 360
Selection of Hymns, A, Rippon's (1787), 425
Shaker song, 606
Shurtleff, Ernest W. (1862–1917), 448
Sill, Edward Rowland (1841–1887), 566
Smith, Elizabeth L. (1817–1898), 625
Smith, Samuel F. (1808–1895), 476
Smith, Walter Chalmers (1824–1908), 433
Southern Harmony (1835), 608
Spannaus, Olive Wise (b. 1916), 465
Spencer, Robert Nelson (1877–1961), 356
Stone, Samuel J. (1839–1900), 582
Stowe, Everett M. (b. 1897), 417
Struther, Jan (1901–1953), 638
Sveeggen, Peter A. (1881–1969), 467
Symphonia Sirenum Selectarum (1695), 597

Tate, Nahum (1652–1715), 643

Taylor, Sarah E. (1883–1954), 499
Tennyson, Alfred (1809–1892), 578
Tersteegen, Gerhard (1697–1769), 384
Theodulph of Orleans (ca. 755–821?), 284
Threlfall, Jennette (1821–1880), 424
Thring, Godfrey (1823–1903), 349, 458
Tisserand, Jean (d. 1494), 527
Toplady, Augustus M. (1740–1778), 419
Troutbeck, John (1832–1899), 314
Trueblood, Elton (b. 1900), 603
Tucker, F. Bland (b. 1895), 290, 294, 366, 546, 588
Tweedy, Henry Hallam (1868–1953), 357

Van Dyke, Henry (1852–1933), 446
Vories, William Merrell (1880–1964), 451

Wade, John Francis (ca. 1711–1786), 486
Walworth, Clarence A. (1820–1900), 420
Watts, Isaac (1674–1748), 306, 373, 376, 443, 444, 477, 549, 558, 628, 635
Webb, Benjamin (ca. 1819–1885), 273, 518
Webster, Bradford G. (b. 1898), 509
Weisse, Michael (ca. 1480–1534), 291, 328
Weissel, Georg (1590–1635), 454

Wesley, Charles (1707–1788), 330, 332, 342, 411, 440, 471, 493, 553, 562, 645
Wesley, John (1703–1791), 306, 377
Whiting, William (1825–1878), 356
Whittier, John Greenleaf (1807–1892), 350, 434, 484
Wile, Frances Whitmarsh (1878–1939), 281
Williams, John, 409
Williams, Peter (1772–1796), 409
Williams, William (1717–1791), 409
Winkworth, Catherine (1827–1878), 279, 283, 287, 309, 328, 336, 347, 351, 405, 431, 442, 454, 461, 481, 500, 521, 544, 557, 577, 614, 622, 633
Winter, Miriam Therese (b. 1938), 381
Woodford, James Russell (1820–1885), 324, 599
Work, John W., Jr. (1871–1925), 380
Wortman, Denis (1835–1922), 398

Yamaguchi, Tokuo (b. 1900), 417
Ylvisaker, John (b. 1937), 598
Young, Andrew (b. 1885), 457
Young, John Freeman (1820–1885), 567

Zinzendorf, Nicolaus L. von (1700–1760), 441

Index of Composers, Arrangers, and Sources

Abels, Paul (b. 1937), 321, 598
"Agincourt Song, The," England (ca. 1415), 273, 518, 531
Ahle, Johann Rudolph (1625–1673), 309, 310
Ainger, Geoffrey (b. 1925), 312
Allgemeines Katholisches Gesangbuch (ca. 1774), 420
Anonymous, 333, 360, 388, 455, 473, 476, 554, 560, 581, 598, 632
  England, 273, 281, 357, 401, 504, 518, 526, 531, 585, 602, 630
  France, 299, 305, 313, 319, 449, 527, 556, 605
  Germany, 328, 332, 406, 622
  Hebrew melodies, 482, 587
  Ireland, 304, 428, 590
  Italy, 458

  Latvia, 321
  Netherlands, 324, 573, 601, 624, 627
  Russia, 268, 269, 480
  Slovak melody, 465
  United States
    American Indian, 263
    Appalachian, 253, 271, 610
    Negro, 253, 380, 432, 436, 452, 507, 535, 570, 572, 600
    Other, 296, 341, 425, 474, 583, 608
    Southern, 267, 345, 591
  Wales, 289, 313, 404, 418, 433, 447, 448, 468, 497, 498, 605, 618
  West Indies, 547
Antes, John (1740–1811), 453
Arnatt, Ronald (b. 1930), 603
Arnold, J. H. (1887–1956), 599
Atkinson, Frederick C. (1841–1897), 575

COMPOSERS, ARRANGERS, AND SOURCES

Bach, Johann Christoph (1642–1703), 338
Bach, Johann Sebastian (1685–1750), 309, 310, 314, 336, 351, 397, 442, 464, 485, 500, 521, 524, 614
Barnby, Joseph (1838–1896), 637
Bash, Ewald (b. 1924), 321
Beethoven, Ludwig van (1770–1827), 446, 642
Bender, Jan (b. 1909), 569
Benoit, Paul (b. 1893), 641
Billings, William (1746–1800), 636
Bishop, John (1665–1737), 631
Bohemian Brethren Hymnal (1544), 344
Bohemian Brethren Hymnal (1566), 568
Book of Psalmody, A, Chetham's (1718), 566
Book of Psalm Tunes, A (1724), 566
Bourgeois, Louis (ca. 1510–1561), 272, 288, 297, 347, 363, 364, 366, 398, 405, 423, 456, 492, 494, 576, 611, 625, 640, 646
Broadwood, Lucy (1858–1929), 526
Buchanan, Annabel Morris (b. 1888), 583
Burleigh, Harry T. (1866–1949), 436
Burnap, Uzziah C. (1834–1900), 434

Caldwell, Mary Elizabeth (b. 1909), 399
Carter, Sydney (b. 1915), 359, 426
Carwithen, Robert (b. 1933), 339, 343, 444, 590
Chetham's *A Book of Psalmody* (1718), 566
Choralbuch, J. G. Werner's (1815), 332, 622
Choral-Buch, Schicht's (1819), 420
Chorale Book for England, The (1863), 557
Church Hymn Tunes (1853), 470
Clark, Jeremiah (1669–1707), 589
Collection of Hymns and Sacred Poems, A (1749), 488
Coller, Percy E. B. (b. 1895), 326
Common Service Book (1917), 633
Compleat Psalmodist, The (ca. 1750), 440
Conkey, Ithamar (1815–1867), 437
Copes, V. Earle (b. 1921), 558, 571
Croft, William (1678–1727), 530, 549
Crotch, William (1775–1847), 456, 492
Crüger, Johann (1598–1662), 280, 314, 351, 481
Crüger's *Praxis Pietatis Melica* (1653), 368, 442, 574
Cummings, William H. (1831–1915), 411

Dakota Indian melody, 263
Darwall, John (1731–1789), 562
Davies, Hugh (ca. 1900), 313, 605
Day, George Henry (b. 1883), 479
Day's Psalter (1562), 470
Decius, Nikolaus (ca. 1485–ca. 1541), 283

Douglas, C. Winfred (1867–1944), 348, 414, 505, 534
Drese, Adam (1620–1701), 441
Dykes, John B. (1823–1876), 356, 421, 563

Ebeling, Johann Georg (1637–1676), 287
Edwards, John D. (ca. 1805–1885), 546
Elvey, George J. (1816–1893), 346, 349
Emerson, L. O. (1820–1915), 404
English Hymnal, The (1906), 447, 449, 460, 484
English Psalters, 288, 398, 625
Este's Psalter (1592), 371
Evans, David (1874–1948), 304, 311, 330, 333, 365, 384, 392, 418, 499, 552
Evans' *Hymnau a Thonau* (1865), 448, 497, 498
Excell, Edwin O. (1851–1921), 296
Eyn Enchiridion . . ., Erfurt (1524), 565

Foundery Collection (John Wesley's) (1742), 323, 553
French Processional (15th century), 489
Freylinghausen's *Geistreiches Gesangbuch* (1704), 337, 415, 577
Fritsch, Ahasuerus (1629–1701), 500

Gardiner's *Sacred Melodies* (1815), 533, 642, 645
Gastorius, Severus (ca. 1650–1690), 633
Gauntlett, Henry J. (1805–1876), 539
Gay, Annabeth McClelland (b. 1925), 501
Geistliche Kirchengesäng, Cologne (1623), 282, 373, 644
Geistliche Lieder, Wittenberg (1535), 623
Geistreiches Gesangbuch, Freylinghausen's (1704), 337, 415, 577
Gesangbuch der herzogl. Wirtembergischen Katholischen Hofkapelle (1784), 424, 628
Geystliche gesangk Buchleyn, Johann Walther's (1524), 327
Geystliche Lieder, Leipzig (1539), 279, 461, 464
Giardini, Felice de (1716–1796), 339, 343
Gibbons, Orlando (1583–1625), 358, 422, 451
Gläser, Carl G. (1784–1829), 493, 621
Goodman, Joseph (b. 1918), 234–252
Gore, Richard T. (b. 1908), 616
Goss, John (1800–1880), 551, 580
Greiter, Matthäus (1500–1552), 558
Grooters, Robert E. (b. 1914), 570
Grüber, Franz (1787–1863), 567

Handel, George Frederick (1685–1759), 444, 643

COMPOSERS, ARRANGERS, AND SOURCES

Harvard University Hymn Book, The (1926), 397
Hassler, Hans Leo (1564–1612), 524
Hatton, John (d. 1793), 443, 495, 517
Havergal, William H. (1793–1870), 593
Haweis, Thomas (ca. 1734–1820), 410
Haydn, Franz Joseph (1732–1809), 378, 379, 595
Haydn, J. Michael (1737–1806), 533, 645
Helmore, Thomas (1811–1890), 489
Hemy, Henri F. (1818–1888), 361
Herbst, Martin (1654–1681), 550
Herman, Nikolaus (ca. 1490–1561), 450
Hillert, Richard (b. 1923), 331, 374, 465, 634
Holden, Oliver (1765–1844), 285
Howard, Samuel (1710–1782), 377
Hughes, John (1873–1932), 393, 409
Huijbers, Bernard, 412
Hutcheson, Charles (1792–1860), 514
Hymnal, The (1933), 518, 531
Hymnal for Colleges and Schools (1956), 273, 451, 477, 489, 538
Hymnau a Thonau, Evans' (1865), 448, 497, 498
Hymnbook, The (1955), 303, 452, 602
Hymns Ancient & Modern (1861), 342, 523
Hymns for the Celebration of Life (1964), 631
Hymns of the Kingdom of God (1923), 468, 618

Irvine, Jessie Seymour (1836–1887), 592

Japanese gagaku mode, 417
Johnson, David N. (b. 1922), 211–223, 225–233, 354, 396, 473, 591, 610
Jones, Griffith Hugh (1849–1919), 353
Jude, William H. (1851–1922), 439

Kentucky Harmony (ca. 1815), 505, 638
Kettring, Donald D. (b. 1907), 345, 353, 428, 462, 541
Knapp, William (1698–1768), 408, 529, 545
Kocher, Conrad (1786–1872), 302, 372
Koizumi, Isau (b. 1907), 417
Kremser, Eduard (1838–1914), 624, 627

Laufer, Calvin W. (1874–1938), 579
Leich, Roland (b. 1911), 613
Leupold, Ulrich S. (1909–1970), 338
Lindeman, Ludvig M. (1812–1887), 320
Lloyd, John Ambrose, Sr. (1815–1874), 295
Lovelace, Austin C. (b. 1919), 450
Luther, Martin (1483–1546), 274, 276

Lyon, Meyer (1751–1797), 587
Lyra Davidica (1708), 440

MacMillan, Ernest (b. 1893), 375
Maker, Frederick C. (1844–1927), 308, 350
Mason, Lowell (1792–1872), 376, 493, 621, 635
Mason's *The Modern Psalmist* (1839), 444
Memmingen MS. (17th century), 586
Mendelssohn, Felix (1809–1847), 411, 481, 532
Messiter, Arthur H. (1834–1916), 561
Methodist Hymnal, The (1966), 327
Miller, Edward (1731–1807), 578
Minchin, James (b. 1942), 490
Modern Psalmist, The, Mason's (1839), 444
Moe, Daniel (b. 1926), 509
Monk, Willlam Henry (1823–1889), 278, 302, 372, 597
Moyer, Harold (b. 1927), 600
Munson, Kenneth (b. 1916), 638
Musikalisches Handbuch, Hamburg (1690), 528

Neander, Joachim (1650–1680), 384, 544
Negro melodies, 253, 380, 432, 436, 452, 507, 535, 570, 572, 600
Neumark, Georg (1621–1681), 431
Neuvermehrtes . . . Meiningisches Gesangbuch (1693), 532
New Universal Psalmodist, The (1770), 626
Nicolai, Philipp (1556–1608), 521, 614
Nunn, E. Cuthbert (1868–1914), 319

Old Church Psalmody (1864), 528
Oliver, Henry K. (1800–1885), 510
Owen, William (1814–1893), 403

Palestrina, Giovanni P. da (ca. 1525–1594), 597
Paris Antiphoner (1681), 311, 365, 392
Parry, Joseph (1841–1903), 617
Pattison, Olive, 547
Peace, Albert L. (1844–1912), 519
Peek, Richard M. (b. 1927), 318, 466
Piae Cantiones (1582), 375, 538
Pilgrim Hymnal (1958), 291, 297, 299, 305, 319, 335, 344, 347, 407, 456, 482, 492, 513, 527, 576, 646
Plainsong, 283, 335, 348, 534, 599
Porter, Ethel (b. 1901), 328
Porter, Hugh (1897–1960), 380
Powell, John (1882–1963), 608
Praetorius, Michael (1571–1621), 455, 516, 581, 632

COMPOSERS, ARRANGERS, AND SOURCES

Praxis Pietatis Melica, Crüger's (1653), 368, 442, 574
Prichard, Rowland H. (1811–1887), 322, 419, 471
Pritchard, T. C. L. (1885–1960), 592
Prys's Welsh Psalter (1621), 459, 525
Psalmodia Evangelica (1789), 454
Psalmodia Sacra (1715), 342, 523
Psalmody in Miniature (1783), 578

Redner, Lewis H. (1831–1908), 511
Reimann, Johann Balthasar (1702–1749), 629
Reinagle, Alexander R. (1799–1877), 316, 435
Repository of Sacred Music, A, Wyeth's, 2d part (1813), 341
Richardson, John (1816–1879), 502
Roberts, Caradog (1879–1935), 289
Röntgen, Julius (1855–1932), 324, 573, 601
Russell, Frederick George (1867–1929), 512
Russian melody, 268, 269, 480

Sacred Melodies, Gardiner's (1815), 533, 642, 645
Salmon, Joan M. (b. 1938), 432, 535
Sateren, Leland B. (b. 1913), 467
Schicht, Johann Gottfried (1753–1823), 457
Schicht's *Choral-Buch* (1819), 420
Schlesische Volkslieder (1842), 360
Scholtes, Peter (b. 1938), 619
Schop, Johann (ca. 1600–ca. 1665), 314
Schreiber, Lawrence P. (b. 1933), 290
Scott-Gatty, Alfred (1847–1918), 460, 484
Scottish chant, 272
Scottish Psalter (1615), 391, 430, 496, 515, 559
Scottish Psalter (1635), 405
Service Book and Hymnal (1958), 283
Shaker melody, 426, 606
Sharp, Cecil J. (1859–1924), 388
Shaw, Geoffrey (1879–1943), 362, 514
Shaw, Martin (1875–1958), 389, 560, 566
Sheppard, Franklin L. (1852–1930), 602
Sherwin, William F. (1826–1888), 317
Shrubsole, William (1760–1806), 286
Smart, Henry (1813–1879), 298, 325, 584
Smith, Alfred M. (b. 1879), 340
Smith, Henry Percy (1825–1898), 520
Songs of Syon (1910), 337, 371, 565
Southern Harmony (1835), 318, 477, 608
Stainer, John (1840–1901), 401, 406, 585
Steurlein, Johann (1546–1613), 569
Stevenson, John A. (1761–1833), 480
Stralsund Gesangbuch (1665), 557
Sullivan, Arthur S. (1842–1900), 542

Tallis, Thomas (ca. 1505–1585), 292, 503, 588, 594
Tans'ur, William (1706–1783), 294
Taylor, Cyril V. (b. 1907), 386
Taylor, Virgil C. (1817–1891), 463
Teschner, Melchior (1584–1635), 284, 506
Tochter Sion, Cologne (1741), 502
Trier MS. (15th century), 516, 581, 632

United States Sacred Harmony, The (1799), 293
Universal Psalmodist, The, Williams' (1763), 626

Vaughan Williams, Ralph (1872–1958), 281 282, 303, 334, 357, 369, 373, 471, 504, 526, 556, 644
Venua, Frédéric M.-A. (1788–1872), 306
Vulpius, Melchior (ca. 1560–ca. 1615), 291 336, 407, 485, 513

Wade, John Francis (ca. 1711–1786), 486
Wallace, William V. (1814–1865), 434
Walter, Samuel (b. 1916), 301
Walter, William H. (1825–1893), 564
Walther, Johann, *Geystliche gesangk Buchleyn* (1524), 327
Walton, James G. (1821–1905), 361
Ward, Samuel A. (1848–1903), 483
Warren, George William (1828–1902), 394, 416
Webbe, Samuel, Jr. (ca. 1770–1843), 410
Werner, J. G., *Choralbuch* (1815), 332, 622
Wesley, John (1703–1791), Foundery Collection (1742), 323, 553
Wesley, Samuel S. (1810–1876), 307, 582
Wetzel, Richard D. (b. 1935), 253–271, 312, 359, 381, 388, 395, 412, 413, 536, 547, 606, 619, 636
Wilkes, John B. (1785?–1869?), 453
Williams' *The Universal Psalmodist* (1763), 626
Williams, Robert (ca. 1781–1821), 330, 552
Williams, Thomas John (1869–1944), 382, 540
Willis, Richard Storrs (1819–1900), 438
Winter, Miriam Therese (b. 1938), 381
Woodward, George R. (1848–1934), 516, 581 586, 632
Wyeth's *A Repository of Sacred Music*, 2d part (1813), 341

Ylvisaker, John (b. 1937), 598
Young, Carlton R. (b. 1926), 293

Alphabetical Index of Tunes

Aberystwyth, 617
Abbot's Leigh, 386
Adeste fideles, 486
Adoro te devote, 599
Allein Gott in der
   Höh', 283
Amazing Grace, 296
America, 476
Amsterdam, 553
An die Freude, 554
Antioch, 444
Ar hyd y nos, 404
Arfon, 313, 605
Arnsberg, 384
Audrey, 462
Aurelia, 582
Aus der Tiefe, 550
Austrian Hymn, 378, 379
Ave virgo virginum, 344
Aylesbury, 566
Azmon, 493, 621

Baker, 399
Bangor, 294
Battle Hymn of the
   Republic, 474
Beatus vir, 465
Bethlehem, 473
Blaenhafren, 468, 618
Boundless Mercy, 345
Bread of Life, 317
Bring a Torch, 319
Bryn Calfaria, 403
Built on the Rock
   (Kirken), 320

Carol, 438
Charlestown, 293
Charlotte, 466
Charterhouse, 499
Cheshire, 371
Christ ist erstanden, 328
Christ lag, 327
Christe sanctorum, 365
Christian Love, 641
Christmas, 643
City of God, 509
Clay Court, 331
Conditor alme, 348
Coronation, 285
Creation, 595

Crimond, 592
Crusaders' Hymn, 360
Cwm Rhondda, 393, 409

Darwall's 148th, 562
Das neugeborne Kindelein,
   336, 485
Deirdre. *See* St. Patrick
Deo gracias, 273, 518, 531
Diademata, 349
Divinum mysterium, 534
Dix, 302, 372
Donne secours, 363, 364,
   423
Down Ampney, 334
Duke Street, 443, 495, 517
Dundee (French), 391, 430,
   496, 559
Dunfermline, 515

Easter Hymn, 440
Ebeling (Warum sollt ich),
   287
Ebenezer (Ton-y-botel),
   382, 540
Ein' feste Burg, 274, 276
Ellacombe, 424, 628
Elton, 376
Epworth Church, 571
Erfyniad, 418
Ermuntre dich, 314
Es flog ein kleins
   Waldvögelein, 586
Es ist ein' Ros', 455
Evan, 593
Eventide, 278

Federal Street, 510
Festal Song, 564
Forest Green, 281, 357
Foundation, 425
Frankfort, 521
French (Dundee), 391, 430,
   496, 559

Galilee, 439
Gallery Carol, 560
Gelobt sei Gott, 291, 407,
   513
Geneva, 479
Germany, 642

Gloria, 299
Go Tell It, 380
God of the Ages, 396
God Rest You Merry, 401
Gosterwood, 504
Gott sei Dank, 415, 577
Gottlob, es geht, 397
Gräfenberg (Nun danket
   all'), 368, 574
Greensleeves, 630
Grosser Gott, wir loben
   dich, 420
Gud er Gud, 467

Hall, 579
Hamburg, 635
Herzliebster Jesu, 280
High Popples, 301
Hyfrydol, 322, 419, 471
Hymn to Joy, 446

In Babilone, 324, 573, 601
In dulci jubilo, 406
Irby, 539
Irish, 488
Italian Hymn (Trinity),
   339, 343

Jesu, meine Freude, 442

King's Weston, 303
Kingsfold, 526
Kirken (Built on the
   Rock), 320
Komm, O komm, du Geist
   des Lebens, 338
Kremser, 624, 627

Ladue Chapel, 603
Lancashire, 584
Land of Rest, 583
Langham, 362
Lasst uns erfreuen 282, 373,
   644
Lauda anima (Praise,
   My Soul), 551, 580
Laudes Domini, 637
Leicester, 631
Leoni (Yigdal), 587
Liebster Jesu, 309, 310
Llanfair, 330, 552

ALPHABETICAL INDEX OF TUNES

Llangloffan, 448, 497, 498
Llef, 353
Lobe den Herren, 557
Lobt Gott, ihr Christen, 450
Lombard Street, 512
L'Omnipotent, 297, 576, 646
Louvan, 463
Lyons, 533, 645

McKee, 436
Madrid, 333
Mannitto, 541
Marion, 561
Maryton, 520
Materna, 483
Meine Armuth, 337
Melita, 356
Mendelssohn, 411
Miles Lane, 286
Mit Freuden zart, 568
Monkland, 453
Mooz Tsur (Rock of Ages), 482
Morecambe, 575
Morning Song, 505
Munich, 532

National City, 290
National Hymn, 394, 416
Neander (Unser Herrscher), 544
Nettleton, 341
Neumark, 431
New Dance, 413
Nicaea, 421
Nun danket, 481
Nun danket all' (Gräfenberg), 368, 574
Nun freut euch, 623
Nun komm, der Heiden Heiland, 565
Nunc dimittis, 494

O filii et filiae, 305, 527
O Gott, du frommer Gott, 500
O Jesu, 629
O quanta qualia, 311, 392
Old Hundredth, 288
Old 107th, 405
Old 113th, 558
Olwen, 289
Orientis partibus, 556

Palestrina (Victory), 597
Park Street, 306

Passion Chorale, 524
Personent hodie, 538
Picardy, 449
Pittsburgh, 613
Praetorius (Puer nobis), 516, 581, 632
Praise, My Soul (Lauda anima), 551, 580
Prospect, 591
Psalm 22 (abr.), 640
Psalm 42, 347
Puer nobis (Praetorius), 516, 581, 632
Purpose, 389

Rathbun, 437
Ratisbon, 332, 622
Regent Square, 298, 325
Rendez à Dieu, 366, 611
Resignation, 477
Rest, 350
Rhosymedre, 546
Rhuddlan, 447
Richmond, 410
Rock of Ages (Mooz Tsur), 482
Rockingham Old, 578

St. Anne, 530, 549
St. Bernard, 502
St. Bride, 377
St. Catherine, 361
St. Christopher, 308
St. Columba, 590
St. Denio, 433
St. Drostane, 563
St. Dunstan's, 414
St. Flavian, 470
St. George's, Windsor, 346
St. Gertrude, 542
St. Joan, 326
St. Louis, 511
St. Magnus, 589
St. Margaret, 519
St. Michael, 456, 492
St. Patrick *and* Deirdre, 428
St. Peter, 316, 435
St. Theodulph, 284, 506
St. Thomas, 626
Salvation, 638
Savannah, 323
Schmücke dich, 351
Seelenbräutigam, 441
Serenity, 434
Shepherding, 374
Shepherds' Pipes, 501

Sicilian Mariners, 458
Sine nomine, 369
Slane, 304
Song 1, 358
Song 13, 422
Song 34, 451
Song 67, 459, 525
Stille Nacht, 567
Stracathro, 514
Stuttgart, 342, 523
Sursum corda (*Smith*), 340

Tallis' Canon, 292, 594
Tallis' Ordinal, 588
Tempus adest floridum, 375
Terra beata, 602
The Babe of Bethlehem, 608
The First Nowell, 585
Third Mode Melody, 503
Tōkyō, 417
Ton-y-botel (Ebenezer), 382, 540
Toulon, 398, 625
Trinity (Italian Hymn), 339, 343
Truro, 454

Unser Herrscher (Neander), 544

Vater unser, 464
Veni Creator Spiritus, 335
Veni Emmanuel, 489
Vesper Hymn, 480
Victory (Palestrina), 597
Vom Himmel hoch, 279, 461

Wachet auf, 614
Walker, 318
Wareham, 408, 529, 545
Warum sollt ich (Ebeling), 287
Was Gott tut, 633
Wedlock, 388
Welwyn, 460, 484
Whitford, 295
Wie lieblich ist der Maien, 569
Wigan, 307
Winchester, 528
Witmer, 395
Wooster, 616

Yigdal (Leoni), 587

Zu meinem Herrn, 457

Metrical Index of Tunes

S.M.
Aylesbury, 566
Festal Song, 564
St. Bride, 377
St. Michael, 456, 492
St. Thomas, 626

S.M. with Refrain
Marion, 561

S.M.D.
Diademata, 349
Terra beata, 602

C.M.
Amazing Grace, 296
Antioch, 444
Azmon, 493, 621
Bangor, 294
Cheshire, 371
Christian Love, 641
Christmas, 643
Coronation, 285
Crimond, 592
Dundee (French), 391, 430, 496, 559
Dunfermline, 515
Epworth Church, 571
Evan, 593
Irish, 488
Land of Rest, 583
Lobt Gott, ihr Christen, 450
McKee, 436
Miles Lane, 286
Nun danket all' (Gräfenberg), 368, 574
Richmond, 410
St. Anne, 530, 549
St. Bernard, 502
St. Flavian, 470
St. Magnus, 589
St. Peter, 316, 435
Serenity, 434
Shepherding, 374
Song 67, 459, 525
Stracathro, 514
Tallis' Ordinal, 588

C.M.D.
Carol, 438
Ellacombe, 628
Forest Green, 281, 357
High Popples, 301
Kingsfold, 526
Materna, 483
Old 107th, 405
Resignation, 477
Salvation, 638
Shepherds' Pipes, 501
Third Mode Melody, 503

L.M.
Audrey, 462
Beatus vir, 465
Conditor alme, 348
Das neugeborne Kindelein, 336, 485
Deo gracias, 273, 518, 531
Duke Street, 443, 495, 517
Elton, 376
Federal Street, 510
Germany, 642
God of the Ages, 396
Hamburg, 635
Llef, 353
Louvan, 463
Maryton, 520
Old Hundredth, 288
Park Street, 306
Prospect, 591
Puer nobis (Praetorius), 516, 581, 632
Rockingham Old, 578
St. Drostane, 563
Song 34, 451
Tallis' Canon, 292, 594
Truro, 454
Veni Creator Spiritus, 335
Vom Himmel hoch, 279, 461
Wareham, 408, 529, 545
Winchester New, 528

L.M. with Alleluias
Lasst uns erfreuen, 373, 644

L.M.D.
Creation, 595
Schmücke dich, 351

P.M.
Arnsberg, 384
Battle Hymn of the Republic, 474
Christ lag, 327
Ein' feste Burg, 274, 276
Frankfort, 521
Go Tell It, 380
Gud er Gud, 467
In dulci jubilo, 406
Jesu, meine Freude, 442
Lobe den Herren, 557
New Dance, 413
St. Patrick *and* Deirdre, 428
Wachet auf, 614

4.6.8.6.
Wooster, 616

5.5.8.8.5.5.
Seelenbräutigam, 441

5.6.8.5.5.8.
Crusaders' Hymn, 360

6.4.6.4.D.
Bread of Life, 317

6.5.6.5.D.
King's Weston, 303

6.5.6.5.D. with Refrain
St. Gertrude, 542

6.5.6.5.6.6.6.5.
St. Dunstan's, 414

6.6.4.6.6.6.4.
America, 476
Trinity (Italian Hymn), 339, 343

6.6.6.D.
Laudes Domini, 637

6.6.6.4.8.8.4.
Wigan, 307

6.6.6.6.D.
Madrid, 333

686

METRICAL INDEX OF TUNES

6.6.6.6.6.
with Refrain
Personent hodie, 538

6.6.6.6.8.8.
Darwall's 148th, 562
Rhosymedre, 546

6.6.6.7.
with Alleluias
Bethlehem, 473

6.6.7.D.
Nunc dimittis, 494

6.6.8.D.
Olwen, 289

6.6.8.4.D.
Leoni (Yigdal), 587

6.6.11.D.
Down Ampney, 334

6.7.6.7.6.6.6.6.
Nun danket, 481
O Gott, du frommer Gott, 500
St. Joan, 326

7.5.7.5.D.
Tōkyō, 417

7.6.7.6.D.
Aurelia, 582
Ave virgo virginum, 344
Boundless Mercy, 345
Ellacombe, 424
Es flog ein kleins Waldvögelein, 586
Gosterwood, 504
Lancashire, 584
Llangloffan, 448, 497, 498
Munich, 532
Passion Chorale, 524
St. Theodulph, 284, 506
Tempus adest floridum, 375
Wedlock, 388
Whitford, 295
Wie lieblich ist der Maien, 569

7.6.7.6.6.7.6.
Es ist ein' Ros', 455

7.6.7.6.7.7.7.6.
Amsterdam, 553

7.6.8.6.8.6.8.6.
St. Christopher, 308

7.7.7.7.
Aus der Tiefe, 550
Clay Court, 331
Gott sei Dank, 415, 577
Monkland, 453
Nun komm, der Heiden Heiland, 565
Orientis partibus, 556
Savannah, 323
Song 13, 422

7.7.7.7.
with Alleluias
Christ ist erstanden, 328
Easter Hymn, 440
Llanfair, 330, 552

7.7.7.7.
with Refrain
Gloria, 299

7.7.7.7.D.
Aberystwyth, 617
St. George's, Windsor, 346

7.7.7.7.D.
with Refrain
Mendelssohn, 411

7.7.7.7.5.7.6.7.
Rock of Ages (Mooz Tsur), 482

7.7.7.7.7.7.
Arfon, 313, 605
Dix, 302, 372
Pittsburgh, 613
Ratisbon, 332, 622

7.8.7.8.7.7.
Grosser Gott, wir loben dich, 420

7.8.7.8.8.8.
Liebster Jesu, 309, 310

8.3.3.6.D.
Warum sollt ich (Ebeling), 287

8.4.7.D.
Meine Armuth, 337

8.4.8.4.8.8.
O Jesu, 629

8.4.8.4.8.8.8.4.
Ar hyd y nos, 404

8.6.8.6.7.6.8.6.
St. Louis, 511

8.6.8.6.8.6.
Morning Song, 505

8.6.8.8.6.
Rest, 350

8.7.8.7.
Charlestown, 293
Galilee, 439
Rathbun, 437
St. Columba, 590
Stuttgart, 342, 523

8.7.8.7.D.
Abbot's Leigh, 386
An die Freude, 554
Austrian Hymn, 378, 379
Blaenhafren, 468, 618
Ebenezer (Ton-y-botel), 382, 540
Geneva, 479
Hyfrydol, 322, 419, 471
Hymn to Joy, 446
In Babilone, 324, 573, 601
Ladue Chapel, 603
Nettleton, 341
The Babe of Bethlehem, 608

8.7.8.7.4.4.8.8.
Was Gott tut, 633

8.7.8.7.4.7.
Bryn Calfaria, 403

8.7.8.7.6.8.6.7.
Greensleeves, 630

8.7.8.7.7.7.
Komm, O komm, du Geist des Lebens, 338
Neander (Unser Herrscher), 544

8.7.8.7.7.7.8.8.
Psalm 42, 347

8.7.8.7.8.6.8.7.
Vesper Hymn, 480

8.7.8.7.8.7.
Cwm Rhondda, 393, 409
Irby, 539
Lauda anima (Praise,
 My Soul), 551, 580
Picardy, 449
Regent Square, 298, 325
Rhuddlan, 447
Sicilian Mariners, 458

8.7.8.7.8.7.7.
Divinum mysterium, 534

8.7.8.7.8.8.7.
Allein Gott in der Höh', 283
Mit Freuden zart, 568
Nun freut euch, 623

8.7.8.7.8.8.7.7.
Ermuntre dich, 314

8.8.8.
 with Alleluia
O filii et filiae, 305

8.8.8.
 with Alleluias
Gelobt sei Gott,
 291, 407, 513
O filii et filiae, 527
Victory (Palestrina), 597

8.8.8.D.
Old 113th, 558

8.8.8.8.6.
St. Margaret, 519

8.8.8.8.8.6.
Charlotte, 466

8.8.8.8.8.6.
 with Alleluias
Lasst uns erfreuen, 282

8.8.8.8.8.8.
Gottlob, es geht, 397

Leicester, 631
Melita, 356
St. Catherine, 361
Vater unser, 464
Veni Emmanuel, 489

8.8.8.8.8.8.8.8.
Kirken (Built on the Rock),
 320

8.9.8.9.D.
Baker, 399

9.8.9.8.D.
Rendez à Dieu, 366, 611

9.8.9.8.8.8.
Neumark, 431

10.4.10.4.10.10.
Witmer, 395

10.4.10.4.12.10.
Mannitto, 541

10.10.9.10.
Slane, 304

10.10.10.
 with Alleluia
National City, 290

10.10.10.
 with Alleluias
Sine nomine, 369

10.10.10.6.
Psalm 22 (abr.), 640

10.10.10.10.
Adoro te devote, 599
Erfyniad, 418
Eventide, 278
Hall, 579
Morecambe, 575
National Hymn, 394, 416
O quanta qualia, 311

Sursum corda (*Smith*), 340
Toulon, 398, 625

10.10.10.10.10.10.
Song 1, 358

10.10.11.11.
Lyons, 533, 645

11.10.11.10.
Charterhouse, 499
City of God, 509
Donne secours, 363, 364, 423
Lombard Street, 512
L'Omnipotent, 297, 576, 646
Walker, 318
Welwyn, 460, 484
Zu meinem Herrn, 457

11.10.11.10.10.
Langham, 362

11.11.11.5.
Christe sanctorum, 365
Herzliebster Jesu, 280

11.11.11.11.
Foundation, 425
Gallery Carol, 560
O quanta qualia, 392
St. Denio, 433

11.12.12.10.
Nicaea, 421

12.11.12.11.
Kremser, 624, 627

Irregular
Adeste fideles, 486
Bring a Torch, 319
Purpose, 389
Stille Nacht, 567
The First Nowell, 585

Irregular
 with Refrain
God Rest You Merry, 401